LANDSCAPE ENCYCLOPAEDIA

DAY LOAN

Retur **1 WEEK LOAN**
Fine es are charged at £2 per **day**

No renewal

19 APR 2010

# Landscape Encyclopaedia

## A Reference Guide to the Historic Landscape

*Richard Muir*

**WIND*gather***
P R E S S

*Published by*: Windgather Press Ltd, 29 Bishop Road, Bollington, Macclesfield, Cheshire SK10 5NX, UK

*Distributed by*: Central Books Ltd, 99 Wallis Road, London E9 5LN

*British Library Cataloguing-in-Publication Data*
A catalogue record for this book is available from the British Library

*hardback*  ISBN 0-9545575-0-6
*paperback*  ISBN 0-9545575-1-4

Typeset and originated by Carnegie Publishing Ltd,
Chatsworth Road, Lancaster
Printed and bound by Biddles Ltd, King's Lynn

# Introduction

This encyclopaedia can serve as a reference book and be employed to interpret all the most significant cultural features in the countrysides of the British Isles. It can also be used as a research aid for use in local fieldwork projects involving landscape history and landscape archaeology. In general terms, the length of particular entries reflects their relative importance as features of, or forces in, the rural landscape, so that the *Clearances of the Scottish Highlands* has a length of 966 words, *Flax Kiln*, one of 51 words, and *Lousy Land*, just 23 words. A determined effort has been made to avoid the bias towards the countryside characteristics of southern England and the English Midlands that has so frequently occurred, so that salient features from landscapes as far apart as Shetland and the Atlantic shores of Ireland are represented. Questions of inclusion have been encountered throughout and, for example, in the case of Lowland Scottish dialect terms decisions were made to include relevant dialect words while excluding those which seemed only to represent only an accented form of an English word.

Decisions that are at least partly subjective were taken regarding which of the thousands of archaic and obselete words that endure, for example, in the form of field-names, should be listed, and which not. Rural communities in the past lived in an intimate association with their settings, and this resulted in the development of vocabularies of a richness that we, today, can scarcely imagine. Just as the Inuit people are so often said to have had a multitude of words for different qualities of snow, so there are thought to be 130 words in Ireland specific to bogland alone. Rural communities that survived in some localities within living memory conversed about matters of day-to-day living in dialects composed of words imported in the centuries before Domesday and shared between culturally diverse communities. They used words coined more recently to denote important aspects of existence, like the nuances of the qualities of soil, and sometimes they attached different meanings to words to those applied by groups living on the other side of a watershed.

The countrysides of Britain and Ireland are cultural constructions and the emphasis here is on the man-made features of the landscape. The natural setting of human life does, despite a current and doubtless short-lived tendency to devalue environmental influences, exert a considerable effect on human activities and their manifestations in the landscape. At the less technological levels of human history, these influences were much more compelling. Reference to a limited range of physical landforms and to their evidence in place-names is provided. The rural landscapes of these islands are the products of interactions between people and places and between the many components and facets of the scene. This is reflected in a system of cross-referencing: terms in capitals have entries elsewhere in the book. Attempts have been made to make this comprehensive, yet not too obtrusive. All the entries included have been compiled from hundreds of published sources, as well as from personal observations and research. For major and some minor entries, suggestions for further reading have been provided. I have also attempted to humanise and enliven the text by including short quotations and examples from medieval and later sources. In this respect, two sources proved particularly rich: George C. Homans's *English Villagers of the Thirteenth Century*, first published in 1941, and the volumes of *West Yorkshire: An Archaeological Survey to AD 1500*, published in 1981 (to the great credit of West Yorkshire Metropolitan County Council). The core of the long entries was derived from an earlier reference book and this has been brought up to date and greatly expanded, while a multitude of new and short entries have been added, giving this text little resemblance to the predecessor. Thanks are due to Sarah Harrison for her excellent proof reading and suggestions with regard to further reading, and to the Cambridge University Committee for Aerial Photography (CUCAP) for permission to reproduce the aerial photographs.

It is very much hoped that this work will stimulate numerous episodes and adventures in local discovery. Historic interest is disappearing so swiftly from the countrysides of Europe's Atlantic margins that any reliable local surveys of a vanishing heritage are likely to become records of considerable value.

RICHARD MUIR
University of Aberdeen
Editor and Co-founder, LANDSCAPES journal

## Table of dates

The system of dating used in the text is as follows:

Up to *c.* 5000 BC: Mesolithic

*c.* 5000 to *c.* 2200 BC: Neolithic

(*c.* 2700–*c.* 2000 BC: Beaker)

*c.* 2200 to 650 BC: Bronze Age

*c.* 650 BC to 43 AD: Iron Age

43–410 AD: Roman (Romano-British)

410–1066: Dark Ages (Early, Middle and Late Saxon periods)

1066–1536: Medieval

## Dedication
For friends in the North.

# A

**Abbey**. Usually a large monastic house of high status, though a few PRIORIES were comparable to abbeys in almost every respect. An abbey was presided over by an abbot, who was presumed to represent Christ within the abbey and who served as the father of the community. Differences between the monastic orders were reflected in the lay-outs and architecture of their buildings. The Cistercian houses had substantial accommodation for lay brethren and favoured architecture that was more austere than that employed by the Benedictines or Cluniacs, while the abbey churches of the Augustinians often survived the Dissolution because they were shared with lay communities. Sometimes, the early years in the life of a community were glamorised in foundation myths which invented or exaggerated hardships endured and overcome in establishing the house, thus making the community seem blessed, and more worthy of admiration and donations.

*Further reading:* Aston, M., *Monasteries*, Batsford, London, 1993.

Menuge, N. J., 'The Foundation Myth: Yorkshire Monasteries and the Landscape Agenda', LANDSCAPES, **I.I**, 2000, pp. 22–37.

Bond, J., 'Landscapes of Monasticism' in Hooke, D. (ed.), *Landscape the Richest Historical Record*, Society for Landscape Studies, 2000.

**Acre**. Originally an expanse of land of indeterminate extent, though the term came to be associated with an open field STRIP of a size that could be ploughed by a team of oxen in one day. It was standardised by Edward I as 40 × 4 Rods, equalling 4840 sq. yds. Even so, different acres remained in different parts of the British Isles, with Westmorland and Scotland having their own acres, the Scottish acre measuring 6084 sq. yds, while in the English Midlands an acre was sometimes a linear measurement of around a chain (22 yds) to 1½ chains.

**Acredyke, acregarth, acrewall**, see HEAD DYKE.

**Acreland**. Indeterminate area of land of between around 8 and 20 ACRES.

**Aerial archaeology**. The leading British pioneer in the development of aerial archaeology was O. G. S. Crawford, who had served as an observer in the Royal Flying Corps. In 1924, he tested ideas he had derived from RFC and RAF materials in a series of flights over Wessex, funded by another First World War flyer, A. Keiller. The impressive results were published in *Wessex from the Air* (1928) and demonstrated the invaluable nature of air photography in archaeological discovery and interpretation. As editor of the journal *Antiquity*, which he had founded in 1924, Crawford encouraged the use of air photographs, including those taken by the private pilot, Major G. W. G. Allen, in the vicinity of Oxford. On the eve of the Second World War, Crawford undertook a programme of aerial photography in Scotland with J. K. St Joseph. Later to become a Professor, St Joseph, who remained secretive about his wartime intelligence work, developed the Cambridge University Committee for Aerial Photography, obtaining RAF material and initiating a flying programme that led to the collection of more than ¼ million items. In the mid 1960s, the National Monuments Record gained a flying unit and various other permanent or periodic flying units appeared, while the amateur tradition was perpetuated by aerial archaeological photographers like D. N. Riley. See also CROP MARKS.

*Further reading*: Bewley, B., 'Understanding England's Historic Landscapes: An Aerial Perspective', LANDSCAPES, 2.1, 2001, pp. 74–84.

Bowden, M., 'Mapping the Past: O. G. S. Crawford and the Development of Landscape Studies', LANDSCAPES, 2.2, 2001, pp. 29–45.

**Aftermath**. Stubble, the aftermath of the harvest, normally thrown open to the livestock of a community. Known as the eff-crop in Scotland.

**Agger**, see ROMAN ROADS.

**Agistment**. A movement of animals to summer grazings, often on high ground but possibly in a FOREST or a DEER PARK, that were rented out at a fixed per capita charge for each grazing animal. The agister was a royal official who took payment from commoners whose pigs enjoyed PANNAGE in the FOREST. The practice of agistment normally differed from the use of SHIELINGS in that in the former case the animals were driven up to the summer grazings and left alone or in the charge of a local herdsman. It therefore involved animals that did not require regular milking and the rent of the grazings was on a per capita basis rather than being incorporated in the rent of a tenancy. Occasionally, agistment involved the use of winter pastures. Farmers concerned in agistment with the introduction of 'foreign' livestock were frowned upon by the manor courts – perhaps mainly because the lord had not received anything from the deal. However, lowland farmers were keen to gain access to summer grazings and tenants in the hill country welcomed any extra income. The real threat that the introduction of foreign cattle posed was that of over-grazing and the disregard for the rule of LEVANCY AND COUCHANCY could imply an overstocking of the summer pastures. Normally, agistment allowed a grazing to support more cattle over summer than could be supported by local resources over the winter, and the removal of livestock around Michaelmas also removed the problems of over-stretching the winter fodder reserves.

*Further reading*: Winchester, A., *The Harvest of the Hills*, Edinburgh University Press, 2000.

**Agricultural depression**. Agricultural depressions have left distinctive marks upon the rural landscape. A major depression occurred during the last quarter of the nineteenth century after the British domestic market became flooded with cheap foreign agricultural produce. Some of this reflected the colonisation of vast new granaries in the New World and some of it was a consequence of technological advances, notably refrigerated ships. Very considerable acreages of land in Britain were abandoned by agriculture. This was mostly marginal land that required special treatment, like the heathlands that depended on the extraction of calcareous material from nearby MARLPITS. Land that fell out of agriculture was often redeveloped for forestry PLANTATIONS or for shooting. Meanwhile, with agricultural investments offering such low returns, the owners of the rural ESTATES no longer responded to the messages of HIGH FARMING. With the fall in profitability, farm rents were also obliged to fall and landowners sought to amalgamate tenancies into more viable holdings, while all agricultural employers strove to cut their wages costs. This was generally a time of decay, when VILLAGE communities shrank and workers gravitated to urban employment.

Depression of a special kind was experienced at the start of the twenty-first century with the return of foot and mouth disease, and by June of 2001, 3.4 million animals had been slaughtered, 80 per cent of them sheep. A by-product of the epidemic and the resulting closure of footpaths was an estimated loss of £1.7 billion to the tourist industry. The long

term consequences of the epidemic will include the psychological and social consequences for a pastoral farming community already hit by economic crisis, and also the reluctance of many consumers to buy meat products following media exposure of disturbing aspects of practices in the livestock industry. Rough grazing land could, increasingly, be converted to grouse moors and coniferous plantations, or be left unmanaged and revert to peaty ground. Hill pasture could revert to bracken or scrub, while livestock raising could be concentrated in lowland grazings, where SET ASIDE and invasion by scrub will also be apparent. At a time when hill farmers on very low incomes needed a maximum of public support it was found that the arrogance and the destruction of the rural landscape by 'barley barons' and the use of practices in food production that masses of people considered abhorrent had alienated much sympathy.

*Further reading*: themed papers on the landscape consequences of the foot and mouth outbreak in LANDSCAPES, 2.2, 2001.

**Aisled barn**, see BARN.

**Aisled hall**, see HALL.

**Aisled wheelhouse**, see WHEELHOUSE.

**Aith**. An INFIELD in Lowland Scots.

**Aitliff-crap**. Lowland Scots, the crop grown after barley, usually oats.

**Amad**. An old word for a hay meadow. See also MEADOWS.

**Ana, anay**. Lowlands Scots, a river island or river meadow.

**Anchorage**. A place free of dangerous shoals and sheltered from prevailing winds or gales where a ship could take refuge en route to harbour, or where a crew could await a change of wind or tide before proceeding on the next phase of their journey. Lundy Island provided a sheltered anchorage for vessels about to navigate the approaches to the Bristol Channel.

**Ancient and planned countryside**. For a very long time it has been recognised that lowland

3

England contains two distinctive types of countryside. Periodically, serious students of the landscape have discussed this fact, but surprisingly it has made little or no impact on the 'popular' literature of the countryside or on the public imagination. The two types of countryside have been described by different names at different times and by different writers. Medieval travellers were aware of the difference between 'fielden' and 'arden' – field and woodland countrysides. In the sixteenth century Thomas Tusser compared the 'several' countryside, where land was held by many small farmers, with the 'champion' countrysides of the OPEN-FIELD FARMING areas. Other writers used the word 'woodland' to describe Tusser's 'several' areas – not because they were covered in woodland, but because of the richness of their hedges. The Elizabethan writer William Harrison described the contrast:

> It is so, that our soile being divided into champaine ground and woodland, the houses of the first lie uniformelie built in everie town together, with streets and lanes; whereas in the woodland countries (except here and there in great market townes) they stand scattered abroad, each one dwelling in the midst of his owne occupieng.

Writing in 1941, the historian George C. Homans explained that:

> In England, four hundred years ago, when people first began to take an interest in such matters, they distinguished between two main kinds of English countryside, which they called *woodland* and *champion*. The word *champion* is of course derived from the Low Latin *campania*, by way of the French *champagne* and the English *champaigne*, which was in use, in something like its later sense, at least by the beginning of the fourteenth century.

More recently, the contrasting characters of the two countrysides have been studied by both Oliver Rackham and Tom Williamson, the former using terms 'ancient' and 'planned' to identify the types. But in essence all the writers are describing the same two kinds of countryside, so that the labels are interchangeable:

| Ancient Countryside | v. | Planned Countryside |
|---|---|---|
| arden | v. | fielden |
| several | v. | champion |
| woodland | v. | champion |

Each countryside has its own characteristics, yet these characteristics do not seem to be determined by the geographical qualities of the areas concerned, but rather by differences in their history of development. Much remains to be discovered, but the planned or champion areas were associated with open-field farming. The introduction of this system of farming was an act of planning by somebody, while the dismantling of open-field farming by PARLIAMENTARY ENCLOSURE introduced a new form of planning expressed by the superimposition of new geometrical field boundaries.

Ancient countryside was never transformed by the adoption of extensive open fields. In some places small open fields shared between a few tenants appeared, but they were localised (and usually partitioned away by the end of the seventeenth century) and the essential traditional aspects of the landscape survived. Land in ancient countryside areas was held 'in severalty', or divided between many independent farmers, rather than existing in vast common fields. The large nucleated villages which were so characteristic of the champion areas were rare in ancient countryside, where the settlement pattern is mainly composed of small hamlets and dispersed farmsteads – 'each one dwelling in the midst of his owne occupieng'.

It is possible that the planned or champion countrysides appeared in areas where the fragmentation of old estates during the Dark Ages had not gone so far as to prevent the introduction of coherent manorial farming systems incorporating an extensive set of open fields along with a complement of common or waste and meadowland. If, however, the patterns of land ownership had fragmented to a greater degree, the estates and holdings would be too small to accommodate open-field systems, and so ancient field and settlement patterns would endure. But as yet such an explanation is unproven.

Each countryside has its own distinct character. Ancient countryside is a place of hollowed winding lanes, many rich old HEDGEROWS, abundant footpaths, scattered FARMSTEADS and numerous small woods. Planned countryside often bears the hallmarks of PARLIAMENTARY ENCLOSURE: there are few woods but those that exist may be large and with long histories of organised commercial exploitation; lanes and footpaths are fewer and are often straight and not sunken; while the settlement pattern is composed of old nucleated villages and the dispersed farmsteads of the eighteenth and nineteenth centuries which derive from Parliamentary Enclosure.

Planned countryside is characteristic of the English Midlands, while ancient countryside is still recognisable in the West Country, Essex, the Weald and parts of the Welsh Marches. Within these broad patterns there can be abrupt transitions from one type of countryside to the other – for example, Cambridgeshire is typical planned countryside, though the change to ancient countryside comes abruptly as one crosses the boundary into the less spoiled parts of neighbouring Essex. Interestingly the juxtaposition of contrasting countrysides is not confined to England and can be seen in France in the contrast between the open *champagne* landscapes and the heavily hedged *bocage*. In all too many English parishes the agri-business movement has wiped all character and expression from the face of the countryside, but where the local scene is largely unspoiled the reader should have no difficulty in identifying the planned or ancient character of the setting.

*Further reading:* Rackham, Oliver, *The History of the Countryside*, Dent, 1986.

Williamson, T., *Shaping Medieval Landscapes: Settlement, Society, Environment*, Windgather Press, 2003.

Williamson, T., and Bellamy, L., *Property and Landscape*, George Philip, 1987.

**Ancient trackways**. Thousands of our lanes and trackways are likely to be ancient, although it is normally virtually impossible to identify them as being such. Moreover, several trackways have been billed as 'ancient' without there being a shred of evidence to support the claims. For example, it was once assumed that prehistoric farmers exploited only the downs and uplands, while the vales and plains were thought to have been blanketed in forest. Hence it was claimed that ridgeways are prehistoric routeways which stood high above the impenetrable wildwood. Now serious students of the countryside have realised that the archaeological evidence against such visions of the past is overwhelming. For a routeway to be shown to be prehistoric it should satisfy more rigorous tests; it must be associated with finds made along its length of ancient trade goods, like stone or bronze axes, be flanked by prehistoric monuments (in the way that Wayland's Smithy chambered tomb stands beside the Ridgeway) or yield evidence of having been redeveloped by the Romans, like the Peddars Way in East Anglia. Of course, a trackway could *be* prehistoric and yet not have revealed any of these characteristics – but then one has no grounds for arguing that it *is* prehistoric. Even when a trackway does seem to have good prehistoric qualifications it can pose problems – for example, the famous Ridgeway runs about a mile to the east of the great Neolithic temple at Avebury yet appears to show no interest in the monument and just carries blithely on its way. Even so, the pattern of prehistoric fields (now largely destroyed) which flanked the route did seem to respect it and confirm its antiquity. The Ridgeway and the Icknield Way, its eastward continuation into Norfolk, do seem to be credible as ancient trackways. However, ancient routeways have sometimes been confined between boundaries and robbed of their real form as zones or corridors of movement; different tracks would be developed and then abandoned and relocated within the corridor as they became rutted or muddy. Some of the candidates for 'ancient' have poor credentials, and it is not clear why the identifiers of ancient trackways have singled them out from the adjacent maze of similar routeways – components of which could be equally old or still older. There is no problem with supposing that a hollowed track running up to the entrance of an Iron Age HILLFORT has been walked since Iron Age times or that the entrances to monuments like Stonehenge or Avebury are as old as the monuments themselves. Most long-distance trackways pose sterner problems, and it is best to assume that masses of lanes and trackways have been used since prehistoric times – though normally we cannot produce provenances for specific examples.

*Further reading*: Harrison, S., 'The Icknield Way: some queries', in *Arch. J*, 160, 2004.
Taylor, C. C., *Roads and Tracks of Britain*, Dent, 1979.

**Applegarth**, see ORCHARD.

**Ash-houses**. In the days when all farmers were concerned for the health and quality of the soil, the conservation of natural fertilisers was a vital factor in farming. One minor but often significant source of goodness was represented by the rich potash content of household ash. The ash destined for the fields was sometimes stored away from the farmstead in a little ash-house, generally a small circular stone building with a conical thatched or corbelled roof and a diameter and height of less than 12 feet (4 metres). Sometimes DOVECOTES were converted to serve as ash houses. A number of examples can still be seen on the eastern flanks of Dartmoor.

**Assart (ridding)**. An assart is a field or group of fields created by medieval clearance, most usually of WOODLAND. The word appears to derive from the French word *essarter* 'to remove or

grub up woodland', and sometimes it was used to refer to the agricultural colonisation of heathland or fen. In the north of England, assarts were often known as 'riddings': land rid of trees. Although the fields created by assarting were normally privately owned, the woodland that was cleared in their creation was frequently common land. Where the woodland under threat was in the hands of the Crown, as with the royal hunting FORESTS, special licences to assart were required – and the sale of such licences, coupled with the taking of fines for illegal assarting, constituted a useful source of royal revenue.

While the term 'assarting' is conventionally applied to the medieval clearances, episodes of woodland clearance had been experienced since Mesolithic times, and the assarting of the Middle Ages must have been preceded by a great deal of felling in the later centuries of the Saxon period. It was then that some of the woodland which had colonised the countrysides depopulated in the centuries following the Roman withdrawal in AD 410 was removed. In England, the population rose quite rapidly in the years after the Norman Conquest of 1066 and, to a certain extent, the agricultural colonisation of woodland and waste provided a safety-valve for population pressure. During the thirteenth century the assarting movement was very active, but it appears to have slowed down as economic and environmental problems were encountered early in the fourteenth century – and then the process came almost to a standstill with the arrival of the Great Pestilence or Black Death after 1348, which created a myriad of untenanted peasant holdings.

Assarting took place in many forms. Often it involved the hacking of small, privately owned hedged fields from the retreating woodland margins. Sometimes several members of a village community were simultaneously engaged in assarting, and at times whole villages assaulted the woodland and the new lands created were divided into STRIPS, shared amongst the tenants and added to the village OPEN-FIELD system.

Monastic communities, notably the Cistercians in northern England, also engaged in assarting. Sometimes the lord of a manor would sanction or assist assarting by his tenants, and sometimes he assarted to expand his personal DEMESNE – in which case he was obliged, according to the statutes of Merton and of Westminster, to ensure that his free tenants still had sufficient pasture for their stock. Some individuals made assarting their speciality and acquired surnames like 'Sart'.

Occasionally, assarting took place on a grand scale, and great inroads would be made into the local woodland – in 1316 some fourteen different tenants paid their 'entry fines' to take over lands assarted from the common wood of Hipperholme on Wakefield manor, while during the early thirteenth century about 1000 acres (405 hectares) of land on the Bishop of Winchester's manor of Whitney in Oxfordshire were assarted. Normally, assarting was a more piecemeal process which expanded gradually from successive bites at the woodland apple. The fields produced were generally small – sometimes very small – often existing as a zone of hedged pastures with irregular shapes and curving boundaries which were sandwiched in a zone between the wood and the earlier village open fields or older pastures.

Assarts can sometimes be recognised from their shapes and settings, while certain field-names are very frequently associated with assarts. They include: 'Stocks', 'Stubbings' and 'Stubbs', which relate to tree stumps; 'Assart', 'Sart', 'Ridding', 'Royd, 'Brake' and 'Breach', which describe land newly colonised for farming; and 'Hay', a name commonly associated with the hedge planted around new assarts (though it could signify small woods). See also WOODLAND.

*Further reading*: Broad, J. and Hoyle, R. (eds), *Bernwood, the Life and Afterlife of a Forest,* **Harris Paper Two**, University of Central Lancashire, Preston, 1997.

**Avenue**. In LANDSCAPE PARKS avenues of trees were planted to line the straight roads leading to a mansion, thus having the visual effect of enhancing its importance, to provide straight alignments and vertical notes in formal arrangements of a geometrical kind or to direct the gaze towards some focal point in the landscape, such as an EYECATCHER, BELVEDERE or GAZEBO. Sometimes the trees were planted on low banks, and sometimes avenues extended beyond the confines of the park and lined the approach roads, signifying the imminent arrival of a new landscape based on status and aesthetics. At Studley Royal, near Ripon, a lime avenue and drive formed a line between Ripon Minster and a specially-built eyecatcher church of St Mary. The trees employed were generally of the taller kind and favoured species included lime, poplar, beech and horse chestnut. See also PARKLAND.

**Awald, award**. In Lowland Scots, the second crop of oats grown after a spell under grass, sometimes the second of two grain crops.

**Axe factory**, see STONE AXE FACTORY.

# B

**Bachille**. In Lowland Scots, a small portion of ploughland.

**Back-faulds**. In Lowland Scots, fields that lie behind or at some distance away from a farmstead.

**Backit dyke**. Lowland Scots, an earth bank boundary revetted in stone on its outer face. See also CONSUMPTION DYKE, CORN DITCH, DRYSTONE WALLS, ORTHOSTAT WALLS.

**Badgergate**. A road associated with 'badgers' or itinerant dealers in corn, who operated from medieval times through until the Industrial Revolution. Complaints from badgers resulted in the improvement of a track at Greenhow Hill, between Nidderdale and Wharfedale, in the 1630s. Various roads and lanes with names associated with badgers can be found in the Pennines, like Badger Gate on Denton Moor near Beamsley.

*Bakehouse*
A communal village bakehouse at Papworth St Agnes, Cambridgeshire

**Bakehouse**. Many villages supported a baker, and it was a common custom for the women of the community to pay a small fee to have their Sunday roasts cooked in the local baker's oven. Less common were the communal bakehouses, like the one that still stands on a small green in the Cambridgeshire village of Papworth St Agnes. It dates from the mid-nineteenth century.

In the Middle Ages, however, manorial bread-ovens were very common and were frequently rented out to a free tenant who was, in effect, a baker. A Leeds account of 1323 records a payment of 8*s.* 4*d.* (42p) 'for rebuilding the common oven of the borough which had fallen down, that is, for carrying stones there and for the wages of one man constructing the said oven by contract'. The non-free tenants of a manor were obliged to give all their custom to the manorial oven or face a fine, though free tenants could bake at home or patronise cheaper bakers. If, however, they wanted to sell the produce of their own ovens, then they had to have a licence and provide loaves of a weight that conformed to the regulations of the Assize of Bread and Ale.

**Bakestone, bakstane**. Slabs of fine-grained shale that could be heated on an open fire and used to bake oatcakes and the like. From at least medieval times, seams of suitable rock were quarried for this purpose and the stones were used until the industrial era. The little quarries associated with the practice have left a legacy of field- and place-names of the 'Bakestone' and 'Backstone' variety.

**Balk, wall, mere**. This term can be used loosely to describe any long narrow stretch of grassland. Towards the end of the Middle Ages some narrow STRIPS in the OPEN FIELDS were sometimes allowed to become grassed over, and were then used as permanent access-tracks through the ploughlands. See also BAULK.

**Balk and burral**. Lowland Scots term for RIDGE AND FURROW.

**Balloch**. A narrow mountain pass in Scotland.

**Band**. In northern Britain, a ridge running down from an upland mass, e.g. The Band in the Langdale Pikes region of the Lake District.

**Bandstane**. In Lowland Scots, a through stone in a DRYSTONE WALL that helps to bind the faces of the wall together.

**Bank**. The cutting face in a peat working. See also BANKS, TURBARY.

**Bank barrow**, see LONG BARROW.

**Banks**. In Lowland Scots, steep crags or sea cliffs but in northern England, the sloping sides of a valley.

**Barescrape**. In Lowland Scots, very impoverished and unrewarding land.

**Barmkin**. A fortification of late- or post-medieval date in Northern Britain, which could sometimes be a bridge tower or a barbican. Normally, the term was used to describe a walled courtyard attached to a stone tower or TOWER-HOUSE. See also PELE TOWER.

**Barn**. Barns are buildings where agricultural produce is stored or processed. They come in many different shapes and sizes and serve a number of different purposes. Well-preserved timber-framed barns are objects of great functional beauty, more appealing to some eyes than stately homes. The word 'barn' is thought to derive from Old English words meaning 'barley-house'.

*Tithe barns*. Any big old barn is likely to be known locally as a tithe barn, but this is no sure indication of its former role. Tithes were first instituted in late Saxon times and existed in one form or another until their abolition in 1936. During the Middle Ages, the rector of each parish had the right to take a tithe of a tenth of the annual income of each man in his parish. In practice not all tithes could be collected – it was not easy to take a tenth of a pig or a tenth of five chickens – and the main tithes involved crops and cattle. Often the rector would take the harvest from the tenth acre of a holding or the tenth sheaf harvested – and these would be stored in the parish tithe barn, the rector being largely supported by tithes and the produce of his GLEBE land. Not every parish would have had a tithe barn, for often a vicar was provided by an external institution, like a monastery or college, which controlled the tithes of parishes concerned, so that abbey and priory tithe barns can also be found. The size of a tithe barn partly reflected the productivity of the contributing lands, and many of the most impressive barns were associated with monasteries. The largest surviving example is the Great Coxwell tithe barn in Berkshire, associated with a GRANGE of Beaulieu Abbey and some 152 feet (46 metres) in length. However, the tithe barn at Cholsey, another Berkshire grange of the abbey, that was destroyed in 1815, was twice as long as the Great Coxwell barn. In 1836 the Tithe Commutation Act replaced tithes in kind with a fixed money rent. By this time, many parishes had already achieved such a conversion and the tithe barns had been demolished or taken over by lay farmers. Parochial tithe barns may be indistinguishable from other barns, and their recognition may depend on archival research.

*Aisled barns*. Aisled barns are built in a manner that is reminiscent both of parish churches and of a type of medieval dwelling known as an 'aisled hall'. They consist of a long central nave that is flanked on either side by rows of stout aisle-posts which support the roof. On each side of the nave, aisles ran between the posts and the low walls of the barn, occasionally continuing around the short ends of the barn to surround the nave completely. Sometimes the aisles were sectioned into cattle-stalls, but more usually they were used for storage. The advantage of the aisled form of construction was that of allowing the construction of buildings of increased width by bearing much of the weight of the roof on the internal posts rather than on the outer walls. The actual width of the aisles tended to depend upon the nature of the roof. Thatched or tiled roofs were normally steeply pitched, and the aisle space was usually rather limited as a result, but where stone flags were employed the roof would be heavy and have a shallow pitch of around 35 degrees, allowing a greater aisle space. When seen from inside, aisled barns are unmistakable, the larger ones having a cathedral-like grandeur. From the outside they

can usually be recognised by their high roof-ridges, massive roof areas and by their low walls, which can be of stone, timber-framing or weatherboarding. By around 1150, the expertise in building very large aisled barns had been acquired, and such barns continued to be developed until early in the nineteenth century.

*Barn*

A cruck-framed threshing barn from Cholstrey in Herefordshire, reconstructed at the Avoncroft Museum of Buildings near Bromsgrove. Here black poplar was used to create the cruck frame and split oak places were woven to fill the spaces between the framing timbers.

Many examples from the fourteenth and fifteenth centuries still survive.

*Threshing barns.* Many tithe barns were aisled, and most tithe and aisled barns were also threshing barns. The typical smaller threshing barn had a three-bay construction. The central bay contained the threshing floor where, during the winter months, grain was threshed using a hand flail – a heavy, hinged stick which was used for beating the opened sheaves of corn to separate the grain, chaff and straw. The bays on either side of the threshing floor were used for the storage of sheaves and straw. Intact threshing barns can easily be recognised by the large double doors at either end of the threshing floor. Not only did these allow cart access to the interior of the barn for the unloading of sheaves, but also they could be opened during threshing to allow the wind to waft away the choking chaff. Large threshing barns, like the Bradford-on-Avon and Bolton Abbey tithe barns, have double sets of doors indicating two threshing floors, and this design dates right back to the thirteenth century and continued to the end of the eighteenth century. The Cholsey barn had four threshing floors.

During the nineteenth century barn designs were modified to accommodate mechanical forms of threshing, the first functional machine being developed in East Lothian in 1786. Some machines were housed on the old threshing floors, others operated in the open, beside the ricks. Steam power was first applied to threshing in 1798, but horse-powered machines were also developed in the nineteenth century, with between two and six horses walking round and round, revolving a vertical spindle which was geared to a horizontal shaft, powering the belt-drive of a threshing machine installed in the barn. Sometimes, the horses operated in the open outside the barn, but often a covered *horse-engine house*, which could be square, circular, pentagonal or octagonal, was built abutting the side of the barn. During the second half of the nineteenth century steam threshing engines became very widespread, and since their power could be transmitted by belt and pulley they allowed more flexible arrangements, though sometimes porches or annexes were erected to shelter the portable machines.

*Field-barns.* In some places it was found practical to have accommodation for crops and animals dispersed amongst the fields rather than huddled around the farmstead. Many field-barns combined a small threshing barn or a hay-storage area with shelter for a few cattle and they eliminated the need to haul the harvest from the field to the farm, while manure from cattle was available for spreading on the field which housed the barn. Where the field-barn was associated with a sheltered CREW or FOLDYARD where a number of cattle could be penned in winter, the term *outfarm* is sometimes used to describe the little complex. In the Dales and uplands, where pastoral farming predominated, the field-barns were often partitioned to provide a space for stall-fed cattle, a hay-loft in the upper storey and a ground-level 'sink mow' also for storing the hay crop of the surrounding field. Most field-barns date from the period 1750–1850, coinciding with the Agricultural Revolution and PARLIAMENTARY ENCLOSURE. Following enclosure, land was partitioned and privatised, and often a village- or hamlet-based farmstead would be inconveniently separated from its allocated fields, which helps to explain the popularity of field-barns in areas of mixed farming. Many field-barns have been demolished or converted into dwellings, partly explaining the current demise of the barn owl in many areas. But in Swaledale, particularly in the vicinity of Muker and Gunnerside, the multitude of field-barns is still a remarkable feature of the fieldscape. *Three tier barns* are southern equivalents of the more numerous field barns of the north and have hay and other goods stored in the higher level of the roof, winter feed in the level below and the cattle, or sometimes sheep, at ground level. *Bank barns* are especially associated with the south-western half of the

Lake District. They employ terrain, in the form of a bank or slope to allow direct access (sometimes employing a ramp) to the upper level, entered on the upslope side of the barn, as well as to the lower level, which is entered on the downslope side. Carts carried grain to a threshing floor at the upper level, while livestock and possibly a sink mow for storing hay were on the level below. Barns exploiting steep slopes can be found throughout the northern and western uplands.

*Dutch barns or hay-barns.* These buildings consist of a roof supported on brick or stone piers and date from the late nineteenth century onwards. They were used for storing hay, straw or sheaves in conditions that allowed a free circulation of air. Twentieth-century examples often consist of a curving corrugated-iron roof standing on an iron frame. See also BARNYARD, HEMMEL.

*Further reading*: Brunskill, R. W., *Traditional Farm Buildings of Britain*, Gollancz, 1982.
Peters, J. E. C., *Discovering Traditional Farm Buildings*, Shire Publications, 1981.

**Barnyard**. The stockyard or CREWYARD adjoining a BARN.

**Barrow**, see LONG BARROW, ROUND BARROW, SQUARE BARROW.

**Barth**. A sheltered pasture, suitable for delicate lambs or calves.

**Barton, Barken, Burton, Berton**. These words, occurring in place-names, can designate the DEMESNE land of a manor, often a detached portion of the desmesne, but also sometimes a barley field or a chicken house.

**Bastle house**. The bastle house was to some extent the poorer man's equivalent of the PELE TOWER. Like pele towers, bastle houses developed in parts of Cumbria and Northumberland which were particularly vulnerable to Scottish raiding, and most examples date from the sixteenth century. They were defensible farmhouses with ground-floor accommodation for livestock and domestic quarters on the first floor. The walls, of boulder rubble, were built to a thickness of around 4 feet (1.2 metres) at the base, and access to the upper storey was originally provided by a ladder which could be dragged inside for safety, though later external staircases of stone were added. Downstairs, the door-jambs had deep slots which took the thick drawbars which helped to barricade the entrance. The Borders farmers who occupied bastles must have been a doughty breed, and logic suggests it would have been safer to hide in the woods or moors waiting for danger to pass than huddle entrapped in a bastle with a raiding party just outside.

The bastles, of which several examples survive, were a remarkably individual but homogenous class of dwellings. They are confined to a narrow strip of territory of about 20 miles (32 kilometres) in width which runs along the border, they almost all measure about 36 feet (11 metres) by 20 feet (6 metres) and all date to the century 1550–1650, though after 1650 some less genuinely defensive examples were built.

**Batch, Beck, Bourne, Burn**. Dialect words from different parts of the country for a stream.

**Battlefield archaeology**. This youthful and popular branch of archaeology is applying the techniques of archaeology to a subject previously dominated by military historians. Concentrations of missiles gathered from the ploughsoil by FIELDWALKING may demonstrate the focus of an attack and be used to refute or confirm traditional views of the development, tactics and strategies of a battle. Grave pits may indicate the probable murder of prisoners or reveal the ways in which warriors and camp followers were slain and with what weapons. Battlefield finds may also highlight the exploitation of terrain by the opposed forces. The new field of study is to be welcomed, not only because it enhances our understanding of history, but also because it issues reminders of the hideous brutality of battle at times when displays of martial skills may mask the true nature of conflict.

*Further reading*: Hill, P. and Wileman, J., *Landscapes of War*, Tempus, Stroud, 2002.

Various authors, LANDSCAPES, 4.2, 2003, themed issue on battlefield landscapes.

**Battock**. In Lowland Scots, a river floodplain or island; also a tussock of grass.

**Bauk**. In Lowland Scots a narrow footpath or trackway though a field (see BALK and BAULK) or a boundary between adjacent ESTATES.

**Baulk**. A boundary in open fields, frequently between FURLONGS, which was grassed-over. Animals were tethered to graze on the baulks, and often they broke loose, damaged crops and ended in the POUND. As the harvest time approached so the tethering of animals within the arable fields was increasingly resented. See also BALK.

**Bawn**. A defensive enclosure attached to an Irish TOWER-HOUSE. See also BARMKIN.

**Beacon (beacon hill, toot hill)**. Beacon hills were the topographical components of early-warning systems which pre-dated the radio or the telephone, and the sight of a fire burning atop a beacon hill was a warning of approaching danger and a signal to muster the local forces. The antiquity of the system is unknown, although it is hard to believe that beacons would not have been used in prehistoric times and the concept was echoed by the coastal Roman SIGNAL STATIONS which may, like their lighthouses, have employed beacons. Related to the beacon hills were those which may still be known by names like 'Toot', 'Tout' or 'Tot'. These were hills where men scanned or 'toted' for danger. The name derives from the Old English *totaern* and it is likely that toot-hill lookout posts were employed when Viking raiders threatened.

Beacons were normally operated in chains or systems, which were revived and redeveloped to meet successive invasion threats or scares.

Place-name evidence suggests that some form of beacon system existed in the twelfth century, and a signalling network was produced during the fourteenth and fifteenth centuries, when French raiding threatened the south coast, and a different beacon system operated in the northern counties of England to give warning of advances from Scotland. During the reign of Henry VII a coherent national system of coastal defence was introduced, with a chain of artillery forts to guard the southern invasion coast. This was supported by an elaborate system of beacons running from Land's End to the Thames, capable, in theory, of transmitting coded messages. In 1558, in the reign of his daughter, Elizabeth I, the Cornish beacons were fired to signal the sighting of the Spanish Armada, and beacons were rebuilt at the time of the Napoleonic invasion scare. Like other, more sophisticated early-warning systems, this one was prone to giving false alarms, so that the accidental firing of Hume Castle Beacon (Berwickshire) in 1804 produced an unintentional muster of auxiliaries across the Scottish Lowlands. Ceremonial beacons were lit to mark two of Queen Victoria's jubilees and the coronation of Elizabeth II.

The beacon itself could consist of a large bonfire, sufficient to be seen ablaze from the next site in a beacon chain, perhaps 5–10 miles (8–16 kilometres) away. Sometimes the fire was carried on a stone fire-turret, like the one on Culmstock Beacon in Devon, though frequently the fire was contained in an iron basket held aloft on a pole and reached by a ladder. A similar reconstructed beacon, standing on the ruins of a Bronze Age hilltop barrow, can be seen on Beacon Hill on the North York Moors. In some cases beacons lit at ecclesiastical sites could provide valuable LANDMARKS for mariners and occasionally beacons may have been built upon church towers, as at Blakeney in Norfolk.

Beacon Hill and Toot Hill place-names are very common: there are Toot Hills in Essex, Hampshire, Staffordshire and West Yorkshire, Tote Hills in Hampshire and West Sussex, a

Totham Hill in Essex, a Tothill in Lincolnshire, a Tottenhill in Norfolk, while Dorset has Hambury Tout, Worbarrow Tout and Hounstout to guard its coast, Gloucestershire has Tutshill, and Kent has Tutt Hill. The Beacon Hill place-names are too numerous to mention, but among the most celebrated are Cothelstone Beacon in the Quantocks with a view over eleven counties, and Herefordshire Beacon on the Malverns with a magnificent HILLFORT and, according to John Evelyn, 'one of the goodliest vistas in England'.

**Bear-feys.** In Lowland Scots, land devoted to the cultivation of barley.

**Bear-reet.** In Lowland Scots, land that has just borne a crop of barley.

**Beck head pastures**. Grazings on high ground in northern England which were accessible, via the HOPES or valleys of becks, to surrounding lowland communities, though they may not have operated strictly as COMMONS.

**Bee bole**, A nook in the wall of a Tudor or Jacobean house or garden wall at about waist or chest height deliberately created to accommodate bee skeps. Other niches were used for hens, hawks or rabbits. They were most common in the damper north-west of England, where more shelter was needed for the hives.

**Bee garden**. Circular or square turf-walled enclosures within which beehives were placed. They were about the same area as a house, with the enclosing banks being about a metre tall. Most were associated with commercial honey production in southern Britain but are now decaying.

**Beel**. In Lowland Scots, a place where cattle are gathered together in the open to spend the night. Also a building that offers shelter. See also BIELD-WALL.

**Beestone**. A stone on which a beescap, -skep or –hive was placed. See also BEE BOLE, BEE GARDEN.

**Bell pit (day hole)**. Bell pits are relics of medieval or seventeenth-century mining, mainly for iron ore and coal. A circular shaft at least 6–7 feet (about 2 metres) in diameter was dug downwards to the seam or ore body and then the shaft was widened as the material was extracted to produce a bell-shaped pit. Abandoned bell pits could collapse, be filled with spoil or form ponds, and their relics are frequently associated with areas of medieval woodland and common. They are usually found in groups – sometimes large groups – as on Catherton Common in Shropshire. Bell pits can often be recognised as circular hollows with slight rims, though the earth-works may be obvious or very faint, some only being visible only when the pasture is very closely grazed. Bell-pit mining, which was no more advanced than the technique used in Neolithic FLINT MINES, was superseded by shaft mining when practical water-pumping techniques were developed to drain the workings.

The term 'bell pit' is now under fire from industrial archaeologists, who tend to avoid the words. Where the mineral resource that was being mined existed as a seam that outcropped at the surface – as with many early lead workings – bell-shaped pits were not formed. Miners had immediate access to the ore and worked their way along the vein leaving a trench or chain of cavities behind. Such methods of mining would make sense at any period of history, so the sinking of series of small shafts into an outcropping vein need not necessarily be indicative of 'primitive' exploitation. See also MEER.

*Further reading*. Roe, M., 'The Changing Face of Lead Mining in the Yorkshire Dales', LANDSCAPES, 4.1, 2003.

**Bellware**. A type of seaweed from which KELP was made.

**Beltie**. In Lowland Scots, a narrow plantation often serving as a SHELTER BELT.

**Belvedere**. A small but often ornate building in

a palladian or gothic style, normally of the eighteenth century and erected within a LANDSCAPE PARK to serve as a place of contemplation or retreat and as venues for picnics. There were some quite imposing examples, like the Temple of the Four Winds at Castle Howard, near York, the Octagon Tower of the 1730s at Studley Royal, near Ripon, whose view of Ripon Minster were obscured as trees matured. Some took the form of a circular temple and also acted as EYECATCHERS. A spacial variant was the gazebo, which served as a place to look from rather than at; these were popular resting places for groups of ladies and were often placed to provide views of traffic moving along a road. See also FOLLIES.

**Bent**. This word occurs quite frequently in Englaish and Scottish place-names and will usually refer to the presence of bent, a kind of grass.

**Berewick**. A subordinate or outlying estate.

**Bield-wall**. In the northern uplands of England, a short length of wall built to shelter livestock in gales and blizzards. The compression of the air on the windward side causes wind to blow over the wall, taking any snow with it.

**Biggin**. A cottage or coarsely-built dwelling in Scotland and the north of England

**Bilbie**. In Lowland Scots, a residence or shelter.

**Birk**. An archaic form of 'birch', denoting woods where birch once grew, as in Birkenthwaite or Birkenshaw.

**Black and white houses**, see TIMBER-FRAMING.

**Black house**. The black house is a form of the LONGHOUSE which developed in the Hebrides. The name seems to be of a recent coinage and makes a distinction between the 'old' black houses and the more conventional modern 'white houses' which have superseded them. Black houses adopt the characteristic longhouse form of one or two domestic rooms that share their roof with a byre. They were adapted to

exploit locally available materials and provide the maximum insulation against wind and weather, some being built with walls more than 6 feet (2 metres) thick. In the Outer Hebrides, the low walls of the black house were built of turf sandwiched between inner and outer courses of rubble, and water from the thatch dripped into this turf packing to improve its windproof qualities. On Skye, in contrast, the walls were of boulders and rubble, and the thatch overlapped the walls and was held in place by a net weighted with stones. The antiquity of the black

*Black house*
The interior of a black house open to the public at Colbost on Skye.

house is not known, although the basic design harks back to the Dark Ages. Thousands of black houses were still occupied at the start of the twentieth century, but now such dwellings are either seen as decaying ruins or have been restored as tourist attractions. Good examples include the Arnol black house on Lewis and those at Kilmuir, Colbost and Luib on Skye. See also CROFTING, RUNRIG.

**Bleachfield**. This and similar names usually indicate the former presence of bleachyards or bleach works, often associated with a cottage based linen industry and with access to a river.

**Bod or booth**. Places on the coasts of Shetland where fish, caught and cured by the islanders, were stored and traded with merchants from Hamburg, Bremen and other North German cities for goods like salt. See also LODGE.

**Booley**. In Ireland, a temporary stockpen used when herds were grazing the summer pastures. This is an Anglicisation of *buaile*, denoting the summer huts associated with the SHIELING and with butter-making.

**Booley house**. Summer dwelling associated with a BOOLEY. See also SHIELING.

**Bookland**, see FOLKLAND.

**Booth**. A term for a cow house in the north of Britain (but see also BOD OR BOOTH).

**Borders**. The Anglo-Scottish border landscape retains many relics of the hostility that frequently erupted between the two countries. During times of relative peace it was in the interests of all concerned that the life of the border region – a territory which united as well as divided communities – should proceed as normally and profitably as possible. Until the Union of the Crowns in 1603, there were sections of the boundary, like Wark Common, that remained in dispute or uncertain, though the marchlands of each kingdom had its own distinct organisation. In Scotland there was the West March, comprising the two Stewartries of

Kickubright and Annandale, most of Wigtownshire and Dumfries; the Middle March, with Peebleshire, Roxburghshire and Selkirkshire, and the East March, which covered most of Berwickshire (with Liddesdale often functioning as a discrete entity). The most significant officers overlooking the affairs of each march in the early post-medieval period were Wardens (Keepers in Liddesdale). They were drawn from the leading families in each march, with the wardenships becoming virtually hereditary. They had both judicial and diplomatic functions and on truce days the Wardens, along with six Scots and six Englishmen, met and negotiated. Occasionally, their near-autonomy was compromised when an armed royal force would descend upon part of a March and apprehend any law-breakers that it could find. In England there was also a threefold division into Marches, with the Liberty of Berwick-upon-Tweed and Cheviot in the East March and Cumberland in the West March. Warders were responsible for enacting the body of practices that had become the Border Laws, which concerned the rites of pursuit, sanctuary and surrender. The gradual natural harmonisation of relations through intermarriage was retarded by Wardens, who generally banned cross-border marriages.

Meetings between the leading knights and wardens to regularise the affairs of the Borders were held at 'gates' or crossings on drove roads high in the fells and often at the heads of streams and burns. Thus representatives of the Kerrs and Douglases from the Scottish Middle March might meet and negotiate with the equivalent English appointee. In reality, the international diplomacy was complicated by feuds between leading families on the same side, like that between the Kerrs and the Scotts on the northern side of the Border, and also by the emergence of local warlords and robber barons, like Johnny Armstrong, who renounced all authorities. When diplomacy failed, fiercely destructive raids could be launched, like the invasion of northern England by the Earl of Douglas in 1388 which culminated in the Battle of Otterburn. The almost continual presence of 'mosstroopers' or raiding bands, who 'lifted' cattle and burned crops and buildings in the perpetuation of feuds or pursuit of wealth, ensured that every family of substance had its castle or TOWER HOUSE. A response to the insecurity was the appointment of 'setters and searchers' to organise the watching of the border passes. Raids not only gave rise to prolonged feuds, they also provoked reprisal raids and the periodic devastation of the landscape of the Borders resulted in the reduction of its population, the distortion of its commerce and the devaluation of its resources. With England as the greater power, any efforts at castle-building by the Scots was likely to be regarded as a provocation and to provoke a punitive invasion. After the Union of the Crowns, many of the causes for enmity were removed, a joint border commission oversaw the affairs of the Borders and commerce between the two lands quickened.

*Further reading*: Rae, T. I., *The Administration of the Scottish Frontier, 1513–1603*, Edinburgh University Press, 1966.

White, J. T., *The Scottish Border and Northumberland*, Eyre Methuen, London, 1973.

**Bote**. This comprised a series of rights which tenants on particular manors might (or might not) enjoy. They concerned the rights to take certain materials from the common and normally included cartbote (getting materials to make transport vehicles), firebote (gathering sticks for fuel), foldbote (taking timber to build a sheep fold), haybote (taking timber to repair fences and gaps in hedges), housebote (taking materials for house-building) and ploughbote (taking timber for making ploughs). The old English custom was replaced by the Norman-French term 'estovers'. See also COMMONS.

**Bothie, bothy**. In Lowland Scots, a cottage occupied by farm servants or 'bothie-men'.

**Boundary**, see HEDGE AND DITCH RULE, BALK, BAUK, LAND-MARCH, MARK.

**Boundary stone**. In the old countrysides, boundary stones, MARK STONES, mere stones or HAIR STANES marked a whole heirarchy of divisions, from the bounds of kingdoms, shires, sherrifdoms or Forests at the higher level, to the limits of DOLES in common ploughlands or MEADOWS at the other. All divisions were jealously guarded and tenants accused of moving a stone that marked a division between two holdings would frequently be brought before MANOR courts. Large stones or small boulders will often be encountered in former communally-worked fields, but generally their significance has long since been forgotten and it will be impossible to know whether or not they were boundary-markers.

**Boundary tree**. Ancient trees that are recorded in charters or place-names in association with personal names were frequently boundary-markers on the borders of ESTATES or HUNDREDS. Occasionally, the person referred to can be identified, as in the case of Godwin's Oak at Ripley, North Yorkshire, which grew on the boundary between the estates of the early thirteenth-century Godwin and the King's Forest of Knaresborough. It lived until the mid-eighteenth century.

*Further reading*: Gelling, M., *Place-Names in the Landscape*, Dent, London, 1993.

**Bovate, Oxgang**. A widely varying area of land sometimes equating with a half-VIRGATE and sometimes with a whole one. It notionally represented the amount of land that could be ploughed by an ox team in a year.

**Bow**. A word with several agricultural associations in Lowlands Scots, including a cow pasture or cattle fold, a dwelling or the principal FARMSTEAD on an ESTATE.

**Box-framing**, see TIMBER-FRAMING.

**Bracken**. Today bracken, with its carcinogenic qualities and its invasion of upland grazings and heather MOORS, is seen as an unwelcome feature of the fellside landscapes. Formerly, however, it had considerable uses. It was harvested on the COMMONS and used as a substitute for straw as a bedding, thatching and packing material. It was also burned on quite a large scale, the resultant ash providing potash used in the manufacture of soap and glass. In the seventeenth century bracken beds in the north of England were conserved and shares or 'dalts' were allocated amongst the tenants of a manor. The season for harvesting the fronds was restricted to a few weeks around the end of August, when the cutting or pulling of individual fronds as thatching materials could take place, while the mowing of the bracken for burning could not take place before the end of September.

**Brae, brow**. In Lowland Scots, a hillside, hill or knoll, also a steep road. A braeside is a hillside and a brae head is the top of a slope.

**Brairded-dyke**. In Scotland, a dead hedge made of thorns and furze. See also HEDGEROWS.

**Breasting**. Revetting an existing earth field boundary bank with stone, as took place on some northern upland manors in the immediate post-medieval period. See also DRYSTONE WALLS, DITCH.

**Breck, break, breach, brack**. Land taken in from the waste and improved, as with the Brecklands of the Norfolk/Suffolk borders. In Lowland Scots, a 'brack' or 'breck' can be untilled land between two cultivated plots or else an area of barren ground, while a 'break' is a piece of ground broken-up for cultivation.

**British Fisheries Society**. Founded in 1786 as an offshoot of the Highland Society of London, this represented the growth of more enlightened attitudes towards clan communities. It attempted a reorganisation of society in coastal settlements. Boat fishing was encouraged by bounties paid on barrels of fish caught. Ullapool, Lochbay and Tobermory were among the new settlements.

*Further reading*: Munro, J., 'The planned villages of the British Fisheries Society' in Smith, J.S. and

Stevenson, P., *Fermfolk and Fisherfolk*, Edinburgh, 1992.

**Broch**. Brochs are remarkable defensive stone towers, built only in Scotland, mainly in the north of the country, and in the Northern Isles around the first century AD. They were built with double DRYSTONE WALLS of an exceptional quality, the hollow space between the walls accommodating a number of chambers or cells. The brochs seem to have appeared suddenly and in a fully refined form, and their origins are still mysterious and controversial. One interpretation regards the brochs, which have a largely coastal distribution, as being native defences against seaborne Roman slavers. However, it may be more reasonable to regard the brochs as a defensive response by native leaders to the destabilisation of coastal communities caused by a shortage or deterioration in land. No broch survives to its original height, which could approach 50 feet (15 metres), the best preserved being the broch on Mousa in Shetland. More accessible are the pair of neighbouring brochs, Dun Telve and Dun Troddan, which can be seen in Glenelg in the Western Highlands.

*Further reading*: Smith, B. B. and Banks, I. (eds), *In the Shadow of the Brochs*, Tempus, Stroud, 2002.

**Brook**. In Lowland Scots, an accumulation of seaweed washed onto a beech.

**Bruntlin**. In Lowland Scots, a burnt muir or MOOR.

**Buildwall**, see FOLD.

**Bullaun**. Bullauns are found in Ireland and exist as stones or small boulders that have been ground and hollowed to contain basin-like depressions. They can be found scattered and forgotten in the countryside but are most frequently associated with Celtic monastic sites. They may have been used as mortars, perhaps for the pounding of herbs used in some ritual concoction. Subsequently, other myths have developed, like that which claims that rainfall

*Broch*
The ruins of a broch at Dun Carloway on Lewis. Note the double wall construction.

collecting in a bullaun acquires curative powers. It is also claimed that pebbles rolled three times in a bullaun against the movement of the sun would fix a curse.

**Burh (burgh).** *Burhs* (see photograph on page 20) were defended Saxon towns, mainly the creations of Alfred the Great, his son, Edward the Elder, and daughter, Aethelflaed of Mercia, in the period *c.* 880–920. They were intended to serve as strongpoints during Danish invasions and were built to a regular street-plan and surrounded by earthwork defences. Some, like Stamford (developed from both a Saxon *burh* and a nearby Danish one), survive as towns today; some failed; and some, like Langport in Somerset, now exist as villages. Probably the

*Burh*

Lydford in Devon may have originated as a hamlet associated with a church dedicated to St Petrock around AD 600. In the reign of King Alfred it was developed as a *burh* and in 997 it repulsed a Danish attack.
The course of the Saxon wall can be seen running from right to left just above the V-shaped road junction.
The mound of a Norman motte is visible in the upper right corner of the Saxon defensive structure. (CUCAP)

most interesting of the *burhs* are Wallingford and Wareham, both preserving features of the Saxon defences and street-plan. In medieval Scotland the towns were royal burghs or burghs of barony, depending on the status of their feudal founders and masters.

From the point of view of the countryside detective *burhs* are most relevant because their name, usually surviving in the form 'burgh' or 'bury', provides place-name clues to former strongholds – though often, defences no more imposing than those of a moated homestead (see under MOAT) or a small MOTTE. The extremely numerous examples include the fieldname 'Bury Close' at Walkern in Hertfordshire, associated with a castle moat. These place-names, as well as others, like HALSTEAD, can be exploited in the detection of mottes, moats and manor houses that were the local power-centres of post-Conquest England.

**Burnt mound**. These are heaps of burnt stones that have been subject to great heating. The mounds sometimes have a kidney-like plan with a central depression. It is believed that the stones were roasted on fires and then used to heat water held in a stone box or wooden trough, with the resultant steam giving rise to a sauna effect. In Ireland, where these sites are very numerous, the heated water was thought to have been employed for cooking, though the sauna interpretation seems equally apt. Burnt mounds appear to date from the late-Neolithic to early-Bronze Age period. They are normally situated close to a source of water, employed not only to fill the traugh, but also for bathing by those emerging from the sauna. They have a relatively recent equivalent in the SWEAT HOUSES of Ireland.

**But and a ben**. In Scotland, a two-roomed cottage, the 'but-a-hoose' being the outer room

or kitchen and the 'ben-hoose' being the better, inner room or parlour.

**Butt**, see HEADLAND.

**Butts**. Archery butts certainly existed in medieval times, when the sport of archery was actively encouraged by the state for obvious military reasons. One knows of only one place where such butts survive as recognisable earthworks: Wold Newton in East Yorkshire. Here, a pair of earthen mounds dating from the thirteenth century stand in a field close to the green and pond, and they will have been used to prevent a reduction of the local populace caused by stray arrows. 'Butts' or 'butt' place-names are very common, but in virtually every case they relate to HEADLANDS within medieval OPEN FIELDS.

**Byre**. A cow house. See also BOOTH.

**Byrlaw, Birlie, burlaw, barley**. A local court in northern England and the Scottish Borders somewhat resembling the COURT BARON. The word derives from the Old Norse *byjar-log*, denoting a law community or legal territory. The courts were concerned with creating regulations relating to a particular locality and community and were normally presided over by the lord or his bailiff. Such courts were particularly useful in settling disputes between neighbours and regulating the affairs of individual townships that lay within much larger jurisdictions whose head courts might have been somewhat remote. Sometimes there was a requirement that estate tenants should attend their local byrlaw courts on a regular basis, as on the manors of Fountains Abbey, where tenants were required to attend the appropriate court each year and observe its rulings.

*Further reading*: Winchester, A. J. L., *The Harvest of the Hills*, Edinburgh University Press, 2000.

# C

**Cairn, currough**. A loose pile of stones, sometimes developing on summits as climbers add a stone on the highest point and sometimes accumulating in the commemoration of a person or event or in the marking of a boundary.

**Cairnfields**, see CLEARANCE CAIRNS.

**Cairt-sheuch**. In Lowland Scots, a rutted cart track (while a carr gate is a road over steep, rocky country).

**Capital messuage**, see MESSUAGE.

**Carr**. Land in the central and northern parts of Britain that is badly-drained, flood-prone and often colonised by alder. Alder carr bordered rivers on many northern floodplains and could offer shelter for outlaws and wolves. Now the alders may be gone, or else reduced to a single line of trees, followed by flocks of siskins, helping to stabilise the river bank, and perhaps exploited for timber by clog makers until a century or so ago.

**Carrick**. In Scotland, a crag.

**Carse, kerse**. In Scotland, an expanse of flat, fertile land flanking a river.

**Cartshed**. Cartsheds were provided to protect carts and other farm vehicles against rain damage. Built of a variety of materials, they had an open side – or occasionally an open end – to allow free access, and the 'parking spaces' were divided at the front, by the posts or piers which helped to support the roof. Unlike the open-fronted cowhouses which they faintly resemble, cartsheds were usually orientated to face away from the farmyard, CREW or foldyard, preventing farm animals from wandering amongst the vehicles. The space above the vehicles often served as a granary.

**Carucate**, see HIDE.

**Cashel**. A stone ringfort associated with parts of Ireland with shallow soils and readily-available building stone. The encircling wall might be compared with the enclosure of a farmyard, and the dwelling and farm buildings would have stood inside. Some cashels appear to contain the remains of temporary accommodation used in the summer, and some contain clocháin (see CLOCHAN) and may date from the early Christian period. Cashels may range in age from the Neolithic to the early modern period. Most seem to be integrated with the surrounding fields and are likely to date from the Iron Age and early Christian era. See also RATH.

**Cat and clay**. A Scottish form of WATTLE AND DAUB construction, involving building walls of clay and chopped straw around a framework of wooden laths. The wall was built-up in layers or 'clats'. See also MUD AND STUD.

**Catch meadow**. MEADOW irrigated by water flowing down an adjacent slope.

**Catchland, Catchpole Acre**. Land which had escaped early partitioning between PARISHES and which was therefore available to the first clerk to establish a claim.

**Cattle close**, see CREWYARD.

**Cattle creep**. A tunnel passing through a railway embankment allowing livestock to pass in safety from one side of the track to another.

**Cattle raik**. In Scotland, a common or an extensive pasture where cattle grazed.

**Caul or cauld**. In Scotland, a floodbank of cobbles and boulders protecting riverside land from inundation, or a weir used to deflect water into a mill stream. See also WATERMILL.

**Causeway camp**, see CAUSEWAYED ENCLOSURE.

**Causewayed enclosure (causeway camp).** In their heyday, between about 4300 and 3300 BC, causewayed enclosures will have appeared as spectacular as any form of prehistoric monument. Today, after perhaps six millennia of erosion and silting, there are no examples which are really impressive when seen from the ground, and the best of the aerial photographs only offer hints of the former grandeur of these mysterious creations.

The enclosures consist of a roughly oval central space, sometimes a hilltop, which is girdled by between one and four sets of hyphenated or interrupted banks and ditches. In this respect – as well as those of age and, possibly, function – the enclosures differ from HILLFORTS. Plainly the builders of these remarkable monuments sought to define and surround a large central stage, which must have had enormous ritual, social or economic significance, with a most imposing girdle of banks and ditches. Causeways of undisturbed ground, far too numerous for the simple needs of access to the interior, were left untouched, though the massive ditches between the causeways were the result of enormous exertions, presumably those of labour gangs swinging picks made from red-deer antlers. The rubble from the ditches was piled up to form concentric rampart-like banks that were built to lie just inside the ditches. These banks are completely or virtually eroded away now, but it is possible that they were originally more continuous than the interrupted quarry ditches.

The construction of a causewayed enclosure imposed enormous demands of time, labour and commitment upon the Neolithic society concerned. It has been calculated that the most celebrated of the monuments, on Windmill Hill near Avebury in Wiltshire, with its maximum diameter of 1200 feet (365 metres) and its three rings of roughly concentric ditches would have taken a labour force of a hundred men about six months to construct. That the contemporary community of the region was able to divert such massive resources of manpower from the day-to-day necessities of farming and also support the labourers with food and shelter during the construction work tells of a capable, motivated, reasonably secure and well-organised society. When one walks over the Windmill Hill site today the remains are unobtrusive, and in many sections the earthworks are invisible from the ground. Yet excavation has shown that originally the ditches were 10 feet (3 metres) deep, while the banks could have stood taller than a man.

While excavations at causewayed enclosure sites have produced a wealth of detailed information, the function of these majestic monuments is still debated. Given that prehistoric societies probably did not categorise and pigeon-hole ideas and functions in the way that we do, it is probable that their monuments served a mixture of important religious, ritual, social, political and economic roles. The enclosures certainly had important ritual connotations, for the excavations of their ditches have shown that quantities of human and animal bones as well as stone axes, which served as both functional and ritual objects, were frequently deposited in them. These 'ritual deposits' were sometimes covered with earth, while occasionally ditches were recut after they had become choked by silt washed down from the banks. At Hambledon Hill in Dorset the last recutting of the ditch took place a thousand years after the initial building of the causewayed enclosure, demonstrating the remarkably long currency of some of these monuments. It has been suggested that the animal bones concerned could represent the debris of ritual feasts. The human bones could have been removed from CHAMBERED TOMBS for use in religious ceremonies, and it is possible that corpses which did not qualify for burial in a chambered tomb – perhaps those of common people – were often placed in the ditches of these enclosures. At the Crickley Hill enclosure in Gloucestershire a gruesome collection of thirty skulls had been positioned in one of the ditches.

Plainly the ditches of the causewayed

*Causewayed enclosure*
The best-known Neolithic causewayed enclosure is Windmill Hill, close to the famous henge and stone sicrle of Avebury, Wiltshire. Excavated sections of the hyphenated ditches are plainly displayed, though the concentric shading is produced by recent farming operations. (Crown Copyright/MOD)

enclosures were used during the performance of important rituals, but this does not prove that they were primarily ritual sites – the religious ceremonies could have accompanied or sanctified other, less spiritual activities. Previously the enclosures were known as 'causewayed camps', it being presumed that they accommodated settlements. This was probably not the case, though some, like Whitesheet Hill in Wiltshire, had secondary enclosures and at Hambledon Hill both ritual and domestic enclosures existed. The settlement interpretation was generally discarded in favour of one that regarded the causewayed enclosures as livestock corrals, and then in turn ritual interpretations were invoked. Defensive possibilities should also be considered. A number of the causewayed enclosures, like Hambledon Hill, occupied sites which were later selected by the builders of hillforts – though many others adopted lowland sites with few if any defensive advantages. Battles were certainly fought at some causewayed enclosure sites – at Crickley Hill excavations found 400 flint arrowheads fired by opposing ranks of Neolithic archers standing about 130 feet (40 metres) apart, while a fortified enclosure standing close to the main Hambledon enclosure was destroyed during a violent encounter. These and some other great prehistoric enclosures may have been built on COMMONS that stood between communities and were shared by them. They could have been associated with the conduct of diplomacy, and have experienced the consequences of its breakdown.

Modern archaeology regards the causewayed enclosures as important focuses of Neolithic regional (tribal?) life. They were certainly associated with ritual and were occasionally the scenes of encounters between hostile forces. It is also very reasonable to assume that they could haved been the great gathering and trading centres of their day. Perhaps they might be compared to the sites of the great medieval rural fairs, where trading experienced a much broader dimension than was known at run-of-the-mill markets? Perhaps, too, they were the venues for cultural, ritual and economic events where parochial or tribal norms were set aside?

During the last two decades, aerial photography has produced more discoveries of causewayed enclosures – like the one which surrounds the great tomb of Duggleby Howe, North Yorkshire. These monuments appear to have served as the leading regional foci or 'central places' in most parts of England. Unfortunately, only a few hilltop examples plainly display the earthworks of interrupted ditches, and most are only seen from the air, as CROP MARK sites. See also CHAMBERED TOMB, HENGES, LONG BARROW.

**Causey or causeway.** Paved roads were made from at least Roman times until the nineteenth century and the tracks surfaced in paving stones (or in Scotland, 'causey-stanes') can be extremely difficult to date. The author has discovered one example (overgrown by turf in a deer park), that had led to a village that was deserted around the thirteenth or fourteenth century yet it appeared very much like the paved roads built to service northern textile mills and markets in the early decades of the Industrial Revolution. Where stone slabs were readily to hand they made excellent paving materials, while elsewhere river cobbles might be rammed into a sand or gravel bed to provide a durable surface. Often less than 10 feet (*c.* 3m.) wide, the old causeys sometimes had a raised centre or 'causey-crown' to assist the shedding of water and they gave rise to a number of dialect terms, like 'causey-talk' or common gossip and 'causey-faced' or brazen. See also MEDIEVAL ROADS, HOLLOWAY.

**Cave.** There are two main natural forms of cave formation: by the solution and erosion of rock by subterranean water bodies, and by the differential erosion of sea cliffs by wave action. Artificial cavern networks could be undertaken for occupation or storage, e.g. Nottingham. Human uses of caves have been diverse. They were used for both shelter and ritual in the Palaeolithic period, while burials in caves occurred throughout the prehistoric and Roman eras. Some were dwellings and places of worship for now-obscure early Christian saints, like St. Fillan's cave, Pittenweem, Fife or the abodes of medieval hermits or of soothsayers, like Mother Shipton at Knaresborough.

**Celtic cross**, see CROSSES.

**'Celtic' fields**. The language of archaeology includes some highly inappropriate terms. Perhaps the best (or worst) example is 'HENGE' which derives from the unique hanging or lintel stones of Stonehenge. 'Celtic fields' is another unfortunate term. It was used freely to describe prehistoric fields – and the implication that all such fields were created and formed by Celtic people is quite unacceptable. 'Celtic' is a cultural term, associated with speaking one or another of the Celtic dialects, some of which still endure, with the use of certain artistic motifs and so on. Currently, the science of genetic fingerprinting is exploring the truth behind many myths. Though much remains to be discovered, the ancient

character of populations and the importance of pre-Celtic elements in those of Britain and Ireland; the relative confinement of strong Viking influences to the Northern Isles; and the similarity between the populations in the east of England and Lowland Scotland seem to emerge.

Ancient field-patterns are extremely difficult to date even when archaeological techniques are available. Some 'Celtic' field systems are likely to be of a Neolithic date. In Co. Mayo, the Céide Fields, consisting of two conjoined CO-AXIAL systems, became overrun by blanket bog. The fields were dated by pollen analysis allied to radiocarbon dating (which dated pine stumps in the bog overlying field walls), to a farming phase running from around 3700 to 3200 BC. The system was not of a 'primitive' or 'localised' nature, but extended across an area of at least

*'Celtic' fields*
'Celtic' fields near Grassington, North Yorkshire, outlined in the snow above the line of the much later field-wall.

*'Celtic' fields*

A fine system of 'Celtic' fields can be seen above the wood on Fyfield Down, Wiltshire. The remains are extensive: originally 'Celtic' fields would have covered virtually all the land in this photograph. (CUCAP)

1000 hectares (*c.* 2471 acres). Several prehistoric field systems are known to belong to the Bronze Age, while others date from the Iron Age and Romano-British periods. Although the term 'Celtic' has been applied to 'fossil' field-patterns, recognisable as earthworks or discernible only in aerial photographs, there is strong evidence to suppose that fields of a Roman or older vintage are still being cultivated as living fields in Cornwall, various parts of East Anglia and probably other localities in Britain as well. Small, irregular fields on the margins of Dartmoor, presumed to have been abandoned in the Bronze Age, easily mesh with and match adjacent working pastures.

'Celtic' fields can be seen in numerous localities of Britain where the subsequent patterns of land-use have favoured their survival. They are visible at various locations on the south-western moors, in the Pennines, most notably above Grassington or at the foot of Malham Cove, while until the modern introduction of PRAIRIE farming there were numerous prominent 'Celtic' field systems to be seen on the Wessex downlands. Such field systems were not originally localised, but covered most of the modern countryside and built-up areas.

'Celtic' fields varied in form as well as in age. Most typically, they existed as small rectangular enclosures bounded by 'lynchet banks' which had accumulated as a by-product of the ploughing of adjacent fields. It seems highly probable that a large proportion of such lynchets would originally have carried hedgerows. Where stone was abundant, as in Cornwall or Dartmoor, then stone cleared from farmland would be used in the construction of field-walls. The small size and roughly rectangular form of most 'Celtic' fields are probably explained by the use of the simple 'ard' plough, little more than a pointed branch, which lacked a mouldboard to turn the sod. Consequently, fields were ploughed in a criss-cross fashion, and in a few cases delicate excavations have revealed the scratches in the subsoil left by the snout of the ard.

'Celtic' fields could form 'nuclear' patterns with a small group of fields radiating outwards from an ancient farmstead, 'brickwork' patterns with the arrangement of the fields resembling that of bricks in a wall, or less regular systems. In some parts of the country vast networks of 'CO-AXIAL FIELDS' have been recognised, with the fields sharing a common orientation and being set out in great blocks which are bounded

by droves or DRIFTS. Such systems must indicate the large-scale reorganisation of farming according to a deliberate plan. In parts of Wessex and the Berkshire Downs there is evidence that conventional networks of 'Celtic' fields were, at some point in the Iron Age, cut across by great 'ranch boundaries', implying another type of wholesale reorganisation of the ancient countryside. See also ORTHOSTAT WALLS, REAVES.

*Further reading*: Fowler, P. J., *The Farming of Prehistoric Britain*, Cambridge University Press, 1983.
For a discussion on the Celtic myth see James, S., *The Atlantic Celts*, British Museum Press, London, 1999.
Cooney, G., *Landscapes of Neolithic Ireland*, Routledge, London, 2000.

**Chambered tomb**. These Neolithic monuments date from about 4100–3000 BC. In Britain they form a distribution which is complementary to that of the earthen LONG BARROWS, being found where necessary building materials, in the form of tough slabs of stone, were available. However, these 'megalithic' ('big stone') tombs are not confined to Britain but also occur on the Continent in many parts of Europe's Atlantic fringe, strongly suggesting that a common religious inspiration united the tombbuilders. This may have been so, but as the construction of chambered tombs evolved and spread, so a varied range of distinctive monument types developed.

The essence of the chambered tomb was the provision of one or more stone-built burial chambers and an entrance that could be sealed and reopened. The chambers could be placed at the mouth of the tomb, in its sides, at the terminus of an entrance passage or flanking such a passage, while the stone-built structures were usually covered in a substantial mound of earth and rubble. As with the long barrows, bodies were normally installed in a decomposed and disarticulated condition, and chambered tombs were similarly associated with the rite of collective burial. The chambered tombs differed from the long barrows in that their burial chambers could be periodically reopened to accept new interments.

Chambered tombs of the 'PORTAL DOLMEN' type, known loosely as 'quoits' in Cornwall and as 'cromlechs' in Wales, were widely distributed, also occurring in Scotland and Ireland. They are relatively simple structures, with a massive capstone being supported (generally in a sloping position) on a number of upright slabs. Two of these slabs serve as great portals, flanking the entrance to the burial chamber. While portal dolmens seem generally to have been covered in a mound of earth or rubble, it has been suggested that prior to the construction of the covering mounds corpses may have been exposed and allowed to decompose on the sloping capstones – this ritual of 'excarnation' being shared, as we shall see, by the builders of both chambered tombs and long barrows. Some of the best examples of portal dolmens, like Chun Quoit, Zennor Quoit and Trethevy Quoit, can be seen in Cornwall. Ireland has good examples, like the tomb at Glenroan, Co. Tyrone. The distribution of the portal dolmens in Ireland has been used as a basis for arguing that they evolved from 'court tombs', which have a small courtyard bounded by orthostats in front of the long, segmented stone burial chamber, in the Ulster region. Later, a sea-borne expansion is said to have carried the tomb form southwards, to Leinster.

Portal dolmens are generally thought to represent an early chapter in the development of the chambered tomb, and examples were occasionally incorporated into subsequent, more elaborate constructions. It is also possible that the earliest chambered tombs represented attempts to translate the timber mortuary houses associated with long barrows into the medium of stone. Chambered tombs of what has been termed the 'Cotswold-Severn group' seem to

combine the trapezoidal plan of the covering mound of the typical long barrow with entrances which are reminiscent of portal dolmens. Their internal structures are frequently of the 'gallery grave' type, with an entrance passage flanked and terminated by stone-built burial chambers. Sometimes gallery graves were provided with impressive façades of standing stones, such façades being imposing features at tombs like West Kennet near Avebury and Wayland's Smithy in Oxfordshire. Chambered-tomb architecture reached its most grandiose and sophisticated expression in the construction of massive 'passage graves', like Newgrange in County Meath and Maes Howe on Orkney, where the burial chamber was placed at the end of an impressive entrance passage and the whole stonework was covered in a gigantic

*Chambered tomb*
The portal dolmen known as Trethevey Quoit in Cornwall with its characteristic sloping capstone.

dome-shaped mound. These magnificent
constructions might seem to represent the
culmination of the megalithic tomb-building
tradition, although much smaller and simpler
tombs of a passage-grave type which exist in a
cluster at Carrowmore near Sligo have been
dated to the period around 4000 BC, when the
community concerned had scarcely advanced
beyond the Mesolithic hunter-gatherer stage of
development. Megalithic art, based on concentric
circle motifs, is found in passage graves ringing
the Atlantic coast of Iberia, in the Pyrenees,
lining the coast of Brittany, flanking the Severn,
punctuating the north-eastern half of Ireland and

occurring in Caithness and the Hebrides and
Northern Isles. It provides good evidence for
supposing that the passage graves, at least, were
evidence of far-reaching cultural influences.

A distinct variation of the passage-grave type
is the 'stalled cairn' of northern Scotland and
the Northern Isles, where upright slabs of
flagstone segment the flanks of the passage into
burial chambers, twenty-four such chambers
existing at the famous Midhowe tomb on
Rousay island. A more outlandish development
of the megalithic tomb is represented by the
'Clava Cairns' tombs of the Inverness region.
These tombs, often standing inside stone circles,
had doughnut-shaped rings of rubble with
stone-slab revetments to their inner and outer
faces. Sometimes the interiors of the rubble rings
were roofed over by a 'corbelling' of overlapping
slabs, and sometimes they were open to the

skies. A less bizarre late stage in the development of the passage grave was the 'entrance grave', a passage grave of a small and simple type which is very largely confined to the west of Cornwall and the Isles of Scilly and which belongs to the early Bronze Age rather than to the Neolithic period.

Whenever their structures are tolerably well preserved, chambered tombs are invariably impressive and evocative monuments. For decades, experts have attempted to establish a

*Chambered tomb*
Stoney Littleton chambered tomb in Avon: the view along the entrance passageway.

chronology and pedigree for the different types, but so far their efforts are incomplete. It was once thought that the development represented a degeneration from spectacular prototypes like Newgrange and Maes Howe, but current archaeological thinking favours the idea of elaboration from simple beginnings, with the different regions of Britain developing their own distinctive versions of the chambered tomb. Even so, the evolution was complicated, for several regions boast an array of quite different tomb types.

As with long barrows, the chambered tombs were the last resting places for a favoured minority of the population, and most seem to

have served a distinct community and locality. Thus, those people interred at Carrowmore seem to have belonged to a community occupying the Knocknarea peninsula and exploiting the resources of the surrounding beaches and rivers. Impressive territorial symbols, the chambered tombs were frequently sited so as to be seen silhouetted on the skyline, announcing to any intruder that the spirits of the ancestors were watching over the communal homeland. Whether the Neolithic tomb-builders actually indulged in ancestor worship is still uncertain, but the bones placed in chambered tombs were normally set down in a jumbled fashion and existing accumulations of bones would be unceremoniously swept aside to create space for new interments. Bones may also have been removed from these tombs for use in special rituals. See also LONG BARROW, ROUND BARROW.

*Further reading*: Renfrew, C., *Before Civilisation*, Jonathan Cape, 1973.

**Champion countryside**, see ANCIENT AND PLANNED COUNTRYSIDE.

**Charcoal burning pan**. For many centuries wood was converted into charcoal, which was used as domestic and industrial fuel, by stacking lengths of timber around a central post, then removing the post and covering the mound with a coating of turf, loam or clay in which ventilation holes were made. The wood was then fired, 'cooking' slowly, and when the covering was raked away the charcoal was extracted. The pan was a shallow circular scoop in the soil, around 10 to 30 feet in diameter, in which the timber was burned and many survive as slight earthworks within old woods.

**Chase**. The exclusive hunting reserve of a medieval lay land-holder or churchman of high status, in which they had rights to hunt and conserve game. The legal measures for the protection of game were not as intimidating as those operated by the kings in their FORESTS. Only the Dukes of Lancaster were allowed to

operate Forest Law, otherwise, common law applied. There were twenty-six medieval chases and though the chases have gone, their names may endure in localities like Cranborne Chase and Hatfield Chase. During the time of their currency as township reserves, many chases were referred to as 'forests'.

**Cheese loft**. An upper room in a dairy where cheese was stored and ripened. Below would be the cheese vat which held the cheese as it was pressed, the heavy cheese stone, turned with a screw to press hard on the cheese, and the cheese-breaker or curd crusher.

**Chiminage**. A toll taken by a feudal lord from travellers for use of a track that he had made through manorial woods.

**Church dedications**. In different cases the dedications of churches are unremarkable, misleading or extremely revealing – the problem being that one often will not know which description to apply. Different dedications were fashionable at different times, in much the same way that Christian names rise and fall in favour: there are, so far as I know, no saints Wayne, Tracy or Darren. It is normally safe to say that a dedication to a Celtic saint denotes an early foundation, for the Celtic church began a gradual retreat following the theological triumph of the Roman cause at the Synod of Whitby in 664. Celtic dedications in parts of southern and eastern England which lie far from the conventional arenas of the Celtic church may represent the efforts of particular Dark Age Celtic missionaries, like St Cedd. Within the Celtic lands, the most 'authentic' dedications are thought to be those which are unique. Celtic saints were very numerous, for the title was applied to anyone who pursued a religious vocation. Many saints are now known only from a single church dedication, while in other cases it is impossible to discriminate between myth and reality: Brocagnus is said to have brought a dozen daughters and a dozen sons from Wales to Padstow – all of them saints – and it is certainly true that a wealth of obscure and ancient dedications is found in the hinterland of Padstow. One of the prettiest legends concerns St Endellion in Cornwall. Said to be the daughter of a Welsh king, this hermit was killed by the owner of fields where her goat had trespassed. She asked for her body to be placed in a cart drawn by young cattle and buried where they stopped. The church is said to mark this spot.

It is sometimes said that the journeys of a Celtic missionary can be traced by the dedications that the evangelist would leave in his wake – but this is dubious. Missionaries often dedicated churches to early and celebrated saints, like St Peter, while a chain of similar dedications could easily just reflect later imitation or mythology.

Unusual dedications – like the church of St Ethelbert and All Saints at Belchamp Otten in Essex, which has Norman architecture but a dedication to a Saxon king of East Anglia – always suggest an interesting history. In many localities villages share a similar name, normally because they crystallised in the same ancient estate, and frequently church dedications were adopted to distinguish between the different settlements. Thus we have Pulham St Mary, with its church dedicated to St Mary the Virgin, and Pulham Market close together in Norfolk – Pulham Market having a church dedicated to St Mary Magdalene and therefore adopting the 'market' suffix. But such simple rules do not always apply: at Belchamp St Paul in Essex the church is dedicated to St Andrew and the village name reflects the fact that the church was given to St Paul's Cathedral by King Athelstan.

The most remarkable of the dedication mysteries concerns the St Michael churches – partly because the dedication was so popular for so long and partly because such a high proportion of isolated hilltop churches carry this dedication. The most concentrated stipple of St Michael churches is found in Lancashire, while Wales has almost seventy and England as a whole, more than 600 examples. To some extent the association between the cult of St Michael and hilltop sites may be explained by Professor Finberg's suggestion that many of these were previously the places of pagan worship and the warrior Archangel was regarded as an acceptable successor to gods of the Hermes and Mercury types who guarded and escorted the dead. The longstanding popularity of St Michael may reflect his attraction to the militaristic societies of Saxon, Viking and Norman times, while his continuing appeal after the Reformation could derive from his position as a saint who did not owe his canonisation to the Vatican.

The most dramatically situated St Michael church can be seen on Brentor, an outpost of Dartmoor, where the hilltop is ringed by the earthworks of a presumed HILLFORT. The tiny church is thought to have been begun as an act of contrition by the Norman landlord, Robert Giffard, about 1130, though the long previous association of such a site with pagan worship is quite likely.

*Further reading*: Arnold-Foster, F., *Studies in Church Dedications, or England's Patron Saints*, 3 vols, 1899.
Everitt, A., *Continuity and Colonization: the evolution of Kentish settlement*, Leicester University Press, 1986.

**Churchyard**. The village churchyard is quite likely to be far older than the church building which it contains today. It is possible that the form of a churchyard may provide evidence about the antiquity of worship and burial at a particular site, for while churchyards tend to have adopted roughly rectangular shapes since Saxon times it seems that circular or oval churchyards were associated with the cemeteries and monasteries of the older, British church. Such forms are certainly evident at ruined early-Christian monastic sites in the 'Celtic' west, and where they are found in England there is reason to suspect a religious site of great antiquity. Another very loose indication of the age of a churchyard is provided by its height above the level of adjacent land, since over the centuries repeated burials will gradually result in the elevation of the churchyard.

Circular or oval churchyard shapes combined with a raised land-surface can be seen at a number of places, such as Bramham in West Yorkshire. (The ruined church at Knowlton in Dorset is a special case, for it stands inside a circular prehistoric HENGE.) In a small number of cases a churchyard contains two churches. The best example is Swaffham Prior in Cambridgeshire, with the two medieval churches of St Mary and of St Cyriac & St Julitta, the latter disused. Apparently, the village was divided between two parishes which shared a common burial ground but required separate churches. The burial ground here could well date from the days of paganism or British Christianity and so pre-date any church.

Today the churchyard may be a rather sombre and soulful place, but this was certainly not the case in medieval times. Despite the regular protests of a succession of bishops, it was a venue for village games, gatherings, dancing and dalliance. Whenever a particularly engaging item of scandal was discovered, the gossip would be sure to attract an audience of villagers in the churchyard after mass. Within the churchyard, the church and the churchyard CROSS stood supreme – there were no gravestones to get in the way of players or traders, and one can search hard and long without finding a gravestone which is older than the seventeenth century and few churchyards boast any older than eighteenth century. Within the churchyard, the social values extended to the dead as well as to the living, with the virtuous receiving burial on the sunny south side of the church, and suicides and outcasts being consigned to the shadowy north side. See also KILLEEN.

**Churchyard cross**, see CROSSES.

**Cider-house**, see POUNDHOUSE.

**Clachan**. The *clachan* was the traditional form of settlement in the Celtic lands until the gradual evolution of the settlement pattern, as in Wales, or more traumatic events like the eighteenth- and nineteenth-century CLEARANCES

in the Scottish Highlands, removed it. In Ireland, the Anglo-Scottish plantations, the evictions and famine and later, the well-intended efforts of the Congested Districts Board eradicated most traces of the ancestral pattern of settlements. *Clachans* could be as small as English HAMLETS or as populous as medium-sized English VILLAGES, but they had only limited similarities to villages. Dwellings were cramped and squalid, and were normally loosely clustered amongst yards and paddocks in a haphazard and formless manner. In the parts of Scotland where Lowland Scots rather than Gaelic was spoken, the *clacharn* were generally known as 'fermtouns' (farmtowns) – or as 'kirktouns' or 'milltouns' if they were distinguished by the possession of a church or a mill. 'Cottouns', occupied by the most impoverished cottagers or farm labourers, also existed. The name *clachan* derives from a word signifying 'stones', probably deriving from the boulders and rubble used for walling the dwellings.

Under the Scottish clan system, which endured in the Highlands until its erosion after the English victory at Culloden in 1746, land was held by the clan chieftains and let and sublet down through a hierarchy of tenancies. These descended to the peasant classes who worked the land on short leases with very little security of tenure or opportunities for improvement. The smaller clachans were group farms, with the land shared between as few as a couple of households. The *clachans* which accommodated the farming families tended to cluster or straggle beside pockets of arable land where RUNRIG cultivation was practised. The dwellings were of the LONGHOUSE type, normally with the byre component sited at the downslope end of the house, and each dwelling would stand amongst its stack-yard, kail-yard and modest outbuildings. Gardens (GARRAÍ) generally intervened between the dwellings and the IN-FIELD, while in Ireland and the upland areas the community had access to summer pastures. The arrangement of components was

*Clachan*

The dwellings of a deserted clachan on Pabbay in the Western Isles. The island is now deserted and the isolation of the settlement is complete. (CUCAP)

normally disordered, in comparison to the more structured lay-out of many English villages: there would be no defined street-pattern, no services or shops and often no throughroad. Many *clachans* were only occupied or fully occupied in winter, for in summer a large proportion of the community would migrate with their livestock to upland SHIELINGS. This pattern of life was extinguished by the Clearances in the Highlands and the Improvements in the Lowlands and North East of Scotland. In the Highlands, tenants tended to be evicted to make way for sheep ranges and deer forests. Where the less rugged terrain and greater accessibility of the low-lying estates offered greater agricultural or industrial opportunities, eviction was less severe and many *clachan* communities were resettled into new purpose-built villages, like New Deer and New Leeds in Grampian.

In Wales, English feudal influences led to a more gradual transformation of the Celtic settlement pattern. Early medieval sources suggest an intricate division of large estates into subordinate TOWNSHIPS with hamlets, which were often of equal size but which were sometimes occupied exclusively by tenants of a particular free or unfree grade and which specialised in particular spheres of estate production. In Ireland, wherever the traditional chiefdoms survived the advances of English feudalism or Anglo-Scottish plantations, a settlement pattern of *clachans*, which were often linked to summer shielings or 'booley houses', persisted. In some places, like Clare island, clachans associated with RUNDALE endured until the activities of the C.D.B. around a century ago. Many were not ancient settlements but reflected the great rises in population and divisions of township land that had been underwritten by the cultivation of potatoes in LAZY BEDS, often on poor OUT-FIELD land. The splitting-off of new *clachan* populations and the subdivision of *clachan* land-holdings continued until the horrors of the potato blight struck in the second half of the decade. Thereafter, many decaying *clachans* were broken-up and their RUNDALE lands were re-allocated to produce dispersed LADDER FARMS. See also CLEARANCES, RUNRIG, SHIELING.

*Further reading*: Smith, J.S. and Stevenson, D., *Fermfolk and Fisherfolk*, Mercat Press, Edinburgh, 1992.

**Clam, staff and daub**, see MUD AND STUD.

**Clamp**. A small heap of peats or turf.

**Clamp-kill**: A Scottish LIME KILN built of sods.

**Clapper bridge**. Clapper bridges are in appearance the most primitive of all stone bridges, normally being built without mortar or squared stones and consisting of heavy horizontal slabs supported by low boulder-built piers. While the design is very likely to be of a prehistoric vintage, surviving clapper bridges are unlikely to be very old in their current forms. Their vulnerability to flooding virtually ensured the periodic need for a fairly comprehensive rebuilding, as experienced by the Tarr Steps on Exmoor, one of the most celebrated examples, which suffered damage in 1947, 1952 and 1980, but whose origins are obscure. Clapper bridges are found in upland areas where the financial resources for bridge-building were modest but where suitably massive stones or moorstone boulders were readily available. Their distribution is concentrated in the moors of south-western England and the Pennine Dales.

Clapper bridges can vary quite considerably in appearance as the two best-known examples show. Tarr Steps, mainly associated with a PACK-HORSE ROAD, has seventeen spans of locally obtained stone flags which stand only a little above the normal level of the Barle, which has a width of 180 feet (55 metres) at this point. The clapper bridge at Postbridge on Dartmoor, thought by some to date from the thirteenth century, has a much more robust appearance and consists of three spans of massive moorstone slabs supported, man-high, by two piers and abutments built of large, thick, roughly rectangular slabs. Although the historical documentation is meagre, it appears that clapper bridges can variously date from any period from the Middle Ages to the nineteenth century.

**Clayland revolution**. This was the heavy lands equivalent of the LIGHT LAND REVOLUTION and it involved the expansion of arable farming into areas which, at the start of the eighteenth century, had been dominated by dairy farming and the fattening of livestock. Here, the Agricultural Revolution was not spearheaded by nobles and the owners of enormous estates, but by the lesser gentry and freeholders. The soils concerned were generally quite fertile and their main problems were those of waterlogging and 'coldness'. The heavy ground was slow to warm and encourage germination in the spring, while the penning of animals on ploughland, which has a fertilising effect, also increased the compaction of the clay and intensified its difficult characteristics. The solution to these difficulties was found in DRAINAGE, firstly involving boundary ditches, then bush drains, which were narrow trenches filled with brushwood, and then drains made of commercially produced earthenware tiles and pipes, which became numerous after the 1840s. The revolution mostly affected the small, irregular, heavily-hedged pasture of the ANCIENT COUNTRYSIDES commonly associated with the claylands. As the land was drained and converted to arable uses, so the small fields were amalgamated, with the uprooting of many of the ancient, POLLARD-studded HEDGEROWS. Those hedgerows that survived were severely cut back to prevent the shading of the crops and the long-established hedgerow pollards were particularly hard-hit. Meanwhile, PARLIAMENTARY ENCLOSURE was removing the COMMONS and smaller GREENS or 'tyes' and partitioning the former OPEN FIELD ploughlands with straight hedgerows of hawthorn. Marling played a significant part in sweetening some soils, though it was far less important than on the lighter, acid soils.

*Further reading*: Williamson, T., *The Transformation of Rural England*, Exeter University Press, 2002.

**Clay lump**, see COB, WATTLE AND DAUB.

**Clearance cairns**. These are mounds of stone accumulated by pioneer colonists during the clearance of land for farming. They are generally of a prehistoric, often of a Bronze Age, date, though more recent examples can be seen. These historical examples include the remarkable large mounds of stone lying between or incorporated into the field-walls at Wasdale Head near Wastwater in Cumbria. Clearance cairns can often be seen in large groupings, sometimes known as *cairnfields*, as at Iron Howe, overlooking the upper Rye valley in the North York Moors, where there are around 2500 clearance cairns. Such cairns have often been mistaken for Bronze Age burial cairns and can be so similar in appearance that only an excavation can provide the answer. Often, some of the low stony mounds in a prehistoric cairnfield will be burial cairns, though the majority will be clearance cairns or HUT CIRCLES, and sections of tumble-down field walling are often associated with them and are likely to be of a roughly similar age.

**Clearances (of the Scottish Highlands)**. For so many people the grim realities of Scottish social history are masked by a tartan veil, and more is known about haggis and bagpipes than about the grinding poverty and injustices of old Highland life. During the Middle Ages, Scotland was a kingdom divided between the Lowlands, where a feudal system not unlike that of England prevailed, and the Highlands and Islands, where the clan system was supreme. The clan system was based on loyalty and kinship (real or imagined) which bound the chief to his tenant clansmen. In the hierarchy of the clan the level below that of the chief was composed of 'tacksmen', or lesser gentry, who held 'tacks' or leases and sublet their lands via a complicated system of subtenancies to the subordinate members of the clan. Under the turbulent conditions of endemic warfare and feuding between rival clans, chieftains tended to measure their power in terms of the size of their armies, each clansman being both a peasant farmer and a warrior. This encouraged the gross over-population of the Highlands, while the poverty of the common folk and the very short term of the leases, which were seldom of more than one year's duration, worked against any attempts at land improvement. Meanwhile, the deforestation of the Highlands and over-grazing by the herds of black cattle, which were the main resource and currency of the area, ensured the continuing deterioration of the environment. After 1739, the introduction of the potato temporarily sustained another surge of population growth.

Despite its failings, the archaic organisation of the plague-ridden society and the recurrent outbreaks of famine, the clan system remained virtually intact until the middle years of the eighteenth century. Then, the collapse of the Jacobite uprising, political polarisation of the clans and the crushing defeat of the badly-led Jacobite forces by the English and Scottish forces under the Duke of Cumberland at Culloden in 1746 signalled the end of the old Highland lifestyle. The clansmen were disarmed, their dress, language and martial culture proscribed and their territories were exposed to the 'modernising' economic forces of British life. Lairds who sought to emulate the grandeur of the English gentry resorted first to rack-renting, giving another turn to the screws of extortion that weakened and impoverished their still-loyal subjects. There was, however, a limit to the revenue which could be squeezed from peasant paupers, and landlords cast around for alternatives. It had been assumed that sheep were insufficiently hardy to flourish in the mountains and glens, but in the 1770s Linton sheep were introduced on a Ross-shire estate and proved successful. With an insatiable demand for wool in the swelling mill towns and a market for mutton in the southern cities, the future of the Highlands could hardly be in doubt – all that was necessary was the removal of the clansfolk and their cattle. The supposed kinsfolk who had formerly furnished the strength, security and wealth of their masters were now no more than an encumbrance.

On some estates the evictions were quite ruthless, on others the lairds attempted to create alternative employment in new fishing villages or mills, or finance the emigration of families to better lives in the New World. The nature of policies adopted seem not to have been related to the background of the laird concerned, whether as a Highland chieftain of illustrious pedigree or as an English interloper who bought-up forfeited estates.

The bulk of the clearances took place in the closing decades of the eighteenth century and the early decades of the nineteenth century, although between 1840 and 1880 around 40,000 people were evicted from estates on Skye. As a consequence of a belated humanitarian outcry an inquiry was held which resulted in the Crofters' Holdings (Scotland) Act of 1886, which provided more security of tenure for the surviving crofters. Even so, Jura and Mull experienced clearances at the end of the century, and even in the early years of the twentieth century there were evictions on the mainland and islands to create depopulated environments where international 'sportsmen' could shoot the red deer.

Some of the most notorious clearances were accomplished on the estates of the Countess of Sutherland in the second decade of the nineteenth century. In 1854 the second Duke of Sutherland called a meeting at Golspie to raise recruits to fight in the Crimea. He achieved a large audience but no volunteers and, according to the recollections of Donald MacLeod, an old Highlander came forward to explain why:

I am sorry for the response your Grace's proposals are meeting here today, so near the spot where your maternal grandmother by giving some forty-eight hours' notice marshalled 1,500 men to pick out the 800 she required, but there is a cause for it and a genuine cause and, as your Grace demands to know it, I must tell you as I see none else is inclined in the assembly to do so. These lands are now devoted to rear dumb animals which your parents considered of far more value than men. I do assure your Grace that it is the prevailing Opinion of this county that, should the Czar of Russia take possession of Dunrobin Castle and Stafford House next term that we could not expect worse treatment at his hands than we have experienced at the hands of your family for the past 50 years … But one comfort you have; though you cannot find men to fight, you can supply those who will fight with plenty of mutton, beef and venison.

Memorials to the shameful – yet ecologically perhaps inevitable – clearances can be seen throughout the Highlands and Islands in the form of tumbledown walls at deserted CLACHANS. See also CLACHAN, RUNRIG, IMPROVEMENTS.

*Further reading*: Prebble, John, *The Highland Clearances*, Secker & Warburg, 1963.

**Clet**. In Scotland, a sea stack, a rock detached from the mainland by the sea.

**Click mill**. These archaic mills with their small wheels set horizontally in streams survived until recently in the Northern Isles. See WATERMILL.

**Cliff castle**, see PROMONTORY FORT.

**Clochán**. This is a drystone structure with a corbelled roof and can be either rectangular, round or oval in plan. Clocháin are found in the west of Ireland and are numerous in Kerry, where they seem to have served a variety of purposes. The oldest examples appear to have provided cells for anchorites or dwellings for the most impoverished members of CLACHAN society, while later ones could be well-covers, saunas and animal shelters. The domed, corbelled roofs of overlapping stones were commonly covered in sods.

**'Clon-' place-names**. Names with a *'clon-'* prefix are very numerous in Ireland, and they normally signify pasture or meadow.

**Close**. This abbreviated form of 'enclosure' or 'inclosure' could apply to any enclosed field, but it is generally used today to describe the little squarish hedged fields and paddocks which contain or lie just beyond old village house-plots, particularly in the Midlands and in southern England. Some such closes could be as old as or

even older than the village itself, but others will date from the sixteenth and seventeenth centuries and result from the creation of paddocks out of old OPEN-FIELD land so that breeding livestock could be reared conveniently close to the village-based farmstead. In terms of field-names, 'close' is extremely common and can be attached to almost any enclosure, though if one discovers an island grouping of little closes within an unspoilt network of larger fields then a deserted village, hamlet or farmstead site may be suspected. At undisturbed deserted-village sites former closes can often be recognised from their boundary banks (some with ancient POLLARDS surviving from their HEDGEROWS) or ditches, and some of them may contain discernible housesites. See also TOFT.

**Closed Village**, see OPEN VILLAGES AND CLOSED VILLAGES.

**Clough, cleugh**. A deeply-incised northern valley.

**Co-axial field system**. An extensive system composed of fields all of which share the same orientation and one which could only credibly result from a deliberate act of landscape reorganisation. While such a system may have been very regular at the time of its creation, the abandonment of some boundaries and amalgam-ation of fields, the superimposition of younger cultural features, the cutting of corners on lanes and natural drifting of hedgerows could all blur the original outlines. In the course of the last quarter century, numerous co-axial field systems with a variety of dates have been discovered. Examples found in Co. Mayo are demonstrably Neolithic in age, some in Norfolk are demonstrably pre-Roman, while the author has discovered a system in the vicinity of Borough-bridge and the Great North Road that seems to have been set out using ROMAN ROADS as axes.

*Further reading*: Fleming, A., *The Dartmoor Reaves*, Batsford, 1988.

Williamson, T., 'Early co-axial field systems on the East Anglian boulder clays', *Proc. Prehis. Soc.* **53**, 419–31.

**Cob**. Cob is the most frequently encountered form of walling using clay. Excavations have shown that it was commonly used in the Dark Ages and medieval times, and building in cob persisted until quite recently – in 1962 a man mentioned his recollection of having built cob houses in Northamptonshire. Cob is a mixture of earth and straw, often with the inclusion of chalk and pebbles and with cow hair or horsehair as strengthening fibres. Cob walls were built up in layers each about 2 feet (0.6 metre) thick. After each layer was built, it was allowed to set for at least a week. This would therefore seem to have been a slow method of building, but firsthand estimates of the time taken to erect cob-walled dwellings range from six months to as little as six weeks. In 1438, however, it was recorded that some cob cottages were completed in 22½ days, though it is not clear whether these were just the days on which building work could take place.

Surviving cob buildings are quite common in Devon, Cornwall and Dorset, the majority being farmsteads and cottages of the seventeenth to early nineteenth centuries. In earlier times, cob was used in the construction of some relatively important buildings, including a fifteenth-century manor house at Trelawse in Cornwall, but cob was also the material used in the houses of many of the poorest members of the rural community. This is apparent in the description of Cornish husbandmen's houses in the 1580s, with their 'walles of earth, low thatched roofs, few partitions, no planchings [ceilings], or glass windows and scarcely any chimneys other than a hole in the wall to let out the smoke'. It also emerges in a rhyme of 1689 by Matthew Prior:

As folk from Mud-wall'd Tenement
Bring Landlords Pepper-corn for Rent
Present a Turkey, or a Hen
To those might better spare Them Ten.

Though once abundant, the poorer-quality cob houses have decayed, dissolving back into the earth from which they came, but a good number of substantial cob farmsteads and cottages survive and will continue to do so as long as they have thatch or tiles to keep the damp out of their walls and a good coat of limewash to protect the cob beneath. Thick cob walls keep a dwelling cool in summer and warm in winter, and the slight irregularities in their walls provide a more homely appearance than do the tradesman's brick or plaster.

A close relative of the cob of Wessex and the West Country is the 'wichert' of Buckinghamshire, made of the locally abundant white chalky clay. Both the cob and the wichert dwellings employ unbaked clay, while a bridge between cob and brick was provided by the 'clay lump' of East Anglia, where clay and straw were pressed into large rectangular moulds and sun-baked to set as building blocks.

*Further reading:* Mercer, Eric, *English Vernacular Houses*, Her Majesty's Stationery Office, 1975.

**Cockpit**. Cock-fighting was popular in medieval and later times and has given rise to some 'cockpit' place-names. Cockpits were circular hollows in the ground, sometimes combined within houses, and some earthwork examples survive, as at Embsay, North Yorkshire, and Stourpaine, Dorset, where the cockpit, with a diameter of about 100 feet (30 metres) is surrounded by a low bank and ditch. On the Boverton estate near Llantwit Major, South Glamorgan, there are the remains of two cockpits, one of them walled. Given the continuing coarsening of standards in the visual media, perhaps a revival of this activity should be expected.

**Cockshoot (cockroad, cockglade, cockshut)**. This is a glade associated in former times with the hunting of woodcock. Nets were strung across the end of the glade to trap the birds as they made their low evening flight from woodland to wetland. The names endure in a number of local place-names, like Cockshut Hill in Birmingham and Cockshot Point on the shores of Lake Windermere. The word was also used in a more general sense as a clearing in a wood made to facilitate the shooting of game crossing it.

**Coed**. A word occurring in Welsh place-names and signifying woodland.

**Combe, coomb**. A narrow valley or hollow, often a dry valley in chalk country that was cut when the rainfall regime was different or when permafrost prevented the absorption of surface streams.

**Commandery**. A manorial estate in the charge of a member of the Knights Hospitaller.

**Commons (waste)**. Commons which survive are relics of a system of great but indefinable antiquity whereby communal rights to grazing and other resources were available to populations who generally, but not always, lived on the immediately adjacent areas, where the quality of the farmland was usually better. Most commons perished as a consequence of PARLIAMENTARY ENCLOSURE but during the Middle Ages the typical village would stand amidst its TOFTS or CLOSES beside or in the middle of its OPEN FIELDS. A zone of enclosed and privately tenanted pastures might intervene between the open plough-lands and the open expanse of the common, which normally comprised less productive hill or marsh land. Yet the common did not always lie close to the village, and in Kent, for example, individual villages had rights of land in woodland clearings or 'denns' which lay some distance away. The common normally belonged to the lord of the manor, but his tenants enjoyed various rights to the resources of the common (see BOTE and ESTOVERS). The most valuable of these rights would usually be AGISTMENT, that of summer grazing, but others were TURBARY, the right to dig peat for fuel, and ESTOVERS, or rights to timber – like 'husbote', the rights to wood for house-building, 'heybote', the right to timber for hedge-making and various other rights, like gathering bracken for bedding. Other rights enjoyed by commoners concerned beastgate, cattlegate, oxgate, kinegate, horsegate and sheepgate, the rights to graze fixed

numbers of the animals concerned on the common and piscary, the right to fish in manorial waters. Commonable rights involved practices of mutual forbearance whereby villagers allowed each other's cattle to graze the stubble on arable land after harvest as though it were a common, though a few communities established the practice as a legal right.

Although commons are regarded as large expanses of completely open land, in many places there was a differentiation of uses and the livestock did not roam freely together. In the Lake District and on some other northern fells the lower slopes or BANKS which immediately overlooked the HEAD DYKE and FARMSTEADS functioned as grazing for the milk cattle, and though the land here was technically part of the common its use might be monopolised by the tenant of the adjacent farm. Further up the slope was the 'MOOR', extending across the lower plateaux and providing summer grazing for bullocks, heifers and horses. Overlooking the banks and the moors were the high fells, with their bleak, windswept pinnacles, scree slopes and ridges, and these were the abode of the flocks, each flock tied to its HEAF. Many so-called 'commons' were STINTED COMMONS and subject to so many special arrangements regarding the ownership of beastgates and rights concerning agistment of outside cattle that it is debatable whether they really were 'commons' in the generally understood meaning of the word.

Commons varied greatly in their terrain and ecology, ranging from Lakeland and Pennine fells to lowland heaths, woods and marshland grazings. Most readers may envisage commons as vast tracts of open hill land, but there were many other forms. In Norfolk, for example, there were ribbon-like commons forming wide grassy roads between some villages as well as 'low commons' which followed some stream-courses. The presumed commons of the Lake District were organised between free-holding 'statesmen' for centuries, yet in Victorian Ireland there were still CLACHAN communities who used BOOLEY grounds in the

*Commons (waste)*
Commons were frequently exploited for mining and quarrying. The earthworks below the postmill at Brill in Buckinghamshire result from the digging of clay for the local pottery industry.

hills in an essentially prehistoric manner. There was also variation in the particular rights of tenants and the nature of ownership. The arrangements could also evolve through time. In the Dark Ages people of Devon and Cornwall seem to have exploited the grazings on Dartmoor quite freely, but after AD 850 the folk of Dartmoor appear to have developed their own common rights to the moor, which served meanwhile as a hunting reserve for the Saxon kings. After the disafforestation of the Norman hunting FOREST in 1239 a number of farms in Dartmoor enjoyed 'venville rights', paying small fees to the Crown or the duchy in return for rights to pasture on the commons or Forest by day – an extra charge being levied for the right to keep the animals in the forest at night – and the rights of turbary, husbote and heybote were also provided. Devonian householders living beyond the moor were 'foreigners' but had free common rights outside the forest area.

Common rights, however they varied, were crucial to most peasants and small farmers. All manner of disputes arose when there were claims of over-stocking or accusations that cottagers had driven or 'dogged in' the stock of strangers (so that the humble cottagers were often allowed rights on the common but forbidden to keep dogs). Disputes arose when farmers living on the edge of the common enclosed INTAKES of common land; or when larger enclosures were proposed by superiors attempting more sweeping privatisations. There were always those who gazed avariciously at the common, often from the windows of the manor house. Attempts to expropriate common land into private ownership would periodically disrupt local life, though the Statute of Merton of 1235 empowered the manorial lords to enclose portions of the waste providing that sufficient pasture remained to meet the needs of the tenants. Those who exploited commons did not necessarily dwell right on their margins; as recently as the early years of the nineteenth century around fifty parishes in Devon and Cornwall would send their flocks under the charge of shepherds to exploit the summer grazings on Exmoor, which supported around 25,000 sheep. As shown by the Dartmoor example, the form of rights enjoyed could depend partly on status, partly on local/regional custom and partly on whether one lived beside or away from the common. Residents living within the bounds of the ancient forest of Clee in Shropshire had full common rights of agistment, turbary and estovers on Brown Clee only if their TOWNSHIPS actually occupied the hill; residents from other parts of the old forest were out-commoners with fewer privileges and subject to restrictions which prevented the disturbance of deer found amongst their crops. The out-commoners arrived by tortuous tracks known as 'outracks' or 'straker ways' that are still visible as deep HOLLOWAYS.

As well as the conventional commoners' rights, commons were also associated with digging for MARL or clay, quarrying and mining activities, so that many now have pock-marked surfaces. In the course of the Middle Ages, the area covered by commons began to decline as a result of controversial enclosures by some landlords and by the taking of 'intakes' by farmers and squatters living on the common margins. However, Parliamentary Enclosure was responsible for the wholesale removal of commons, so that now only a minute portion of the medieval endowment remains. Norfolk, for example, still had 143,346 acres (58,000 hectares) of common in 1808, when enclosure had already reduced the county's waste, and today only 8339 acres (3375 hectares) remain.

Estimates of the extent of commons in England and Wales existing at the start of the eighteenth century range from 7 million to 10 million acres (2.8 million to 4 million hectares). The enclosure of a common could have dire effects for the neighbouring community; a note in the *Annual Register* for 1767 tells:

... a great number of farmers were observed going along Pall Mall with cockades in their hats ... it appeared they all lived in or near the parish of Stanwell in the county of Middlesex, and they were returning to their wives and families to carry them the agreeable news of a Bill being rejected for inclosing the said common, which if carried into execution might have been the ruin of a greater number of families.

See also FOLD, GREEN, INTAKE, INTERCOMMONING, GIBBET SITES, OVERLEAP, PARLIAMENTARY ENCLOSURE, SQUATTER, STINTED COMMONS, WASHPOOL.

*Further reading*: Birtles, S., 'Common Land, Poor Relief and Enclosure: the use of manorial resources in fulfilling parish obligations, 1601–1834', *Past and Present* **165**, 74–106.

Hoskins, W. G., and Stamp, L. Dudley, *The Common Lands of England and Wales*, Collins, 1963

Winchester, A., *The Harvest of the Hills*, Edinburgh University Press, 2000.

**Coneygarth**, see WARREN.

**Coniferisation**. A practice of removing indigenous deciduous trees from woods, that were often ancient, and substituting alien conifers. Coniferisation has been popular on ESTATES since Victorian times and results in a more rapid return on capital and it may be associated with the ancillary rearing of pheasants. In terms of natural history, however, it is a retrograde development. Frequently the boundaries of the original wood will be retained, along with wood walls or WOODBANKS and any ancient POLLARDS growing on the bank. Where light is able to penetrate, normally only at the margins and in any rides, then species of the old woodland flora, like bluebells or wild garlic, may survive. See also WOODLAND, PLANTATION.

**Consecration cross**, see CROSSES.

**Consumption dyke**. A massive DRYSTONE WALL built to 'consume' stones gathered from adjacent fields during IMPROVEMENTS, particularly in North East Scotland. One of the most impressive examples is the Kingswells Dyke to the west of Aberdeen, which is half a mile long and as wide as 25 feet (7.6 metres) in places. See also BACKIT-DYKE, DRYSTONE WALLS, IMPROVEMENTS.

**Contested landscape.** In cultural geography this concerns the idea that different individuals and groups have different perceptions or visions of the nature and relative importance of landscapes. In the ensuing contests, some of these views are recognised by officialdom or otherwise legitimated, while others are marginalised. Thus, some interpretations of landscape are silenced and unrecognised, while others are loudly proclaimed or imposed. For example, in terms of grouse MOORS, up to the 1914–1918 war it was the visions of the estate owner, his guests and his gamekeeper and other leading employees that monopolised the perceptions of the moors, but in the years after the Great War the views of ramblers and others campaigning for access to the countryside came to be heard. See also ICONIC LANDSCAPES.

*Further reading*: Bender, B. (ed.), *Contested Landscapes, Movement, Exile and Place*, Berg, Oxford, 2001.

**Contextual approach.** Seeing landscapes in the contexts in which they were (partially) created. For example, medieval people had perspectives on landscape that were strongly influenced by Biblical associations as well as by non-scriptural allegorical influences. Symbolism, often of quite an intricate kind, had powerful effects on their attitudes towards their setting, with landforms and different plants exerting influences that may seem 'invisible' to our eyes. Similarly, one could only appreciate the Neolithic RITUAL LANDSCAPE of, say, the Avebury locality if one could visualise the known world as it was perceived by the contemporary tribespeople of Wessex.

**Convertible husbandry**, see UP-AND-DOWN HUSBANDRY.

**Coom.** In Scotland, the timber framework employed in constructing a bridge. See also PACK HORSE BRIDGE, MEDIEVAL AND LATER BRIDGES.

**Cop.** When found in place-names this can denote a domed or pointed hill, or perhaps a POLLARD.

**Coppice (copse).** A coppice is an expanse of deciduous shrubs or trees which are cut back to their bases at regular intervals in time, according to an established coppicing cycle, to provide a crop of light timber which could be used as fuel or for a wide variety of other uses. Coppicing is an ancient craft, which can be traced right back, for example, to the harvesting of masses of elm, oak, ash, lime, hazel and other poles which were used in the construction of artificial timber trackways across the Somerset Levels from the Neolithic period onwards. The Romans recorded the advantages of coppicing woodland, and the Saxon records contain various mentions of coppicing. Only in quite recent times has the craft been neglected, but today working coppices are few and are often associated with the cutting of hazel to make thatching pegs, or 'sways', or conservational work designed to improve bird cover or to stimulate the growth of woodland flowers, like orchids, oxlips, violets and bluebells, which flourish in the light and airy coppice environment.

One might imagine that a treatment as severe as coppicing a tree just above ground level would be at best severely debilitating and at worst fatal. However, in the case of most deciduous woodland trees this was far from being the effect. If one cut down a young ash tree, for example, one will find that not one but several strong stems rise from the base; cut these down and in due course even more straight and sturdy poles will grow up from the base or 'coppice stool'. Coppicing was applied to a wide range of different deciduous trees, including the elm, ash, lime, hazel, oak and sallow amongst others. In some cases, the stump or stool remained alive, while in others, like cherry and some kinds of elm, the regeneration was accomplished by suckering, with the new growth arising not from the stump but from the root system. Ultimately, the effect of regular coppicing is to invigorate and revitalise the trees concerned. It is hard to generalise about the lifespan of trees, but there seem to be a few living coppice trees which have been in existence since Norman times. After repeated coppicings, the stool becomes elongated and tortuous, while the suspension of coppicing will lead to 'trees' composed of tightly clustered trunks, rather resembling the upward-reaching tentacles of an inverted octopus. Some fine and very old hornbeam coppices can be seen in parts of Epping Forest.

Medieval woods were certainly not wildernesses, and usually more like farms or workshops than playgrounds – this is not surprising given all the uses that were made of wood. Timber provided not only the main fuel and building material, but also the main industrial raw material. Even platters and cogwheels were made from timber. Consequently almost every coppice wood was kept at work yielding a regular supply of timber of many different grades. In the years preceding the Dissolution it is recorded, for example, that the kitchen, brewhouse and bakehouse of Ulverscroft Priory, a relatively modest establishment, consumed so much fuel cut in the Charnwood Forest that seven men were employed solely in felling the coppice and lopping the POLLARDS 'to the number of four to eight cart loads a day and so for most part of the year during ... ten years'. In 1636, coppice poles cut in The Outwoods in Charnwood Forest were sold by the Hastings family to buyers drawn from no fewer than twenty-eight surrounding villages.

Within the encircling WOODBANK a medieval wood was normally divided into a number of distinct coppices. These in turn could be surrounded by banks, and grazing animals might be excluded from each coppice for up to ten years after coppicing, until the young growth

was tall and strong enough to resist browsing. After a period of perhaps twelve to twenty years a coppice would be felled, and the rotational cutting of the various coppices within a wood ensured a constant supply of light timber. Coppice timber had a multitude of uses. Timber cut on a short cycle of, say, seven years could yield thin flexible branches useful for wattle- or hurdlemaking or the shafts for tools or weapons, while timber from a longer coppice cycle might provide wood for fuel, turnery, rafters, poles and light construction work. Heavier timber was also needed for beams, boards, machinery and the main components of timber-framed buildings, and this was often obtained from oak trees which were not coppiced but allowed to grow straight and tall as STANDARDS towering above the coppiced 'understorey' and felled at ages of perhaps eighty or a hundred years.

The coppice was an essential resource to any community and was governed by rules and protected by the courts. Thus, when the trees in a wood near Wakefield were sold to four tenants in 1307 the agreement demanded that they 'cut the wood as close to the ground as possible, and to clear the place of twigs, so as not to impede the fresh growth of the wood'. People were also expected to respect and maintain the protective boundaries of the coppice to prevent the entry of browsing animals. Records show that coppices were banked and fenced or hedged, and in 1316 one suggestively-named Robert Hood of Newton was fined 6*d.* (2½p) at Wakefield court for 'breaking the coppice hedge'. In the following year Thomas the Roller was fined the substantial sum of 13*s.* 4*d.* (67p) for receiving and selling rods cut and stolen in the coppice.

For countless centuries the coppice was an invaluable servant of day-to-day life in Britain, but eventually the more widespread use of coal as fuel, changing building practices, the development of factory processes and metalworking and the availability of cheap imported softwood timber all undermined the traditional woodmanship. Oliver Rackham quotes from an inquiry into Hayley Wood in Cambridgeshire of 1816, where a complainant records:

> I have a fine wood of 120 acres, which formerly was a never-failing resource in all times of emergency, as I could sell any quantity of oak timber at 4s. 9d. [25p] per [cubic] foot, and now I cannot find a purchaser at 2s. 4d. [12p] for the fall of that spring ... with the greatest of ease I would sell a hundred pounds' worth of underwood annually; this winter my woodman has effected sale of about thirty pounds' worth with much difficulty; this I attribute solely to the want of money, which is experienced in this neighbourhood to a ruinous degree.

Ramblers in most old woods will see plenty of evidence of coppicing – but it will generally take the form of heavy trunks arising from stools which have not felt the woodman's axe for many decades. Traditional woodland scenes, with bright leafy shoots of the coppiced understorey arising from recently cut stools, is much more seldom seen. A few thatchers still exploit old hazel coppices, and some conservational bodies have reactivated coppicing, as in Wolves Wood, Suffolk. Most old coppices are badly neglected and serve only as game cover. They are likely to remain in this state unless the fashion for wood-burning stoves increases along with rises in the price of alternative fuels so that it again becomes profitable to manage and exploit a coppice system. A variety of place-names are associated with coppiced woods, they include: 'spring', 'fall', 'hag', 'copse' and 'copy'. When associated with a wood 'Spring' almost invariably denotes a coppice rather than a seasonal reference, while 'Hag' is linked with divisions in medieval coppiced woods. See also WOODLAND.

*Further reading*: Rackham, Oliver, *Ancient Woodland, Its History Vegetation and Uses in England*, Edward Arnold, London, 1980.

Helen Read, *Veteran Trees a Guide to Good Management*, English Nature, London, 1999.

**Copyhold**. An ancient form of land tenure that was eventually abolished in 1926. The title of the tenant was set-out in the rolls of the manor court. Before the Black Death tenure normally carried obligations to perform certain services for the lord and/or render certain gifts, but after 1349 these services were increasingly commuted to money rents. For property to be transferred to another tenant it had to be surrendered to the lord, who would then admit a new tenant to the holding. See also FREEHOLD.

**Cord rig**. Very narrow RIDGE AND FURROW created in late prehistoric times which survives in some upland areas and was only recognised after 1980.

**Corn circles**, see CROP CIRCLES.

**Corn ditch**. A name sometimes given to old DRYSTONE WALLS in Devon with cores composed of earthbanks that are revetted on either side with stones.

**Corn loft**. In Northern Britain a GRANARY, a place for storing grain.

**Corpse road (corpse way, lychway or lick-way)**. In medieval times, the parishes of most upland districts were very large and composed of numerous TOWNSHIPS. An obvious consequence of this was that many households lived several miles from the parish church. Sometimes subsidiary chapels of ease were provided to serve the remote outposts of a large or elongated parish, but the right of burial could still be monopolised by the main church. As a result, the burial of folk who died in distant farmsteads or hamlets required an arduous and sometimes horrific journey by the bearers, particularly in winter when blizzards flew across the fells and rivers were flooded. It was at times like this that the neighbourliness of the rural communities faced its sternest test, and some remarkable examples of steadfast courage are recorded.

A number of tracks are named as corpse roads or corpse ways, though they were normally PACK-HORSE ROADS and DROVE ROADS which were occasionally used by funeral parties. In the Yorkshire Dales in the seventeenth and early eighteenth centuries, corpses were carried not in coffins but in wicker baskets, and journeys of around 15 miles (25 kilometres) would occupy the bearers for two full days. Hubberholme church in Langstrothdale was a chapel of ease of Arncliffe church in Littondale. This relationship brought complaints from the Langstrothdale community in the late fifteenth century after a party of eight bearers had almost died in snowdrifts and another party had lost the corpse in attempting to cross the flooded wharfe. Some time later, Hubberholme was granted the right of burial. Lydford churchyard on the fringes of Dartmoor was reached from the recesses of its parish by large moorstone stepping stones placed across the Tavy, each stone long enough to accommodate two bearers and their burden.

**Coster**. In Lowland Scots, a piece of arable land.

**Cot, cote, cottar house**. A cottage or small farm house, the home of a cottar or 'cottar-body' or, in Scotland, of a 'cotlander' who had a croft and a horse to plough it. See also COTTAGER, COTTAR-TOUN.

**Cottage ornée**. The cottage ornée was a picturesque building designed under the influence of romanticism and whimsy rather than considerations of cost, domestic functions or convenience. The vogue was greatly stimulated by the building of the fanciful Royal Lodge in Windsor Great Park in 1814. All manner of fashionable and exotic features could be incorporated into the cottage ornée, but most popular were aspects culled from English vernacular building traditions and executed in an exaggerated and incongruous manner. Steeply pitched thatch, dormer windows, Elizabethan-style chimneys, bargeboards and rose-trellises were all grist to the architect's mill. Architectural motifs that had caught the eye of a patron in the course of a continental tour, like Swiss gables, might also be included. Some of these cottages were built as country retreats for middle-class romantics, and some to provide eye-catching accommodation for estate workers, which could be built singly or in larger hamlet-sized groupings to prettify the approaches to a mansion. The degree of ornateness varies considerably, so that the distinction between bona-fide vernacular estate housing and the cottage ornée can be difficult to draw. Subsequently the Arts and Crafts movement produced admirable developments of the cottage ornée, incorporating vernacular themes and materials in grander scales and less flamboyant manners.

Villages composed of cottages in a relatively restrained ornate style include New Wimpole in Cambridgeshire, of around 1840, and Ripley in North Yorkshire, dating mainly from the first half of the nineteenth century. Both villages employ a vaguely Tudor or Elizabethan form of architecture, and this is far more effectively adopted in the northern village, though not without references to Alsace and Lorraine. To see cottage ornée architecture in its most exuberant and uninhibited form one should visit Blaise Hamlet in Avon, built at a very early stage in the movement, around 1810–12, by the Quaker and banker J. S. Harford, who employed John Nash as his architect. Although earlier examples of the cottage ornée had appeared and a measure of picturesque influence had been incorporated in estate villages, like Nuneham Courtenay in Oxfordshire, of the 1760s, Blaise Hamlet was the first group of such cottages to be built in an unrestrained Picturesque style. One would not normally have expected that a Quaker like Harford would have been associated with such florid designs, though it was in keeping with his calling that the cottages were provided for elderly people. At Lord Ongley's village of Old Warden in Bedfordshire, built in the middle of the nineteenth century, the villagers themselves were made ornée, being expected to move between their fanciful dwellings decked out in tall hats and red cloaks! Tyrrellspass, Co. Westmeath was a late eighteenth-century Irish village of English design,

*Cottage ornée*

A large *cottage ornée* at Somerleyton in Suffolk. The dwellings in the original village were demolished during emparkment in the mid-nineteenth century and replaced by homes in the 'Picturesque' manner.

the white, slate-roofed cottages being arranged in crescentic form around a green. See also FERME ORNÉE.

*Further reading:* Darley, Gillian, *Villages of Vision*, Paladin, 1978.

**Cottager, cottar, cotman, cottar-folk**. A member of the lowest stratum of medieval rural society, who had a cottage but generally no land holding. Since cottagers did not normally have land holdings they had, in theory, no rights to the COMMON, for if they lacked land they could not produce hay upon which to feed their stock in winter. In reality, the lines were more blurred and more variable, for in some places cottagers did, indeed, put animals on the common, while people like the post-medieval cotlanders of

Scotland had both crofts and plough beasts. See also COTE, COTTAR-TOUN, GERSS HOUSE.

**Cottar-toun, cottoun, cotton**. A loose hamlet occupied by low-status COTTAGERS or COTTARS, who seem, sometimes, to have formed separate communities in Scotland before the IMPROVEMENTS. The cottouns will have resembled CLACHANS in form. They seem to have existed as colonies attached to the township of tenants of higher rank, though some may have housed cottars displaced to the coast by evictions. The cottars or cottar-folk were generally dependent for work on the tenants of neighbouring farms and the ESTATES in which they stood, while the farmer holding the ground on which their COTES were built could stipulate 'cottar-wark' that had to be performed (see DAY-WORK). Potatoes might be grown on adjacent land in return for giving seed or manure. Some cottouns developed during the IMPROVEMENTS, housing poor tenants evicted from their holdings. In some cases their settlements evolved into modern hamlets and small villages, while in other cases they were deserted as their inhabitants sought more rewarding employment. In Lowland Scots the verb 'cotter' concerns communal life in a state of fellowship.

**Court Baron**. A division of the medieval MANOR court for the free tenants. With the COURT CUSTOMARY it administered manorial property, such as the COMMON and its use by livestock.

**Court Customary**. A division of the MANOR court for the unfree (see COURT BARON).

**Court Leet**. An institution of the medieval VILLAGE or TOWNSHIP concerned with the jurisdiction over the OPEN FIELDS, while the COMMON was subject to the MANOR court. The court leet was subordinate to the court of the HUNDRED and that of the shire. Sometimes it fell under the control of the lord and was effectively integrated into the manor court.

**Courtyard farm**. This is a common farm layout in which the various farm buildings are arranged around a central rectangular yard. Courtyard layouts are apparent at a number of deserted

medieval farmstead sites and were still favoured in the designing of new farming complexes in the nineteenth century. In some cases a systematic arrangement of farm buildings can be recognised, with the great barn being placed at the northern side of the yard to give shelter from chilling north winds, the stables being placed on the western side and facing eastwards so that the rising sun would illuminate the buildings as carters and ploughmen prepared for work, while cartsheds were placed on the south side of the yard, facing north so that sunlight and rain carried on the westerly winds would not warp or damage the timber vehicles. Sometimes the farmhouse is included in the buildings around the courtyard, but sometimes it stands alone to the south of its yard and outbuildings. In Ireland, various farm lay-outs are found. In the north and west, with warm Atlantic influences, the need for animal shelters is reduced and farm buildings tend to be arranged in a single long range. Elsewhere, different types of courtyard arrangements may be

*Courtyard farm*
A courtyard farm near Westbury in Wiltshire.

*Courtyard house*
One of the courtyard houses at Chysauster in Cornwall.

seen. In the far south-west, the farmstead and its compact farm buildings may occupy different sides of a 'street' that leads to the adjacent through-road, and in the south and east 'improved' nineteenth-century courtyard farm lay-outs influenced by English designs and landlords can be seen.

*Further reading*: Wade Martins, S., *The English Model Farm*, Windgather, Macclesfield, 2002.

**Courtyard house.** Courtyard houses are distinctive rural dwellings that date from about the last century of the Iron Age through most or all of the Roman occupation period. They are almost entirely confined to Cornwall, though a Breton influence has been suggested for their peculiar design. The dwellings are roughly circular in plan, with the thick boulder wall that encircled an open, central courtyard being breached by an entrance passage. Various individually roofed chambers that opened on to the courtyard were built within the thickness of the great boulder wall.

Some courtyard houses are solitary and must have existed as dispersed farmsteads, while others are found in hamlet or small 'village' groupings. The best sites to visit are Chysauster and Carn Euny, both in the west of Cornwall. At Chysauster the nine dwellings are arranged in four pairs with the ninth house standing alone. The slight terraces which can be seen adjacent to the dwellings were the gardens of the community. Excavation at Carn Euny has shown that here, courtyard houses superseded a previous generation of timber dwellings in the first century BC. Both Carn Euny and Chysauster had FOGOUS, that at the first-named site being one of the best surviving examples. Modern visitors may find the courtyard houses to be archaic and bizarre buildings that are far removed from current perceptions of what a 'home' should be. Even so, the land holdings worked from these centres seem to have been long-lived and there must remain a possibility that some of the farm territories worked from courtyard houses even survive as farm units today.

**Coutch**. In Scotland, the process of laying-out land in consolidated private holdings, rather than with the strips intermixed in RUNRIG. To 'coutch by cavel' was to divide out by lots.

**Cow pasture**. In some northern upland localities the entire COMMON served as a summer cow pasture, while in other cases, separate STINTED COMMONS were set aside for milk cattle on the slopes below the main common or 'out moor'. Sometimes this sub-division seems to have taken place at the end of the Middle Ages or in the decades immediately after. In the period that followed, those who held stints in the cow-pasture might agree upon a further division of the resource between themselves, thus causing it to pass from the public to the private countryside.

**Cow's grass**. A unit of land measurement in various parts of Ireland, that varied according to the quality of the pasture and its ability to support cattle.

**Craig-sitting**. A position on the rocks of the seashore used in Scotland as a perch for fishing.

**Cranks, cruke**. In Scotland, meander loops in a watercourse.

**Crannog**. Crannogs were lake dwellings that stood on artificial islands constructed of branches and brushwood weighed down by boulders and earth and pegged in place by timber piles. They were common in the lochs and loughs of Scotland and Ireland, and in 1973 an archaeological survey of Loch Awe showed that the loch had accommodated some twenty crannogs, though not all will have been in

occupation at the same time. Currently, nearly 1,000 crannogs (*crannóga*) have been recognised in Ireland. Their distribution is strongly concentrated in the hillfoot hollows in the lake-rich drumlin zone to the north of the central plain. Crannog-building was more time consuming than the work needed to construct a contemporary RATH and they were assumed to reflect the insecurities of life in the late Iron Age as well as the aristocratic nature of their occupants. Archaeological work has suggested that crannog-dwellers had similar day-to-day possessions as the land-based commuinbities, though early Irish documents do reveal some crannogs as royal sites. Excavations have shown that the first generations of crannogs appeared in the Bronze Age, while in Ireland, a few crannogs were inhabited and occasionally defended throughout the medieval period. The most recent evidence of dating, based on dendrochronological studies of timbers, indicates two concentrated phases of crannog construction in Ireland, one in the fifth to sixth century AD and one in the eighth to early tenth century AD. Thereafter, they fell out of use as strongholds, perhaps perishing in the face of superior power, like the baronial castles in Tudor England? Crannog-dwellers can only have been a minority amongst the local populations – but a minority which perhaps could sleep a little more easily than its land-bound neighbours. Crannogs can still be seen as small blister-like scrub-covered islands, though of course the dwellings which stood on the crannogs have long since decayed. At Craggaunowen in County Clare visitors can explore a reconstructed crannog settlement.

**Craw steps ('crow steps')**. The stepped gables seen in some Scottish vernacular architecture. It was perpetuated in track-side building created by the old London North Eastern Railway (LNER) and exported into northern England. See also VERNACULAR BUILDINGS.

**Creel-house**. A cottage in Northern Britain build with a framework of wattle in the manner of a woven basket or creel. See also WATTLE AND DAUB.

**Crew, crewyard, garston, foldyard**. A small cattle enclosure, often close to a farmstead. In Scotland the term 'cattle close' is often employed. A revival of arable farming in the eighteenth century sometimes resulted in cattle being displaced by plough horses from the area beside the farmstead to outlying sites in the fields, where their manure was still greatly valued as a fertiliser. In time these sites could develop into farmsteads with a dwelling for the chief cowman. From the second half of the nineteenth century, the employment of sheltered accommodation for cattle increased, it being considered that the cold winds weakened the stock and the rain washed away their by-products. Massive brick cowhouses constructed in areas like the Yorkshire Wolds were, effectively, manure factories.

**Crinkle-crankle or ribbon wall**. These are brick-built walls that pursue courses that are weaving or scalloped rather than straight. They were popular in East Anglia, particularly in Suffolk, and most date from the seventeenth and eighteenth centuries, though examples were built, intermittently, through the nineteenth century.

**Crof, croft**. A shed used in the fishing season in Scotland and abandoned for the rest of the year.

**Croft**. A holding of land. See also CROFTING.

**Crofting**. In the Highlands and Islands of Scotland the development of crofting was largely a consequence of the breakdown of the traditional clan system that accompanied the terrible CLEARANCES. Those clansmen and their families who survived the clearances were obliged to adopt a subsistence lifestyle which was tempered by small-scale activities in fishing, KELP-burning (providing fertilier, iodine and materials for the glass industry) and weaving. The crofters were the residue of the Highlanders who, for one reason or another, had escaped eviction or who had abandoned their ancestral CLACHANS and come to rest on the bleak coasts of Scotland. In many cases, the exploitation of the crofters continued beyond the initial onslaughts of clearances, and some crofting squatters were allowed to struggle to improve their holdings only to have them taken away and absorbed into large farms once most of the hard work was over.

In the 1880s, an eruption of discontent led to the 'Crofters War' and a Highland Land League was formed in 1882 to seek the reform of land tenure; a breakaway group of Liberals formed a Crofters' Party. Meanwhile, an awareness of the injustices which had afflicted the Highlanders began to trouble the national conscience, and in 1885, Joseph Chamberlain echoed the government view at a meeting in Inverness:

> The history of the Highland Clearances is a black page in the account with private ownership in the land ... Thousands of hard-working, industrious, God-fearing people were driven from their lands ... their houses were uprooted and burnt down and they were turned out homeless and forlorn, exposed to the inclemency of the winter season, left to perish on hillsides or to swell the full flood of misery and destitution in places overseas to which they were driven for refuge.

The Crofters Act of 1886 attempted to compensate for such injustices by providing security of tenure to the crofters residing in the old crofting counties of Zetland, Orkney, Caithness, Sutherland, Ross and Cromarty, Inverness and Argyll. Although they had now gained security, the crofters found themselves so hidebound by bureaucratic controls from Edinburgh that there was little scope for entrepreneurship and self-betterment. After the First World War, the promise to resettle ex-servicemen on land holdings was accomplished with the transfer to state ownership of crofting land administered by the Crofters Commission.

Within the crofting areas, a way of life

developed which was associated with dual or multiple occupations, most crofts being too small to provide more than a minimal subsistence. The Free Church, greatly favoured for its sympathetic attitudes to the under-privileged, established strong support amongst the crofting communities, while the security of tenure enjoyed helps to explain the radical and liberal political attitudes still current in the crofting areas. Meanwhile, the remoteness and limited opportunities associated with crofting have fostered very high levels of mutual support within the crofting communities. The closed world of crofting came to represent a unique blend of the idyllic and the stagnation of opportunity. The typical croft comprises a small homestead standing amongst a group of perhaps two to eight small enclosed fields together with rights to graze a certain number of animals on the STINTED COMMON pastures. Homesteads are sometimes grouped in clusters, with their

landholdings radiating outwards in dartboard fashion. See also CLEARANCES, INFIELD.

*Further reading*: Hunter, J., *The Making of the Crofting Community*, John Donald, 1976.

**Croftland**. Land in Scotland that was of good quality and kept in production by frequent applications of manure. See also INFIELD-OUTFIELD CULTIVATION, INLAND, RUNRIG.

**Crop circles**. Geometrically-shaped areas of flattened plants encountered within fields of wheat or other cereals which are created, normally at night, by young farmers, university students and small groups of local villagers who

53

take an interest in exploring the limits of human credibility.

**Crop marks**. Crop marks are produced by variations in the height and condition of plants within a growing crop (usually a cereal crop) which are caused by differences in the soil and subsoil. They have become by far the most important means of recognising significant or potentially interesting archaeological sites. Plants growing in silted-up pits and ditches will stand above their fellows, and their deeper root runs will give protection against drought, while others, growing on buried walls, will be relatively stunted. When a low sun shines across the crop the differences in height produced by buried features cause shadows to be cast, and when seen from the air these shadows may neatly trace out a Roman villa, deserted village or ancient system of field-ditches. Prominent crop marks can also be seen from ground level, but one needs the airman's advantage in order to recognise the plan of the patterns produced.

*Further reading:* Edis, J., MacLeod, D. and Bewley, B., 'An Archaeologists' Guide to Classification of Cropmarks and Soilmarks', *Antiquity* **63**, pp. 112–26.

**Crosses**. The Christian cross was *the* almost universal symbol in Dark Age and medieval Britain; and, though the symbolism of the cross itself was known to all, crosses were erected for a wide range of purposes, and they evolved and differed in many important respects. Consequently crosses are best treated under a series of headings. If one sees a freestanding cross on a village GREEN, with its cross-shaft (with or minus a cross-head) standing upon a stepped plinth, then one can be quite confident that this is a medieval MARKET cross. But other examples can be more difficult to interpret. (This entry ranges and includes stones that are not strictly crosses).

*Dark Age memorial stones.* These belong to the Christian tradition but may not actually display a cross symbol – though many have the 'chi-rho' symbol, which derives from the first letters in

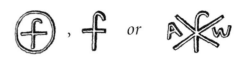

Greek of Christ's name. The alpha and omega letters are found on a third type of 'cross' and are the first and last letters of the alphabet and symbolise the message 'I am the beginning and the end'. These stones survived, as Roman Christianity may have done, in parts of the 'Celtic' lands. Their crudely carved inscriptions are in Latin, which may or may not be accurate, or occasionally in Celtic or OGHAM, and consist of simple epitaphs which often include standard phrases like *Hic Iacit in Pace* ('Here he lies in peace'). Examples include the sixth-century 'Tristan's Stone' near Fowey in Cornwall: 'Tristan lies here, son of Cynvawr'; the 'Men Scryfa', or written stone, near Chun in Cornwall: 'Rialobran, son of Cunoval' of the late fifth or sixth century; the sixth-century stone preserved at Margam Abbey near Swansea: 'The stone of Boduocus, here he lies, the son of Catotigirnus, great-grandson of Eternal is Vedomavus'; and the tantalising and important fifth-century grave-marking stone amongst the trio of stones at Kirkmadrine in Galloway inscribed 'Here lie the holy and principal priests, Ides, Viventius and Mavorius'. Comparable inscriptions may also be found on later crosses,

*Crosses*
A Celtic tomb slab at the early monastic site of Clonmacnois, County Offaly.

like the tenth-century decorated cross-shaft at Llantwit Major near Cardiff: 'Samson set up this cross for his soul, for that of Illtut, of Samson the King, of Samuel, and of Ebisar.' Most memorial stones represent the lingering of Roman Christianity or the early conversion of communities in the Celtic lands and pre-date the conversion of the Saxon kingdoms of England. Where the cross symbol is displayed it may derive from 'Chi' rather than from the symbol of Christ's passion and death.

*Christianised monoliths.* These are not uncommon in Ireland and represent the Christian conversion of local communities and the carving of simple crosses on ancient pagan standing stones. This activity would have begun around AD 400, and as it proceeded, the cross symbol adopted evolved, apparently in the sequence Latin cross–Greek cross–crosses made up of arcs-crosses with wedge-shaped tips.

*Cross pillars.* Unshaped or crudely shaped upright stones with simple inscriptions or symbols are found in other 'Celtic' countries and can be entirely the products of early Christianity.

*Ogham stones.* Ogham is an alphabet composed of strokes that intersect a baseline in different ways. It appeared in the fourth century and was used in the fifth, sixth and seventh centuries for simple inscriptions in Ireland and the parts of western Britain that experienced Irish contacts and settlement. Ogham stones are not crosses, but the currency of the alphabet spanned the conversion era and ogham inscriptions could appear on Christian stones, some of which are 'bilingual' in Latin and ogham. One of the most accessible ogham stones can be seen incorporated as a window-sill inside the medieval church at Nevern near Fishguard. See also OGHAM.

*Pictish symbol stones.* See entry for SYMBOL STONE.

*Celtic crosses in Cornwall.* These crosses, ranging from little waist-high 'lollipops' to grander churchyard crosses, like the ones at Boscastle and

A Saxon cross of the ninth century at Irton in Cumbria.

Altarnun, are in the Celtic tradition of the wheel-headed cross, but are carved in uncompromising granite (moorstone) so that it was not possible to pierce the space between the enclosing circle and the arms of the cross. They appear to span the centuries from the later Dark Ages to the early Middle Ages, and their function is uncertain and variable. Some may have been preaching crosses, others boundary- or

The 'Cross of the scriptures' at Clonmacnois in County Offaly is a superb Irish high cross of the tenth century.

track-markers and several appear to have marked the limits of church land and sanctuary.

*Cross slabs.* These date from the Dark Ages, and the cross is presented not in a freestanding form

but as a relief carved on one or both faces of an unshaped or partly-shaped stone. They are creations of early Celtic Christianity and include Irish gravestones and tomb slabs and the later Pictish symbol stones. Some, like the superb Pictish example in Aberlemno churchyard near Forfar, can be expertly and intricately decorated. Most date from the seventh to the ninth centuries, and some of the decorative inspiration for the more ornate and later slabs of Scotland and Ireland appears to be partly derived from Northumbrian artistic motifs. The slabs vary considerably in their sophistication and, as with many other crosses, it is hard to be sure of their original sites, positions and functions. Some that are now upright were originally placed horizontally over burials, and so they were tomb slabs rather than crosses.

*Irish high crosses.* These are arguably the most refined and beautiful of all crosses and represent a development of the earlier cross-slab tradition and appeared after AD 800. However, most adopt the form of the wheel-headed cross, and it has been argued that this evolved from an earlier tradition of carved wooden crosses, the wheel deriving from braces used to strengthen the arms of a wooden cross – though Mediterranean Christian traditions presented the cross within a circle. Of the hundred-or-so known examples in Ireland, most are relatively plain, but a celebrated minority, like those at Castledermot, County Kildare, Monasterboice, County Louth, and Kilfenora, County Clare, are superbly carved with scriptural scenes or elaborate interlace motifs. Most are associated with Irish-Celtic monastic sites.

*Preaching crosses.* It is generally assumed, and probably true, that many places in Britain gained a preaching cross as a venue for services conducted by priests travelling from MINSTERS before adequate resources, congregations and patronage allowed the building of a local church. Scores of churches have evidence of a Dark Age freestanding and decorated cross, though usually the cross is broken or fragmentary rather than intact. The cross, or its fragments, may stand or lie inside or outside the church, or the cross may have been incorporated into the actual walls as building stone in the course of building or rebuilding, as at the Saxon Kirkdale minster in the North York Moors. However, one can hardly ever know for sure that such crosses were preaching crosses and did actually pre-date the church concerned. Some may have been churchyard crosses erected close to existing houses of worship. In many cases, the crosses now displayed in churches and churchyards have been removed from other locations, which are generally long forgotten. Decorations can take the form of interlace or vine-scroll motifs, birds and animals and scenes from the Scriptures. The remarkable Gosforth cross in Cumbria dates from the late tenth century, stands 15 feet (4.57 metres) and has both Christian motifs and scenes from Norse mythology on its slender shaft.

*Churchyard crosses.* Some of the older crosses that stand in churchyards may originally have been preaching crosses. Most surviving churchyard crosses are medieval (a few are quite modern) and, as well as sanctifying the churchyard, they were closely associated with the Palm Sunday rituals. As part of this procession a mass was said at the foot of the cross and it was wreathed in 'palms'. The most typical medieval designs had a small cross-head or an oblong tabernacle carried on a tall shaft above a rectangular, round or polygonal stepped base. Since the tabernacle often carried images of Christ crucified, the Virgin and saints, such crosses were popular targets at the time of the Reformation and Civil War for those offended by 'Popish' images. Most medieval churchyard crosses now consist only of a base and shaft.

*Consecration crosses.* These small crosses were installed in newly built churches to protect them against the devil. A full set of consecration crosses amounted to twelve inside and twelve outside, and when the bishop consecrated the church he ascended to each cross and anointed it with chrism, a cream of oil and balm, and repeated a prayer beginning 'Blessed be this church ...'. The crosses were normally placed at heights of around 8 feet (2.43 metres). They consisted of a small stone circle containing a red-painted, incised or metal cross and were provided with a bracket to hold a candle: twelve consecration crosses with candles symbolising the twelve apostles who illuminated the world. Several churches still display one or several of these crosses, but few full sets remain. Edington in Wiltshire still has ten outside and eleven inside. Crosses on door-jambs of churches were also intended to keep out demons.

*Penitential or weeping crosses.* These have worn grooves for knees around their bases marking the places where penitents would kneel to pray. They are rare, but there is a good example in Ripley churchyard, North Yorkshire, an early example that appears to have been removed to the present church when the original one was abandoned about the late fourteenth century.

*Wayside crosses.* When provided to mark the course of routeways across difficult ground wayside crosses are usually medieval in date and crude or simple in execution, some being mere upright boulders. The North York Moors, in particular, and Dartmoor, to a lesser extent, are rich in such crosses. Some consecrated a crossroad site or the place where a local disaster occurred and some were spaced at intervals on routes used by corpse-bearers, as places for rest and prayer on the way to the funeral. They can easily be confused with *boundary crosses*, erected to mark the limits of monastic lands. The Abbots of Fountains Abbey erected small crosses with simple plinths to mark some of the places where routeways entered their estates. *Sanctuary crosses* were set up where roads entered ecclesiastical liberties. There were eight sanctuary crosses around Ripon, of which the Sharow cross survives. The *Eleanor crosses* are a special category of wayside cross: ornate crosses erected at the eleven places where the body of Queen Eleanor rested on the route to Westminster after her death at Harby, Northamptonshire, in 1290.

sanctify the sites of medieval trading, but they mainly existed as prominent indications of the sites of markets, with their size and elaboration often reflecting the importance of the market concerned. Sometimes they are associated with STOCKS, with the step of the plinth giving seating to the prisoners. Designs vary, but often market crosses resemble the description given of churchyard crosses, though often the base or a broken shaft or the square socket that held the shaft are all that remains to symbolise a settlement's commercial aspirations. The market cross seen at any village might easily date from the time when the market charter was granted, which is usually recorded. Not all market crosses are medieval; the one at Carperby in Wensleydale is archaic in style but seventeenth-century in date.

Towards the end of the medieval period, an interesting evolution affected market crosses in some of the more successful trading centres, like Chichester. Benefactors sometimes left money for the building of polygonal roofed shelters pierced by arches and carrying the lantern or cross above the canopy. In a few villages, which could not afford such elaborations, like Cheddar in Somerset, a shelter was built over the old village cross. In the sixteenth century, John Leland described such arrangements and explained that the late fifteenth-century cross at Malmesbury was built and vaulted 'for poore market folkes to stand dry when rain cummith'.

While it is possible to group crosses into different categories, as attempted here, not all the answers can be found. Stylistic features can be used by experts roughly to date a cross, but even with the problem of dating solved other questions remain. These relate both to the fact that crosses were adopted for so many different roles and to the fact that crosses have so often been moved from the original settings: incorporated into church masonry, gathered together in churches or churchyards, pillaged for gateposts or demolished as 'Popish' symbols. Elsewhere, this author has argued that the presumed market cross at the shrunken/deserted

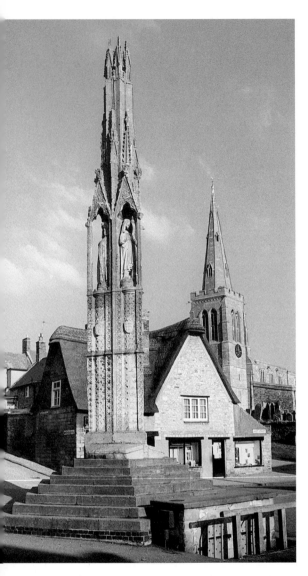

An Eleanor Cross at Geddington in Northamptonshire.

Three examples survive: at Geddington and Hardingstone in Northamptonshire and at Waltham Cross in Hertfordshire. Roadside crosses were sometimes carved by *pilgrims;* an example can be seen cut on a small rock-face beside a track near Nevern.

*Market crosses.* These may have been intended to

village site of Clint in North Yorkshire is, in fact, a monastic boundary cross that has been transported a few hundred yards down a lane from its original setting on the boundary between abbey estates and the Forest of Knaresborough.

*Further reading*: Vallance, Aylmer, *Old Crosses and Lychgates*, Batsford, 1920.

**Cruck-framing**, see TIMBER-FRAMING.

**Cryw**. A name associated with FORDS in Wales.

**Cultural landscape**. In the words of the American geographer, Carl Sauer, who regarded 'cultural geography' in rather the way that landscape history is now regarded in Britain: 'The cultural landscape is fashioned from a natural landscape by a culture group. Culture is the agent, the natural area is the medium, the cultural landscape is the result. Under the influence of a given culture, itself changing through time, the landscape undergoes development, passing through phases … With the introduction of a different – that is, alien – culture, a rejuvenation of the cultural landscape sets in …' (1925).

*Further reading*: Leighly, J. (ed.), *Land and life: selections from the writings of Carl Ortwin Sauer*, University of California Press, Berkeley, CA, 1974.
Muir, R., *Approaches to Landscape*, Macmillan, London, 1999.

**Culture, couture**, see FURLONG (the name probably derives from the blade or 'coulter' on the plough).

**Cup marks, cup and ring marks**. These are symbols that can be found pecked into rock outcrops and boulders and standing stones in various parts of the British uplands. Where one example is discovered there are likely to be several others in the vicinity. They are, for example, particularly numerous in the vicinity of Ikley, and upland Northumberland, while a standing stone at Ballymeanoch in mid-Argyll is thickly covered with cup marks and cup and ring marks. The symbols consist of cup-like depressions, cups within circles and concentric circles which often have a 'duct' running radially from the central depression to the outer ring. Occasionally, other symbols are seen. Some of the decorated stones are small enough to be portable, though others appear on massive, earthfast boulders. They were presumed to date from the Bronze Age but late-Neolithic/early-Bronze Age dates are more credible, evidenced by the facts that cup marks are found on portal dolmens and a cup-marked slab was incorporated in the covering mound of the LONG BARROW at Dalladies, near Aberdeen. Occasionally, spiral and rectangular motifs are found in association with cup and ring marks.

Presumably, the symbols had a meaning for the people who carved them, but this meaning remains mysterious despite the many interpretations that have been offered – most of them extremely bizarre. One of the less extreme suggestions regarded the symbols as mineral surveyors' marks, but the elaborate nature of many assemblages of symbols would argue against this. The representations seem to have symbolic meanings, and as some decorated stones seem to be associated with burial mounds, the meaning may concern life, death and the transition from one to the other.

*Further reading*: Beckensall, S., *Prehistoric Rock Art in Northumberland*, Tempus, Stroud, 2001.

**Currie**. A deep pool or embayment in a Scottish river where fish may lie.

**Cursus**. Cursūs or cursuses are seldom seen as prominent monuments today, but in their late-Neolithic heyday they must have appeared as very imposing avenues defined by high earthen banks built about 200–600 feet (60–185 metres) apart. The most famous example is the Dorset Cursus which consists of two cursuses joined end to end and runs across the countryside of the Cranborne Chase for about 6 miles (10 kilometres). The monuments appear as components in RITUAL LANDSCAPES. A cursus is associated with Stonehenge, and the monuments often run close to or incorporate LONG BARROWS. In the past they were regarded as prehistoric racecourses, but modern archaeologists tend, cautiously, to interpret them as great processional and ritual avenues. The Gussage Cursus aligns on the mid-winter solstice and can be interpreted as a processional avenue between existing groups of long barrows.

An enormous effort was expended in cursus construction – some 260,000 cubic yards (200,000 cubic metres) of earth and chalk being shifted to create the Dorset Cursus, the longest example at a length of over 6 miles (10 km).

Most of the monuments are now so eroded as to be scarcely visible, but from time to time the parallel ditches of formerly unknown cursuses are recognised in aerial photographs. In places like the lower valley of the Ure in Yorkshire and Rudston in Humberside they are associated with great ritual areas with HENGES and standing stones.

*Further reading*: Green, M., *A Landscape Revealed*, Tempus, Stroud, 2000.

**Cwealmstow**. Early English execution place. See also GIBBET SITE.

# D

**Daffin Green**. Village green or public space in Scotland where people gather to play games and 'daff' or sport in a light-hearted or foolish manner. See also GREEN (VILLAGE), PLAISTOW.

**Dale-land**. The shared arable land of a northern community, inhabited by 'dale-landers'. See also INFIELD-OUTFIELD CULTIVATION, INLAND, RUNRIG.

**Dalloch**. In Lowland Scots, a piece of land that is flat and fertile. The ground would be described as rich or 'daichy'.

**Dams and weirs**. Frequently the building of a WATERMILL was accompanied by associated works in river engineering. A weir was built across the river to divert water into an artificial channel or 'GOIT', while a dam placed just above the mill, on the goit or the millpond which it fed, impounded the head of water necessary for milling operations.

A special type of weir which existed in the Dark Ages and medieval times was the fish-hedge, FISH GARTH or fish-weir, and some of these were particularly associated with

catching eels and lampreys. Such weirs must have a much longer history, for excavations on former meanders of the River Trent near Castle Donington revealed the birch upright posts and wattle partitions of a fish-weir which was dated to 800 BC. Excavations on other old meanders of the Trent, at Colwick near Nottingham, recently revealed a Saxon, a Norman and seven Tudor fish-weirs, while Domesday Book tells of some twenty-one 'piscarae' or fish-weirs which existed in Nottinghamshire. The Norman weir that was excavated consisted of wattle screens supported by six rows of oak and holly posts. The rows were arranged in the form of a funnel that narrowed downstream and was probably used to catch silver eels during their autumn migration. The Saxon weir, which was constructed of boulders, posts and wattle, had run obliquely across the river to funnel fish into a basket of wicker. Similar fish-weirs appear in Saxon documents, and the records of Tidenham estate in Gloucestershire of around 1060 mention twenty-one weirs on the Severn and thirty-eight on the Wye; and 'at every weir within the [ESTATE] every alternate fish belongs to the lord of the manor, and every rare fish which is of value – sturgeon or porpoise, herring or sea fish – and no one has the right of selling any fish for money when the lord is on the estate without informing him'.

Around 1394 there were complaints to the Archbishop of York about the various artificial obstructions which threatened navigation from the Trent river system to York, and 'weirs called fish garths' were specifically mentioned. Apparently the enlargement of one of the weirs on the Ouse had caused the sinking of two ships carrying valuable cargoes of cloth, said to have been worth £60. Both the mill-weirs and the fish-weirs constituted serious impediments to navigation. When the primitive locks or sluices in the weir were closed to raise a head of water for milling, navigation was prevented, not only in the vicinity of the weir, but also downstream, where the reduction of flow led to a shallowing of the river. Millers operating downstream of their rivals similarly suffered from the interruptions to their water-supply. Acts of 1352 and 1399 attempted to regulate milling activities, but may not have been widely observed.

As well as the problems concerning navigation, there were always likely to be conflicts about weirs, dams and ponds when the different sides of a river were held by different owners. Often, agreements were reached establishing the maximum water-level which a neighbour across the river would be expected to experience. Sometimes, however, the harmony was lacking, and in the entry on the GRANGE is described the thirteenth-century affair involving the abbeys of Fountains and Sawley and the disputed mill-dam on the Skirfare. A similar kind of dispute involving the vill of Foxton in Cambridgeshire was recorded in Domesday Book, which reported that 'in the same vill there is half a mill worth 10s. 8d. [54p] which Robert Gernon annexed in defiance of Geoffrey [the new landowner] as the men of the hundred testify'. The other half of the mill was held by the Abbess of Chatteris, and it seems likely that the mill was divided following an earlier dispute

over rights to the stream and its weir between parties living on the opposed banks.

From the evidence of surviving medieval accounts it seems that weirs and dams were constructed with a core of boulders, clay or turf retained by a carpentry framework and had a system of planking to stabilise the core. Even so, regular damage by flooding and, perhaps, occasional sabotage by navigation interests resulted in repeated repairs to the medieval weirs. This burden fell on the peasant tenants of the manor concerned, and there is some evidence that different tenants were responsible for specific sections of a dam or weir. For example, in 1427 a heavy fine of 40d. [17p] was levied on an errant tenant of Baildon manor in West Yorkshire 'that he do sufficiently repair the part falling to him to be repaired'. The mill-dam at Otley was 45 yards (41 metres) long and composed of sections or 'doles', each 11 feet (3.4 metres) wide, and each the responsibility of a particular tenant, the obligation remaining in force until the mid eighteenth century.

While medieval weirs do not survive, many milling sites are very old indeed and several surviving later weirs and dams occupy the sites of their medieval or even Dark Age predecessors. The watermill at Houghton in Cambridgeshire, for example, is associated with a site which has a connection with milling that goes back at least as far as AD 964, when a mill here was granted to Ramsey Abbey. At the deserted village site of Wharram Percy near Malton, the Saxon mill-dam has been excavated and the medieval millpond has been restored. See also FALL TROUGH, POND, WATERMILL.

**Davoch**. An old Scottish land measurement, normally of around 400 ACRES.

**Day hole**, see BELL PIT

**Day math**. A term formerly used in the countryside around Chester to describe the amount of meadow that a man might mow in a day – around 2 ACRES.

**Day work**. A term used in the north of England

to describe three ¼ ACRE land units. The equivalent in Lowland Scots is a 'darg' or 'dargue', which imitates the sound of a spade in yielding earth. 'Darg-days' were the amount of work given as rent by a cottager to the farmer on whose holding his cottage stood and a 'darger' was a day labourer.

**Dead hedge**, see BRAIRDED DYKE, HEDGEROWS, GARTHING.

**Debatable land.** Land on the Anglo-Scottish border whose attribution to England or Scotland was uncertain or in dispute. See BORDERS.

**Deer park.** Hunting was the major recreation of the medieval nobility; the monarchs had their FORESTS, the nobles their CHASES and the gentry obtained rights of 'FREE WARREN' to hunt lesser game. An important extra element in the bloodsporting spectrum was the deer park, a large, enclosed area where deer were contained by a deer-proof 'pale'. Deer parks had a long tradition on the Continent, and a few existed in England under the last Saxon kings, but they multiplied rapidly after the Norman Conquest. By 1086, about thirty-six parks had been created, but when the deer park reached its peak of popularity, around 1300, some 3200 examples were in existence, and the woodland historian, Oliver Rackham, suggests that at this time some 2 per cent of England's area was covered by deer parks. In northern England the movement to create hunting parks was sustained through the Middle Ages, and into the seventeenth century.

Before the Norman Conquest, Britain contained two types of deer, the red and the roe. Fallow deer were normally used to stock deer parks and, although these beautiful creatures were present in interglacial times, they did not return to Britain after the last Ice Age. The Romans may have attempted to reintroduce the fallow deer, but it was the Normans who successfully re-established it in Britain. The typical deer park could almost be regarded as a farm for raising venison, and it supplied a reliable quota of meat for the great feasts of the

*Deer park*
Fallow deer were introduced by the Normans and were the deer most commonly found in deer parks.

adjacent castle, manor or abbey. In size it would normally cover 100–200 acres (40–80 hectares), though a few were much larger. It would generally be of a roughly elliptical shape, and before it could be enclosed, the aspiring owner would normally need to obtain a licence to empark from the King, though permission might be concealed in a 'grant of *free warren*' or a licence to crenellate or fortify a home.

Since fallow deer are very difficult animals to confine, the perimeter defences needed to be unusually strong, with a tall paling of cleft posts, a dense hedge or a stone wall often set upon a massive earthen bank. The natural terrain could be exploited in hilly or undulating areas, with the wall or paling being placed on a scarp in a way that made it difficult for deer to get out, but easy for them to leap in. Sometimes, an initial stocking of a gift of deer by the King was obtained, while efforts were made to allow wild deer to enter but not to leave the park. This was made possible by the provision of a *deer leap*, a cunning juxtaposition of bank and ditch. However since the Crown owned all wild deer the privilege to build deer leaps was often refused. The Statute of Winchester of 1285 stipulated that the wall or paling of a park should be set 200 feet from the king's highway, with the area between the park and the road being cleared of bushes and undergrowth to prevent robbers hiding there to ambush travellers. It is doubtful that the statute was properly enforced.

Deer parks were often sited in wooded country, and the trees within the parks would be POLLARDED rather than COPPICED to allow timber to grow above the reach of browsing. Often the interior of the park was segmented to provide '*launds*', or lawns, where the deer could graze and protected coppice areas from which the deer were excluded when the timber was soft and young. The laund landscape of deer lawns interspersed with lollipop-like pollard trees gave rise to what is still regarded as 'parkland' scenery. While vermin, like the fox, may have been hunted inside deer parks, it appears that space might too limited for the conventional chase, and sometimes the deer were released and hunted across the neighbouring fields – to the consternation of the working population. In other cases, *hunting towers* were built on the highest ground within a park and driven deer were shot at by the hunting party. Later, feasting and drinking could take place in the tower.

Some deer parks were resented because they had been created through the forfeiture of peasant land, while the confined deer were irresistible to outlaws and poachers. There were numerous instances of poaching and many complaints about the injustices and damage to crops caused by the bloodsports. The case was put most eloquently by a foreigner, Jonas of Orleans:

> It is a most wretched and lamentable thing that, for the sake of wild beasts which no human care has nurtured but which God has granted for the common use of mankind, the poor are despoiled by great folk and scourged and cast into prison and subjected to many other sufferings … Who can deny that this is un-Christian this infliction of so manifold injustices on so many of Christ's poor, for the sake of one man's pleasure; yet this thing is

practised almost in more ways than I can rehearse.

Haverah Park near Knaresborough was one of a group of parks created under dubious circumstances and it encompassed 2250 acres (910 hectares) of peasant common land seized in the late twelfth century. As usual, a bizarre local mythology developed, partly to explain the odd name of the park. It invoked a cripple with the improbable name of Taverah who hobbled up to John of Gaunt to beg a little piece of land in the forest. He was promised as much land as he could hop around in a long summer's day – and promptly hopped around the entire circuit of the park by nightfall. Because of the high concentrations of deer which they contained, deer parks were particularly vulnerable to poaching. In 1289, for example, Whitwick Park in the Charnwood Forest lost fifteen deer that were valued at the incredibly high price of £40. A gang of nine or more members had broken into the park, armed with swords, sticks, bows and arrows. Three members of this poaching gang were local clergymen. Park breaking sometimes amounted to more than simple poaching, for to break into an enemy's park and hunt his deer was regarded as a supreme insult.

It is claimed that the greatest multiplication of parks occurred in the period 1200–1350, but the park was later in the North. The deer park became a much sought after status symbol – but ii was costly and needed a great deal of labour to be maintained properly. From the outset, deer parks were venues for the AGISTMENT of cattle, while permanent cultivation existed within closes in some parks. The parks could also be useful sources of quarried building stone, clay, charcoal, ores and various other resources. With the arrival of the Black Death in 1348, labour became scarce and costly; and, though new parks appeared in areas ravaged by the plague and falling out of cultivation, in the fifteenth, sixteenth and seventeenth centuries many parks were disparked. Others became VACCARIES or general amenity parks rather than venison farms, and their tree-studded lawns provided the image which would be cultivated and refined by the later creators of the English LANDSCAPE PARKS, some of which, like Studley Royal near Ripon or Ripley near Harrogate, had a medieval deer park nucleus. Some parks reverted to tillage and others became stud farms. A number of deer parks, like those just mentioned, still contain deer. Partly because of escapees from derelict deer parks, and partly as a result of the fewness of farmworkers found in today's countryside, the English countryside probably now contains more wild deer than at any time in the Middle Ages.

Former deer parks can be identified through documentary research, while in the countryside evidence comes from the survival of massive curving perimeter banks which may be hedged and embrace networks of fields created at the time of disparking, while 'park' place-names are usually found in the vicinity of a former deer park, like Park End hamlet by the old Stevington deer park in Bedfordshire. Because the institution of a deer park generally protected the enclosed area against later tillage, the earthworks preserved in deer parks provide invaluable indications of the details of the medieval rural landscape.

*Further reading:* Canton, Leonard (ed.), *The English Medieval Landscape*, Croom Helm, 1982.
Birrell, J., 'Deer and Deer Farming in Medieval England', *Agricultural History Review* 40/2, 1992.
Liddiard, R., 'The Deer Parks of Domesday Book', LANDSCAPES 4.1, 4–23.

**Demesne.** This medieval word is used in some slightly different contexts. The royal demesne consisted of MANORS which were held directly by the King rather than by his vassals and which contributed revenues to the royal purse. Likewise a great lord might hold several manors, some of them subinfeudated to his vassals and others held directly by him as demesne manors. Most commonly the term is used to describe the portion of the lands of a manor which the lord of that manor held for himself as opposed to the lands which were held by his peasant tenants.

Of course, the lord did not cultivate the demesne himself; the work was performed either by labour services imposed upon the peasant tenants, or by paid estate workers ( *famuli* ) or by a combination of the two. The demesne was in a sense the 'HOME FARM' of the manor and in some cases attempts were made to extract the dispersed demesne lands from the milieu of open-field cultivation and create a consolidated demesne holding. In the late fourteenth and early fifteenth centuries high labour costs encouraged many lords to lease out the demesne lands. Occasionally 'demesne' will occur in a field-name, revealing the old ownership.

**Den.** A glen or ravine.

**Dendrochronology.** A method of dating timber and timber structures and artefacts by measuring the age 'fingerprints' provided by successions of annual growth rings, which reflect variations in climate and growth conditions from season to season. These 'fingerprints' can be linked to established local growth patterns, thus obtaining probable dates for the materials concerned. By obtaining new patterns that overlap the ends of the established chronology, the chronology can be extended.

**Dene hole,** see MARLPIT.

**Denn.** A woodland pasture where pigs could feed on fallen acorns or beech mast.

**Deserted village,** see LOST VILLAGE.

**Designed landscape.** A landscape with several deliberately contrived components, such as lakes, avenues and tree clumps. See also ORNAMENTAL LANDSCAPE.

**Devall.** In Scotland, a sunk fence. See also HA-HA.

**Devil, The.** Former rural communities were steeped in superstition and generally fearful of spirits and devils. Hob, a traditional name for Satan, occurs in various place-names, but is most likely to derive from an Old English word denoting tussocks of grass. More probably related to the Devil are field-names of a euphemistic nature which are associated with land linked to 'Good Man', like Goodman's Hey. Direct references to the Devil and Satan in field-names will probably be relatively recent and they often embody a derogatory reference to bad farming land.

**Dew pond**, see POND.

**Dike**. In Northern Britain an ambiguous term that can variously signify a wall, a ditch, a track or CAUSEWAY, the act of digging or that of walling. See also CONSUMPTION DYKE, DRYSTONE WALL, DRAINAGE, HEDGE AND DITCH RULE.

**Dike-end**. In Northern Britain, a wall that continues a boundary across the seashore to prevent livestock wandering on the beach from gaining access to growing crops.

**Ditch**. Normally a narrow trench that is filled with water or dug to carry water away. In Ireland the term comprises not only the ditch, but also the adjacent hedge bank made of stones cleared from the adjacent land and covered in mud and silts derived from the wet ditch as well as the HEDGEROW that stands on it. The construction of such 'ditches' was a key element in the eighteenth-century agricultural improvements in the east of Ireland. See also HEDGE AND DITCH RULE.

**Divot-dyke, fail-dyke**. In Scotland, a wall built of 'divots' of turf. See also BACKIT DYKE.

**Divot house, fail-housie**. A Scottish house or cottage roofed in turf.

**Dole, dale**. A share in a communal resource of farmland. Dole MEADOWS were divided into shares or strips like those in the arable land. These might be permanently held, or if the meadow was a LOT MEADOW then the doles could be reallocated each year. In Northern Britain, the share delivered to one in a lottery was known as a KEAVLE.

**Dolver**. Marshy ground or land reclaimed from the Fens in East Anglia.

**Domesday Book**. This is often regarded as a complete description of the villages and countrysides of early Norman England, but is likely to prove to be a very deficient guide unless an effort is made to understand the meaning of the entries. The Anglo-Saxon Chronicle (a record of events compiled over many years by English monks) tells us that while William I was spending the Christmas of 1085 at Gloucester he had 'much thorough and deep discussion with his council about this country – how it was occupied, and with what sort of people'. As a result, he sent his men 'over all England into every shire and had them find out how many hundred hides there were in the shire, or what land and castles the King himself had in the country, or what dues he ought to have in 12 months from the shire ...'. The result was a record which, so the common people believed, would last until Domesday, the final day of reckoning. William's realm, then lying south of the Westmorland hills and the Tees, was divided into seven circuits and noble commissioners were despatched to each region.

William was not attempting to compile a guidebook to Norman England, as so many later writers have assumed, but principally to discover who owned what, who owed him what, and to record the imposition of feudal law and tenure on his kingdom. The terse entries seek to answer a number of questions: What is the place called? Who owned it before the Norman takeover? How much taxable ploughland was there? How much is there now? Who owns it now? How many feudal peasants does he have? How much pasture, etc., is there? What was it worth in King Edward's time? What is it worth now? All these answers were obtained from sworn groups of local men and recorded in a form of Latin shorthand. A typical entry runs:

> In *Kirk Hammerton*. Turchil, Gamel and Heltor had 6½ carucates of land to be taxed. There is land to 6 ploughs. John, a vassal of

Osbern's, has there 2 ploughs, and 5 villeins with 1 plough. There is a priest and a church, and 1 mill of 2 shillings [10p], and 1 fishery of 3 shillings [15p]. The whole ½ mile long and 1½ mile broad. Value in King Edward's time 4 pounds, now worth 45 shillings [£2.25].

This entry shows that Kirk Hammerton, North Yorkshire, had a Saxon church – it still has – and a village may have accompanied the church (the decline in value since King Edward's time was probably a consequence of the Normans' terrible Harrying of the North in 1069–71). In fact there is no proof that a village existed here – none is mentioned – and the most important thing to remember is that Domesday Book selectively lists the contents of manorial estates and TOWNSHIPS. Theirs are the names recorded, not the names of villages, which may or may not have existed. For example, the 'village' of Birstwith (North Yorkshire) is 'named' in Domesday, but the village did not exist until groups of estate cottages and a church were built in the nineteenth century! It is the township that is named.

All kinds of other problems can flow from a misreading of Domesday; numerous churches and even the occasional castle are overlooked, it is not clear if woodland was always COPPICE or more open WOOD PASTURE, and while an effort was made to list feudal peasants and their status we are not told about their families, while the records themselves are sometimes erratic and groups of villages and hamlets are sometimes masked under a single entry.

*Further reading*: Darby, H. C. (ed.), *Domesday England*, Cambridge University Press, 1977.
Galbraith, V. H., The *Making of Domesday Book*, Clarendon Press, 1961.
Hallam, E. M., *Domesday Book Through Nine Centuries*, Guild Publishing, 1986.

**Doocot, dooket, dow-cot**. Scottish terms for DOVECOT.

**Door-land**. In Scotland, the plot of land lying outside the door.

**Dovecot**. Doves, taken from a dovecot, 'culvery' or 'pigeon house', provided a useful source of fresh protein to relieve the diet of salted meats in winter and spring. Dovecots continued in use from the Middle Ages, when they were monopolised by the manorial lords, to the eighteenth and nineteenth centuries, when they were common features of the larger farms. The doves, domesticated from the wild, cliff-nesting rock-dove, could fly freely from their 'cots' and could be expected to gorge themselves on the village corn, explaining the manorial monopoly on this potentially destructive form of farming. However, the medieval peasants may have had their own ways of catching doves, for a Gloucester case records how boys and girls had been 'carolling' for doves: '... and one boy said that one of the girls carolled well, and he gave her doves, but this being heard by Nicholas Calt and Thomas le Prute who put up the doves, they said that he lied and that she should not have the doves and beat the said boy over the head with a certain stick.' Whether it was the taking of the doves or the unseemly gaiety of the carolling which offended is not clear. However, an Act of 1761/62 allowed freeholders and all landlords to build dovecots, while tenants could erect them if they obtained permission from their landlords.

The dovecot is usually a distinctive building, although a number of different designs were employed. In the latter part of the Middle Ages, cylindrical towers were favoured, exemplified by one beside the church at Garway, Herefordshire, or the dovecot at Avebury, Wiltshire. The remains of a different, tower-like monastic dovecot can be seen near Bruton in Somerset, but the finest old dovecot of all is at Willington in Bedfordshire, built at the time of the Dissolution of the Monasteries, by Sir John Gostwick. This is a grandiose example of the lectern-shaped type of dovecot – a double lectern in fact – with a open clerestory midway up the roof to provide free access for the birds. There is also some evidence that church towers occasionally served as dovecots, and in one case a complaint was taken to the archdeacon after a falconer priest had loosed his birds at such a tempting target in a neighbouring church. The offended priest put his case in verse:

> To hawke in my church of Dis
> This fond franktyte fauconer
> With his polutid pawternar
> As priest unrevenent
> Streyght to the sacrament
> He made his hawk to fly
> With hugeous showte and cry
> The hye auter he strypt naked
> There on he strode and craked ...

By the end of the seventeenth century England had around 26,000 dovecots, while in 1808 one writer guessed that there were 1,125,000 domestic doves in England and Wales. In these and the following periods, most of the cots constructed took the form of a box-like square tower of timber-framing, brick or stone with a roof that could be conical, pyramidical or four-gabled, though circular and octagonal dovecots were also built. Birds entered and left via a roof dormer or

*Dovecot*
This dovecot, at Willington in Bedfordshire, dates from about 1540.

a cupola-like structure, or 'glover', at the top of the roof. The inner walls of the dovecots were lined with stacks of niches, providing nesting and roosting places. These were reached by ladder, and often a revolving axle and projecting arm (a 'potence') were provided high up in the dovecot as a rest for the ladder so that it could be moved easily around the stacked niches. Such an arrangement favoured the circular dovecot form.

A dovecot of average size might have accommodation for 1000 nests and a population of 2000 birds, plus their young, and a succession of two-egg clutches were produced throughout much of the year. The benefits of this protein-rich bounty of birds, fledglings and eggs had to be measured against the losses inflicted on green and cereal crops, although the dove guano was collected as a particularly potent fertiliser. During the eighteenth century, pigeon-lofts with just a few openings or niches were often incorporated in the gables of barns and hay-lofts.

With the development of winter root fodder crops, canning and refrigeration, the cold-season meat provided by the dovecots had much less importance, and the cots were converted or abandoned. One of the last to be recorded in use existed at Walton Hall in Yorkshire, yielding up to a hundred young birds for the table each year as well as fertiliser for the barley. Occasionally, one will still see doves frequenting an old dovecot, as at Great Yeldham in Essex.

The internal construction of an octagonal dovecot in Cumbria. A revolving beam supported the top of a ladder when eggs or young birds were being taken from the nest niches.

The keeping of 'doos' in lectern-shaped cots was particularly popular in Scotland, while many villages in the East Midlands of England have an example surviving – one should look out for the small, square, towerlike dwelling houses with pyramidical or gabled roofs, which are often dovecot conversions. Dovecots were almost invariably built close to the parent manor house or farmstead, and even after their demolition, small paddocks with names like 'Dovehouse Close' will often endure. Often the name has become corrupted and lives on in a form like 'Duffers (i.e. dovehouse) Field, 'Ducket' or 'Duffousyard'. Dovecots were very numerous in some parts of Scotland, such as Fife, where they were associated with improved estate farming (see IMPROVEMENTS). A good example, resembling a miniaturised version of the one illustrated at Willington, is seen standing in arable land near Anstruther.

*Further reading*: Cooke, A.O., *Book of Dovecotes*, 1920.

**Dower house**. A dower was a gift given to the bride by her husband on the morning of their marriage, though it was later broadened to denote the part of the estate, ⅓ or ½, that the bride could claim until she remarried. The dower house was a house upon the estate that was occupied by wife of the lord after she was widowed. Depending on her relationship with her offspring, it might be placed close to or as distant as possible from the manor house. Before he died (in 1854), Sir William Amcotts Ingilby of Ripley confessed that his wife, Mary Anne, had endured a miserable time with him and he asked that she be given a bit of 'Terre' within the deer park for a Dower House. She pursued his wishes with gusto, building a house with ten bedrooms and accommodation for two coaches and eight horses.

**Downs, downland**. An environment character-ised by escarpments of chalk overlooking vales formed in softer materials. The landscape is one of dry COMBES, rounded hills, steeply-sloping scarps, often crowned by HILLFORTS or older prehistoric monuments and freely-draining, calcareous soils. The downland countryside has a distinct personality, based on its chalk bedrock and subsoil, which are alkaline, porous and absorb most surface drainage. They support lime-loving plants that are tolerant of relative drought. Variation is provided by local occurrences of sandstone, lically occurring in the form of fragmenting a hard, sarsen capping, as well as deposits of gravels, loam and flint seams. Though traditionally existing as springy, herb-rich pastures forming uninterrupted sheep walks, the chalks downlands were originally wooded, and the rolling chalk hills of the Yorkshire Wolds have a name signifying 'wald', or woodland.

*Further reading*: Brandon, P., *The Sussex Landscape*, Hodder & Stoughton, London, 1974.
Brandon, P., *The South Downs*, Chichester, 1998.

**Drainage**. This is often essential to farming. Badly-drained land will remain 'cold', delaying the germination of crops and the waterlogging of soil prevents the take-up of nutrients by plants and stunts their root development. Where permanent, waterlogging will lead to the accumulation of acidic organic peat deposits. In pasture land bad drainage will encourage foot rot in sheep, the spread of diseases in cattle while the feet of the livestock will tear up the sward and compact the clay. OPEN FIELD ploughland was drained by the creation of the corrugated surface associated with RIDGE AND FURROW, the ridging up of land being pronounced on the clay lands but much less marked on the light soils of the heathlands and Downs. When old open field land was partitioned into private holdings under EARLY ENCLOSURE it was commonly the practice for the margins of a field to be ditched, and sometimes these ditches were given the forms of stone-lined culverts. In East Anglia at the end of the Middle Ages, STITCHING involved ridging-up land in temporary ridges which lasted just one or a few years. In the eighteenth century the practice of underdrainage became widespread, with drains being cut in such a way that water passed down through the field below the rooting level and was then conducted laterally away from the field. Bush drains existed as narrow trenches filled with brushwood and capped with heather, straw or gorse and then backfilled. They normally conducted water into one of the ditches hemming a field. When earthenware tiles and pipes became available around the middle of the century, the cultivation of heavy soils was greatly facilitated and countless miles of new drains were installed, sometimes employing curved tiles set on flat tiles to produce drains with the cross sections of railway tunnels. See also DITCH, DRAUCHT.

*Further reading*: Phillips, A.D.M., *The Understanding of Farmland in England in the Nineteenth Century*, Cambridge University Press, 1989.
Williamson, T., *The Transformation of Rural England*, Exeter University Press, 2002.

**Draucht**. In Scotland, a farm boundary ditch or the land enclosed by such a ditch. See also HEDGE AND DITCH RULE.

**Drech, draig**. In Lowland Scots, an unpleasant, low-lying place.

**Drift, driftway**. Drift is more or less a synonym for DROVE ROAD and is common in the eastern counties of England. Some of the lanes or green roads known as drifts in East Anglia may be very old indeed. Pre-Roman field-patterns in Norfolk and Suffolk have been recognised, with the fields, which share a common orientation, being divided into blocks by parallel drifts of a similar or older age. In Cambridgeshire, Cuckoo Drift, which forms the boundary between Cottenham and Oakington parishes, is thought to be a prehistoric trackway. See also DROVE ROAD.

**Drove road or Drovers' road**. A drove road might be a general-purpose road that was quite often used by drovers (that is, men/children driving animals to market on the hoof over quite long distances) or a road that was

specifically forged for the purpose of droving. It is likely that some forms of droving took place in prehistoric and Roman times, but the growth of the trade reflected the expansion of urban markets and the specialisation in some more distant places on the commercial production of beef and mutton. Droving was quite important in the Middle Ages, when a precarious Anglo-Scottish trade had developed: a letter of safe conduct survives from 1359, granting a safe passage through England to two Scottish drovers accompanied by three horsemen and servants and their merchandise of horses, oxen and cows. In the north of England the large Cistercian abbeys, like Fountains and Rievaulx, had vast, far-flung sheep ranges, and old lanes, such as Mastiles Lane near Malham, were used by the monastic flocks. However, it was during the post-medieval centuries leading up to the railway age that droving became a very important traffic. In the reign of Queen Mary (1553–1558) droving became a respectable profession which depended upon the issue of an annually renewable licence. At the peak of the droving trade, around 1800, the annual drove from Scotland to England involved about 100,000 cattle.

Droving existed in a variety of regional forms – for example, the walking of geese from farms in East Anglia to supply the Christmas market in London – but two of its facets were particularly important. One involved the assembly of herds of black cattle gathered from upland grazing grounds in the Highlands and Islands of Scotland at 'trysts', or markets, at places like Falkirk in the Scottish Lowlands and their droving down the Pennine spine of England to centres like Malham, where they would be bought and fattened by English dealers for sale in the Midlands and south. Many of them were then resold at the great October fair at Bullock Hill, Horsham St Faith, near Norwich. The second involved a similar droving of Welsh cattle to markets in the Welsh Marches at centres like Shrewsbury or progressing to Tewkesbury cattle fair and the great cattle fair at Barnet, north of London.

A herd consisting of around 200 cattle or a flock containing ten times as many sheep might be divided into four parts, each in the charge of a drover and his dogs. The animals would be driven in the form of a long narrow column, it being easier to control the course of the small number of leading beasts. While such columns sometimes used conventional roads, there were obvious advantages in adopting a drove road across the COMMONS of the upland plateaux, away from other road-users and constrictions, growing crops, tolls and a route furnished with adequate route-side grazings. At intervals of about a dozen miles there were halting places. Many of these supported an inn which had pasture attached. Most of the old 'Drovers' inns have since decayed or have been converted into private dwelling places. As well as the obvious 'Drovers' inn-names there are others like the 'Highland Laddie' or the 'Scotsman's Pack'. Cattle were shod, their cloven hoofs requiring eight shoes per beast. Sheep walked unshod, while geese were walked through a mixture of tar, sand and sawdust that gave their feet a protective coating.

Droving survived into the first age of the train, the Scottish drovers were still active in the 1880s, and Horsham St Faith fair survived until 1872. When the practice perished some of its routeways died with it, and they may only be recognised as slightly hollowed tracks with hoof-smoothed rocks which are gradually vanishing into the moors. Some drove roads were also used by pack-horse traders, peat diggers, coal workers and other travellers, though in the Yorkshire Dales the main market routes tended to run north-west to south-west along the valleys, while the drove roads ran north to south, across the grain of the country. Sometimes, the lines of the old roads are perpetuated by walls built along their margins at the time of PARLIAMENTARY ENCLOSURE. Some drove roads were partly incorporated into the TURNPIKE network, while sections or fragments of others exist as minor branches of the contemporary network, like the spectacular Swaledale–Wensleydale link between Muker and Askrigg. Sewstern Drift on the Leicestershire–Lincolnshire border is a GREEN LANE once used by Scottish drovers bound for Stamford.

Any cow or bullock that eventually met its fate at Smithfield in the eighteenth century could at least have had an interesting history. It might have been the booty of clan raiding in some misty Highland glen, or have been swum across to the mainland from a Hebridean island. Then it would have been driven to a tryst in the Lowlands and incorporated in a herd walking southwards down the spine of England. Then sold to a Midlands dealer or butcher at Hawes or Malham, it might have been fattened and bound for London. This contrasts with the animals of today that are so filled with chemicals that their droppings are gradually killing the old trees on whose roots they fall.

One of the most colourful contemporary accounts of droving was quoted by the historian Arthur Raistrick. In 1792 the Hon. John Byng stopped at the inn at Gearstones near Bainbridge:

> … the seat of misery, in a desert; and tho' filled with company, yet the Scotch fair held upon the heath added to the horror of the curious scenery: the ground in front crowded by Scotch cattle and the drovers; and the house cramm'd by the buyers and settlers most of whom were in plaids, fillibegs etc. … the Scotch are always wrap'd up in their plaids – as defence against heat, cold or wet; but they are preventions of speed or activity; so whenever any cattle stray'd, they instantly threw down the plaid, that they might overtake them.

See also DRIFT.

*Further reading:* Bonser, K. J., *The Drovers*, Macmillan, 1970.
Brown, C., 'Drovers, Cattle and Dung: the long trail from Scotland to London', *Proceedings of the Suffolk Institute of Archaeology and History* 38, 428–31.
Haldane, A. R. B., *The Drove Roads of Scotland*, Edinburgh University Press, 1952.

**Drowned landscape**. The relative heights of land and sea have not remained constant throughout time, and as a result there are various places in which ancient cultural landscapes extend beneath the sea beyond the low tide mark. Some landscapes are destroyed in the process of submergence, as has occurred in regions like Holderness on the east coast of England, where landscapes formed behind unstable cliffs of glacial drift have disintegrated as the cliffs retreat and the sea advances. Where, however, a gradual rise in sea level has taken place as the result of isostatic process then facets of the cultural landscape may survive the inundation. The post-glacial emergence and submergence of land results from a 'see-saw'-like effect on the British mainland, with land in the north that had been depressed by the weight of glacial ice rising, with a compensatory sinking of land in the south. At the time when the ice melted, masses of water were added to the oceans, and this produced a eustatic rise in sea level, and it occurred much more rapidly than the isostatic re-elevation of depressed lands. On the western seaboard of Scotland, step-like sequences of raised beaches mark stages in the uplift. As the northern uplands, which had borne such heavy burdens of ice, rose, the submergence of land was greatest in the far south. On the Isles of Scilly, the sea rose relative to the land at a rate of 9½ inches per century. The gradual inundation of lands fragmented a more coherent group of islands to form an archipelago, with the drowning of the core of 'Ennor' island creating separate islands of Bhryher, Norwethel, St Helen's, Tean, St Martin's, Tresco, Samson and St Mary's. Flooding engulfed woods of the late-Neolithic and early Bronze Age periods, whose roots can be seen at low tide in Mount's Bay, and drowned systems of early fields and causeways between islands. In places like Pentle Bay the remains of late-Iron Age or Roman houses as well as field walls lie beneath the sea.

*Further reading:* Thomas, C., *Exploration of a Drowned Landscape*, Batsford, London, 1985.

**Dry dyke**. Scottish term for a DRYSTONE WALL.

**Drystone walls**. In Britain the distribution of drystone walls complements that of HEDGEROWS. Hedges tend to predominate in the lowlands, where the underlying rocks are often unsuitable for walling – soft clays, marls and sandstones – while in the uplands, where the climate discourages the vigorous growth of hedging plants, tough walling materials tend to be found in abundance. Even so, there are some exceptions to this rule, and field-walls may be found in lowland areas, like Northamptonshire and the Portland area, if the local geology provides a good supply of useful stone. Because it was never economical to transport walling stone over long distances, each locality exploits its own stone resources, so that stone walls echo the geology and harmonise with the landscape. The qualities of the stone vary enormously, from the intractable granite 'moorstone' boulders and rubble of the south-western moors, to the Jurassic limestone of the Cotswolds, which splits conveniently into small slabs.

Field shapes, like the straight-line geometry of PARLIAMENTARY ENCLOSURE boundaries or the irregular curves and 'reversed-S' strip margins of EARLY ENCLOSURE, may enable one to relate the age of a wall to that of the field which it delimits, though this cannot always be done with certainty. In the north of England at least there is evidence of drystone walls superseding hedgerows in the post-medieval centuries – as well as evidence of 'spontaneous' hedges colonising tumbledown walls.

The use of drystone walls to demarcate fields goes back to Neolithic times, as evidenced by excavations following peat-stripping at remote localities in County Mayo. Bronze Age field-walls are visible in the REAVES of Dartmoor and at various other places, like Rough Tor in Cornwall. During the clearance of land for farming, walls provided a convenient repository for the gathered stone, as exemplified by the CONSUMPTION DYKES of Scotland or the maze of very thick walls incorporating

CLEARANCE CAIRNS at Wasdale Head beside Wast Water. The earlier generation drystone wall may have incorporated turf or earthen banks and 'free-standing' walls may have developed in northern England. In the northern uplands of England in the sixteenth century, tenants found themselves under pressure from the MANOR courts to replace old earthbanks and dead hedges with drystone walls, the dimensions of which were sometimes specified in the orders. In some cases, the requirement involved 'BREASTING' or revetting an existing earthen bank with stones. In other cases, flat-topped walls of stone seem to have been built, according to the Dales farmer, Tom Lord. In return for the high initial input of labour, the resulting walls and stone-breasted

*Drystone wall*
A classic drystone wall landscape, at Wharfedale in Yorkshire. The walls are of various ages.

banks offered more permanent and more stock-proof boundaries. By superseding dead hedges the walling work reduced the pressure of demands of STAKE AND RICE HEDGES on the dwindling timber resources of the common.

Just as the Parliamentary Enclosure movement launched a mighty bustle of hedge-planting operations in the lowlands, so it also launched a massive programme of field-wall building in the uplands, with straight walls advancing from the valleys to ascend the steep fells and partition the

Local limestone has been used in this field-wall at Malham in North Yorkshire.

old COMMONS. Generally, the forms and dimensions of the Parliamentary Enclosure walls were plainly specified, as at Linton in Wharfedale, enclosed in 1792–93, where the walls were to be 6 feet (1.8 metres) in height and battered from a base width of 3 feet (0.9 metre) to a top width of 14 inches (0.36 metre), while the frequency of 'through stones' (running right through the wall to increase stability) was also specified. Linton is interesting, for a study of its walls by Dr A. Raistrick led to the probable identification of a Dark Age village boundary-wall of massive construction and walls bounding the village ploughlands which had come into existence by the time of Domesday Book. It is not normally possible to date a wall from its appearance (which gradually changes as a result of periodic repairs so that eventually an original wall will be patched out of existence), though certain unusual walls may be dated – like the medieval boundary-walls of the lands attached to Fountains Abbey. Estate boundary-walls are usually taller or more massive than those of the internal field-divisions while need to exclude deer may result in tall, wide-topped walls.

A variety of regional forms of drystone wall exist, and atypical forms include the use of upright slabs of flagstone seen in parts of Orkney, the ORTHOSTAT WALLS of parts of western Britain and Ireland, and the use of sheets of slate built in herringbone fashion in parts of Snowdonia. The so-called 'Danes fences' of Northern Ireland seem to be of considerable antiquity and were built of stones placed in the spaces between rows of stone uprights, though frequently only the uprights now remain.

The typical post-medieval drystone wall is built of double thicknesses of stone with the space in between packed with small stones to form a filling, or 'hearting'. The stones of the outer faces may be roughly coursed and shaped in places like the Millstone Grit areas of the Pennines where the stone is amenable to shaping, and the wall is 'battered', being much broader at the base than at the top. The largest stones are built in the foot of the wall, which should be set in a shallow trench, and the stones in the courses become progressively smaller towards the top of the wall. No mortar is used in the construction of the wall, hence its designation as being of 'drystone', though the top of the wall may consist of topstones or 'combers', which span the full width of the wall and which are bedded in mortar.

A proficient drystone-waller, or 'dyker', should be able to build about 20 feet (6 metres) of wall in a day. In addition to his stone hammer his main tools are an 'A'-shaped frame of wood, which establishes the cross-section of the wall, and a length of twine to set out its intended height. In the past most hill farmers were reasonably competent wallers, but now these skills are often lost and many walls are in dire need of repair, while others are being removed to create larger enclosures. Professional dykers now tend to work at roadsides or the gardens and paddocks of gentrified former cottages and farmsteads, with most of the stone that they use being recycled from old walls that have been removed. See also BACKIT-DYKE, CONSUMPTION DYKE, CORN HEDGE, HEAD DYKE, ORTHOSTAT WALLS, REAVES.

*Further reading:* Hodges, R., *Wall-to-Wall History*, Duckworth, London, 1991.

Mitchell, W. R., *Drystone Walls of the Yorkshire Dales*, Castleberg, Settle, 1992.

Raistrick, A., *The Pennine Walls*, Dalesman, Clapham, 1946.

**Duck decoy.** During the Middle Ages, ducks were caught by gently shepherding the birds into a narrowing arm of a lake, around which nets were suspended. Subsequently the techniques were refined, and by the early nineteenth century designs had more or less standardised on the form of a steep-sided shrub-fringed artificial pond with narrow, curving, tapering arms, or 'pipes', usually three or four in number, running off from its corners. Nets were hung over a pipe, and rectangular wicker screens were erected at close intervals along the sides of the pipe. A dog, often loosely of the 'gingery' golden Labrador type, was trained to walk in a weaving manner in and out of these screens. Ducks floating on the pond were fascinated to see this appearing and vanishing 'fox', and their curiosity attracted them further and further towards their fate in the narrowing nets.

These starfish-shaped ponds became numerous in England, particularly in the east-coast counties, and as late as 1886 there were forty-four of them still in use. A few are still used for the purpose of ringing, and a working example can be seen at Boarstall in Buckinghamshire.

**Dumble.** A small, wooded ravine in the Midlands and north of England.

**Dun.** Duns were heavily defended homesteads first built in Scotland around 600 BC, but used and redeveloped in the course of the following millennium. Various forms existed, but essentially the dun comprised a very robust drystone wall, with a rubble core sandwiched between boulder facings, which defended an occupied interior area where lean-to timber buildings were built against the inner wallfacing. They were most numerous on the western seaboard and islands. In Scotland 'Dun' place-names signifying a fortress are very common, though not all of them relate specifically to strongholds of the dun type. In England most 'Dun' place-names do not derive from the Gaelic *dun*, but from the Old English word *dun*, which denotes a hill and 'dun' can also signify a hill in Lowland Scots.

**Dutch barn,** see BARN.

**Dyke,** see DIKE and LINEAR EARTHWORK.

# E

**Earding**. A medieval term for a dwelling.

**Early enclosure**. In some parts of England OPEN-FIELD FARMING endured for at least a thousand years. Yet in many places, the gradual dismantling of the system began within a few centuries of its introduction. This was largely achieved by the enclosure of components of the common fields and their conversion into 'private' fields. In the eighteenth and nineteenth centuries PARLIAMENTARY ENCLOSURE achieved a more formalised assault on the traditional world of the village peasant, but the loose term 'early enclosure' covers various different forms of land privatisation which took place before the era of the Enclosure Acts.

Some enclosure was achieved by agreement between various members of the peasant farming community – though disagreement was often more common in the negotiations. Some of the enclosure was technically illegal, though for various reasons the manorial authorities might overlook the misdemeanour, while some involved the creation of ASSARTS or INTAKES. Often the problems concerned a clash between individual and communal interests, and where the 'privatisation' of common resources was taking place on a scale to great to be resisted, lords would often 'legitimise' enclosures by taking a rent for the newly privatised lands. There were also the often illegal but widespread and comprehensive sheep enclosures of the Tudor period, as described in the entry on LOST VILLAGES.

In 1235 and 1285, the Statutes of Merton empowered manorial lords to enclose whatever portions of the 'waste' were not being used by their free tenants, and the enclosures involved may not have been particularly controversial. Later in the medieval period, the manorial lords often deemed it an advantage to extract their demesne STRIPS, or 'doles', from the common ploughland and meadows, organising a redistribution of land to produce a compact DEMESNE holding. An early recorded example of this was carried out by three generations of the Berkeley family from the early thirteenth to the early fourteenth century. Enclosure of open-field land was also undertaken by members of the peasant classes. Two or three of them might agree to exchange strips lying within the same or different furlongs in order to achieve more convenient consolidated blocks of land, and sometimes whole communities organised an enclosure by agreement. However, trouble was always likely to arise after the harvest when the village livestock were put out to graze the open-field stubble or when the new hedges obstructed traditional rights of way. Problems could also arise over ASSARTS; thus, Henry, son of Walter, agreed with the community of Killinghall near Harrogate that he would fence his new assart while the corn was growing but throw the land open as common pasture after the harvest. However, in 1344, his neighbours complained that he had broken his promise.

Enclosure by agreement – or at least with the agreement of the more influential members of the local community – achieved a piecemeal but considerable reduction of common land during the centuries preceding Parliamentary Enclosure. It produced plenty of little squabbles and doubtless some injustices, but nothing to compare with the outrages and deprivation caused by the Tudor sheep enclosures. The eviction of whole communities and the enclosure of their traditional lands, often producing large hedged sheep enclosures, is commemorated in a famous passage in Sir Thomas More's *Utopia* (the English version appearing in 1551):

... your shepe that were wont to be so meke

*Early enclosure*
Small, irregularly shaped fields with sinuous,
curvilinear hedgerows characterise this area of early
enclosure near Moretonhampstead in Devon.

and tame, and so small eaters, now, as I heare
say, be become so great devourers and so
wy'lde, that they eate up, and swallow downe
the very men themselfes. They consume,
destroye, and devoure whole fields, howses
and cities …

In 1517, the King set up a commission to
enquire into enclosure and its unfortunate
consequences. Peasant revolts in 1536 and 1549
were largely caused by popular grievances about
the continuing alienation of common land. The
popular sentiments were expressed by William
Tyndale in 1525: 'Let them not take in their
common neither make park nor pasture, for
God gave the earth unto men to inhabit and
not sheep and wild deer.'

While the despised sheep enclosures dwindled
away as the medieval period came to its close
other forms of enclosure, notably enclosure by
agreement, continued. Enclosure of one kind or
another was responsible for the creation of all
hedged, walled or fenced fields. Those that are
the product of Parliamentary Enclosure can
generally be distinguished by their arrow-straight
boundaries, while early enclosure tended to

create less regular fields, and one can often
recognise walls and hedgerows with characteristic
'reversed-S' shapes which were established along
the curving margin of a parcel of open-field
strips at the time of enclosure. See also
PARLIAMENTARY ENCLOSURE.

*Further reading*: Tate, W. E., *The English Village
Community and the Enclosure Movements*, Gollancz,
1967.

**Earthworks**. The study of earthworks is a
cornerstone of non-invasive archaeology, and
their investigation, whether in air photographs or
on the ground, can provide essential clues to the
nature and development of past landscapes. They
are all components of the CULTURAL
LANDSCAPE, though great care may be needed
to differentiate between naturally-created
landforms and cultural features – for example,
HOUSE PLATFORMS are hard to recognise when

found on level river terraces. Some earthworks are 'freestanding' and difficult to date, while in other cases relative dating may be possible, as where the earthworks of a medieval barn cut across those of an older abandoned track. One set of earthworks will be younger than any other features that are slighted by it. Normally, interpretation depends on being able to picture the earthworks concerned in plan form, so survey and mapping are necessary. When features are identified as being cultural rather than natural (the first step in an analysis) it is still necessary to determine their nature. This may not be easy, for some, like WINDMILL mounds, small MOTTES, prospect mounds and rabbit WARRENS can present at least superficially similar appearances.

*Further reading*: Bowden, M. (ed.), *Unravelling the Landscape*, Tempus, Stroud, 1999.

**'Eccles' place-names**. These names, which are said to derive from the vulgar Latin '*eclesia*', signifying a church, are though to indicate locations where Roman Christian worship may have survived the collapse of Roman rule in Britain. Later 'church' names employed the Old English '*cirice*', giving 'church' and 'kirk' place-names. A cluster of Eccles names, including Ecclesfield and Ecclesall, seems to be associated with the Dark Age southern Yorkshire kingdom of Elmet.

*Further reading*: Cameron, K., 'Eccles in English place-names' in Barley, M.W. and Hanson, R.P.C. (eds), *Christianity in Britain 300–700*, Leicester, 1968, pp. 87–92.

**Edge**. A ridge or watershed.

**Eleanor cross**, see CROSSES.

**Elf stone, elf shot, elfer-stone, fairy dart, fairy hammer**. Worked flints of the Neolithic or Bronze Age periods that were assumed by country people to be the works of elves.

**Enclosure by agreement**, see EARLY ENCLOSURE, ENCLOSURE: SCOTLAND.

**Enclosure road**. Any modest country road which runs arrow-straight will probably either be a ROMAN ROAD or else an enclosure road. These roads were part of the package of transformations which were encountered in parishes which experienced the effects of an Act of PARLIAMENTARY ENCLOSURE, and so most of them date from the main period of the movement: 1750–1850. Occurring abruptly within the network of winding older routeways, these planned roads contrast with the winding older routes, but since Parliamentary Enclosure mainly took place on a piecemeal parochial basis, enclosure roads frequently terminate abruptly at the parish boundary. Often, but not always, they result from the rationalisation and straightening of an existing route and they revert to the old pattern on crossing the parish boundary. Where enclosure roads span more than one parish a slight change of alignment may be noticed on crossing the parish boundary. Most enclosure roads were built to a standard width between their boundary walls or hedges of 30 or 40 feet (9.14 or 12.19 metres), though in a few cases a 60-foot (18.29-metre) standard was employed. They are most common in localities that had experienced little field-enclosure before the great enclosure movement, and their straight forms were adjusted to the rectangular geometry of the new fields. Sometimes the curving HOLLOWAY of the superseded country lane can be seen close to the track of the enclosure road.

**Enclosure: Scotland**. Much of the enclosure by stone dykes and hedges of land in Scotland was associated with the IMPROVEMENTS of the eighteenth and early nineteenth centuries. Some land was enclosed at earlier dates – the estates of Sir David Dunbar of Baldoon, Wigtownshire were enclosed for the breeding of livestock in the seventeenth century. Such enclosures were encouraged by the Scottish Parliament in the years leading up to the Act of Union of 1707. The movement continued, with the enclosure of pastures suitable for raising cattle for the English market being particularly encouraged. In the south-west of Scotland, the Levellers of Galloway attempted to resist the partitioning of communal lands in the 1720s, but the hardships of enclosure seem to have been tempered by the fact that at least to begin with, the new privatised and modernised farming still provided plenty of employment for rural populations. The process of enclosing the countryside rose steadily until the 1760s and in the next century the rate remained at a high level throughout the first half of the century. The impetus came from the landowners and there was less formal, statutory involvement than in England, where the processes of PARLIAMENTARY ENCLOSURE were followed. Being more responsive to conventional farming techniques, the Lowlands very largely escaped the horrors of CLEARANCES that took place in the Highlands and Islands. See also CONSUMPTION DYKE.

**Encroachment**, see INTAKE.

**End**, see GREENS AND ENDS.

**Enfeoff**. There are two meanings, both concerning a change of tenants. The feudal term can either denote the giving up or surrender of a property or the legal installation of a tenant into the possession of a holding. See also ENTRY FINE.

**Engrossment**. An amalgamation of tenancies which would often lead to migration and the creeping depopulation of settlements. Numerous smaller villages in East Anglia perished in this way. A rationalisation of tenancies also played an important part in Scottish IMPROVEMENTS.

**Entry fine**. Money, more a tax than a fine in the modern understanding of the words, paid by a tenant to his lord on taking over the tenancy of a property. 'Relief' was similar, but more normally it applied to the larger estates which had military duties attached to them. On a KNIGHT'S FEE, the relief was 100 shillings, a quite considerable sum to pay to a superior for the right to succeed to an estate, but the

practice of exacting reliefs persisted in some places until 1661.

**Envisioning landscape**. The process by which we form our mental images of landscape. Photographs, art, maps and literary sources may all be involved. Those who build their visions of countryside on selective, sentimental sources – like postcards, chocolates boxes and the worst kind of glossy books – will acquire inaccurate and misleading visions and be blind to the problems of rural life and conservation.

*Further reading*: Brace, C., 'Envisioning England', *Landscape Research* **28**, 4, October 2003, 365–82.

**Erws**. Welsh equivalent of an ACRE.

**Escheat**. The reversion of an estate to the crown or to a feudal lord when a tenant died without heirs old enough to inherit or after he had forfeited his lands for committing a crime. The practice was ended in 1925.

**Estate**. The ancient MULTIPLE ESTATES fragmented during the Saxon era and the redistribution of lands after the Norman Conquest blurred the old patterns of landholdings. Estates continued to form and reform according to the accidents of marriage, inheritance and royal favour or disfavour. The landscapes of large estates tended to differ from those associated with small freeholders in that the owners of great estates were not preoccupied with subsistence and the need to maximise short term income in order to settle bills, meet rents or pay taxes. Instead, they could use the extensive acreages that they controlled to satisfy recreational needs (pheasant cover, grouse moors, gardens etc.) or to indulge in specialised commercial activities (land reclamation, horse studs), including those which would be slow to yield returns on investment (commercial forestry and softwood plantations). Estate owners could plan on a grand scale and use the resources of the estate to finance developments that could not be contemplated on a small, freehold property. In exceptional circumstances, the estate could even have its own canal, like the one that conveyed quarried stone from Skipton Castle to the Leeds and Liverpool canal. Bettey points out that as well as having a church that has been drastically restored by the local dynasty and dwellings which bear the family arms: 'Neatly enclosed fields, wide roads, uniform woodlands, game coverts and landscape features such as obelisks, towers or other 'eye-catchers' are also hallmarks of ownership by a great estate'.

He defined such an estate as being: '... any landholding of at least 3000 acres, subject to a single owner, whether an institution or an individual, not necessarily made-up of a single compact territory, but which has been administered as a unit and where the effects of a single ownership can be recognised'.

During the medieval centuries, and earlier, this effect could be seen in the way that different tenants on the estate had different roles and obligations. On many feudal estates certain tenants were responsible for tending and exercising their lord's hunting dogs, while others operated his mill or held offices concerned with administration or regulating grazing. The situations of different tenants on the estate could be reflected in the renders that they were obliged to make, with those living by woods perhaps rendering beeswax or honey, while others brought eggs or other forms of produce. Estates had functional components like VACCARIES and others concerned with status, notably DEER PARKS. There were other components, like FISHPONDS and WARRENS with exclusive and utilitarian functions that combined both aspects. Many of the great estates were controlled by the Church, some being held by Bishops or Abbots and some by the chapters and officers of cathedrals. This ownership did not, however, make them obviously different from estates held by lay nobles and the bishops and abbots delighted in hunting as well as the more contemplative pleasures associated with a garden.

The Dissolution of the Monasteries by Henry VIII profoundly affected estates, as did Edward VI's suppression of the chantries. The

extensive ecclesiastical estates reverted to the Crown, and when these lands were disposed of nobles and speculators struggled to secure the lands. The old monastic estates were recycled, some being added to existing aristocratic estates, some obtained by the newly rich classes, people like courtiers, lawyers and merchants, while some were bought in large blocks by speculators and then divided into many freeholds and resold. The monastic buildings were sometimes robbed for stone and lead roofing, used in building lay mansions like Fountains Hall, North Yorkshire, and sometimes they were converted for domestic uses (Buckland Abbey, Devon) or storage purposes. The instant demolition of such buildings in order to sell the materials as a means of recouping purchase costs robbed the countryside of many fine buildings. On the whole the monastic estates were sold cheaply and many of the profits accruing to the purchasers were invested in great houses, like Lanhydrock, Cornwall. DEER PARKS and LANDSCAPE PARKS often graced their settings.

In the centuries that followed, the wealth produced by the great estates allowed their owners to be as eccentric, reclusive or flamboyant as they wished. The nucleus of the estate was the great house, which was almost invariably set in an expanse of tastefully manipulated and manicured countryside. The house, its park and its gardens, if these were in fashion, existed not only to please their incumbents but also as symbols of the family's status. Therefore they did not remain set in a particular stylistic mould, but were constantly being redesigned in order to emphasise the fashionable taste and wealth of the dynasty. Much if not all of the wealth needed to sustain this glittering core to the estate derived from the HOME FARM and tenanted farmsteads, woods, quarries and mines in the surrounding estate. The attitudes of estate owners varied. Some sought to extract every last penny of income from tenants and estate workers, some saw 'good farming' as being virtuous in the highest degree and indulged in HIGH FARMING, while others adopted benevolent and paternalistic attitudes. Most were concerned with what are regarded today as 'image' questions, so that when an innovation was praised it would rapidly be imitated by other estate-owners. Sometimes these activities would impose a burden on the public at large, as when useful roads were diverted to run outside parks or when estate housing was not maintained. Sometimes they were self-indulgent, as when estate workers were obliged to occupy fancifully-contrived cottages in an estate VILLAGE where Tudor, Elizabethan or Swiss architectural styles were parodied. At other times there was a fascination with efficiency and wholesome production, as in the creation of MODEL FARMS. In some cases there was a genuine desire to improve the conditions of workers and tenants, by providing fountains for drinking water, laying drains, building almshouses or schools and so on. The 1914–18 War was a watershed in the history of the estate, which had up till then survived the threats posed by death duties, other forms of taxation and the decline of domestic farming in the face of cheaper imported produce. Rising costs and shortages of cheap labour as well as the devastation of aristocratic families by the high level of casualties encountered among officers all conspired to make the great house an encumbrance rather than an asset. Houses were disposed of, often to the National Trust, while estates were sometimes dismantled piecemeal to meet the demands for taxation incurred each time that the holder died. The remaining estates are generally associated with activities that give a rapid turnover on investment, like shooting, raising Christmas trees, commercialised fishing, and so on. Distinctive estate landscapes are still frequently seen and easily recognisable. Driving across the Yorkshire Wolds, for example, the estates, with their coniferous plantations, beech coverts and root crop fields providing pheasant cover and their more extensive softwood plantations have a different appearance to adjacent farming landscapes.

*Further reading:* Williamson, T. and Bellamy, L., *Property and Landscape*, George Philip, London, 1987.
Bettey, J. H., *Estates and the English Countryside*, Batsford, London, 1993.

**Estovers**, see BOTE and COMMONS.

**Extinctions and introductions (of animals).**
Under natural conditions Britain would support a range of wild animals characteristic of northern cool temperate latitudes, but because most parts of the country have supported a reasonably dense rural population since at least Bronze Age times the range of native animals has decreased. A Pictish SYMBOL STONE provides a credible illustration of a reindeer, so these animals may have survived in the north of Scotland until the Dark Ages. Bears were known in Saxon times, but they may only have been performing bears and the name Bear Park near Durham actually comes from the French *beau* meaning 'fine' or 'good'. The beaver survived into Saxon times and might be commemorated in the place-name Bewerley near Pateley Bridge in North Yorkshire. Wild boar were hunted to extinction in the wild by the mid-twelfth century, though on various occasions they were imported from the Continent to restock hunting parks, and a few swine parks, like that of the Earl of Oxford in Chalkney Wood, Essex, existed in late medieval and Stuart times. The boar is recalled in a few place-names like Evensholt in Bedfordshire and Eversden in Cambridgeshire, derived from the Old English word for boar, *eofor*. By the time the boar became extinct, the wolf in England had been driven into a few of the wilder fastnesses of the realm, the last pack apparently being killed in the marshes of Holderness in the years around 1400. The prior of Whitby had thirteen wolf skins tanned in 1396, probably the remnants of a wolf pack on the North York Moors. The wolf lingered in northern Scotland into the seventeenth century, and possibly into the eighteenth century. By the late nineteenth century persecution by gamekeepers had restricted the wildcat to the Scottish Highlands,

but its former presence in England is evidenced by various place-names, like Catstone Wood in Nidderdale, Catcliff in Derbyshire, Catshill in Worcestershire, and many others.

As well as persecuting some animals to the verge of extinction and beyond, man has been responsible for various introductions and reintroductions. The pheasant, fallow deer and rabbit are probably all Norman introductions. The black rat may have found its way to Britain in Roman times, and it carried the rat flea that in turn bore the infection which caused bubonic plague, the Black Death. The displacement of the black rat by the brown rat from eastern Europe in the seventeenth or eighteenth century may have been partly responsible for the elimination of bubonic plague in Britain, since the brown rat tends to seek a less intimate

association with man and his dwellings. The North American grey squirrel was released on numerous occasions in the nineteenth and early twentieth centuries. It may well have spread at the expense of the red squirrel, though red squirrel populations are also subject to extreme fluctuations which are not fully understood.

Both the coypu and the mink have escaped from fur farms. The coypu is a pest in the Norfolk Broads, where it devours waterside vegetation and thus destabilises the banks of the water-courses. The mink is a much more serious pest, a vicious predator on waterfowl and riverine wildlife and one that may never be eliminated.

**Eye-catcher**, see FOLLIES.

# F

**Fail-dyke**, see DIVOT DYKE.

**Fail-housie**, see DIVOT HOUSE.

**Fair**, see MARKETS AND FAIRS.

**Fair house**, see MARKET HOUSE.

**Fald dyke**. Turf walled sheep FOLD.

**Fall trough**. A trough or channel leading to a water mill. In upland areas, like the Pennines, where rivers were likely to rise rapidly and with devastating effects, mills could be placed safely apart from the river in an artificial backwater, with water to fill the pond and power the wheel being taken from the river in an artificial channel or GOIT. Traces of medieval mills operated by fall trough methods and the associated ponds and leats can be found beside various northern rivers and streams, as exemplified by the earthworks by the River Cover near Middleham in Wensleydale.

See also DAMS AND WEIRS, FULLING MILL, GOIT, WATERMILL.

**Far haaf**, see LODGE.

**Farm**. Traditionally, an area of land that was let on a lease. See also FARMSTEAD, FEE, HOME FARM, FERME ORNÉE.

**Farmstead (farm)**. A farmstead, often surrounded by a small complex of outbuildings, is the home of a farmer and the operational centre for the surrounding holding. The word 'farm' is a relatively recent adoption with a peculiar derivation, and the rough medieval equivalent of 'farm' was 'MESSUAGE'. The new term was adopted in association with the piecemeal enclosure of OPEN-FIELD land and the adoption of fixed money rents. The fixed rent was a *firma* in legal Latin, and in Middle English a *ferme* was a consolidated holding which became 'farm' in common usage. The term 'farmer' was adopted to replace the very loosely equivalent terms which had been current at different times in the Middle Ages: 'yardling', 'acreman', 'husbond' and 'yeoman'.

The oldest surviving farmhouses may date from the thirteenth or fourteenth centuries onwards, but the building may provide no reliable clues to the duration of the occupancy of a site by a farmstead. Some sites are no older than the period of PARLIAMENTARY ENCLOSURE, while there is little doubt that some other sites have been occupied since the Iron Age, like ones in Cornwall where the farmstead occupies a courtyard house site. Dispersed farmsteads and hamlets were the fundamental ingredients of the settlement pattern throughout Britain until the emergence of large numbers of villages engaged in open-field farming during the latter part of the Saxon period. At this time, a contrast developed between ANCIENT COUNTRYSIDES and the planned or champion countrysides, where open fields spanned most of the better farmland and where farmsteads were clustered together within villages. Away from the champion areas the pattern of dispersed farmsteads remained the norm, and in some cases we can recognise a continuity of settlement which goes back to Domesday Book and probably much further still. In the case of Exbourne, near Okehampton in Devon, Prof. W.G. Hoskins has shown that the TOWNSHIP's contents of ten isolated farmsteads and one village remained unchanged from 1086 to the present day. Of course, given the sparse nature of the Domesday information, it is not possible to identify the exact site of any farmstead, and it is quite possible that the positions of some farms changed, even if their numbers remained the same. Even so, one must suspect that in areas of ancient countryside many of the farms that we see today are occupying sites which have supported farmsteads for a very long time indeed. In stretches of ancient countryside, like parts of Essex, a number of farms stand within medieval moats – or the remains of these moats

– and many of them bear the name of a medieval owner, perhaps the man who colonised the site or who built a new farmstead on an established site. Glancing at the map of the Saffron Walden area, one can find examples like Maynards, with a moat, Rayment's, Latchley's Farm, also moated, Godfrey's Farm, Swan's farm, and so on. In areas such as this, with scattered farmsteads and hamlets, we are probably seeing the elements of a very ancient tradition of settlement. There is a common myth that Iron Age and Roman countrysides were but thinly peopled, but where archaeologists have had the opportunity to carry out a detailed study of the evidence through a programme of FIELD-WALKING a different picture emerges. In the Somerton area of Somerset, for example, a survey by Roger Leech showed that Romano-British farmsteads and hamlets were scattered evenly across the countryside and stood only ½–1 mile (0.8–1.6 km) apart, and evidence of a similar norm in spacing has come from several other studies in different parts of the country.

Many of the dispersed farmsteads which existed in medieval England will have occupied ancient sites, but new farmsteads were also created in the course of the Middle Ages. Some were established in newly cleared ASSARTS, some developed from monastic GRANGES, and others could result from the breakdown of the old SHIELING tradition, with a permanently occupied sheep farm taking over from the shepherd's summer hut. Various new farmsteads appeared in the medieval attempts to colonise or recolonise difficult areas, like fenland or the south-western moors, and on moors like Dartmoor and Bodmin there are numerous ruined medieval farmsteads which tell of the failure to re-establish cultivation. Similarly, many hamlets contracted to become solitary farmsteads. A good example is Challacombe Farm on Challacombe Down, Dartmoor, which results from the implosion of a medieval hamlet and stands beside an impressive group of STRIP LYNCHETS which were engraved into the hillside

*Farmstead*
A farmstead near Blubberhouses, North Yorkshire.

by the ploughmen of the hamlet, probably during the thirteenth century.

In the champion countrysides most farmsteads existed within the village, and indeed almost every medieval village house was, in a sense, a farmhouse. Within the area of open-field cultivation isolated farmsteads would only be found where the enclosure by agreement of compact blocks of strips formed a sizeable parcel of land worthy of supporting a farmstead, or where consolidated parts of the demesne were devoted to special uses, like VACCARIES or studs. Beyond the open fields isolated farmsteads might be found standing on blocks of land reclaimed from the WASTE.

This situation was transformed by Parliamentary Enclosure. Once farmers were allocated compact holdings carved from the former open ploughlands and commons, then they had every incentive to leave their old village-based farmhouse and reside in a new, purpose-built dwelling which was conveniently situated close to the centre of their lands. Such farmsteads display the architecture of the eighteenth and nineteenth centuries and

sometimes have names associated with the Enclosure era, like Waterloo Farm, Trafalgar Farm, California Farm and so on. Occasionally, the Parliamentary Enclosure Commission attempted to alleviate the need for migration from the village by arranging their land divisions so that they each converged on the village dwellings of the impending holders, as at Middle Barton in Oxfordshire, but in practice such an arrangement was generally impossible to achieve. The migration to a new, isolated farmstead might only occur many years after the Enclosure award, for first the farmer had to pay his share in the costs of the enclosure and establish the hedgerows, walls or fences that defined his new fields. In the meantime, the village-based house might receive only the most urgently needed of repairs and then be partitioned to provide cottage accommodation for labourers.

The farmstead patterns of England tend to emphasise the distinction between ancient and planned countrysides. In the former are farmsteads and farmstead sites of many different ages, but in the latter, as Professor Hoskins has described:

> Nearly all the farmhouses we see between compact villages of the country between Yorkshire and the Dorset coasts date from the century 1750–1850. The few that are older may be either the result of Tudor or Stuart enclosure, or examples of monastic granges … But probably four out of five of these farmsteads in the field are the consequence of Parliamentary Enclosure.

*Further reading:* Darley, G., *The National Trust Book of the Farm*, Weidenfeld & Nicolson, London, 1981. Taylor, C., *Village and Farmstead*, George Philip, 1983.

**Farthingdale, Fardel, Ferling or Farthinghold**. An area of land a quarter of a VIRGATE or 10 acres in extent, though, most confusingly, it was occasionally used for an area of just ¼ ACRE.

**Faughs**. Land that was not manured and was only fallowed between episodes of ploughing. See also INFIELD-OUTFIELD CULTIVATION.

**Fee**. A piece of land or freehold property that could be inherited. See KNIGHT'S FEE.

**Fell dyke, fell garth**, see HEAD DYKE.

**Ferme ornée**. Like the COTTAGE ORNÉE, the *ferme ornée* was as much decorative as functional. This marriage of agriculture and Picturesque whimsy seems to have originated in the *ferme ornée* created on Thames meadows near Chertsey by Philip Southcote in the late 1730s, and it produced numerous imitations and variations. The *ferme ornée* could be a working farm which sported some fanciful additions, such as a mock-Gothic farmhouse, dandified outbuildings and exuberant untrimmed hedgerows, or it could be a complex of ornate farm buildings set within a park and serving as the home farm of a great mansion. The enthusiasm for the more extravagant applications of the idea did not last for more than a few decades, and the *ferme ornée*

received some wounding criticism from the celebrated landscape gardener, Humphry Repton. He proclaimed that 'if the yeoman destroys his farm by making what is called a *ferme ornée* he will absurdly sacrifice his income to his pleasure'. Even so, other noted arbiters of taste had dabbled with the concept, as evidenced by the castellated cow-shelter designed for Rousham in Oxfordshire by William Kent in 1738. While the *ferme ornée* was largely a fad of the eighteenth century, various individual farm buildings of an unfunctional and unashamed splendour were built in Victorian times, like the Royal Dairy of the home farm in Windsor Great Park of 1858. See also MODEL FARM.

*Further reading:* Wade Martins, S., *The English Model Farm*, Windgather Press, Macclesfield, 2002.

**Fermtoun**, see CLACHAN.

**Fey-land**. In Scotland, the best land that was heavily manured and was kept in continuous cultivation. See also INFIELD-OUTFIELD CULTIVATION, FAUGHS.

**Ffridd**. Enclosed land close to the farmhouse on a farm in Wales.

**Field-barn**, see BARN.

**Field-names**. Most old fields had names. Many of these names have been forgotten or else have been lost when neighbouring fields have been dehedged and amalgamated into the featureless anonymity of modern PRAIRIE FIELDS. Plenty of old field-names can be recovered simply by asking the farmer concerned, while many others are recorded on old maps of the post-medieval centuries. Any reader interested in the history of a locality will find research into its field-names to be a fascinating and worthwhile undertaking.

Plainly, a field-name can be no older than the field that bears it, but it could be younger. This might result from renaming, so that, for example, a field could be renamed Dovecote Close after a dovecote was built in it to provide a prominent landmark. Its name could also change along with the evolution of language and dialect. The meaning of many old words associated with the land has been forgotten, while local dialects have shed some of their colourful words. In Middle English the word *pightel* or *pichel* referred to a small enclosure of land, but as it has lapsed from the language so farmers have tried to make something intelligible out of such field-names – and new names like Pig Hill have been coined which completely confuse the original meaning. But sometimes even the most peculiar names could endure, like 'Great Plaster Pightle' near Kingsclere in Hampshire, preserving both Pightle and the medieval PLAISTOW, or playing field. Field-names could evolve for all kinds of reason; one cannot imagine that a farmer who was a strict Nonconformist would persevere with a field-name like 'Great Bare Arse', for example. When we look at field-maps of the post-medieval centuries we find that virtually every enclosure had a name, while names were commonly given to the new fields which resulted from PARLIAMENTARY ENCLOSURE. The vast medieval OPEN FIELDS also had names, usually of a simple and self-explanatory kind – like North Field, Mill Field, Hedge Field, East Field and so on. The FURLONG subdivisions of the open fields had names, too, and sometimes these were preserved after the enclosure of the field system, while the STRIPS or selions were named only in association with their current tenants.

In different cases field-names can evolve rapidly or prove to be remarkably durable. For example, between 1765 and 1838 the name of a field at Chiddingstone in Kent had evolved from Upper Daniels to Little Donalds, though on the other hand the aptly named field-name expert John Field has described some remarkably persistent examples: Dead Hills Field near Ely being known as Dedhil around 1195; Clay Furlong at Everdon in Northamptonshire being Claifurlong in 1240; and Sowerbutts near Winmarleigh in Lancashire being recorded as Le Sourbut around 1220.

Field-names can be sorted into a number of different categories. John Field offers twenty-six which can be summarised as: size of field; distance from village; direction; order (e.g., First Close, Middle Leys, etc.); shape; nature of soil; relative fertility; topographic features; type of cultivation (e.g., meadow, assart); specific crops grown; wild plants and trees; domestic and farm animals; wild animals; buildings; roads and bridges, etc.; name of owner; profession of owner/tenant; person or object maintained by income from the land (e.g., Priest Acre, Charity Close); money value of land; archaeological features; supernatural and folklore associations; arbitrary names (e.g., Nelson, Xenophon); boundary associations; legal terms (e.g., Copyhold, Tenantry Down); industrial uses; and games.

Many field-names that will be encountered are common, simple and not particularly informative – such as Great Close, Small Heath or Triangle. Others may be very interesting because they provide information about the landscape. Names such as Warren Close, Cunning Garth or Cunning Flat tell us about old warrens and the conies that lived in them. There are scores of similarly useful names, like Gallows Ground, Fishery Meadow, Orchard Close, Dove Cote Garth, Wrestling Piece, Windmill Post, Galloping Field, Garden Hill and so on, that tell us about former features of the landscape and activities. There are many others that tell us about the plants and wildlife of the countryside in days gone by, such as Brockholes (badger setts), Cockle Close (with the now almost extinct corn cockle growing there), Woodcock Mead, Blue Button (where scabious grew), or Tansy.

Fields that were a long way from the farmstead were often given the names of distant places. This habit must go back a long way, for a medieval field called Antioch has been recorded and more recent examples include Botany Bay, Fan Damons (a corruption of Van Diemen's Land) and Zululand. The rustic sense of humour is also evident in the derogatory names given to fields of poor land, like

Pickpocket, Bare Bones, Starvation, Greety Guts (for 'hungry' ground) and Twistgut. Field-names can also tell us the condition of the land before improvements, like drainage or woodland clearance. Names like Plash Field, Carr Field, Moorish and Moss Close denote marshy land, and ASSART names like Royd, Sarts, Sarch and Stubbs together with wood names like Shaw, Hurst and Hanger tell of former woodland. Other names tell us about which crops were frequently cultivated on a particular piece of ground, some of the names being archaic, like Aver for oats as in Averhill, and some of the crops being unusual today, as with Woad Meadow, Saffron Garth or Balsam Ground.

Local studies of field-names can be most interesting if one begins with a survey of the current and remembered field-names, picking the brains of old members of the farming community. These names can then be regressed and related to those recorded on the nineteenth-century tithe maps (if available), and then one may search for older maps of the locality, like ESTATE maps, which record field-names, thus discovering how the names have evolved. Because the names discovered are likely to include archaic elements, it is necessary to have a good dictionary of field-names to hand, but a selection of some of the more common name-elements is provided as follows:

*Balk, edge, mere, linch, rean*: unploughed access-way or boundary between furlongs
*Bury, berry, borough*: old fort or moated homestead
*Butt 1*: a strip or selion of shorter than normal length
*Butt 2*: tree stumps
*Brake, breck*: wasteland or wasteland brought into cultivation
*Chart*: a rough common
*Close*: an enclosed field
*Clough, cleugh*: steep valley
*Copy, copse, grove*: coppice
*Cot, cote*: cottage
*Croat, croud*: croft

*Dell, fardel*: a group of strips or selions
*Dole, dale, dalt, dote*: share in a common field or meadow
*Eddish, etch*: enclosure
*Ersh*: ploughland
*Essart, assart*: land cleared of trees
*Farrow*: path
*Field*: a large expanse of common land sub-divided into furlongs and strips
*Flash*: a shallow pool
*Flatt*: a furlong in a field of open ploughland
*Fit*: meadow or pasture by a stream
*Flonk*: pen in front of a pig stye
*Fold*: pen
*Forschel*: ribbon of land beside a routeway
*Foss*: a ditch
*Frith*: land that was or had been wooded
*Garth, garston, hoppett*: small grass enclosure
*Gill, gut, lake, keld, pill*: a stream
*Gore, gair*: small triangle of land at junction of two furlongs
*Gospel tree, mark/march tree/oak etc.*: tree growing on a parish or estate boundary
*Grip*: ditch or stream
*Ground*: large pasture some distance from the farmstead
*Hafod*: upland pasture grazed in summer
*Hagg*: a wood, often a division of a medieval coppiced wood
*Hale, hall*: small corner of land
*Half-year land*: Lammas land
*Half year field/close etc.*: an enclosure used seasonally for grazing
*Ham*: enclosed meadow or pasture, sometimes a settlement.
*Harve, haw*: small enclosure or yard near the farmhouse
*Hatch*: fence or fenced enclosure
*Haugh, herne*: a nook of land, sometimes inside the loop of a river
*Hay 1*: hedged enclosure, sometimes a deer park
*Hay 2*: small wood
*Headland, hade, furhead*: the area at either end of a furlong where the plough was turned
*Heaf*: sheep pasture

*Hempland/field*: land where hemp was grown in medieval times

*Hern, hirn, scoot*: oddly shaped piece of land, e.g. within a river meander loop

*Heugh, hoe, hoo*: bank, steep slope

*Hollins*: wood where holly was grown

*Holme*: water meadow, ground standing just above flood-level

*Holt, shaw, shay, hurst, hag*: a wood

*Homestal, hamstal, haw, home field, inland*: field beside a farmstead

*Hop, hope*: land enclosed from marsh

*Hoppet*: little enclosure

*Howe*: hill or burial mound

*In-by land*: enclosed and most intensively-worked land in English uplands

*Ing, eng*: meadow

*Inlandes*: demesne land rented out to tenants

*Innings, gainage*: land reclaimed from a wetland

*Intake, inning*: land enclosed from the common

*Inwood*: a wood lying within the demesne

*Jack*: a small unused piece of land

*Knap*: hillock

*Land, loon*: a strip or selion

*Lawn*: pasture in wood or park

*Lea*: confusing word, can denote wood, meadow or track

*Leas, leaze, leys*: meadow, generally one held in common

*Leasow*: enclosed pasture

*Leat, leet*: an artificial channel associated with flooding watermeadows or industrial ponds

*Leighton/laighton*: a garden

*Ley, 1*: a medieval clearing or else a place with trees

*Ley, 2*: also lay, leah, lee: land alternating between arable and pasture

*Ley, 3*: a meadow or piece of unploughed land

*Low, law*: often refers to ancient burial mound

*Mains*: demesne land on a Scottish estate

*Mark, mere march*: boundary

*Mark stone, mere stone, mere stake, mark soil etc.*: boundary marker

*Moor*: can mean marsh as well as moorland

*Oldland*: land converted from arable to pasture

*Over*: a slope

*Park 1*: a deer park

*Park 2*: demesne land, sometimes including recreational areas near the mansion

*Park 3*: enclosed land in Scotland and Ireland

*Parrock*: small enclosure, paddock

*Patch, pickle, pightle, pingle, plack, plackett, hoppet, tye*: small enclosure

*Plashet*: marshy field

*Piking, pilch, nook*: little triangular piece of land

*Plash, moss, slough*: waterlogged ground

*Pre, mead*: meadow

*Quillet*: ribbon of land or small croft

*Reading, ridding, royd, sart, sarch, stubbs, stubbing*: assart

*Reans, reins, mere*: boundary land

*Severals*: land held individually, not communally

*Shott, flat*: a furlong

*Sike 1*: a meadow beside a stream

*Sike 2*: a ditch or stream, those named 'Black Sike' often marked boundaries

*Slade, sitch*: valley, valley-bottom land

*Sleight*: sheep pasture

*Sling, slang, slip, spong, rap, screed*: narrow strip of land

*Slough*: badly-drained land

*Stank, lachek*: a pond

*Stubbs, Stubbings*: assarted land that was punctuated by treestumps after the removal of woodland

*Thwaite*: generally a meadow

*Tye*: enclosed pasture, sometimes bounded by roads or tracks

*Tyning*: enclosed land

*Vaccary*: land associated with a cattle farm

*Wath*: fording place on a stream

*Waver*: pond serving a village

*Weald, walden*: wooded country

*Wick*: dairy farm or sometimes a roadside village of Roman origin

*Wong*: can be same as 'severals' or be a garden or else enclosed wet meadow

*Wray, stitch, roe, plat, piece, patch, hale*: various words for a nook or portion of land.

*Further reading*: Field, J., *English Field Names*, David & Charles, Newton Abbot, 1972.

**Field-walking**. More grandly known now as 'surface artefact collection' this is an invaluable method of discovering the history of settlement in an arable area, which experienced a wave of popularity in the 1970s and 1980s. It concerns discovering the settlements and activities of former communities from the evidence of lost and broken artefacts littering the surface of ploughland. Since prehistoric times, countryfolk have consumed pottery in large quantities, and broken pots often appear to have ended up on the household muck-heap along with other items of domestic debris. When the manure was spread upon the fields, the sherds of pottery were spread with it, so that any respectable ploughed field will display a scattering of pot fragments of many ages. This 'manuring debris' will be fairly evenly distributed across the plough-soil, but when the field-walker discovers a concentration of pot fragments he or she will be fairly certain that a former settlement site has been located. With experience one may be able to judge from the extent and density of the sherds whether the settlement was a farmstead, a hamlet or a village, and even an abandoned farmstead site can yield a bag full of broken pots. Equally, a field-walking technique can be applied to seaches for flint fragments and tools that were lost or discarded in the prehistoric era.

To discover more about the settlement history of the fields being studied it is necessary to learn to recognise the distinctive qualities of the different types of pottery produced by different societies at different times. Helpful staff in a local museum may identify fragments or produce a range of pot samples of different ages from their stores. Blue and white glazed pottery of the Victorian era is unmistakable, and every field seems to have its fair share, but the grass tempered ware of the Saxons is hard to find, resembling chips of coal. Most prehistoric pottery is coarse; wheel-turned Roman pottery is much more impressive, and a wide spectrum of wares were produced in medieval and later times. It is a poor field that fails to yield plenty of examples of coarse, locally-made pot

fragments of the twelfth or thirteenth century. Other artefacts, like bronze or flint axes, flint arrowheads or flakes of worked flint, and sometimes even bonework or jewelry may also be found.

Were one to find a concentration of fragments of clay roofing tiles, pieces of mosaic, building stones and sherds of imported red 'Samian ware' pottery, there is every likelihood that the site of a ROMAN VILLA has been discovered. Hopefully there would also be associated coins to suggest dates. Similarly, but less obviously, by discovering an extensive spread of pottery including sherds of tenth-, eleventh-, twelfth- and thirteenth-century date in various quantities, but little or nothing later, one might be dealing with a settlement which began in the tenth century, expanded in the two following centuries, then declined and was abandoned by the fourteenth century, while local differences in the occurrence of sherds of different ages might reveal the directions of growth of the settlement.

Field-walking is a very useful technique which can be attempted by anyone who is prepared to study the characteristics of pottery through the ages, but it is only practical in areas of arable farming or periodical ploughing. One should always obtain the permission of the landowner and call a halt to operations when further trampling threatens the growing crop.

It is also vital that any finds should not be regarded as 'treasure', but be taken to the local museum for recording, even if they seem only to be worthless pot fragments. Exponents vary in their ability to recognise sherds amongst the ploughsoil, and conditions may be easiest after harrowing and light rain. Results obtained are more impressive if walking is organised by a set grid rather than as a random ramble. The field concerned should be walked in an organised manner. 'Extensive' walking along parallel lines 25m apart may give a broad picture of what is to be found. 'Intensive' walking can involve careful searching in a system of squares with sides of 25m which have been set out from the National Grid.

*Further reading:* Barton, K. J., *Pottery in England from 3500 BC to AD 1730*, David & Charles, Newton Abbott, 1975.

Steane, J. M. and Dix, B. F., *Peopling Past Landscapes*, Council for British Archaeology, London, 1978.

Schofield, A. J. (ed.), *Interpreting Artefact Scatters*, Oxbow Monogr 4, Oxford.

**First-floor hall**, see HALL.

**Firth**. Topographical terms in Scotland with conflicting meanings. The word can signify an estuary or deep inlet; a wood ('frith') or a place on the MUIR where peat was cut (see TURBARY).

**Fisherland**. A part of the seashore where fishermen spread their nets and dried fish.

**Fish garth**. An artificial loop from a river in which fish were caught in nets slung from stakes or an enclosure within the course of the river made from stakes and wattle within which fish would be trapped. See also DAMS AND WEIRS.

**Fishing (on Shetland)**, see BOD, LODGE.

**Fishpond**, see POND.

**Fish-weir**, see DAMS AND WEIRS, FISH GARTH.

**Fit rig**. Lowland Scottish term for HEADLAND.

**Flatt**, see FURLONG.

**Flax kiln**. In areas of moist climate, like Co. Tyrone and Co. Armargh, flax that had come from the retting ponds, where rotting left just the fibres remaining, might not dry sufficiently in the open air and kilns were built to dry the material. They are associated with the eighteenth and early nineteenth centuries.

**Flint mines**. Around thirty areas with STONE AXE FACTORIES are known, and in addition to these, about twenty flint axe production sites have been recognised. Because of its toughness and particular characteristics of fracturing when struck, flint was an ideal axe-making material – Neolithic craftsmen were prepared to quarry through different seams of material in order to obtain access to the best flint beds. Flint occurs in association with chalk, and so the known sites are associated with the English DOWNLANDS. Until around 3000 BC, most of the inhabitants of southern England may have relied partly upon axe imports from the northern and western stone axe factories, but then they systematically exploited the best local flint sources.

The most famous flint-mining complex is at Grimes Graves in Norfolk, where workers dug through two bands of substandard flint to reach the excellent materials of the 'floorstone' layer. Pits that were 20–40 feet (6–12 metres) deep were dug down to the floorstone level and then horizontal galleries were dug (using picks made from red deer antlers) to radiate outwards from the base of the pits. In all, around 800 shafts were constructed at Grimes Graves, and spoil from the workings forms a large area of hummocky and pitted terrain. Mining at this site continued until about 2100 BC.

More flint-mining sites surely await discovery, and other well-known centres of the Neolithic industry included the site later developed as a HILLFORT at Cissbury in West Sussex, exploited as early as 3500 BC, and the Blackpatch mines on Harrow Hill near Clapham, also in West Sussex. The products of such mines were exported far and wide, usually as 'rough-outs' which would be finished and polished by their 'purchasers'. The ritual associations of both the great flint-mining sites and their products are subjects of considerable recent speculation. See also STONE AXE FACTORY.

**Floated meadow**, see WATER MEADOW.

**Flockrake, flock-raik**. A sheep pasture in Scotland.

**Fog**. In the northern uplands this was the MEADOWS equivalent of the stubble AFTERMATH in the cornfield. After the harvesting of the hay crop, some time around late July or on 1 August, animals entered the meadows to graze on the fog, the 'fogging' helping to fertilise the land for the next haymaking. Their numbers had to be regulated to prevent over-grazing and they were removed on 1 April or during the two weeks that followed.

**Fogou**, see SOUTERRAIN.

**Fold**. These enclosures for sheep were normally built on the commons and they served a variety of purposes. WASHFOLDS were pens beside WASHPOOLS in deep or deepened becks and rivers where sheep were held prior to the annual washing of their fleeces. Lambfolds were built at the lambing places to give the little animals shelter at night, while 'ewe-locks' or 'buchts' were folds where ewes were milked. Sometimes ewes were brought down from the COMMON to the farmstead at evening for milking, at others they were milked on the fells. The milking pens were narrow, rectangular enclosures. All types of folds can be encountered as earthworks, along with any DRYSTONE WALLS built to channel sheep into them. See also FALD DYKE.

**Foldage**. The right of a feudal lord to insist that tenants graze their sheep on the demesne, so as to fertilise it.

**Foldyard**, see CREW.

**Folkland**. A form of land domination and ownership linked with the Saxon nobility that operated according to traditional custom rather than by written titles. Titles of the latter type were associated with the custom of 'bookland' that succeeded folkland in the last centuries of the Saxon era in England. Occasionally, the charters or books associated with bookland have survived and provide very early descriptions of the ESTATE and its BOUNDARIES.

**Follies**. These are buildings with little obvious practical function. Many were built to satisfy the romantic whims and Picturesque enthusiasms of the nobility, though in a number of cases, as with Yorke's Folly in Nidderdale, there was an admirable charitable motive of providing building work for the rural unemployed. Although the craze was mainly associated with the eighteenth century, its roots go deeper, and one could regard Lyveden New Bield in Northamptonshire, an elaborate summerhouse-cum-banqueting hall which was built in the 1590s by Sir Thomas Tresham, as the grand-daddy of the English folly. Tresham's conversion to Catholicism is evident in the cross-shaped plan of the building, the inscribed dedication to Christ and the Virgin Mary, and the symbols of the passion carved in panels around the walls.

Follies span a broad spectrum of English eccentricities, including grottoes, mock hermitages, obelisks, fake prehistoric monuments, the COTTAGE ORNÉE and the Temple of Virtue and it is not easy to decide where ornamental park and garden architecture ends and the folly begins. A number of categories of folly can be recognised. BELVEDERES are lantern-like or turret-shaped rooms added to the roof of a building or on top of mounds to provide an unusual vantage-point over the surrounding countryside, while the *gazebo* is a similar structure, sometimes freestanding and positioned to provide a view of what was going on beyond the garden wall. *Prospect towers* were normally sited on suitable locations within a landscaped park to provide an elevated view across the landscape and came in many shapes and sizes, including the enormous prospect tower in Ashridge Park in the Chilterns and the triangular tower at Cotehele in Cornwall.

While prospect towers, belvederes, gazebos and pavilions were for looking out from, eye-catchers were for looking *at*. They could be sham ruins, façades or gateways and were built to provide a focus of interest in a scene, as Whately explained in his observations on *Modern Gardening* of 1770: 'When a wide heath, a dreary moor, or a continued plain is in prospect, objects which catch the eye supply the want of variety; none are so effectual for this purpose as buildings'. Thus we find a miniature Colosseum overlooking Oban harbour, Norman arches from a derelict church at Shobdon decorating a

Herefordshire ridge and an unfinished Parthenon on Calton Hill, Edinburgh.

Follies could also be created from organic materials: dead trees were actually planted as a presumed embellishment to Kensington Gardens in the early eighteenth century, while a century later the countryside near Amesbury in Wiltshire acquired a multitude of small round tree-clumps, the Trafalgar Clumps, which were planted to

*Follies*

*Left* This folly, near the summit of Carn Brea in Cornwall, was developed from the ruins of a genuine medieval castle.

*Below* Lyveden New Bield, in Northamptonshire, was built as a garden house-cum-banqueting hall in the 1590s and may be regarded as the grandfather of all follies. It was not complete when its sponsor, Sir Thomas Tresham, died, and work was abandoned.

represent the dispositions of English and French ships at the outset of the great sea-battle.

*Further reading*: Jones, Barbara, *Follies and Grottoes*, Constable, 1953.

**Foot and mouth disease**, see AGRICULTURAL DEPRESSION.

**Ford**. A place where the shallowness of a watercourse allowed it to be crossed by wading. Former fords have given rise to numerous PLACE-NAMES, like Fordham and Fordley.

**Fordraught or meer path**. A path between two farms.

**Forest**. While the term 'forest' is now used indiscriminately to describe any large area of WOODLAND or commercial tree PLANTATION, in medieval times the term was not a synonym for 'greenwood' but applied to the extensive areas of the country that were subject to the widely resented Forest Law. There, 'forest' related more to deer and the laws that protected them than to trees. Royal hunting forests often encompassed a certain amount of woodland, but usually they also contained agricultural countrysides and, perhaps, some open moorland or heath.

The creation of vast forests and the imposition of the Forest Law are associated with the Norman kings, though there is evidence that the late Saxon kings also had (less formalised) hunting territories in the New Forest, the upper Pennine Dales and a few other places, though their reserves were less extensive and less controversial. Under the Norman kings, Forest Law was codified. Each designated forest had an existence as a wooded or moorland refuge in which the deer (red, fallow and roe) lived, and a surrounding area of working land across which hunting might take place and within which deer enjoyed legal protection when they strayed. Towns could even exist within the forest, like Colchester, in Essex Forest. As the woodland historian, Oliver Rackham, has described, the pattern of hunting forests did not correspond

very closely to the pattern of medieval woodland. It was, however, closely linked to the distribution of royal estates and manors, so that as the King progressed from one of his palaces to the next he had regular access to hunting. He did not always directly own the land across which he hunted *his* game in *his* forest, while landholders in the forests could suffer damage from the King's deer but be powerless to slaughter the animals or even to hinder their depredations. Peasants were deprived of pannage, or grazing, for their stock in the weeks when deer were fawning and could take only dead wood for fuel. Swine were also banned at this time lest they injure hinds or eat their fawns. At the time of Domesday Book, about twenty-five forests are recorded, and by the time that the noble discontent expressed in Magna Carta brought a virtual end to the institution of new forests in 1216 almost 150 forests had been created. The King would never have had time to hunt in all his forests, and would never even set foot in some of them. Their main function seems to have been to supply venison that was served at prestigious royal feasts. A lesser role was that of providing largesse in the form of gifts of animals for the stocking of private DEER PARKS. They also yielded considerable revenues from fines and the sale of resources and privileges.

Much is still to be learned about how forests were created, but the enlargement of the New Forest caused much injustice and disquiet. In an over-coloured, rather unreliable later account the chronicler William of Malmesbury claimed that William I: 'had desolated villages and destroyed churches for more than thirty miles around – a dreadful sight, indeed, that where once there had been human activity and the worship of God, deer now ranged unrestrained, animals of no real value to mankind'.

Each forest had its own bounds, and within these bounds the Forest Law was enforced. Similarly each forest needed its own institutions, employees and administrators. Lawbreakers did not tend to be mutilated, as is often claimed, for this rendered them a burden on society. Rather, poaching or the unlawful removal of trees was punished by fines or, occasionally, by imprisonment. Dogs were mutilated, or 'lawed', to prevent their use in hunting, but the owner could choose to pay a fine and keep his dog intact. The fines in turn helped to finance the huntsmen, bureaucracy and courts of the forest. (In the Middle Ages fines were often a useful source of income rather than a form of punishment and were more accurately regarded as fees or taxes.) The administration included two justices of the forest, one operating north of the Trent and one to the south, and each individual forest had its warden. The warden was responsible for a large force of foresters, and some villages like Bainbridge in the Yorkshire Dales, are said to have originated as settlements for forest employees. Most forests seem to have contained a hermit (see HERMITAGE), normally living in the more remote parts and perhaps reporting to the warden on matters of deer and poaching.

The hunting forest was a very special kind of status symbol, and it was one to which only the most powerful nobles and churchmen could hope to obtain. Non-royal forests – most properly known as 'CHASES', though the terminology was not rigidly applied – were always much less numerous than the royal forests. The right to hold a chase was given by the King, though most chases were subject to common law rather than Forest Law. An exception concerned the chases owned by the Earls of Lancaster, where the King allowed the operation of Forest Law. Professor Cantor has identified twenty-six medieval chases (see *Further reading* below).

Even in their wooded components the forests were far from being silent refuges. Woodland was managed, cropped and sold; special enterprises like 'vaccaries', or cattle farms, existed inside the forests, and grants of pannage for pigs and herbage for grazing livestock were other sources of revenue. In some forests there was also mining.

Despite these and other sources of income the medieval kings were seldom financially secure, and useful revenues came from the sale of licences to clear woodland or ASSART. During the thirteenth and fourteenth centuries, assarting greatly reduced the deer cover, while the Forest Law, which had been assiduously enforced in the twelfth century, gradually fell into neglect. Meanwhile, the development of new forms of taxation reduced the reliance on forest revenues. By Tudor times the forest was a far less formidable institution than it had been under the Normans, and as the kings lost interest in their devalued rights, the forest courts became forums for organising the day-to-day exploitation of the lands by commoners and landowners. Under Charles I there was an attempt to revitalise the Forest Law, motivated by the hope that the public would be prepared to pay to have the impositions removed – but this anachronism was overtaken by the Civil War. Long before, the Crown could raise enormous sums by removing Forest Law. In 1204, for example, the men of Devon raised 5000 marks to have the Law lifted from all parts of their county apart from Dartmoor and Exmoor. Eventually the forests disappeared piecemeal, were disafforested or were subjected to PARLIAMENTARY ENCLOSURE and the removal of commoners rights – so it was often the peasant who lost rather than gained from the extinction of a forest.

During the Middle Ages the forest did breed resentment, and the poaching fraternity included representatives of almost every class and occupation. Probably the most serious resentment concerned the restrictions that prevented the protection of crops against damage by grazing deer and galloping huntsmen. The records of an inquest of 1251, quoted by Professor Homans, provide a colourful glimpse of what must have been a not unfamiliar scene:

> Henry, son of John of Sudborough, the shepherd says that as he was sitting at his dinner on Whitsunday under a hedge in the

field of Sudborough [in Northamptonshire], and with him William, son of the winnower, and William Russel, herdsmen of the cattle of the town of Sudborough, and Roger Lubbe of Denford, cowherd of the lord, his fellow herdsmen, came William of Drayton by them in a tunic green in hue with a bow and arrows; and two others whom he knew not with bows and arrows, came with William.

He says also that after them came a horseman on a certain black horse carrying a fawn before him on his lap, and he carried venison behind him covered with leaves.

He says also that after them came two pages leading eight greyhounds of which some were white, some tawny, and some red.

Because the forests existed as legal creations, the main legacy is one of names, some now relating to fragments of former forests, like Sherwood, some to deforested areas, like the Forest of Knaresborough, and some to areas which are difficult to map exactly, like the Forest of Galtres near York. Forest bounds were hardly ever marked out on the ground, though on Dartmoor some banks and ditches do seem to have marked sections of the forest boundary. They were, however, quite regularly perambulated. Where records of such perambulations survive they record the gradual evolution of the countryside. See also DEER PARK, HUNTING LODGE, PANNAGE, SWANIMOTE.

*Further reading:* Cantor, L. (ed.), *The Medieval Landscape*, Croom Helm, 1982.
Cantor, L., *The Changing English Countryside 1400–1700*, Routledge & Kegan Paul, London, 1987.
Rackham, O., *The Last Forest*, Dent, London, 1989.

**Four-course rotation (Norfolk system).** This was a sound system of crop rotation which gained great popularity during the Agricultural Revolution of the eighteenth century. Although elements of the rotation were already in use, credit for the development of the system is given to the second Viscount Townshend ('Turnip'

Townshend), who began farming in 1730 and applied the rotation on his estate of Raynham in Norfolk. The four courses ran: turnips–barley or oats–clover–wheat. The root crops and clover provided winter fodder for cattle, and the combination of clover and grazing cattle improved the fertility of the soil for the demanding wheat crop which followed. See also LIGHT LAND REVOLUTION.

**Freehold, Freeland, Frank Tenement.** A tenure that was not subject to the will of the manorial lord or the custom of the manor. On his death, the property concerned could be disposed of in the manner that the free tenant or franklin had wished. The free tenant also paid a fixed rent and was not required to render labour services. Thus, although he might sometimes be poorer than neighbours who were bondsmen, his position was to be envied for the freedoms it embodied. See also COPYHOLD, SOCAGE.

**Freeth.** A HEDGEROW in the West Country and Wales, generally a dead hedge of wattle and posts or wattle spanning a gap in a living hedge.

**Free warren.** A privilege purchased by a lord from the crown which entitled him to hunt small game on his own estates and salt or pickle the meat.

**Fulling mill.** A fuller was a dresser of cloth and medieval fulling mills, where woollen cloth was cleaned and thickened, were generally built in the countryside beside clear rivers and streams. The energy of moving water was harnessed to power paddles that beat the cloth as it was immersed in water. Sometimes these mills are found to have 'WALK MILL' names, suggesting that the water-powered mill succeeded a place where the cloth was beaten by the trampling action of a 'walker' (a profession that has given rise to a common surname; 'fuller' was another). The house of Richard Bosynton, a leading fuller and dyer in Winchester in the years around 1400, was excavated in 1967. In the front of his house was the shop, served by the running water used by his craft, above were his living quarters, and at the back of the house a kitchen, and behind this a courtyard with the rack where cloth was dried.

**Furlong, culture, shott**. Within each OPEN FIELD the STRIPS were grouped into parcels of parallel strips known as furlongs or shots. Each furlong had a name and each could be said to be roughly 'field-shaped'. This latter feature has led to suggestions that furlongs represent the field-divisions which existed prior to the introduction of open-field farming. In some cases this does appear to have happened, although it cannot be assumed to have been the norm. Evidence is emerging that, in some places at least, the furlong-divisions which existed

through most of the Middle Ages were subdivisions of earlier 'long furlongs' composed of 'long strips'. In some communities the crop rotations appear to have been practised on a furlong rather than on an open-field basis. Most furlong divisions disappeared as a result of EARLY ENCLOSURE or PARLIAMENTARY ENCLOSURE, though occasionally hedged furlongs survived longer than the strips that they contained and were preserved in the guise of large privately owned fields. The furlong was notionally one 'furrow long' and its dimensions became standardised as a linear measure of 220 yds (201.2 m).

# G

**Galloway dyke**. A type of DRYSTONE WALL associated with the south-west of Scotland that has a firmly constructed base upon which rough courses of single stones are loosely placed.

**Gallows, gallow ley**, see GIBBET SITE.

**Ganging-gate, gangway**. A field track or footpath in Scotland.

**Garraí (pl.)**. Vegetable gardens associated with CLACHANS in Ireland and usually occurring between the homesteads and their INFIELD arable lands.

**Garth**. In the north of England this word can be used to describe a small enclosure, usually under grass. In the medieval monastery a 'garth' was a space enclosed by walls. The cloister garth was an enclosed lawn, sometimes furnished with a fountain, though Carthusians used the garth as a burial ground. Other monastic garths were used as herb gardens or enclosures near kitchens that were used for storing fuel. Where the word occurs with a descriptive prefix one may learn

more about the use of the garth concerned – 'applegarth' was a common medieval name for an apple orchard and rabbits were kept in CONEYGARTHS. The word comes from the Old Norse *garr*, 'an enclosure', though a few 'garth' names derive from a Cornish and Welsh word for a hill or promontory. In Scotland the word is often associated with a house and the land attached to it. See also GARTHING, FISH GARTH, WARREN.

**Garthing**. In medieval times and the centuries immediately following, garthing involved repairing gaps in GARTHS or enclosures with DEAD HEDGES or STAKE AND RICE HEDGES. These were made of brushwood gathered in the spring by tenants under their rights of haybote (see BOTE). The dry or dead hedging material was woven between stakes that were driven into the banks of earth and turf which marked out the boundaries in the working countryside. During the fifteenth and sixteenth centuries, with the accelerating enclosure and privatisation of the land, the dead hedges tended to be superseded by quick or living HEDGEROWS and later by DRYSTONE WALLS.

**Garthstead**. A house and its associated land.

**Gate**, see STINT. Also an anglicised Old Danish word denoting a routeway.

**Gate or crossing**, see BORDERS.

**Gavelacre**. A reaping obligation; 'gavelerthe' was a ploughing service performed by tenants for their lord, and 'gavelsed' was an obligation to thresh for him.

**Gavelkind**. A form of inheritance associated with Kent, parts of southern England and Wales in which, after the subtraction of his widow's dower, a man's property was divided equally amongst his sons (or daughters, if sons were lacking).

**Gazebo**, see BELVEDERE, FOLLIES.

**Geese**. Like swine and goats, geese, domesticated from the wild greylag goose, were both useful and environmentally unfriendly. They were frequently associated with GREENS and other COMMONS, but their numbers had to be carefully adjusted to the resource or their fouling of the sward would over-enrich and smother the grass. Being able to fly, geese could not be confined by hedges and so they posed a threat to growing crops – one that was solved by pinioning or clipping the long flight feathers. The keeping of geese is preserved in field names like Goose Croft, Goose Lease or Gooselands. They were driven in considerable numbers to urban markets when feast days approached.

**General enclosure**, see PARLIAMENTARY ENCLOSURE.

**Gerss house**. In Scotland, a tenanted house that has no land attached to it; the 'gerss-man' and 'gerss-fouk' would normally be cottars. See also COTTAGER, COTTAT-TOUN.

**Gibbet sites**. In times when conviction rates for criminals were low, gibbets provided powerful and grisly reminders of the possible consequences of crime. They would often stand at former places of execution, and criminals executed at a provincial capital might then have their remains returned to hang in chains from the local gibbet in the parish where their crimes had been committed. Bodies sometimes remained on the gibbet for decades, the better to proclaim the case for good behaviour, while other victims of the executioners found their way to dissecting tables. Apart from the claims of the moral publicist and the surgeon, there was also a religious belief that the corpses of criminals should not be allowed to pollute hallowed ground or be given the opportunity to rise on Judgement Day. Moreover, the public had a morbid fascination with execution as well as a desire to exact vengeance on the criminal, even after death.

Gibbets were frequently sited on parish boundaries and on COMMONS. For example, in 1795 the body of William Bennington was hung from a gibbet in Gibbet Lane on the boundary between the Norfolk parishes of West Dereham and Wereham. In Scotland the field in which a gallows was built was known as a 'gallow ley'. Wooden gallows placed on parish boundaries were frequently seen in the medieval period, and they have given rise to a multitude of 'Gallows' place-names, like the gallows road or Gallowgate in Aberdeen, Gallowstree Common, near Reading and Gallowhill, near Paisley. As well as being sited at boundary locations, gallows were normally at or beside roads, and they were sometimes placed upon artificial mounds, either purpose-built ones or ancient BARROWS. As places of execution, the gallows were at least officially redundant in England by the later medieval period, when the manor courts were overtaken for more serious matters by the royal courts and capital crimes came to be tried at the twice-yearly assize courts held in the county towns. Some gallows went out of use, though some gallows sites became used by gibbets, where the remains of felons executed elsewhere were displayed.

Some gibbet sites were very old and could be

traced back to the CWEALMSTOWS or execution cemeteries of the Anglo-Saxon period. These seem to have been placed on the boundaries of HUNDREDS and PARISHES and to have been sited on tumuli. The seventh-century barrow cemetery at Sutton Hoo in Suffolk remained a place of execution long after it had lost its burial function. The employment of boundaries and, sometimes, crossroads as execution sites related to ritual perceptions. Boundaries were interfaces, between life and death, heaven and hell or home and foreign places. Execution at such a place would consign the victim to a limbo or eternal torture. Crossroads could confuse the ghost of the execution victim, which would not know which way to go and could not return to haunt the community. Later, the peripheral location of a gibbet might have symbolised the exclusion of the victim by the community – suicides, who had also died in an 'un-Christian' manner, were also buried at places on the roadside at the parish boundary. In some cases, stakes were driven through the hearts of corpses in such graves, pinning down the spirits and preventing them from walking. Gibbets were removed at the time that the commons on which they stood were partitioned under PARLIAMENTARY ENCLOSURE; sometimes large numbers of people attended the taking down of a gibbet and the suspended skeleton.

*Further reading*: Whyte, N., 'The deviant dead in the Norfolk Landscape', LANDSCAPES 4.1, 2003.

**Gibloan**. In Scotland, a path or track too muddy to be negotiated.

**Gin-gang**. An engine powered by a horse (or donkey) which walked round repetitively in a circle, the power from its motion being harnessed by a shaft and cogged wheels and applied mainly to threshing but also to various other tasks, like turnip cutting. The engine was housed under a square, circular or polygonal roof and these buildings can still be, serving other uses. Horse engines became popular in the late eighteenth century as threshing by hand

using flails was labour intensive and costly in wages, while efficient steam boilers were not available until the middle of the nineteenth century.

**Girnel house**, see GRANARY.

**Glair-hole**. In Scots, a marsh or mire – a mud-hole.

**Glauroch**. Glaur-hole, similar to GLAIR-HOLE.

**Glebe**. Most medieval parish priests or rectors were men of modest education and means. They derived their income from tithes; the revenues from 'altarage' (payments made by parishioners on important occasions); 'mortuaries', or the taking of the second-best beasts of deceased members of the congregation; and the produce of the glebe land. The quality and extent of the glebe land would vary considerably from parish to parish; some glebes were sufficiently profitable to allow the parson to sublet the lands, but more often he would be seen toiling on his glebe like any overworked villein. Today the old glebe land is not usually easily recognisable, but hedged strip-shaped fields sometimes endure as relics of a glebe, for the glebe was not easily reallocated under the informal arrangements by which land was enclosed by agreement in the era before PARLIAMENTARY ENCLOSURE. Field names may also identify old glebe land, like Parsons Croft, Rector's Close, Glebe Mead, Priestlands, and so on.

Glebe land is interesting to the historian because it would not tend to be sold or swapped around in the way that other STRIPS might, so that post-medieval maps of glebe land may provide clues to the original allocation of OPEN-FIELD land. At Great Givendale in Humberside, for example, a survey of 1684 shows that the parson's strip was always at the end of a FURLONG with the lord of the manor's strip next to it in the penultimate position – suggesting that centuries earlier the division of open-field land was made in a regular, orderly way. A 'glebe terrier' is a survey of church lands and benefices which may provide a useful record of church property in a locality.

**Glen**. In Scotland, a narrow valley.

**Goats**. These useful animals, producing milk, meat and hides while surviving in much more marginal settings than those associated with dairy cattle, have been present in Britain for thousands of years – though archaeologists face enormous difficulties in distinguishing between their remains and those of sheep. The presence of the goat in medieval farming was greatly reduced by the restrictions that were imposed to control the destructive assaults of the animal upon its environment. These were encountered in their most severe form when goats gained access to woodland, where they would strip trees of their bark and thus cause them to die. Manorial and BYRLAW courts would ban the keeping of the animals or else seek to regulate their presence. Goats were likely to be cast out to the COMMONS beyond the HEAD DYKE between Lady Day and Michaelmas, banned from the common arable fields and subjected to strict tethering controls. For all their anti-social foraging and annoyance to others, goats were useful components in a cottage economy and were kept in ones and twos by villagers (sometimes at the cost of fines) or in substantial herds, such as the ones owned by some religious houses.

**Goit**. A northern word for the artificial channel used to carry water diverted from a river to a WATERMILL. See also FALL TROUGH.

**Goodman's croft/Gudeman's field, acre etc**. In Northern Britain, land supposedly devoted to the Devil. It might be a derisory term for very bad ground, or it might be untilled land dedicated to the Devil. In some cases, however, the 'gudeman's acre' was a plot of ground that a farmer kept back for himself when passing his inheritance over to his son.

**Gorse or whin**. This prickly shrub of the lower fells was useful both for making dead HEDGEROWS and as a very combustible material that was suitable for starting fires. It is associated with areas of acid but not impoverished soil. In some localities it appears to have been protected by the local courts in order to conserve fencing materials. As 'quick' hedgerows replaced dead hedges during the post-medieval centuries, gorse lost its significance. See also BRAIRDED DYKE, GARTHING.

**Got**. In Scotland, a drainage ditch or a narrow arm of the sea.

**Gowl**. In Scotland, a hollow between two hill masses, a pass.

**Granary**. Grain needed to be stored in dry airy conditions, and when it was not kept in a purpose-built structure it might be stored above a stable, cartshed or cowhouse. Quite frequently, however, the granary existed as a building in its own right, usually having a square form, a gabled, hipped or pyramidical roof, and walls of brick or of timber-framing or clad in weatherboarding. To assist the circulation of air and provide extra protection against rats and mice, the granary was raised on short brick arches or on 'staddles'. Mushroom-shaped staddle stones are now sometimes seen decorating a garden or arranged beside a roadside lawn, where they are mementoes of a former granary. The door of a granary was sometimes furnished with a cat-hole, while dogs could be kennelled under the granary steps. Most granaries date from the period 1770–1890.

**Grange**. Having become established at centres like Fountains and Rievaulx in the early twelfth century, the monks of the Cistercian order soon became the recipients of what amounted to vast and remarkable endowments of land. Much of it was donated piecemeal by Norman landlords who both admired the piety of the monks and hoped, through their gifts, to find favour in the afterlife. The monastic estates acquired were often too remote to be worked directly from the abbey concerned, and so the system of the *grangia,* grange or outlying farm was introduced, the word actually relating to a barn. Each Cistercian abbey contained both monks and lay brethren, the latter being the numerous 'worker bees' of the colony, who received only a minimal religious education but who performed most of the day-to-day tasks. Granges were established at suitable intervals throughout the monastic estates and were staffed by a team of lay brethren under the supervision of the cellarer. Initially, the scheme proved very successful and could be operated by the monastic communities without recourse to outside help. Furness Abbey in Cumbria sustained no fewer than eighteen granges, and other orders, including Benedictines and Augustinians, soon imitated the system.

Subordinate granges, or *lodges*, also developed, sometimes staffed only by a lay brother and a cowman or shepherd. The grange of Fountains at Kilnsey in Wharfedale, for example, was the focus for no fewer than seven subordinate lodges established along Langstrothdale.

The heyday of monastic life dawned early, and during the thirteenth century the flood of new endowments began to dry up, the life of the monk and the lay brother began to lose its popular appeal, and fewer new recruits could be found. The onslaughts of the pestilence in the fourteenth and fifteenth centuries greatly depleted the monastic communities, while public comment began to highlight the wealth and corruption rather than the piety of the monastic orders. With the shortage of recruits, granges

*Grange*

A well-preserved granary beside the ruins of Cowdray Mansion near Midhurst in West Sussex. Note how the granary is raised on 'staddle stones' above the reach of vermin.

began to depend upon the work of peasants employed from outside the system, while granges were increasingly leased out to laymen, which greatly weakened the monastic connection. Although the Cistercian ideal emphasised the need for detachment from the evils of the lay world, the haphazard pattern of land endowments ensured that the occupants of the granges were often obliged to work cheek-by-jowl with members of the village and hamlet communities – and numerous bitter conflicts ensued. Sometimes, the disputes involved different houses of monks; in 1279 the abbot of Fountains was given a mill at Litton on the Skirfare, and his MILL-DAM extended across the river to the bank which was part of the property of Sawley Abbey, also a Cistercian house. Evidently a fierce dispute soon occurred, for the monks and lay brothers of Sawley were fined £10 for the violence and damage done to Litton mill, though the abbot of Sawley and his tenants were also granted rights to use the mill.

Eventually, a number of granges emerged as villages or hamlets, and, for example, most of the settlements in Upper Nidderdale, like Middlesmoor, Ramsgill and Bouthwaite, have their origins in monastic granges. The granges themselves varied considerably. Some, like Minster, Thanet, were substantial and imposing complexes of buildings, while others were small and might only accommodate a trio of staff. Fragments of a grange or its subsidiary buildings may survive, like Monks Hall at Appletreewick in Wharfedale; or monastic stonework, including decorated pieces, may be incorporated into post-Dissolution buildings standing near the site of the grange. 'Grange' place-names can be informative, although this prestigious house-name, with its hints of monastic precedents, has been indiscriminately adopted and applied to houses that have not the remotest connection with actual medieval granges. In Northern Britain the term can be used to describe GRANARIES, whether attached to religious foundations or to secular farmsteads.

**Great Rebuilding.** This is a term created by the great landscape historian, Professor W. G. Hoskins, who recognised a large-scale rebuilding and improvement in urban and rural housing in England in the late sixteenth and early seventeenth centuries. The movement reflected an Elizabethan sense of optimism and expansion, with lively commerce, good prices for arable produce, relatively secure government and a fairly universal desire for self-betterment all serving as catalysts to a great flurry of new building activity. Although the revival could not be shared with the most impoverished members of the rural communities, whose dwellings were generally to remain flimsy and insubstantial, it did result in the construction of thousands of farmsteads and superior cottages to standards of craftsmanship and robust durability which have allowed many of them to endure to this day.

Like most national fashions, the Great Rebuilding first erupted in the affluent south-east of England and then spread outwards into the provinces. Professor Hoskins dated the movement to the years 1570–1640. More recent studies suggest that this timebracketing is too close.

In his study of the Cambridgeshire village of Foxton, the amateur historian Rowland Parker found that:

> between 1550 and 1620 they rebuilt the entire village. More than fifty houses were either erected on derelict sites or built to replace houses which were in a state of near collapse. Some were built in the old ramshackle way, or built of old material re-used, and lasted no more than a hundred years or so. Most of them were built of new straight beams of oak, or of sound timbers salvaged from a previous house. They were built to last, and last they did, as witness the fact that in this one village alone twenty of them are standing at the present day.

Working further away from the fashionable heartlands of England the historian R. Macbin studied the houses of Yetminster in Dorset.

There it was found that the prices paid for arable farm produce did rise during the period of Professor Hoskins's Great Rebuilding and they encouraged a burst of rural rebuilding. In Yetminster, however, there was a second and more important eruption of building in the late seventeenth century, which was related to rises in the value of livestock products.

Moving further north, the Great Rebuilding appears as a less clearly defined process, but if one looks at the Pennine Dales and associates the Great Rebuilding with the construction of thousands of LAITHE HOUSES, then the broad timespan runs from about 1650 to about 1870. But most of the rebuilding work was concentrated in the period about 1770 to 1830. Looking still further north, to the Scottish Highlands and Islands, if the Great Rebuilding is represented by the replacement of BLACK HOUSES with 'white houses', then the period runs from about the late nineteenth century to modern times. In other words, the Great Rebuilding was not a single event, but rather a wave of affluence and rising expectations that rolled very slowly from the south-eastern lowlands to the northern uplands.

*Further reading:* Currie, C. R. J., 'Time and Chance: modelling the attrition of old houses', *Vernacular Architecture* 19, 1–9.

Hoskins, W. G., 'The Rebuilding of Rural England, 1570–1640', *Past and Present* 4, 44–59.

Hoskins, W. G., *Provincial England,* Macmillan, London, 1963.

Macbin, R., *The Houses of Yetminster,* University of Bristol, Department of Extra-Mural Studies, 1978.

Parker, R., *The Common Stream,* Paladin, 1976.

**Great Sheep.** The Great Sheep was the Cheviot, whose introduction to the clan estates of the Scottish Highlands resulted in the CLEARANCES involving the eviction and replacement of human tenants by 'four footed clansmen'. Word of the changes is said to have reached the Highlands by way of a seer who proclaimed (in Gaelic), 'Woe to thee, oh land, the Great Sheep is coming'. The Cheviot, developed in the

border fells of Northumberland, was bred from the medieval Long Hill strain, into which continental Merino blood had been introduced, with Lincolnshire and Ryeland blood being incorporated in the final stages of breeding. The result was a hardy animal that produced good yields of wool and meat and was applauded by the Society for the Improvement of British Wool. Cheviots entered the Highlands in the last quarter of the eighteenth century, with devastating effects on the cultural landscape.

*Further reading:* Prebble, J., *The Highland Clearances,* Martin, Secker & Warburg, London, 1963.

**Green (village).** Village greens feature prominently in romantic visions of rural England but, even so, the amount of literature which actually attempts to describe the origins and roles of village greens is small – and most of it is misleading. The legal definition of a village (or urban) green is complicated. To avoid delving into the mass of legal jargon one can regard a village green as an area of open COMMON land within a VILLAGE – while remembering that such a definition is open to debate and undermined by exceptions. The evidence of village maps and earthworks show that although greens were communal resources they were frequently reduced by piecemeal encroachment or more sweeping interventions. An oft-repeated myth maintains that greens were original components of villages that were founded by Saxon settlers and were used as safe enclosures for livestock, allowing them to be guarded at night against wild animals and raiders. However, the Saxons who settled here in the fifth and sixth centuries do not seem to have been particularly wedded to village life, favouring looser or more dispersed settlements. When one looks at the evidence of the small number of excavated Saxon villages in England one does not find ordered settlement around a green but, rather, a loose and straggling pattern of farmsteads, outbuildings and paddocks. There is no compelling reason to believe that greens were frequent features of villages existing before the

Norman Conquest, and a number of examples exist which show greens being established or inserted into existing villages during the medieval period. Interestingly, however, in Roman times some coherent new villages sprang up on the edge of Salisbury Plain, and a few, like the one on Meriden Down near Winterbourne Houghton in Dorset, seem to have included village greens in their lay-out.

One needs only to look at a selection of village greens – like the sprawling green acres of Barrington in Cambridgeshire or Long Melford in Suffolk, the neatly planned triangle at Nun Monkton in Yorkshire, the square containing the church at Heighington, County Durham, or the encroached-upon space at Lower Slaughter in the Cotswolds – to appreciate that they come in all manner of forms. So one can suppose that they also have all manner of histories. In other words, the differences between village greens seem to be qualitative as well as quantitative, even if they shared existences as common land as a 'common' denominator. One method by which a village and green could form was by settlement around an area of common grazing. A glance at a few maps of pre-enclosure England will show that straggling HAMLETS lining the edges of commons were not unusual, and this is not

surprising since SQUATTERS and other poor countryfolk could be attracted to the varied resources of grazing, fuel and bedding which unenclosed common could offer. It has also been argued that a number of green villages in East Anglia were formed in medieval times when a shortage of pasture encouraged peasants to migrate from existing villages to set up their homes beside nearby islands of grazing land.

Greens are frequently found in villages that are plainly (because of their neat and regular lay-outs) the creations of medieval planning. The greens found in such villages take a variety of forms. Some consist of ribbons of green which border each side of a through-road or High Street, some are triangular with the road passing through the green or roads following the margins of it and the dwellings arranged around the edges of the triangle, and some are rectangular. In Yorkshire, 'Y'-shaped medieval plans are common, with the green or market area having a triangular form and being placed in the angle where the road bifurcates. One of the most attractive examples of a 'long green'

*Green*
The green at Finchingfield in Essex.

plan is at East Witton in North Yorkshire. The houses in the village date from 1809, when East Witton was completely rebuilt and provided with a new church by the Earl of Ailesbury, to commemorate the jubilee of George III. However, the houses stand around the large elongated green, exactly where dwellings have stood for centuries. East Witton and its green seem to date from the years around 1300 when the abbot of Jervaulx appears to have had an existing settlement removed and a new one built further away from the Cistercian foundation, the monks of this order seeking isolation from the laity. The large and regular green was apparently provided (as Prof. M. W. Beresford described) to accommodate the Monday market and Martinmas cattle-fair which were first held in 1307. Roads or tracks entered the green at each of its four corners.

MARKETS could sometimes be accommodated on a new green or on an existing one, but where no convenient site was available, a market green or square might be created by actually demolishing existing dwellings. In 1299, South Zeal in Devon, then lying on a busy road between London and Cornwall, was granted a weekly market and two fairs. In response to this, the lord completely rebuilt the village to a regular plan. Dwellings were set along the through-road with their narrow burgage plots running back behind them, and the marketplace was formed as a broadening in the street. (The market faded long ago, and South Zeal is by-passed by the road, now the A30.) In the different case of Culworth in Northamptonshire two existing villages, Culworth and Brime, were linked by a marketplace formed as a rectangular expansion in their through-road when a market charter was granted to the lord of the manor in 1264, and the village became one settlement with a central green or square. But while some greens were deliberate additions to a village and frequently associated with the multiplication of markets in the thirteenth century, others were acquired almost by accident. At Shipton, in Shropshire, the green dates from 1587 when the old village was demolished to improve the view from Shipton Hall, which was being built at this time. The new village was then built around the edges of the open space created by the demolition. Great Shelford in Cambridgeshire existed as two old and widely separated hamlets, each centred on a manor house and linked by an area of meadow. As the hamlets gradually expanded towards each other the meadow became a green which in turn disappeared as a result of PARLIAMENTARY ENCLOSURE. A number of greens were lost to enclosure, and as G. K. Chesterton wryly noted:

> The village green that had got mislaid
> Turned up in the squire's back-yard.

Many more were reduced or obliterated by encroachments. (The General Act of 1845 attempted to put a stop to anti-social enclosures, particularly those destroying village greens.) This encroachment could involve gradual constriction of a green by the colonisation of its edges by dwellings, the building of squatter cottages on the green, or the creation of front gardens for the houses lining the green, as at Cold Kirby, North Yorkshire. Some encroachments were subsequently removed, as at East Witton, where five squatter cottages were shown standing on the green on a map drawn in 1627. Others became welded into the fabric of the village, as at Lower Slaughter where several of the much-photographed stone cottages stand upon an older green. Scores of villages seem to incorporate former greens that have been consumed or reduced by encroachment as elements in their lay-outs, but over the centuries the encroachment can become very difficult to detect.

Plainly, it is impossible to generalise about village greens and a wide variety of origins can be demonstrated. There is also much to learn about the functions of greens. Clearly, many were created as venues for markets, most frequently in the thirteenth century. It is also clear that, as areas of common land, greens would have been useful for recreation. They may have provided grazing and overnight accommodation for animals involved in droving – and greens with ponds, like the planned medieval green at Newton-on-Rawcliffe near Pickering, would have been valued. Equally, greens could often have provided grazing for small village livestock, notably GEESE, which have a reputation for fouling the pasture when grazing in conventional fields and GOATS, which needed to be tethered. One possibly significant use for village greens which does not seem to have been explored concerns the role of the village 'neatherd' or cowman. In medieval times he would walk down some village streets early in the morning and blow his horn. Each family would then send out their cattle so that he could drive them to their grazings. So it is possible that some greens existed as assembly areas where the cattle were gathered and marshalled by the neatherd. Evidence of recreational use is provided in William Warner's *Albion's England* of 1612:

> And Lard and Ladie gang tille Kirke [church]
>    with Lads and Lasses gay
> Fra Masse and Eensong so gud cheere and
>    glee on ery Green.

See also MARKETS AND FAIRS, PLAISTOW, VILLAGE.

*Further reading*: St Joseph, J. K. and Beresford, M. W., *Medieval England, an Aerial Survey*, 2nd edn, Cambridge University Press, 1979.
Taylor, C., *Village and Farmstead*, George Philip, 1983.
Roberts, B. K., *Landscapes of Settlement*, Routledge, London, 1998.
Lewis, C., Mitchell-Fox, P. and Dyer, C., *Village, Hamlet and Field*, Windgather, Macclesfield, 2001.

**Greenhews, browsings, 'watter-boughs'.** Leafy stems lopped from a POLLARD or other tree and tossed down as browse for dear or cattle. The trees concerned might stand in WOODLAND, WOODPASTURE or HEDGEROWS.

**Green house**, see MARKET HOUSE.

**Green lanes.** These are simply lanes which, for want of importance in recent centuries, have never been metalled and so consist of a ribbon of pasture bounded by walls or hedgerows. They served all kinds of functions; some are field-access lanes created at the times of PARLIAMENTARY ENCLOSURE or before, while others may be fragments of SALTWAYS, ROMAN ROADS, monastic rights of way, DROVE ROADS or PACK-HORSE ROADS. A few are derived from a band of grass which served to divide the OPEN FIELDS of neighbouring parishes, some of which are known today by a name like 'Mere Lane', from the Old English *gemeare*, 'a boundary'.

*Further reading*: Raistrick, A., *Green Roads in the Mid-Pennines*, Moorland, Buxton, 1978.

**Greens and ends.** These are HAMLETS and small VILLAGES that usually exist within a pattern of larger villages. In the East Midlands, many such settlements are known as 'Ends', as with Duck End, Church End and Park End ranged around Stevington village in Bedfordshire. In East Anglia similar settlements are frequently known

*Green lane*
A green lane representing an unsurfaced enclosure road near Bourne in Cambridgeshire.

as 'Greens' as with Pilson Green, Cargate Green, Upton Green, Tyegate Green and Town Green near South Walsham in Norfolk.

Very little is known or written about the origins of such settlements. It would, according to the old conventions, have been argued that these places are 'secondary settlements' which have been budded off from expanding older villages. Equally, and possibly more convincingly, it can be argued that they represent relics of an ancient and looser settlement pattern which pre-dated the era of the concentrated or 'nucleated' village. Archaeology has yielded a small amount of evidence to support each contention. Presumably the Greens at least were associated with settlement beside a small pasture or green. The nucleation of settlement in the centuries on both sides of the Norman Conquest must have led to a desertion of farmsteads and hamlets, though the medieval shortage of pasture and meadow could have encouraged a reverse movement away from larger settlements to small commons.

*Further reading*: Warner, P., *Greens, Commons and Clayland Colonization: the origins and development of Green-side Settlement in East Suffolk*, Department of English Local History Occasional Papers, 4th series 2, Leicester University Press, 1987.

**Grist**. The fee or multure paid in kind to a miller for grinding grain.

**Grotto**. An artificial cave or an unusual building created for fanciful purposes, often as abodes for real or imaginary hermits. They were often associated with LANDSCAPE PARKS, and at Fonthill and some other parks the hermit was placed on the estate payroll. See also FOLLIES.

**Group farm**, see RUNRIG.

**Grove**. This seems to derive from different Old English words signifying a thicket or a copse and there is a possibility that one of the derivations was associated with woods that were ringed by woodbanks and ditches. 'Grove' names seem often to be related to districts with free-standing, managed woods in agricultural settings rather than to extensive woods where huntsmen might range widely. See also WOODLAND.

**Guildhalls**. Guildhalls are normally associated with the urban craft guilds of the Middle Ages, but examples of various kinds can be found in villages. Sometimes, their presence indicates the failure of a medieval town to grow and prosper, and one of the finest of surviving guildhalls is at Thaxted in Essex, built around 1420 for the town's guild of cutlers, with an open trading area at ground-floor level and guild meeting rooms above. Others reflect the prosperity of local farming, and the fourteenth-century Court House at Long Crendon in Buckinghamshire has a spacious upper chamber which served as a staplehall, the place where the locally produced wool was stored prior to marketing. Other guildhalls had only a local significance, being used by guilds or friendly societies associated with the parish church, like the splendid late-medieval example at Whittlesford in Cambridgeshire. See also MARKET HOUSE.

**Gullet**. In Scotland, a water channel.

**Gypsey, Gypsey Race, Levant, Nailbourne**. A dry valley, often cut in chalk, which contains a stream at times when the watertable is high. The Gypsey Race in the Yorkshire Wolds is an example. See also COMBE.

# H

**Haaf**. In Scotland, a deep-sea fishing ground where 'haafing' or 'haaf fishing' was practised from haaf boats.

**Hafod**, see SHIELING.

**Hag**. An archaic term for a wood, sometimes a hag-wood or division of a medieval coppiced wood, though in Scotland 'hag', 'hagg' or 'hack' can also signify unkempt, uneven and 'moorish' ground. A 'hagger' was employed to cut trees or brushwood, often with a hatchet. Sometimes, the cutting was done 'haggerty-tagg-like' or in an uneven manner.

**Hag-yard**. A coppiced wood cut by a hagger or 'hag-man'.

**Ha-ha**. This is a wall with its top at ground level and its base in a deep ditch. The ha-ha was constructed between a garden and the park or countryside beyond to deprive livestock and deer of access to the home garden or forecourt while allowing unimpeded views across the landscape. Ha-has date from the start of the eighteenth century onwards and were originally referred to as 'fosses' or 'sunk fences'. The peculiar name is said to derive from a French interjection, a warning to stop, or take care, which is directed at any trespassing herbivores. An alternative and perhaps more credible interpretation sees the word as descending from the Old English 'hedge' word, *haya*, while another interpretation suggests that the name comes from the exclamation of surprise vented by those who accidentally fell into the trench. See also PARKLAND, DEVALL.

*Further reading*: Williamson, T., *Polite Landscapes*, Alan Sutton, Stroud, 1995.

**Haigh**. In Northern Britain, a very steep bank.

**Hain**. A Lowland Scottish word signifying a haven and sometimes used to describe the protection of a piece of land, like a hay meadow, by a protecting HEDGEROW or DEAD HEDGE. 'Haining time' was the period when livestock were excluded from the ploughlands and meadows.

**Hair stane**. In Scotland, a BOUNDARY STONE.

**Half-timbered houses**, see TIMBER-FRAMING.

**Hall**. Today the word 'hall' is associated with, amongst other things, the home of the local squire and the entrance lobby of the modern house. But for many centuries, the hall was the most important room (sometimes the only room) in dwellings at every level in the social spectrum of housing from the castle to the hovel. Dark Age epics like *Beowulf* reveal that the lord's hall was already established as the social, administrative and domestic focus of his life and was also the centre of communal affairs. Although no Saxon halls still stand, Norman applications of the hall theme are preserved in a few surviving stone-built 'first-floor halls'. Examples endure in rural locations at places like Boothby Pagnall in Lincolnshire and Burton Agnes in Humberside, as well as in urban expressions of the design in towns like Lincoln and Bury St Edmunds. In these designs the hall, which was the main reception, business and living room, was placed at first-floor level above a vaulted undercroft that was used for storage. Access to the hall was normally obtained via an external stone staircase, while a small private parlour or 'solar' shared a portion of the first-floor level with the hall.

The Norman first-floor hall design was echoed in many castles, and a version resurfaced much later in the BASTLES of the Anglo-Scottish borders. Most medieval dwellings were constructed in TIMBER-FRAMING, and

*Hall*
The hall at Stokesay Castle in Shropshire. Built by Laurence de Ludlow in the mid-thirteenth century, this is one of the best surviving examples of a medieval open hall.

The vaulted undercroft of Burton Agnes Old Hall dates from around 1170 and would have been used for storage.

throughout the period the open hall remained the principal component of the house. In the 'aisled hall' the roof was supported both by the outer walls of the house and by two rows of internal posts which divided the interior of the dwelling in the manner of the stone piers which define the side-aisles in a church. This form of construction allowed houses a greater breadth; width was limited by the length of available roof-truss timbers, and the carrying of the trusses on internal aisle-posts permitted extra space, represented by the flanking aisles, to be obtained below. Aisled halls appear to have been associated with the nobility in the twelfth century, but by the fourteenth century smaller versions of the design were commonly adopted as the homes of people of a much lower status. Around a hundred examples are known to

survive, mostly much altered, and medieval aisled halls can often be recognised at a distance by their large roofs extending downwards to low outer walls.

The hall had its domestic uses, but was essentially a public rather than a private living room. It was a place for feasting and socialising, and also served as an office and focus for business, while in the case of the manor houses it was also a courtroom and estate headquarters. On MANORS that were seldom visited by their owners, the manor house might consist solely of a single hall chamber. In medieval times there was a greater emphasis on public activities, and so the hall component of the house maintained its pre-eminence. But as the period progressed, so more private and specialised rooms were required – private bedrooms and parlours, rooms for storage, brewing and dairying, and in the greater houses, accommodation for servants. The additional rooms could be obtained by lengthening the house or providing cross-wings. The addition of cross-wings gave rise to a variety of hall-and-cross-wing houses, the construction of one cross-wing producing 'L'- or 'T'-shaped plans, the building of two cross-wings giving an 'H'-shaped plan, while in some localities houses were built with three cross-wings, to produce an 'E'-shaped layout.

In the 'Wealden house', a design associated with the Weald of Kent, but also found in East Anglia, most south-eastern localities and places as far afield as York, the hall, open to the rafters in characteristic medieval fashion, was flanked at each end by two-storey bays, one bay containing service rooms at the ground-floor level, the other accommodating private parlours at this level. The upper storeys of the two flanking bays were 'jettied', projecting outwards from the front of the house, though a single roofspan covered the entire building. Hall houses of the Wealden type appear to have developed in the late fourteenth century as successors to aisled halls. They continued to be built in the sixteenth century, but as they evolved, so the ratio of space devoted to 'private' chambers as opposed to the 'public' space of the hall increased. This reflected the gradual decline in the importance of the hall and the drift towards buildings composed of numerous specialised rooms adapted to the convenience of family life rather than public affairs. See also GREAT REBUILDING, TIMBER-FRAMING.

*Further reading*: Johnson, M., *Housing Culture*, UCL Press, London, 1993.

Mercer, Eric, *English Vernacular Houses*, Her Majesty's Stationery Office, 1975.

Wood, Margaret, *The English Medieval House*, Ferodale, 1981.

**Halstead**. A fairly common place-name which generally indicates the location of an early MANOR house or feudal HALL.

**Hamlet**. There is really no standardised way of discriminating between hamlets and small VILLAGES, though hamlets tend to contain less than a dozen dwellings and are usually deprived of public buildings like churches. Meanwhile, a hamlet is, of course, larger than a single FARMSTEAD. While many villages result from the amalgamation of neighbouring hamlets, the hamlet can not simply be regarded as a less-favoured settlement which has failed to make the village grade, for in several parts of Britain, like Cornwall and Cumbria, hamlets are the principal components of the rural settlement pattern and villages are few and far between. Indeed, hamlets were numerous throughout Britain in ancient times and villages only gained their ascendancy over the areas where they are now plentiful – most notably the English Midlands – during the latter part of the Saxon period. In some other areas, like the margins of the uplands of northern England, nucleation continued through the Middle Ages and into the Industrial Revolution.

Excavations have explored different hamlets ranging in age from the Neolithic to the modern eras. As settlements, most of the ancient places explored seem to have been ephemeral, being occupied only for a few decades or centuries before their occupants drifted to settle on a new site, probably at a place not very far away. Although it would be virtually impossible to prove the claim, it seems very likely that most of these hamlets were the abodes of an extended family comprising the dwellings of the local patriarch, his wife and children, and those of a few brothers, cousins and uncles.

While the prehistoric hamlets do seem to have

*Hamlet*
Watendlath in Cumbria has its small in-field on low ground beside the tarn and below the open fell grazings.

been rather short-lived and footloose places, it is also likely that many of our surviving hamlets have pedigrees which are longer than those of almost all villages, and which may extend back to Roman or even earlier times. It was commonly assumed that hamlets originated as 'secondary settlements' which were budded off from swollen villages during the phase of rapid growth in the first half of the Middle Ages. As a general rule this may be unlikely: many small settlements only had their names recorded in documents in the twelfth and thirteenth centuries but by this time they could have been quite venerable. There must be hundreds of hamlets which have remained doggedly stable, supporting just about as many families now as they did in medieval, Saxon or even Roman times. It is known that there were others that merged or expanded to become villages, and also many which just faded away. The relics of some of these 'failures' can be seen today. Hound Tor, close to the imposing tor of this name on Dartmoor is one, an irregular cluster of three or four farmsteads with subsidiary cottages, barns, paddocks and yards that withered away during the later medieval centuries. Lettaford hamlet, North Bovey, Devon, is another good example. There were also numerous hamlets which are now represented by a solitary farmstead. Plenty of Welsh farmsteads include the word *hendref* in their names, denoting an old settlement, and this will frequently reflect the fact that formerly the site was home not to a single farming family, but to a little agricultural community. (The word '*trev*' is another common indicator of a hamlet in Wales). Equally the development of a farmstead with a few adjacent cottages to house farmworkers may be an evolution from a hamlet which does not represent a particularly drastic change.

The fruits of recent research suggest that when we survey a countryside stippled with hamlets we are granted a glimpse of the ancient traditions of settlement in Britain – a dispersed pattern of occupation which pre-dates the advances made by the village in some but not all

lowland regions. Village patterns were favoured in areas where late Saxon and medieval OPEN-FIELD FARMING could be introduced, where later re-organisations of the agricultural landscape drew tenants together and where industrialisation provided concentrated employment opportunities. In other respects the hamlet lifestyle was neither inferior nor superior to that of the village – just different, and older. See also ANCIENT AND PLANNED COUNTRY-SIDE, CLACHAN, GREENS AND ENDS, VILLAGE.

*Further reading:* Aston, M., *Interpreting the Landscape,* Batsford, 1985.
Lewis, C., Mitchell-Fox, P. and Dyer, C., *Village, Hamlet and Field,* Windgather, Macclesfield, 2001.
Roberts, B. K. and Wrathmell, S., 'Dispersed Settlement in England: A National View' in Everson, P. and Williamson, T. (eds), *The Archaeology of Landscape,* Manchester University Press, 1998.

**Hammer pond**, see POND.

**Hanger**. A wood on steeply sloping ground, from the Old English '*hangra*'. See also WOODLAND, DOWNLAND.

**Harepath, herepath**. A road associated with the movement of Anglo Saxon armies, particularly in Wessex. It is unlikely, indeed, impossible that a *Here-paeth* would serve only this purpose, while not all herepaths may be genuinely ancient routeways. See also ANCIENT TRACKWAYS, ROMAN ROADS, MEDIEVAL ROADS.

**Hauch, haugh**. In Scotland, floodplain land beside a river.

**Hay barn**, see BARN, HELM.

**Head dyke, headgarth**. In the northern areas of upland farming, the head dyke was a prominent DRYSTONE WALL or earthwork which marked the boundary between farmland, whether that of a community or of a FARM, and the open COMMONS of the fell. It was therefore a highly significant component of the working countryside and was massive in form, consisting sometimes of a substantial bank of earth or rubble with a ditch on the side of the un-enclosed common, a bank revetted in stone or a boulder-built wall. In spring, often on St Helen's Day (3 May), cattle were driven out from the lower grazings and through the head dyke to pasture on the fell. Some were returned to graze the mown meadows and stubble of the AFTERMATH at 'foggage' or 'edish' time and the remainder returning in the autumn, sometimes at Martinmas (11 November). The practice of having an open season, when the livestock of the community could range freely, and a closed one, when they were confined to the fell, must go back to the prehistoric era. St Helen's Day or Ellenmas was directly related to the pagan festival of Beltane, when fires were lit to purify cattle bound for the high grazings. During the growing season, when crops were vulnerable, the stock-proof head dyke excluded the animals from the meadow grass and arable land below.

Many different names were used to describe head dykes in different localities, including acre dyke, ACREGARTH, ring garth, ring hedge, head garth and fell dyke. Head dykes sometimes survive as stock-proof barriers, but often they are neglected and many were overrun in the process of creating INTAKES, that advanced the enclosed land further upslope. See also INLAND.

*Further reading*: Winchester, J. L., *The Harvest of the Hills*, Edinburgh University Press, 2000.

**Headland, head or butt**. In the course of medieval ploughing small quantities of soil were carried forward by the plough, and when the plough was lifted and turned at the end of each strip and plough ridge in the RIDGE AND FURROW system, a small amount of soil was dropped. Often the ploughman would pause at the end of a furrow and scrape clay from the coulter and mouldboard to speed the progress of the plough. Eventually, substantial ridges of such soil would accumulate in these ways to form long smooth hummocks or headlands formed at the boundaries between two FURLONGS where the strips ran at right angles, while 'joints'

formed where strips on either side of the furlong boundary ran in similar directions. Sometimes an old headland can still be recognised as a swell in a field after recent ploughing has obliterated the other visible traces of ridge and furrow. In Scotland, the term 'hiddrick' meaning 'head ridge' was sometimes used.

**Heaf, heff, heft, lairing place, lyring**. Sheep have territorial characteristics and an established flock becomes bound to a particular locality or heaf on a fell, an area that has become familiar as a secure place for grazing and sleeping. Within an expanse of upland, different flocks are linked to different lairing places and this natural phenomenon aids the shepherd and reduces the need for fencing. Each farmstead in such a hill farming area has its own track or OUT RAKE leading to the heaf used by its flock and the sheep are said to be 'heft to the hill'. If strange sheep are introduced, they are likely to flee beyond the boundaries of the hill farm and be difficult to recover.

**Hearth tax**. A tax levied between 1662 and 1689 (1690 in Scotland, though paupers and occupants of small houses were exempt). The tax of 2 shillings (10p) per hearth in the home was levied twice a year. Records were compiled by the parish constable and passed on to the local Justices of the Peace and where they survive they give useful information of the numbers, ages and sizes of houses in a locality.

**Hedge and ditch rule**. This is a legal presumption, based on the case of Vowles *versus* Miller in 1810, that when two pieces of land are separated by a HEDGEROW/hedge bank and ditch then the precise location of the boundary is marked by the outer rim of the ditch lying furthest from the hedge. The origins of the practice probably go to a phase of ditch-making when it was agreed that a ditch could be dug provided that it did not trespass on neighbouring territory and that no earth from the ditch should be deposited on the neighbouring holding.

**Hedgerows**. Hedgerows have adorned the lowland countryside for a very long time indeed. It is highly probable that many of the lynchet banks of 'CELTIC' FIELDS originally carried hedgerows; and an Iron Age field-ditch excavated at West Heslerton in the Yorkshire Wolds appears to have been hedged on one side, while when a Roman fort was being built at Bar Hill on the Antonine Wall in Scotland brushwood consisting of hedge trimmings was used to fill in the existing ditches on the site. Moreover, surviving Roman fields in the Dengie peninsula of Essex are still bounded by living hedges. Saxon charters make numerous references to hedges, which are often mentioned as boundary features. The word derives from the Old English *haeg*, *hege* or *gehaeg*, which denote enclosures, and *haga*, perhaps a southern dialect form of these words, which denotes a hedge, while 'hedgerow' comes from *hegeræwe*.

Although 'dead hedges' – hedges made from posts and severed branches – were sometimes constructed in Dark Age and medieval times, living or 'quick' hedges were probably more common. Medieval OPEN FIELDS were, by definition, unhedged within, though their peripheries were often hedged, so that the name 'Hedge Field' was sometimes used to identify a particular great field. There is a myth, promoted by some modern farming interests, that our hedges date from the era of PARLIAMENTARY ENCLOSURE, though the majority of surviving hedges are of various earlier dates. In the medieval lowland countryside, hedges bounded the CLOSES grouped around the villages. They also often edged the privately owned paddocks and pastures, the ASSARTS and the fields extracted from the open ploughlands by the process of EARLY ENCLOSURE, and sometimes, the small woods or 'hays' and DEER PARKS as well. In the ANCIENT COUNTRYSIDE areas, unhedged open fields were few, small and relatively short-lived, and various observers commented on the 'woodland' nature of these thickly hedged countrysides. Numerous references to hedgerows occur in medieval documents, mainly in connection with legal disputes. In the thirteenth century, Gilbert de Gaunt sent his forester and a force of eighty men to destroy hedges planted in a submanor he owned in Swaledale because he claimed that the hedges were interfering with his hunting rights, while in 1512 Richard Burhall was fined at Great Canfield in Essex because his hedges were overhanging the King's highway.

During the era of Parliamentary Enclosure in the eighteenth and nineteenth centuries it has been estimated that around 200,000 miles (321,870 kilometres) of new hedges were planted. The recipients of enclosure awards were obliged to hedge (or wall, depending on the locality) the boundaries of their new holdings. Though some of these hedges would soon be removed, many of the allocated fields were subdivided by additional straight hedges to create smaller, more convenient units.

The Parliamentary Enclosure hedgerows were largely but not entirely composed of hawthorn bought in bulk from commercial nurseries, and their straight plans and initially homogenous composition contrasted with the curving lines and varied shrub species found in the older hedgerows. The concept of 'hedgerow dating' was developed by Dr Max Hooper, who produced a formula that, it appeared, would enable anyone able to recognise the different members of the hedgerow shrub community to determine the age of a selected hedge. In its popular simplified form the formula States: *Age of hedge = number of different species per 30 yards × 100*. Thus, in essence the theory claims that each hedge acquires an additional new shrub species every century, so that a three-species hedge will be around 500 years old, a six-species hedge will be around 600 years old, and so on.

The theory has been accepted uncritically by virtually all countryside writers, though it is riddled with deficiencies. Some of the weaknesses are of a logistic nature, and different 'hedgerow-daters' have been inconsistent in their choice of which species 'count' and which do not (some count bramble, honeysuckle and dewberry and

*Hedgerow*

A newly-laid hedge in Cambridgeshire, showing the 'pleachers' linked to their roots by a hinge of living wood, vertical posts and the woven 'heathering' or binding, linking the top of the posts.

some do not; some differentiate between the numerous different wild rose species and others do not; and so on). More serious is the clear-cut documentary evidence that the hedge-planters of old dug up seedlings and saplings from the woods and wastes, so that most hedges began their life as mixed rather than single-species plantings. In his *Boke of Husbandry* of 1554, John Fitzherbert advised his readers to 'gette thy quick-settes [living hedge plants] in the woode countreye and let theym be of whyte thorne and crabtree for they be beste, holye and hasell be good'. In fact there are several references to the planting of mixed hedges in medieval times – for example, in 1558 the lessee of a furlong at Holdenheck in West Yorkshire was allowed to exploit a wood for 'branches, brambles and thorns for making hedges'.

There are numerous other objections to the hedge-dating theory; one of the more important relates to hedgerow invasion, which can lead to a hedge losing rather than gaining species over time as stretches of hedge become monopolised by an invasive shrub. Elm is perhaps the most frequent invader, but one may find numerous stretches of hedgerow heavily invaded by blackthorn, holly and, where conditions are favourable, bird cherry. The hedges surrounding the Roman fields in Essex may be 800–900 years old, but they are very largely composed of elm. Most Parliamentary Enclosure hedgerows are dominated by hawthorn and contain early colonists like elder, bramble and wild roses, while older hedges do tend to have a more varied composition including species like field-maple, hazel, oak, ash, elm and gean. This does not validate hedgerow dating. Rather, it shows that different assemblages of plants develop at different stages in the life of a hedgerow. Species-counting has demonstrated only that counters disagree about what should be counted. To date the age of a hedge to within a few centuries one must resort to a careful study of the *form* of the field-pattern (does it have the reversed-S boundaries characteristic of [former] STRIPS?). All available map and documentary evidence must be examined in any serious attempt at establishing the age of a hedge and a field-pattern.

Different types of hedge are found in different parts of the country. In the West Country and parts of Wales hedges tend to be established upon earthen hedgebanks, whether they be the mainly nineteenth-century beech hedgebanks of Exmoor or the probably ancient and species-rich hedgebanks of Devon. Throughout most of England the hedge type adopted is a variation on the theme of the 'Midlands bullock hedge', which does not normally have a notable hedgebank but is often flanked by a ditch. When properly managed – and today very few hedges are properly managed – hedges are 'laid' every eight to twenty-five years. This involves removing moribund and misaligned growth as well as 'bad' hedging plants, notably elder. Further trimming reduces the hedge to a number of tall, vigorous, bushy-topped stems which are termed 'pleachers'. The pleachers are then cut almost through at their base by a sloping blow from a billhook, leaving an uncut hinge of living bark and cambium. The pleacher is then tipped over at an angle of less than 45°, and the slanting pleachers are held in position by posts hammered into the hedge-line at distances of 2–3 feet (0.6–0.9 metre). The hedge-laying operation is completed by twisting long, pliable wands of hazel or willow around the tops of the posts and pleachers to form a binding or 'heathering'. The newly laid hedge needs protection against browsing, although the bushy tips of the pleachers will provide some protection on one side of the hedge.

Laying rejuvenates a hedge and encourages dense and vigorous growth. The hedge will receive an annual trim, but repeated trimming to the same dimensions results in the formation of an outer scarred twiggy 'crust' and a deterioration of the growth in the dark interior of the hedge – hence the need for laying at periodic intervals. Hedges managed in this manner vary according to local conditions and traditions – for example, in the sheep-rearing areas of Yorkshire the farmers required a relatively low but very dense hedge, while in beef-raising areas, a robust bullock-proof barrier was needed. The Leicestershire 'bullfinch' (probably meaning 'bull fence') was a particularly tall, robust and well-ditched version of the Midlands bullock hedge. In Wales a variety of hedging traditions exist; the hedges may or may not be embanked but they usually exist as low dense sheep-hedges and dead wood is often incorporated into the heart of the hedge to preserve the barrier effect after laying. In the east of Ireland, 'DITCHES', each consisting of a hedge planted on a ditch-fronted bank of stones and earth, were characteristic of the improved farming of the eighteenth century, while hedges of a Scottish character were introduced by colonists in Ulster. One form had the hedge planted on a 'shelf' half-way up one face of the hedgebank, while in another, the shrubs of the hedgerow grew out through the stones of the revetment that guarded the vertical face of the bank.

Most hedges were deliberately planted, using plants gathered from the woods or bought from nurseries, depending on the period and local circumstances. A minority of hedges are 'spontaneous': they came into being as shrubs colonised the ground protected by an older dead hedge, fence, ruined building or wall. The exploration of abandoned railway lines or neglected verges will reveal just how quickly a spontaneous hedge can come into being. As well as providing invaluable refuges, breeding places and food-sources for wildlife, hedgerows constitute the single most important element in the traditional English scene. In the course of the last few decades one has witnessed a terrible era of hedgerow destruction, and this devastation continues largely unabated, as described in the entry on PRAIRIE FIELDS. When the hedge not grubbed out by a tractor, or battered out of existence by mechanical cutting, the death of a hedgerow can be traced through a series of stages. The abandonment of laying results in the development of gaps. These are widened by livestock and the gaps then stopped with rails and items of farm debris. Eventually, the shrub components of the hedge die, leaving the hedgerow trees standing in a hyphenated line. One by one these die, so that in its closing phases the old hedgerow is seen as an alignment of a few trees separated by wide gaps. See also FREETH.

*Further reading*: British Trust for Conservation Volunteers, *Hedging: A Practical Conservation Handbook*, British Trust for Conservation Volunteers, 1984.

Muir, R. and N., *Hedgerows: Their History and Wildlife*, Michael Joseph, 1987.

Pollard, E., Hooper, M. D. and Moore, N. W., *Hedges*, Collins New Naturalist Series, 1974.

Muir, R., 'Hedgerow Ecology and the Landscape Historian', *Naturalist* 120, 1995, pp. 115–18.

Muir, R., 'Hedgerow Dating: a Critique', *Naturalist* 121, 1996, pp. 59–64.

**Helm.** There are numerous references to helms in medieval documents and they appear to have been small barns or shelters, often built against field walls. Presumably, they were named because of their resemblance to an iron helm, with two-sided roofs sloping down from a crest or ridge.

**Hemmel.** A type of arcaded shelter for sheep found mainly in Northumberland. Sometimes the hemmel spans the boundary between two fields to allow animals from each enclosure to enjoy the shelter, though an internal division still marks the boundary between the two properties. See also BARN.

**Hemp.** Hemp was formerly cultivated to produce fibres used in the making of ropes and twine. The foliage was placed in foul-smelling hemp retting ponds to decay. These ponds must survive in some places as earthworks, while the fertile lands used in the cultivation of the crop may be preserved in place-names like Hemp Riggs, Hemplands, Hemp Yards, Hemp Pitts, Hemphaye and so on. Hemp was grown commercially in fields, but also in small crofts and gardens in association with cottage industries, but had gone by the mid-nineteenth century.

**Hendre.** Land in Wales where cattle and their owners would spend the winter until returning to the upland summer grazings.

**Hendref.** In Welsh place-name, an element indicating former settlement.

**Henges.** These Neolithic monuments are today usually less spectacular than STONE CIRCLES, but they are certainly no less mysterious. They appeared around 3500 BC and continued to be built for about a thousand years, perhaps superseding CAUSEWAYED ENCLOSURES as the foci of ritual landscapes in Britain. The henges consisted of circular or oval embankments, with the quarry ditches that yielded the bank-building material set *inside* the embankments. The banks could be breached by one or two causewayed entrances, and where a pair of opposed entrances was adopted the classic 'double banana' configuration resulted. The name 'henge' is as inappropriate as anyone might imagine, for it relates to the 'hanging' lintel stones at Stonehenge, a henge of atypical construction which was developed in stages to become a highly complicated stone circle. In 1986, the discovery of what may prove to be the earliest henge so far found was announced during excavations at Maxey Quarry near Peterborough. The remains consisted of three large concentric ditches and a circle of smaller pits. Various ritual offerings, including a beautifully polished ceremonial stone axe, red deer antlers and pottery were found in the pits. The complex ritual character of the henge was underlined in 1997 with the excavation on a site at Monkton up Wimborne in Dorset, where the outer perimeter was defined by a ring of fourteen unevenly-spaced pits which contained large blocks of chalk, while a fence screening the eastern entrance was preserved as post holes. In the interior there was a huge central pit dug into the solid chalk, with vertical sides and a level floor perhaps smoothed by feet. An oval multiple burial containing the bones of three children and a woman, the mother of one of the children, was inserted into its northern edge.

There is no doubt that henges were religious monuments – if only because it is hard to imagine that they could have served any more practical purpose. It is also clear that stone circles represented a development of the henge theme, as at Stonehenge, Avebury and various less celebrated sites. Perhaps the henge should be regarded as a ritual 'stage' defined by a ditch and surrounded by banks from which the 'congregation' could observe the ceremonies enacted below. For this writer, however, the greatest mystery relating to henges concerns the fact that some little-known sites have several small henges grouped close together and there are also the more famous large henge groupings. The four great henges of the Priddy Circles in Somerset, and the three Thornborough Circles close to the River Ure near Ripon are examples. The question that they pose is that if the henges are likened to medieval cathedrals, why did the Neolithic worshippers need several 'cathedrals' close together where one might have sufficed as a focus for ritual?

Henges vary enormously in size as well as in their degrees of preservation. Even where the remains are not ploughed out the shallow earthworks are sometimes hard to recognise. In other cases, the henges are still stupendous monuments. At Avebury the ditch of the henge, which encloses an area of 28.55 acres (11.5 hectares), is still impressive even though it is now half-filled with silts. Originally it was 30 feet (9 metres) deep, tapering to a flat floor 15 feet (4.6 metres) wide. Less striking today, but only because of the ravages of erosion, are the

other great Wessex henges of Durrington Walls and Marden in Wiltshire and Mount Pleasant in Dorset, which originally contained circular arrangements of great posts, perhaps the supports for gigantic ritual buildings. At Durrington, the original henge ditch was 23 feet (7 metres) deep and 42.5 feet (13 metres) wide. Henges which are visually more impressive today include Maumbury Rings in Dorset, used by the Romans as an amphitheatre, Mayburgh henge and King Arthur's Round Table henge, both near Penrith, and Figsbury Ring in Wiltshire, a HILLFORT which seems to have been converted from a henge.

*Further reading*: Green, M., *A Landscape Revealed*, Tempus, Stroud, 2000

**Hereschip**. In Scotland, the plundering of cattle by raiders sometimes known as 'herd-widdiefows' or Border rievers. Inter-clan raids were endemic in the Highlands, while Lowlanders feared incursions by clansmen. When one was detected, there might be a 'hot-trod' or pursuit with bugles and bloodhounds.

**Heriot**. Originating before the Norman Conquest as an obligation to return to his lord the fighting gear of a slain tenant, the custom of heriot was superseded by that of a lord's right to take the best beast belonging to a deceased tenant. In the course of the medieval period it evolved into a cash payment or ENTRY FINE. In Scotland, 'hereyeld' or 'herezeld' was the equivalent of heriot.

**Hermitage**. In the popular imagination the hermit exists as a solitary religious eccentric living a frugal existence on nuts and berries in some inhospitable and out-of-the-way place. The name comes from the Old French *ermite*. The eremetical element in early Christian life in the eastern Mediterranean area influenced Dark Age religious life in Britain. However, although there were some reclusive hermits in medieval England, most performed useful work as guides and hosts to travellers. In this capacity they would not live far from the beaten track but right beside it. Their dwellings or cells, which were normally insubstantial and unlikely to survive, were often sited at bridges or fords or where roads crossed wild and difficult country. Caves were occasionally occupied by hermits, and cliff chambers exist at Dale in Derbyshire, where there was a Norman monastery.

In general, however, old hermitages have not survived, though they are commemorated by 'Armitage' place-names, as well as by the surname. Armitage Bridge on the River Colne is an example. By the eighteenth century the figure of the hermit had entered the realms of popular whimsy, and 'hermitages' and GROTTOES were built in LANDSCAPE PARKS; at Foothill the former house was itself a kind of FOLLY and a hermit-in-residence was employed. In due course 'The Hermitage' was sometimes a romantic but unfounded choice for naming a house, so that false names arose which can cause confusion.

*Further reading*: Clay, R. M., *The Hermits and Anchorites of England*, Methuen, 1914.

**Heuch**. In Lowland Scots, a crag, cliff or steep ravine. Also a pit, mine shaft or worked quarry face.

**Hide, Carucate, Husbandland, Ploughland, Ploughgate**. An area of land deemed sufficient to support a family. Its actual size varied greatly from around 60 to 180 ACRES from region to region, partly depending on the quality of soil and partly upon local customs and usage, while in parts of Scotland it could be only around 20 acres.

**High cross**, see CROSSES.

**High Farming**. A form of farming associated with the estates of members of the landed gentry of early and mid-Victorian England who were keenly involved in 'progressive' farming. This involved introducing the mechanical innovations of engineers and the new designs for farm buildings that appeared in the architectural press. At first, it also involved recycling materials produced on the farm, such as the careful

conservation of manure and its application as a fertiliser or the exploitation of calcareous resources by MARLPITS. As high farming developed, however, there was much more reliance on the use of factory products, like earthenware drainage tiles and cast iron machines. On the farmstead, these changes saw a pattern of improved farming that was initially quite labour intensive being transformed by the introduction of increasing numbers of machines. Not only did considerable proportions of the labour force disappear but so too did their traditional practices and folk customs. The era also witnessed the disappearance of buildings in the vernacular forms, which were replaced by buildings in brick and slate in designs adapted to incorporate iron machines. Much thought was given to the siting of buildings as well as to their internal lay-outs, and emphasis was placed on complimentary features, so that, for example, straw from the threshing machine was readily on hand for use in the CREWYARDS. The arrangements of the different buildings was partly determined by the pattern of tramlines and the belts running from the engine house and providing power and transport to other parts of the farmyard. The movement, which effectively ended with the agricultural depression of the late 1870s, was severely damaged by the agricultural decline of the last quarter of the nineteenth century. See also MODEL FARM, FERME ORNÉE, HOME FARM.

*Further reading*: Williamson, T., *The Transformation of Rural England*, Exeter University Press, 2002.
Wade Martins, S., *The English Model Farm: Building the Agricultural Ideal*, Windgather Press, Macclesfield, 2002.

**Hill figures**. Hill figures, the white horses and other emblems carved into the steep scarp faces of the English chalklands, are eye-catching LANDMARKS which have attracted a wealth of myth and not a little nonsense. They are created quite easily by removing turf and the thin layer of subsoil to expose the pure white chalk beneath. However, once such a figure has been

created it needs to be maintained by regular scouring, otherwise turf will gradually recolonise the exposed areas and the figure will gradually disappear into the green hillside. Not all hill figures are cut in chalk; the Kilburn horse of 1857 in the west-facing scarp of the North York Moors is formed of clay and grey rubble, while the Mormond Stag, on a hill near Peterhead in north east Scotland, dating from about 1870, is composed of blocks of limestone and quartz. By accident or design, the hill figures often lie close to important prehistoric monuments. Accident applies in the case of the Kilburn horse, for the nearby HILLFORT was only identified at the end of the twentieth century. Despite the aura of mystery that has all too easily attached itself to hill figures the history of the majority is well documented and unremarkable. For example, the nine White Horses of Wiltshire (ten if one counts the almost obliterated Pewsey horse of

1785, but fewer if one discounts the now obliterated Devizes and Ham Hill horses) date from between 1778, when an older white horse at Westhury was completely remodelled, and 1937, when a new horse was cut at Pewsey. The great vogue for creating white horses in Wiltshire was concentrated in the period 1778–1863. They were cut by eccentrics or simply by landowners seeking to imitate the landmarks that their neighbours had created. For example, the creator of the Cherhill horse of 1780 was Dr Christopher Alsop of Calne, who was an admirer of the horse paintings of Stubbs. Other chalk-cut emblems are more recent still, including an aeroplane cut at Dover in 1909 to commemorate Blériot's first cross-Channel flight, various twentieth-century regimental badges and the Whipsnade lion of 1933. Of course, there comes a point where the cutting of hill figures is no longer an amiable eccentricity but a vandalisation of the countryside – the incongruous kiwi cut at Bulford in Wiltshire by New Zealand troops in 1918 might seem to some to belong to the latter category.

There remains, however, a residue of hill figures, both lost and extant, which cannot be precisely dated and whose mysteries have been exploited to the full, sometimes with scant regard for logic or fact. The craft of hill-figure making does have a reasonably long pedigree, for in medieval times Plymouth maintained the figure of a giant, 'Gogmagog', on Plymouth Hoe. An old audit-book of the corporation contains the entries: 1486 'It. pd. to Cotewyll for ye renewing of ye pyctur of Gogmagog a pon ye howe vij d.' and 1566–67 '20d new cutting the Gogmagog'. An idea of the frequency of the scouring needed to maintain a hill figure can be gained from the fact that similar entries occurred in 1500–1, 1529–30 and 1541–42. In the case of several other figures, scouring became an annual event and a good excuse for festivities afterwards in the village inn. In that of the Uffington Horse, scourings in the eighteenth and nineteenth centuries produced fully fledged fetes with races, competitions and generous prizes (in 1776 these included '*Cudgel playing* for a *gold laced Hat* and a pair of buckskin breeches, and *Wrestling* for a pair of silver Buckles and a pair of pumps').

Scouring and the occasional whimsical embellishment would gradually modify the outlines of a hill figure, and there is evidence that the famous Long Man of Wilmington in Sussex has become a more attenuated, El Greco-like figure, over the years. Though various claims have been made to the prehistoric, Roman or Saxon origins of this symmetrical figure of a man holding a staff upright in each hand, the fact remains that he does not seem to appear in any literature until 1779 – though at this date he was old enough to be in poor condition. Throughout the speculative literature on hill figures, authors have tended to vie with each other in their attempts to extend the antiquity of the various figures, using flimsy or even nonexistent evidence to support the conviction of their imaginations.

One of the most celebrated and eye-catching figures is the naked and explicit Cerne Abbas giant in Dorset. He has frequently been identified as the god Hercules and attributed to the Roman period (as well as to Saxon and Iron Age periods and personalities, also to the Bronze Age). Still, to believe such attributions one must also believe that, come war, plague, famine and changes in religion, there was always a local community ready to undertake a scouring every few years and thus preserve the figure. While the Giant is often said to be executed in the style of the Romano-British period, he escaped the attention of writers until 1694 and current serious thinking attributes him to the seventeenth century. The name Cerne Abbas means something like 'the stony river territory belonging to the monastery' – and it is hard to imagine that if the Giant pre-dated the Benedictine monastery and the village, both nearby, then the settlements at the foot of the Giant's hill would not have been Cerne Abbas but something meaning 'place or hill of the giant (or 'god')'. One interpretation, offered by O. Warner in the *Countryman*, suggested that the giant could have been engraved by Clubmen or Club Risers – associations of countrymen who banded together during the Civil War years of 1644–45 to protect their stock and crops against looting by the military. Clubmen were very active in this area, and it is not hard to imagine a band of look-outs passing their time on the hill by carving an image of a 'super Club-man' on the slopes. The local historian J. H. Bettey has shown that a detailed survey of all the Cerne Abbas lands in 1617 contains no mention of a hill figure. However, later a small spate of references comes and in his *History of Dorset* published in 1744, John Hutchins provided the interesting information that the Giant was made by Lord Holles's servants (Denzil Holles was MP for Dorchester and obtained the Cerne Abbas lands by marriage in 1641). But Hutchins added that: 'for some people who died not long before 1772, 80 or 90 years old, when young knew some of the same age that averred it was there beyond the memory of man'.

Probably the best claim to antiquity is that of the White Horse of Uffington on the Berkshire Downs, familiar to all travellers on the main railway line between Swindon and Reading and visible for distances of up to 15 miles (24 kilometres). The horse, if it is a horse, is presented in a very stylised manner. Its strongest claim to great antiquity derives from the fact that it loosely resembles horses represented on late Iron Age coins (actually it also has some resemblance to horses depicted on Swedish rock-carvings of the Bronze Age and to early Iron Age representations of horses in British metalwork). There is documentary evidence that a monk named Godrick held the manor of Spersholt during the abbacy of Aldelm at Ahingdon (1072–84) 'near the place which is commonly called White Horse Hill'. This would seem to take the existence of the Uffington White Horse back to about the time of the Norman Conquest – but how old was the horse then? It might be a representation of the Saxon white horse battle-standard or the emblem of the tribe or clan which occupied the adjacent HILLFORT. The answer is likely to remain a topic for serious debate and fanciful myth-making for many years to come, though Bettey, who helped to demolish the myth of the Cerne Abbas Giant, has accepted a Bronze Age date for the Uffington horse.

Ranking second in popularity as hillside graffiti after white horses are cross emblems, the two examples from the Chilterns, the Whiteleaf Cross and the Bledlow Cross, being the most interesting. The Bledlow Cross has doubled in size during the nineteenth century, showing how scouring can drastically alter the dimensions and appearance of a chalk-cut monument. It is

*Hill figure*
The Cerne Abbas giant has provoked debate as to whether it is of ancient or post-medieval date.

possible that the Whiteleaf Cross was carved by medieval monks, yet the first recorded mention of the cross does not come until 1742, and it is hard to believe that it had existed for at least two centuries without appearing in some commentary or document. The first account of the Bledlow Cross did not come until 1827, though the symbol was said already to be neglected at this time.

To summarise, it seems plain that most hill figures date from the eighteenth, nineteenth and twentieth centuries, and in many cases they are perfectly well documented. A few older chalk-cut figures like the Plymouth Gogmagog which once existed have disappeared as a result of a local loss of interest in scouring. The celebrated Cerne Abbas giant may be no older than the seventeenth century, and the only surviving hill figure which does seem to have a pre-Norman, indeed, a prehistoric origin is the genuinely mysterious Uffington Horse. See also DOWN-LAND.

*Further reading:* Marples, Morris, *White Horses and Other Hill Figures*, Alan Sutton, 1981.

**Hillforts (hill-forts).** Prehistoric hillforts provide many of the most celebrated landmarks in the British countryside. Most people are aware of their existence, many will have marvelled at the spectacular ramparts of hillforts like Maiden Castle or Badbury Rings in Dorset, and it is generally assumed that hillforts were the boltholes of threatened Iron Age tribesmen. The hillforts most certainly have performed this function, but the full role and purpose of the hillfort still presents us with many challenges, and the typical hillfort was certainly much more than a mere bolthole. Currently, speculation concerns the association of hillforts with ancient COMMONS, which were meeting places between different communities and as such, subjected to a special diplomacy, as well as being places where religious monuments developed. A model seems to be emerging in which field systems and associated agricultural settlements occupied the centre of the socio-economic stage, while hillforts

stood at the peripheries. There they served as places in which surplus agricultural production could be stored and re-allocated by their high-status occupants. As a particular hillfort rose in status, it could extend its dominance over neighbours, and these subordinate hillforts might then be abandoned. As hillforts extended their influence, so tribal territories may have developed.

Although hillforts are almost invariably ascribed to the Iron Age (*c.* 650 BC–AD 43) in the popular literature, defenceworks were built even in distant Neolithic times and the historical pedigree of the hillfort is certainly rooted in the Bronze Age. Neolithic defences at Hambledon Hill in Dorset were built on a massive scale around 3500 BC, long before the site was developed as a great Iron Age hillfort. Palisaded hilltop enclosures, whose functions are uncertain, appeared in the later part of the Neolithic period, and during the Bronze Age rather similar palisades were built in a number of defensible situations, and they could represent the first stages in the evolution of hillforts. During the Bronze Age hillforts of a more conventional type, with earthen ramparts fronted by ditches, also appeared, and examples have been excavated at Rams Hill on the Berkshire Downs and Norton Fitzwarren in Somerset. 'Mini' hillforts of compact construction also appeared in the Bronze Age, while around 800 BC a massive artificial fortified island was constructed at a site near Peterborough. It had a diameter of over 100 yards (100 metres) and was built of a latticework of timber fortified by a wooden palisade and stood about 100 yards from the shore of a shallow lake. The imposing Mam Tor hillfort in Derbyshire contains HUT CIRCLES of a Middle Bronze Age date, and if they are contemporary with the hillfort they provide further proof that the hillfort age began centuries before the Iron Age.

While recognising the existence of very early fortifications, in general it seems that numerous simple 'univallate' or rampart-and-ditch constructions appeared in Wessex in the earlier part of the Iron Age. Subsequently, some of these were abandoned, while a few were enlarged and elaborated. The increasing preoccupation with defence may be explained by reference to a marked deterioration in the British climate which became evident around 1300 BC; cooler summers and heavier rainfall were associated with the onset of blustery conditions. The changes will have driven communities from the upland plateaux and the more poorly drained lowlands, which had hitherto supported human occupation. In the lowlands, the intensification of farming and extension of the arable area could have supported higher population densities. Eventually, however, continuing population growth and the competition to control and retain farmland must have increased tensions and conflicts within and between communities. This in turn would have favoured the rise of aristocratic war leaders and protectors of communities and their lands.

New hillforts continued to erupt during the Iron Age. It was argued that hillforts were a

*Hillfort*
A section of the Iron Age ramparts at Bratton hillfort near Westbury in Wiltshire.

response to the new dimension in warfare represented by fearsome iron swords wielded by Iron Age 'invaders' of Britain, and that the forts were built and elaborated in direct response to the arrival of new waves of the supposed invaders. In fact, hillforts appeared long before the introduction of iron, and the actual archaeological evidence for large-scale continental invasions of Britain before the settlement of the Belgae in south-eastern England in the closing phases of the Iron Age is rather weak, apart from evidence of foreign settlement in East Yorkshire. Simon James has recently argued that the obsession with Celtic settlement and identity in Britain is a myth deriving from the rise of nationalism in the eighteenth century. He wrote that: 'Projecting Celtic identity back onto past societies which would neither have recognized nor understood it, obscures the real, complex history of the isles'. Instead most hillforts are best regarded as indigenous responses to indigenous threats – though after the Roman invasion of AD 43 a number of southern hillforts were fiercely defended against the invaders before being overwhelmed by the disciplined legions and their artillery arms.

While many hillforts are still prominent

*Hillfort*
The Iron Age hillfort on Herefordshire Beacon. The ramparts and ditches were designed to fortify the summit and the adjacent spurs. (CUCAP)

features of the landscape – in some parts of Wessex every summit and plateau seems to be nicked by ditches and girdled by ramparts – it is important to remember that the hillforts that we now explore are ruins. The sophistication of the fortifications is no longer apparent. Nor can we really appreciate the enormous effort expended in hillfort construction, while the surviving earthworks may not be a clear guide to the main function of a hillfort. The modest hillfort at Ladle Hill in Hampshire, an oval enclosure with a maximum diameter of about 900 feet (274 metres), was never completed, but provides an example of the immensity of the work embodied. Estimates show that the fortification of the site with a rampart standing about 12 feet (3.7 metres) tall would have occupied a labour force of 200 members for up to 115 days. One then may struggle to imagine the effort needed to construct monstrous defenceworks like Stanwick fort in North Yorkshire, where eventually an area of some 750 acres (304 hectares) was enclosed by massive rampart.

The constructional character of hillforts varied considerably. Where the bedrock was tough and unyielding, as in most parts of Wales and Scotland, the ditches which fronted the ramparts were usually shallow, rock-cut defences and the ramparts were composed of boulder-and-scree rubble which was sometimes stabilised by a timber framework. In more amenable settings, like the chalklands of Wessex, ditches in the bedrock could be excavated to depths of 20 feet (6 metres) and the rampart banks were often revetted with timber and crowned with palisades and walkways, with impressive timber gatehouses dominating the vulnerable entrances. Most of the greater hillforts experienced several phases of improvement and enlargement. Maiden Castle began as a 14-acre (5.6-hectare) enclosure with a single rampart and gradually acquired multiple ramparts which enclosed an area of 47 acres (19 hectares),the enclosure being furnished with elaborate gateway defences. Hillforts with two girdles are 'bivallate', and those with more than two girdles are 'multivallate'. The more elaborate bivallate and multivallate hillforts may be those that survived the rivalries with neighbours and survived to experience successive elaborations. Some hillforts had functional lives of seven or more centuries (though this period could be interrupted by episodes of neglect and abandonment, perhaps reflecting periods of ascendancy by rival strongholds). During such a long lifespan it was normal for improvements and repairs to be made to the defences, while ditches would need to be scoured of accumulating silt.

At Danebury in Hampshire, a ritual monument consisting of a circle of posts set in pits, one of which contained the body of a dog, was erected on the hilltop about 1000 BC. Around 500 BC the first hillfort was built with 'box' ramparts composed of earth and rubble excavated from the fronting ditch, the rampart being revetted to front and rear by timbers. Two entrances breached the rampart ring. About a century later, a settlement of circular dwellings that had become established inside the protective ramparts was redeveloped as regular rows of dwellings, barns and granaries which lined a neat pattern of streets, and a massive new double-gated entrance was built. Danebury now supported what might be termed a 'proto town', and this planned settlement endured for three centuries. The box rampart gradually decayed and was redeveloped as a 'dump rampart' enhanced with rubble obtained from the deepening of the fronting ditch, which then came to exist as a tapering trough, its base some 65 feet (20 metres) below the top of the rampart. Some time around 100 BC, a new programme of improvements was initiated. There must have been doubts about the security of the eastern entrance, for the banks of a new 'hornwork' which flanked and guarded the outer approaches to the gateway were built. Whatever the threat may have been which stimulated these improvements, it proved to be superior to the efforts of the Danebury folk, for the gate was burned and the fort deserted in the period 70–60 BC. The final development of Danebury was probably a response to the Roman invasion of AD 45, and the ditch was recut, the V-shaped cross-section being converted into a more fashionable flat-bottomed form, and the rubble from the excavations was used to heighten and steepen the ramparts. Very few hillforts have experienced a thorough, modern excavation such as Prof. Cunliffe accomplished at Danebury, but comparable sequences of redevelopment must have been the norm at most of the large and successful sites.

The hillfort was a stronghold and bolthole, and the Danebury example has revealed it in the role of a fortified 'proto town'. Danebury was by no means the only hillfort 'urbanised' in this manner. Croft Ambrey hillfort, near Hereford, had its interior packed with barrack-like buildings and granaries set out along neat streets; Hod Hill fort in Dorset had its 54-acre (22-hectare) interior filled with a less disciplined arrangement of circular dwellings. One of these dwellings stood in a separate compound, and excavators found that the Roman invaders had fired eleven iron ballista (artillery) bolts at what they presumed to have been the chieftain's dwelling. Tre'r Ceiri hillfort on the Lleyn peninsula of North Wales is the best preserved of the Iron Age fortified towns, displaying traces of over 150 stone houses, the use of stone rubble as a building material and the survival of occupation here during the Roman period explaining the preservation of many relics of hillfort life.

It has been estimated that some 1420 hillforts are known in the area of Britain to the south of Hadrian's Wall and a further 1100 examples exist to the north of the wall. The variation in size, construction, situation and age is considerable. Some examples reveal no evidence of dwellings; some contained house clusters of varying sizes; and a few, like those mentioned, clearly existed as hill towns – provided that one adopt a flexible definition of the word 'town'. So the hillforts could exist as defended refuges for people and livestock that were occupied only in times of trouble or they could be permanently occupied defensive settlements. The larger examples were almost certainly tribal or clan capitals of some kind, but we still do not fully understand the role of the greater hillforts in Iron Age society. Like the CAUSEWAYED ENCLOSURES they must have served as 'central places' and could have been the venues of markets or fairs. A most credible interpretation also sees the hillforts as 'redistribution centres', places where the produce of the surrounding territory was brought for redistribution among members of the tribe, clan or community with the distribution of largesse perhaps helping to bolster the standing of the chieftain. They seem to be the most convincing of possible candidates as the abodes of the Iron Age martial elite, though marked differences in the items of material culture excavated at hillforts and other settlements are not apparent. The interpretation of hillforts as great granaries controlled by the local or regional aristocracies is most appealing when applied to Wessex, though hillforts were very numerous in parts of Wales where little grain can have been grown.

As the Roman legions conquered southern England many hillforts were unsuccessfully defended by the indigenous people, and at Maiden Castle a war grave containing the mutilated bodies of British men and women was thought to have been discovered just outside the main gateway. During the Roman occupation, hillforts that were considered as threats to security were evacuated, but in remote places, hillfort life lingered on. Many hillforts experienced their last military uses when they were hastily refurbished to cope with the turmoils of Dark Age warfare. For example, around AD 500 the ancient hillfort at South Cadbury was refortified, as was Cisbury hillfort in West Sussex, while in Cornwall, Castle Dore seems to have become the capital of Cynfawr (the father of the legendary Tristan), who built his great hall inside the Iron Age ramparts. But such Dark Age activity was sporadic and localised. The hillforts never again recovered the ascendancy over the countryside which had been such an important feature of Iron Age life. See also PROMONTORY FORT, VITRIFIED FORT.

*Further reading:* Hogg, A. H. A., *Hill-Forts of Britain*, Hart-Davis, MacGibbon, 1975.

**Hilltop Church**, see CHURCH DEDICATIONS.

**Historical geography**. This is said to be the human geography of the past. It is concerned with reconstructing past landscapes, though it also has various other concerns. In contrast with landscape history and landscape archaeology, historical geography appears to place less emphasis on empirical study and much less on fieldwork of the kind undertaken by landscape archaeologists. The perspective tends to be more theoretical and more 'academic'. However, it is difficult to generalise, for just as some historians, like W. G. Hoskins and M. W. Beresford, were intensely interested in field investigation, so several historical geographers are active and capable landscape archaeologists.

*Further reading*: Butlin, R. A., *Historical Geography*, Edward Arnold, London, 1993.

**Holloway or hollow way, howegait**. These are disused or largely abandoned routeways which, before their abandonment, were engraved into the landscape by the regular passage of feet, hoofs and wheels. Holloways are usually seen as long troughs in the fieldscape and can result from the discarding of an old route, like a PACK-HORSE ROAD, or its replacement by a TURNPIKE or ENCLOSURE ROAD. They are a feature of deserted village sites and can also be seen in the vast lawns of landscaped PARKLAND where the former settlements and routeways were evicted from the scene. Many of our living lanes are also hollowed, with the gradual process of deepening continuing until the arrival of the Tarmac age. When cut into soft rocks on convex hillsides these old lanes can be incised to

depths of 10–12 feet (3–4 metres) below the adjacent fields. See also MULTIPLE TRACKS. Holloways often survive in truncated or hyphenated form, with some sections having been ploughed-out or infilled by farmers and builders. One may then seek to project and extrapolate from the surviving sections in order to deduce their probable destinations – possibly discovering deserted settlements in the process. In the case of older holloways, any roadside hedges are likely to have perished with the passage of time, but sometimes some of the hedgerow pollards will still endure.

**Holm**. An Old Norse term signifying an island or damp river floodplain. It is applied to the small islands in the Shetlands archipelago and river islands elsewhere in Scotland.

**Holy wells**. Holy wells exist in their thousands in Britain, although it is seldom clear why a particular well was considered to be sacred. In 1893, R. S. Hope counted sixty-seven holy wells in Yorkshire and forty in Cornwall, but greatly underestimated the true frequency of holy wells, and a later survey of Wales by Francis Jones

*Holloway or hollow way*
An old packhorse road in Nidderdale.

*Holy well*
A medieval well house or bapistry covers the Dupath holy well in Cornwall.

identified 1179 examples in the principality, while Scotland is thought to have about 600 holy wells. Wells, springs and water-bodies seem to have been worshipped by Iron Age communities in Britain, where they must have competed for attention with sacred groves, other topographical features and mythical gods – for the Iron Age assemblage of sacred objects was a broad one. Holy wells and wishing wells were also associated with some Roman religious cults, and the well sacred to the goddess Coventina at Carrawburgh, beside Hadrian's Wall, has yielded more than 16,000 coins and other votive offerings, ranging from pearls to shoes. Even so, wells do not always seem to have had a part to play in pagan Saxon religious belief.

Nevertheless, legends relating to the sanctity of various holy wells must have survived into the Christian conversion period, when numerous efforts were made to wrest the patronage of a well from some dark pagan deity and substitute a Christian saint. However, the Christian legends associated with holy wells are often transparent, and pagan concerns with the letting of blood and the reincarnation of ritual victims may show through the mask of Christianity. Saints who commandeered a good number of holy wells include Anne, Agnes and Helen. St Helen was probably a convenient substitute for the Celtic goddess Elen, while Anne could supersede the Celtic child-devouring goddess Annis. The commandeering of a pagan site could involve considerable inconvenience. The original church at Ripley, North Yorkshire, overlooked a meander of the river Nidd and was physically bracketed by springs, which saturated the narrow river terrace shelf on which the church was perched. The site was considered sacred but in practical terms, it was atrocious and a ramp was needed to ascend to the graveyard on the level surface above.

The physical appearance of a holy well can vary enormously. It may exist as a veritable swamp overhung by trees and ivy, as with the celebrated St Madron's well in Cornwall, or be a spring issuing from a churchyard wall, as at Stevington in Bedfordshire. It may be covered by a baptistry or well-house, like the Dupath well in Cornwall; or by a small chapel, as at Holybourne in Hampshire; or by an important church, as with St Winifred's well, Holywell in Clwyd. During the Middle Ages, certain favoured wells became the destinations of pilgrimages, some of the wells being associated with cures for specific ailments. St Dwynwen's well on Anglesey was thought to cure lovesickness, St Cynhafel's well near Denbigh cured warts, and the Stevington well eased afflictions of the eyes. Faith and interest in holy wells tended to decline after the Reformation, though some wells are still venerated. In Derbyshire the 'well dressing' of five wells at Tissington village, whereby the wells are decorated with flowers, moss and other oddments pressed into panels of clay, dates back to at least the eighteenth century and it has been imitated at several neighbouring villages. Hundreds of other holy wells are gradually losing whatever celebrity they may once have enjoyed as their legends fade into obscurity. However, the ancient holy wells have left a rich legacy of placenames and surnames, like Helliwell, Helen Hill, Holwell, Holywell, Holybourne, and so on.

**Home farm.** The farm on an estate that was often worked directly for the lords rather than being leased for tenants. Such farms could originate during the consolidation of DEMESNE STRIPS, while in the post-medieval period the home farm might be established beside or in sight of the mansion. When operated as a MODEL FARM or a FERME ORNÉE the home farm could be a hub for the dissemination of innovations around the estate and locality. In Scotland the place-name 'MAINS' often refers to the home farm on an estate.

**Homestead moat,** see MOAT.

**Hope.** A word that denotes a side- or tributary valley in northern Britain.

**Hop-kiln,** see OAST-HOUSE.

**House platform.** House platforms are discernible at relatively well-preserved deserted settlement sites and constitute the final visible stage in the decay of a homestead. In the most obvious cases it may be possible to recognise the upstanding outlines of rectangular walls and the gap in one of them which was the doorway. Where erosion or the pillaging of building materials has gone further, the house platform normally only exists as a fairly level shelf. Careful inspection may reveal the positions of one or more corners, thus confirming a house platform interpretation.

Naturally, a cluster of house platforms signifies a deserted village or hamlet, where other features, like HOLLOWAYS, should also be apparent, while a solitary platform may denote a former cottage or farmstead. These features will only survive in permanent pasture and are easily rendered invisible by ploughing. Nettles, which flourish in the phosphate-rich soil of formerly inhabited places, can sometimes indicate a house platform from a distance, before the earthworks become visible. In pasture, tapping and gentle probing with a metal spike may reveal overgrown floors of flags or rubble lying a few inches below the surface.

**Howe.** A hollow, valley, glen or depression, sometimes flat ground, a plain.

**Hundred (wapentake).** The hundred was an administrative division of the shire that emerged in the tenth century. It supported two chief officers: the bailiff, who served writs on behalf of the sheriff of the shire, and the constable, who was responsible for the pursuit of criminals. The hundred had a court which met every four weeks, and the jury of the hundred could be empanelled to provide the state with information on local affairs and conditions. In Yorkshire, Lincolnshire and Nottinghamshire, which had formed part of Danelaw, the wapentake was the equivalent of the hundred, while Cumberland, Westmorland, Durham and Northumberland were divided into wards. The Isle of Wight had 'liberties', while in Wales the equivalent was the cantrev. The hundred was said to have originated as the area of land possessed by a hundred free families. By the nineteenth century the hundreds had ceased to have any functional significance and were superseded by a pattern of Poor Law Unions and registration districts.

**Hunting lodge.** Many miles could be covered in the course of a medieval hunt, and within the depths of the forest a hunting lodge would offer shelter to a hunting party and accommodation for the various forest officials and servants of the hunt. Lodges were also built in some DEER

*Hunting lodge*
The Barden Tower in Wharfedale, developed from a medieval hunting lodge.

PARKS often in prominent positions, to serve as a working base for the parkers. Both lodges and park-keepers' houses were moated and might be provided with fishponds, and these features may endure as earthworks after the decay and collapse of the buildings. Few hunting lodges have endured, and a medieval lodge which survived in Epping Forest was sadly demolished in 1878 by appointed 'Conservators' of the Forest to save the costs of repair.

Hunting lodges have proved vulnerable to change, though Yorkshire contains a few relics of the more imposing types of lodge. The ruins of 'John of Gaunt's Castle' in Haverah Park, near Knaresborough, seem to be the remains of a square tower and gatehouse which stood on a square ditched platform, while the lodge known as 'Neville Castle' at Kirby Moorside consists only of a wall fragment stranded in a housing estate. By far the most interesting example is the Barden Tower in Wharfedale. This was the chief among six lodges that existed in the Barden forest hunting ground of the Cliffords of Skipton. Built originally as a hunting tower, the lodge was enlarged in 1485 and became the favoured home of the tenth Lord Clifford, 'the Shepherd Lord', who had previously forsaken

Skipton Castle to seek refuge from the dangers of the Wars of the Roses in Cumberland. After his death, the lodge decayed, but was repaired by Lady Anne Clifford in 1658–59. The so-called 'Queen Elizabeth's Hunting Lodge' in Epping Forest was actually built by her father as an observation post for watching ceremonial hunts. See also DEER PARK, FOREST.

**Hunting tower**, see DEER PARK.

**Hurst, hirst**. A wooded hill.

**Husband-toun**, see FARMSTEAD.

**Hut circles**. These are the relics of prehistoric dwellings. Most such houses were built to a circular plan, using either low walls of DRYSTONE WALLING, or timber-post and WATTLE-AND-DAUB construction. The choice of building materials depended partly upon the period concerned and partly upon the nature and building resources of the locality. Where stone was employed, the site of a house may still

*Hut circle*
One of many hut circles at Merrivale on Dartmoor. They are probably of Bronze Age date.

be represented by a circular arrangement of smallish boulders, and sometimes the upright slabs that formed the portals of the entrance can still be recognised. Whether walled in stone or in timber and mud, the houses had conical roofs of thatch or turf carried on rafters of poles which were, at least in the larger dwellings, supported by an inner ring of upright posts. Hut circles only survive in places that have escaped subsequent episodes of land clearance and ploughing, so that they are features of the British uplands, where they can be very numerous. It is not easy to go for a long walk on Dartmoor without stumbling across several examples, but hut circles are almost equally common in parts of Wales, Cornwall and the Pennines. Often, they are relics of the Bronze Age abandonment of the uplands when a worsening of the climate coupled with the effects of land exhaustion through cultivation and over-grazing led to the permanent desertion of many areas, like the southwestern moors. In such places any hut circles discovered are likely to be relics of the warmer and drier climates of the Early or Middle Bronze Age. Some hut circles are surprisingly old, and excavations near Holyhead, Anglesey, showed that the dwellings there dated back to the latter part of the Neolithic period rather than to the Iron Age. Hut circles can be found singly, in loose hamlet- or small village-sized groupings, or, as is often the case on Dartmoor, in tighter little groups lying inside circular or oval walled compounds. On Ordnance Survey maps the most prominent examples may be marked 'hut circles', though this is not consistently the case.

**Hythe.** Landing place beside a river or canal. See also LODE.

**Ice-house**. An ice-house may first be glimpsed as a puzzling hummock in the park or former park of a country mansion. Closer inspection will reveal a thick-walled brick vault, usually beneath a covering mound of clay and earth. The ice-house was an innovation adopted from France in the seventeenth century and was used for storing ice which could be used in the preparation of chilly sweets or iced drinks. Ice-houses were normally built in damp-free situations, often close to the lake or pond whose frozen crust provided the ice. This ice was then powdered and pounded to form a mass which was stored in a deep basin-like well inside the ice-house. Shelves or niches on the wall above were sometimes used for storing fresh vegetables in this primitive 'refrigerator'. Accessible examples include a pair of dome-shaped ice-houses set within their own ditch and built of brick covered in earth which stand in the park at Studley Royal in Yorkshire and were stocked with ice from the ornamental lake.

**Iconic landscapes**. Some landscapes – or rather, perceived landscapes – are so closely associated with the identity of a nation that they function as national icons. Examples of these landscapes are the flat tulip fields of the Netherlands and the fjord coastline of Norway. Some iconic landscapes are not typical of the national homeland in its entirety yet still function as national symbols, so that the semi-arid landscapes of canyons, mesas and buttes of the American south-west are much more iconic than the farmlands of the Mid West. Similarly, Scotland tends to be perceived in terms of the Highlands and Islands, with still lochs, heather-clad slopes and mist-hung peaks. In reality, such landscapes cover a minority of the territory and are home to a very small fraction of a population the majority of whose cultural

roots are more closely linked to Lowland Scots traditions. Equally, many English attitudes towards the native landscape have been conditioned by reactions against the urbanisation and industrialisation that launched the modern era and transformed national life. All manner of images and narratives contribute to the formation of perceptions of iconic landscapes: pictures on biscuit tins, advertising by tourist agencies, place-related fiction, place myths, TV dramas, postcards and so on. Strong and singular features, like tartan and Highland cattle, greatly assist the development of a distinctive iconic landscape. These factors may bolster the sense of national identity yet undermine the true cultural and topographical identities. In the process of exploiting iconic landscapes, distinctive character may be distorted and trivialised, as with the Cornish association with wreckers and smugglers' dens. Meanwhile, other landscapes, no less valid than the iconic ones, may be relatively undervalued. For example, the preoccupation with the landscapes of Scotland's Western Highlands distracts from the conservational significance of the coastal lowlands on the opposite side of the country, between Buchan and Fife. See also SITES OF MEMORY, CONTESTED LANDSCAPES.

*Further reading*: Matless, D., *Landscape and Englishness*, Reaktion Press, London, 1998.

**Improvements**. The Improvements were roughly the Scottish equivalent of the Agricultural Revolution in England. In some respects the tasks facing the improving landlord in Scotland were more challenging, for with generally poorer soils and climate, the potential gains could be more modest, while the poor quality of the road network increased the difficulties of improvement. On the other hand, the Scottish landlords were able to act more freely and could

*Improvement*

A typical countryside produced by Scottish Improvement, near Castle Fraser in Grampian, with dispersed farmsteads and consolidated tenancies replacing the old fermtouns and with plantations and shelter-belts in the distance.

attempt the enclosure of common MOORS and RUNRIG ploughlands without the need to obtain the sanction of an Act of Parliament.

In the barren Highlands, the harsh CLEARANCES were the norm, but in the more amenable plains, straths and low plateaux of the Lowlands and North East, the Improvements often had a more humanitarian dimension. The traditional system, involving runrig, CLACHANS or fermtouns and tacksmen was eradicated and replaced by new tenancy arrangements, land divisions and networks of rectangular enclosed fields, which could be hedged in the south or bounded by CONSUMPTION DYKES on the stonier lands. Normally, the enclosures were first introduced on the HOME or 'MAINS' FARM of the estate and then extended to improve the appearance of the grounds or 'policies' surrounding the ESTATE mansion.

The enclosure of moor and runrig land was accompanied by the rationalisation of the tenancies. Since the fermtouns had tended to support an excess of landworkers, only a select minority were offered new farms, but those that were fortunate enjoyed much longer 'tacks' or leases than had been previously available, and were therefore encouraged to improve their holdings. The terms of the lease would often demand ditching, dyking and draining operations, as well as the planting of SHELTER BELTS of nursery-grown trees, which were sometimes provided by the landlord. Other conventional introductions included the planting of root crops and efforts to improve the quality of livestock by developing the Ayrshire and Aberdeen Angus strains.

Many of the landlords concerned were absentees, dwelling in England, where they were exposed to the buoyant climate of agricultural innovation current there, and many of the latest ideas were relayed back to the 'factors' who had day-to-day charge of estate operations. Countless lowland countrysides were transformed by the Improvements of the eighteenth century; those that had existed as bleak treeless expanses of runrig cultivation rising to the edges of windswept moors were now partitioned into rectangular enclosures by hedgerows and walls, drained and diversified by the straight ribbons of shelter belts. Meanwhile, the squalid fermtouns were largely swept away and replaced by new patterns of solitary, stone-built tenant farmsteads, while 'Mains' place-names still marked the demesne land worked directly for the laird.

Enclosure in Scotland gave rise to strong local objections, just as in England. In Galloway peasant tenants known locally as 'levellers' opposed the fencing of land, arguing that it would deprive children of their role as herders of cattle. The surplus populations of the fermtouns were not always faced with eviction, and many landlords dredged the depth of their optimism in attempts to create new, planned villages offering opportunities of employment in fishing or manufacturing. Cuminestown in the North East was a mile-long chain of dwellings, built in countryside notorious for its former famines by the improving landlord, Cumine of Auchry, and was supported, for a while, by specially introduced linen industries. Fochabers was a village built to enhance the approaches of the castle of the fourth Duke of Gordon, New Leeds was another hopeful linen-making centre, Gardenstown and Port Errol were developed as fishing villages and New Mill was provided to accommodate poor weavers. It has been estimated that improving landlords in Scotland were responsible for the foundation of around 150 new villages between 1745 and 1845, most of them rigorously planned according to a long straight street-village plan or to a 'grid-iron' layout of rectangular blocks. Of the many new villages created by the ambitious improvers, some of them men with a genuine concern to improve the lot of their tenantry, few ever

amounted to very much, many have scarcely grown since their appearance and several did not even swell to fill their originally designated areas. But they did represent a genuine attempt to find an alternative to the Highland Clearances and they still do form important contributions to fascinating Scottish landscapes that often derive their essential personalities from the Improvements of the eighteenth century.

*Further reading*: Phillipson, N. T. and Mitchinson, R. (eds), *Scotland in the Age of Improvement: Essays in Scottish History in the Eighteenth Century*, Edinburgh University Press, 1970.

Munro, D., *Loch Leven and the River Leven, A Landscape Transformed*, The River Leven Trust, Markinch, 1994.

**Inbreak**. A portion of an INFIELD or ground newly ploughed from grazing land.

**In-by land**, see INFIELD-OUTFIELD.

**Inch**. An island or the floodplain of a watercourse.

**Inclosure**. A legal concept: inclosed land is privately owned rather than necessarily being fenced, walled or hedged.

**Infield-outfield cultivation**. This is a form of farming of considerable antiquity that has existed in a variety of different forms in different parts of Britain. It was probably used extensively in prehistoric Britain and may have been practised by Saxon settlers in these islands (though they will have inherited it from Romano-British farmers), and it was very widely operated in Scotland until the CLEARANCES of the eighteenth and nineteenth centuries (see RUNRIG). However, despite the assumption that infield-outfield farming has a very long history there seem to be no recognisable descriptions of this system of farming which date from before the fourteenth century – and this is puzzling. Whatever the variations employed – and the system could be operated at the level of the FARMSTEAD, HAMLET, CLACHAN or VILLAGE – the essence of the system involved keeping one ploughed field, the 'infield', in constant production through the generous application of manure. Meanwhile, the poorer-quality land of the extensive 'outfield' existed as pasture and patches of outfield land were periodically ploughed and cropped to exhaustion and then returned to pasture. The infield was commonly about one-fifth of the size of the outfield, while beyond the outfield there was usually an extensive area of moorland or rough pasture providing COMMON grazing in the summer. Infield-outfield farming may have been displaced from lower, richer lands by the adoption of OPEN-FIELD FARMING in the later Saxon period, though it persisted in the more marginal farming localities, where good-quality land was in short supply. In the richer areas the conversion to open-field farming may have been achieved by expanding the infield to the limits of the arable area and subdividing it to produce two, three or more open fields. See also HEAD DYKE.

*Further reading*: Foster, S. and Smout, T. C. (eds), *The History of Soils and Field Systems*, Scottish Cultural Press, Aberdeen, 1994.
Mercer, R. (ed.), *Farming Practice in British Prehistory*, Edinburgh University Press, 1981

**Inland**. This word is used in various parts of the country to describe land lying close to the FARMSTEAD, but it has a special relevance in the Lake District, where it describes a cluster of walled hay-meadows lying close to a farmstead, some of which are occasionally ploughed to grow root crops or oats. Beyond the inland are the pastures of the INTAKE, which meet the rough open grazing of the fell at a HEAD DYKE. Many Lakeland farms were established, along with their walled inlands, after the decay of monastic controls. Their founders were hardy yeomen known as 'statesmen' (that is, estate men) who did much to establish the outlines of the rural scene.

**Inning**, see INTAKE.

**Intake (encroachment)**. This is land enclosed from a COMMON, usually from its margins, and often without the consent of the other parties

concerned. Such encroachments were frequent in medieval times, when cultivators would often take ribbons of land from around the edge of a common. Sometimes the medieval intakes were temporary in nature and associated with short-term cultivation under an INFIELD-OUTFIELD system of farming. Fields created from breaking in new land in this way are sometimes associated with names like 'breck', 'brock' and 'brech', and the Breckland of the Norfolk-Suffolk border is a region named in this manner. Often, the making of intakes would be resisted by other users of the common. In 1292 the parson of Carlton in Lindrick, Nottinghamshire, complained to the King's Bench that the lord of the manor and six others had reaped his rye in a field called Parsones Breck. The lord claimed the land was his. The other men said that it was their common pasture. The parson said that it was church land. The evidence of the field-name argues that this was an intake from the common which the parson or his predecessors had made. The jury decided that the land was not the private property of any of the claimants:

> But is the common of the whole community of the said vill, and from old the custom of the vill was and still is that the lord of the vill and the parson and every free man of the vill may come to the said place on the morrow of Epiphany after sunrise with his plow and as many strips as he can cut with one furrow in each strip so many may he sow in the year, if he pleases, without asking licence, provided that he applies no compost …

Since the right to compost an intake required the consent of the community this custom seems to have been intended to allow temporary breaks, which would soon become infertile and revert to the common, but to control permanent intakes, which would require manuring. In this case, however, the parson had sown the land for fifteen consecutive years, so the court found in his favour.

Intaking came in many forms, but in the

*Intake*
Old intakes outlined by drystone walls in Swaledale.

more recent centuries, intakes tended to be permanent. In various parts of the Pennines lords of the manor often allowed the miners of the seventeenth, eighteenth and nineteenth centuries to build their COTTAGES on the edges of commons and enclose smallholdings to supplement their mining income, and place-names like Intake Lane are very frequent. Some of the intakes supported the pit-ponies and pack-horses associated with the mining operations. Grassington in Wharfedale became a lead mining centre, but its medieval intakes were used to grow light timber, the villagers being excluded from their lord's Grass Wood. The legal disputes associated with intaking continued after the Middle Ages, and in the Forest of Knaresborough the regulations governing intakes resembled those previously associated with ASSARTS. In 1595–96 it was decided that small intakes could be made if the intention to enclose was announced and not challenged at the Honour Court. Elected officials – a grave and a beadle – attempted to control unsanctioned intakes, but juries were generally sympathetic to small enclosures, many of their members probably having made similar intakes.

Today one will often see abandoned intakes in the northern and western uplands, with tumbled walls and bracken advancing on the pasture. But a modern form of intaking, sometimes heavily subsidised by the taxpayer, is evidenced by the enclosure, deep-ploughing and cultivation of MOORS to the scenic and ecological detriment of lovely areas like Exmoor and Dartmoor. See also COMMONS, HEAD DYKE, SQUATTER. In Scotland 'intaking' can also refer to the diversion of waters from a stream by a dam.

**Intercommoning.** This involved the sharing of an expanse of COMMON grazing, usually on hills but sometimes existing as marshland, by the farming communities of a number of surrounding VILLAGES, FARMS and HAMLETS. The practice could be deeply rooted in time, and an area bound together by intercommoning rights might represent a single ancient estate which subsequently became fragmented. In Norfolk, the parishes of Stoke Ferry, Wretton and Wereham had intercommoning rights on a marsh, and the parishes of Banham and Winfarthing shared a vast common of 1200 acres (486 hectares). Meanwhile, in Warwickshire, farmers living in the Avon valley between Warwick and Evesham intercommoned in an area of woodland lying several miles to the north of the river. When the tenants of two or more manors intercommoned the 'common of vicinage' might operate as a permissive right to allow the animals from one manor to stray on

to the land of another. The Statute of Westminster of 1285 allowed manorial lords to enclose commons where common rights were held by tenants of other manors. See also COMMONS, HEAD DYKE, SHIRE MOOR, STINTED COMMONS.

*Further reading*: Fleming, A., 'Prehistoric Landscapes and the Quest for Territorial Pattern' in Everson, P. and Williamson, T. (eds), *The Archaeology of Landscape*, Manchester University Press, 1998.

**Intoun.** In Scotland, the land adjacent to the FARMSTEAD. See also DOOR-LAND.

**Isolated churches.** An isolated church is always likely to raise more interesting challenges than one that stands more conventionally within a VILLAGE. If a church is isolated, this is either because it always had a solitary existence or because the dwellings that once accompanied it have subsequently disappeared. And so, when exploring an isolated church, one may begin by checking the surrounding area for traces of former settlement. If the land has existed as permanent pasture, then the EARTHWORKS of features like HOLLOWAYS and HOUSE PLATFORMS should betray the lost settlement; while if the land is arable, then FIELD-WALKING could produce concentrations of old pottery to reveal the former existence of a neighbouring community. If it is the church itself that has gone, its former presence may be indicated by a CHURCHYARD or KILLEEN, by archival sources, like old maps, or in place-names like Kirk Croft, Chapel Flatt, Kirkstead, and so on. Care must be used as such names, particularly if linked to land, like Kirkacre, could indicate part of a GLEBE rather than a building.

If the church has always been isolated, this could be because it is a very early foundation established not at a settlement but at a place with special, perhaps pagan, religious significance. It might be a church built to command a particularly inviting location, or maybe a church built in a locality that traditionally supported dispersed settlements rather than villages. One of the most

attractive churches in the first category is the ruined Norman building at Knowlton in Dorset, standing in the centre of one of a group of HENGES. The village which it served, long deserted, stood well away from the church, which was apparently sited to sanctify or exploit the religious associations of an ancient and mysterious place of worship. In the second category there is the ruined post-medieval hilltop chapel dedicated to St Michael de Monte which stands on the prominent landmark of How Hill, overlooking Fountains Abbey. Quite coincidentally it is close to the deserted village of Herleshow, destroyed by the monks of Fountains, but it occupied the hilltop both as a chapel and as an eye-catcher. In the third category there is the isolated church of Rivenhall in Essex, which lies in a locality of traditionally dispersed settlement and has been shown by excavation never to have had an associated village beside it.

It is probable that most isolated churches were formerly accompanied by villages. Obvious examples include the numerous churches that are stranded in parks as a result of the emparking of their village, as at Ickworth in Suffolk or Middleton Stoney in Oxfordshire. Frequently,

*Isolated church*
Knowlton Church in Dorset was always isolated from its village, which was deserted in medieval times. The church was built at the centre of a prehistoric henge monument.

the causes of the death of the village are not known, while at Castle Camps in Cambridgeshire, where the church stands alone amongst the earthworks of the Norman bailey defences, the village did not die but drifted away to a new location. The church building was most likely to survive the disappearance of its village if its building materials did not attract pillagers, as with many of the flint-built churches of Norfolk, or if it was used by worshippers from other localities – a factor which helped to preserve the church at Wharram Percy in the Yorkshire Wolds, where the church, now in decay, was used by the congregation of neighbouring Thixendale until they acquired their own church in 1870. Norfolk is particularly rich in isolated churches, the result of a process called common-edge drift.

*Further reading:* Williamson, T., *The Origins of Norfolk*, Manchester University Press, 1993.

# J

**Jack**. A Middle English word that often occurs in place-names relating to land that was vacant or unused.

**Jamb o' a hoose**. In Lowland Scots, a house so badly built that the wind could whistle through it.

**Jarness, jerniss**. In Northern Britain, a marshy place.

**Jig**. A word sometimes occurring in field names, that relates to gig-mills were teasels were used to raise the nap on cloth.

**Jigger Lane, Jagger Lane**. Lanes once used by jaggers or pack-horse traders with their teams of German *Jaeger* ponies. See also PACK-HORSE ROAD, PACK-HORSE BRIDGE.

# K

**Kailyard**. In Scotland, a kitchen or cottage garden.

**Kaim**. In Northern Britain, a ridge or terrace that is corrugated like the comb of a cock.

**Keavle**. The share in a common field that falls to one in a lottery. See DOLE.

**Keechan**. Small stream, beck or burn.

**Keith**. A bar on a northern river, preventing salmon from migrating further upstream.

**Keld**. In areas of Old Norse influence, like north-west England, a spring.

**Kelp**. The rods produced by the seaweed, *Fucus vesiculosus,* were gathered by coastal communities in both Scotland and Ireland and converted into fertiliser. Kelping involved gathering the weed at the shore, drying it and burning it in small kilns on the beaches. Iodine could also be extracted at the kilns and it was bought by Scottish merchants, who operated as far away as Connemara. In Ireland, rights of tenure included the adjacent strand as well as the land, and access to seaweed was particularly valued.

**Kerse**, see CARSE.

**Kill**. In Scotland, a kiln, often a grain-drying kiln, which had a 'kill-fuddie' or aperture in which fuel could be put, a 'kill-ee', or fireplace, a 'kill-pot' in which the grain for drying was kept, and so on. In place-names it could be confused with 'Kil-' deriving from the Gaelic rather than Lowland Scots and denoting the cell of a monk. In England 'kill' place-names usually refer to kilns, but usually ones associated with LIME-burning or brick-making.

**Killeen**. An isolated burial ground in Ireland, often in a circular or oval enclosure and perhaps originally serving a dispersed farming community. Sometimes, traces of stones marking graves and the ruins of an oratory may be detected. After their replacement by burial yards attached to churches, the corpses of unbaptised children and suicides might furtively be added to killeens. The dates of killeens, known as 'lisheens' in the north-west, could range from the conversion period right through to relatively modern times.

**Kindlie tenant**. A Scottish term and concept

relating to one whose ancestors have resided on the farm concerned for many generations and who therefore claims a hereditary right to retain the tenancy. His land is known as a 'kindlie possession'.

**Kippie**. In the north, a small hill.

**Kirk clachan, kirk toun**. A hamlet or village containing a church. See also CLACHAN.

**Kirkgate**. In Scotland, both the gate in the 'kirk dyke' leading to the churchyard and the road or track leading to a church. The track might also be known as a 'kirk wynd'.

**Kirk hole**. A grave.

**Kirklands**. The lands of the old GLEBE.

**Kirkshot**. Rights of fishing in a river beside or near a church that were attached to it.

**Knap**. A hillock, occasionally, the mound of a prehistoric burial.

**Knight's Fee/Service, Chivalry**. An estate sufficient to sustain a knight and his family for a year. It varied greatly in size, partly in relation to the productivity of the land, and could range between about 5 and 50 HIDES. The knight holding a knight's fee was required to provide military services for his feudal superior in return for his holding.

# L

**Lachter, lachter stead, lairach**. In Scotland, the site of a house, sometimes just the traces of its foundations.

**Ladder farm**. A planned farm holding in Ireland, with the farmstead normally placed at a roadside and straight-sided fields behind it. They derive from the work of the Congested Districts Board in the late nineteenth and early twentieth centuries, which dismantled the old CLACHAN and RUNDALE systems and encouraged more dispersed farmstead patterns, thinking the thatched clachans unhygenic. They were replaced by consolidated, STRIPED FARM holdings with replanned roads and geometrical enclosed and 'privatised' fields. Vernacular roofing tended to be replaced by roofs of slate or flags in the 6,000 rural houses and 4,000 outbuildings directly replaced by the CDB and the further 3,350 houses for which improvements were subsidised. A far-reaching re-modelling of the rural landscape across much of the west of Ireland was achieved, with landscapes governed by planning and ideas of social reform replacing the old organic, if run-down, vernacular landscapes.

**Lade**. Scottish equivalent of GOIT.

**Laithe, lathe**. A barn. See also LAITHE HOUSE.

**Laithe-house**. Laithe-houses can be seen in large numbers in the West Riding of Yorkshire and the Dales of the North Riding. Most date from the late eighteenth century and the early nineteenth century, though the oldest example of this type of vernacular FARMSTEAD yet discovered dates from 1650, while the youngest examples were built in the 1870s. The 'laithe' is a combined barn and byre and in the laithe-house it shares a roof with the domestic component of the house. In some cases dwelling and byre are linked by a door, while in other cases human and livestock spheres are kept entirely separate. In most of the larger laithe-houses a tall arched doorway was provided to give a laden hay-cart access to the barn, where the fodder could be stored in the hay-loft and fed to cattle in stalls in the byre below.

*Laithe-house*
A laithe-house in Coverdale, North Yorkshire.

Laithe-houses may have begun as the homes of relatively prosperous farmers, but in the course of time they became the farmsteads of typical tenants and smallholders of the Dales. They were generally built along hillsides amongst the fields of the farmstead, but quite frequently they can be seen lining the roadside in villages and hamlets. They are built of local gritstone or limestone and may be roofed in local flags or 'thackstones' or be re-roofed in imported slate. They belong to the last generations of vernacular farm buildings, and frequently the domestic component of the house was provided with a fashionable symmetrical façade. See also LONGHOUSE.

*Further reading*: Raistrick, A., *Buildings in the Yorkshire Dales*, Dalesman, Clapham, 1976.

**Lammas land**. COMMON grazing that was thrown open to livestock on Lammas Day (1 August on the modern calendar) and where they could remain until the commencement of sowing. The land concerned was normally pasture, but could sometimes be arable land grazed after harvest or in the fallowing period.

**Lammas meadow**, see MEADOW.

**Lamplands**. Land in the north of England whose rents were used to pay for the candles on the altar.

**Land, loon, lawn, paull, rap, selion, stitch**, see STRIP.

**Land-march, landmarch**. In Scotland, a boundary which might be walked by the community or 'beaten' on the relevant land's-mark day. See also BOUNDARY, BOUNDARY STONE.

**Landmark**. A distinctive reference point on the shore that could be seen by mariners and used to locate their position. These could be physical features, like conical hills, or buildings, like the numerous chapels and hermitages that punctuated some European shores, a few of which also had beacons. The chapel of St Nicholas on the headland guarding Ilfracombe harbour is an example.

**Landscape change**. Changes in a landscape tend to be regarded like chapters in a history book, which begin and end. Real change is far more complex, for each change once introduced sets numerous cultural and ecological changes in motion. For example, when one road replaces another, economic decline is likely to affect settlements along the old route. Meanwhile, dwellings are attached to the new one and the new roadside population generates new changes.

*Further reading*: Muir, R., 'On Change in the Landscape', *Landscape Research* **28**, 4, October 2003, 383–404.

**Landscape Park**, see ORNAMENTAL LANDSCAPE, PARKLAND.

**Latch**. In Northern Britain, a swamp, also the place within a moss or TURBARY where peats were spread to dry. The word also refers to the rut cut by a cartwheel.

**Laund**, see DEER PARK, WOOD PASTURE.

**Lawn**. Grassland. See LAUND.

**Lay**. Grassland, pasture.

**Lazy beds**. Travellers in Ireland and the Western Highlands and Islands of Scotland may encounter marginal farmland patterned by what appears to be miniature RIDGE AND FURROW. The features concerned are 'lazy beds', or cultivation ridges produced by hand digging. They are most commonly seen in areas of thin soils and poorly drained ground.

Firstly, the bed was marked out in lines using pegs and straw ropes. Next, manure was laid along the lines and then sods from either side were cut and turned over the manure, grassy face down, leaving a trench on either side of the ridge made of manure and sods. Finally, digging

sticks were used to pierce holes in the ridge, into which potatoes were inserted. In the following year, the ridges would become furrows, and vice versa.

The potato was adopted in Ireland as a garden crop in the seventeenth century and it became popular with the poorer classes towards the end of the century, when it was adopted as a field crop. By the middle of the following century, it had become the staple food of labourers and poorer tenants, and began to underwrite a spectacular acceleration in population numbers, displacing oatmeal and milk from their diets. Just as populations began to depend on inferior and degenerating varieties of potato, the blight arrived in 1845 and famine and mass fatalities followed. Lazy beds are most usually associated with the eighteenth- and nineteenth-century cultivation of the potato on ever-more marginal ground, and in Ireland abandoned lazy beds may be a legacy of the Great Famine of 1845–48. However, the creation of lazy beds in the cultivation of other crops has a much longer history, and lazy beds have been excavated in fossilised fields in County Mayo which date to around 3000 BC, while they could also be confused with traces of prehistoric CORD RIG.

*Further reading*: Whelan, K., 'Settlement and Society in Eighteenth-century Ireland' in Collins, T. (ed.), *Decoding the Landscape*, Galway, 1994, pp. 60–78.

**League**. A variable measure of distance, normally about 3 miles.

**Lea-laik, lea-gair**. Sheltered grazings in Northern Britain formed by glens, hollows or overhangs in a hill-mass.

**Leen**. In Scotland, moist pasture within a MOOR or low-lying grass on a farm.

**Leissure, leizure, leasow**. Pasture.

**Lempit-ebb**. The seashore between high and low tide marks where fisherfolk and people of poor CROFTING communities in Scotland would gather limpets.

**Levancy and couchancy (rule of).** This rule, observed in many northern upland communities in England, sought to link the rights of a holding to COMMON pasture to its size, efficiency and winter stock feeding capacity, so that there was an equitable apportionment of rights. Thus there would be an equivalence between the number of animals that grazed the commons in the summer and the number that a tenant could support on his holding, below, during the winter. While theoretically just, the rule did not take account of the needs of drovers and pack horse traders moving through an area. Sometimes byelaws had to be created to regularise these affairs, limiting the time that the outsiders could be in the neighbourhood and constraining the amount of time that their animals could spend grazing the pastures. See also STINTED COMMONS, OVERPRESS.

**Leven.** In Scotland, a LAWN, LAUND, or an expanse of open country between woods.

**Ley.** Grassland. In place-names, an ambiguous element that seems sometimes to signify cleared land or clearings but sometimes, land with trees.

**Ley lines.** These are claimed to be straight ancient trackways (apparently towing their undiscriminating users through pond, mire and thorn thicket alike). To discover a ley line one joins up two interesting places on a map and then looks for other interesting places or objects which lie along this 'ancient track' – post-medieval churches or commonplace boulders will suffice. If the line just misses an interesting feature, it can be bent somewhat. Ley lines do not exist as real features of the cultural landscape, and it is unfortunate that imaginative people who might discover worthwhile and fulfilling interests in the countryside and its history are diverted into this moribund backwater.

*Further reading*. Williamson, T. and Bellamy, L., *Ley Lines in Question*, Hutchinson, 1983.

**Liberty.** An area in the surroundings of a borough in which the freemen of the town enjoyed certain rights, like grazing. Also a cluster of manors under a single ownership which enjoyed certain privileges from the Crown. In the Isle of Wight, a territory equivalent to a hundred.

**Lickway**, see CORPSE ROAD.

**Lidgate.** These were gates positioned to prevent livestock from straying. They would often be placed across a highway in the place where it left a TOWNSHIP, at the edge of a settlement or the approach to a bridge. Lidgates were erected in the medieval period, if not before, and have given rise to a variety of place-names, many of them attached to lanes.

**Lie.** A warm and sheltered spot.

**Lie out.** Concerning cattle that lie out in fields at night.

**Light land revolution.** A component of the Agricultural Revolution that involved bringing light soils, the alkaline ones found in the chalk DOWNLANDS and the acid ones of the sandy heaths, into cultivation. This involved a return of emphasis to the easily-worked soils frequently ploughed in the prehistoric period. The lands concerned had frequently been used as pastures for sheep, which would be folded on the resting arable land at night to enrich the thin soils with nutrients derived from the adjacent heaths and Downs. The old 'sheep-corn' system was restricted by the low fertility of many soils and the limited availability of manure. One significant step in the light soil revolution involved the floating of meadows (see WATER MEADOWS) which was occasionally recorded at the end of the Middle Ages and spread rapidly in the seventeenth century to become widespread in the lowlands and Downlands in the eighteenth century. Another was the introduction of rotations combining cereals with clover and turnips. The turnips could either be eaten by sheep folded on the ploughland or fed to bullocks kept in yards. A third element was the digging of countless MARLPITS, often working through the peaty soils of a heath to reach the calcareous subsoil and bedrock. The marling neutralised acid soils, making it possible for turnips or red clover to be cultivated, which in turn allowed sheep to fertilise the ploughland as they fed upon the turnip crop. These developments took place against the background of PARLIAMENTARY ENCLOSURE, which provided the legal framework in which private initiatives could be effective. As the light land revolution proceeded, the old countrysides of open field ploughlands set amongst open heaths and Downs gave way to one of arable fields bounded by straight HEDGEROWS of hawthorn or blackthorn and punctuated by farmsteads of a Georgian or Victorian vintage. Ofter these were founded by families who had quit a failing village to live upon their new, consolidated holding. See also FOUR COURSE ROTATION.

*Further reading*: Williamson, T., *The Transformation of Rural England*, University of Exeter Press, Exeter, 2002.

**Lime-kilns**. Lime-kilns, most of them reflecting the improving ethos of the Agricultural Revolution, were set up in large numbers in the eighteenth and nineteenth centuries and most were redundant by the start of the twentieth century. However, excavations and documentary sources reveal that lime-kilns of not dissimilar designs were used throughout the Middle Ages. There was, however, a myth current among upland farming communities that lime would burn the soil and even if useful, would only have a short term effect. During the seventeenth century, word of the benefits of liming the land spread, while during the eighteenth century the virtues of liming were proclaimed by the apostles of agricultural improvements. The heyday of lime-kilns occurred during the Napoleonic Wars, when corn prices were high and lime was needed to improve lands newly brought into cultivation. It is not widely appreciated that the construction of lime kilns featured in many PARLIAMENTARY

ENCLOSURE provisions. Following decades when normally acid lands received very heavy applications of lime, liming came to a virtual standstill during the agricultural depression of the 1880s, and by the 1920s the ill-effects of this were evident in many pastures. In 1937 a special lime scheme was instituted to subsidise the purchase of lime. The remains of lime kilns are numerous in limestone and chalk areas and they suddenly assert a presence in countrysides dominated by other rocks, like the ancient metamorphics of Deeside in North East Scotland, when small outcrops of calcareous rock are found. The kilns burned lime-rich stone to produce lime, either for use as a sweetener to be spread on acid land or to produce lime mortar. In northern England, the early examples, dating from the seventeenth century or before, can be recognised as depressions at the foot of scree slopes where the boulders from the scree were placed in layers that alternated with fuel, and these 'clamp kilns' resembled the pans used in charcoal burning. In Scotland, clamp-kills were kilns built of sods. Most kilns were operated by the farmers who owned the surrounding land and needed the lime fertiliser for their own use, but some were operated commercially.

Most kilns seen today are in ruins, but they usually had the form of a circular or square tower about 10–15 feet (3–4 metres) in height and diameter containing a sandstone-lined bowl which was about 9 feet (2.7 metres) in diameter and 7 feet (2.1 metres) in depth. At the base of the bowl there was a grate and a tunnel with an arched mouth leading inwards towards this bowl and grate. Limestone and fuel were fed into the kiln, and burned lime and ash were raked out through the grate. In the limestone lands of the Yorkshire Dales the ruined kilns are often seen standing beside the outcrops where limestone was quarried, but further south in England chalk was normally carted to a kiln erected on the claylands where the lime was needed. Other kilns were built upon sea-cliffs, close to easily quarried sources of chalk or limestone, and these were often commercial kilns that sent their

*Linear earthwork (dyke)*
Devil's Dyke in Cambridgeshire, looking across the fronting ditch towards the west of the massive linear earthwork.

product inland. Lime ash from kilns was often rammed down as a flooring material for cottages. Chopped wood from specially raised COPPICES fuelled the kilns until the development of the railway network allowed coal to be employed as a fuel in the second half of the nineteenth century. See also MARLPIT.

*Further reading:* Johnson, D., *Limestone Industries of the Yorkshire Dales*, Tempus, Stroud, 2002.

**Lin, Linn**. In Scotland, a waterfall or sometimes a shrub-girt ravine, but see LINT.

**Linear earthworks (dyke)**. These are long banks fronted by ditches that apparently existed as territorial boundary-markers. Individual examples may prove very difficult to date by archaeological methods, while the span of possible dates is extremely wide, ranging from the Bronze Age to the Norman period. The best known of these earthworks is quite precisely dated, for Offa's Dyke, which marked the frontier between Mercia and the Welsh principalities, was constructed in the reign of Offa of Mercia, 757–96. Visually the most impressive of the linear earthworks is Devil's Dyke in Cambridgeshire, which divides the racecourses at Newmarket and has a length of about 7 miles (11 kilometres) and still stands around 30 feet (9 metres) tall in its best-preserved sections. It is dated only loosely, being built between late Roman and middle Saxon times. Less spectacular but more famous is Wansdyke in Wessex, which is really two dykes, West and East Wansdyke, that are separated by a 12-mile (19-kilometre) gap. These dykes probably belong to the same loose time-bracket quoted for Devil's Dyke.

But not all linear earthworks are related to the territorial struggles of the Dark Ages. The Bokerley Dyke on the Hampshire-Dorset border appears to be a hastily built defencework of the late Roman period, while the Cleave Dyke system of watershed earthworks in the Hambleton Hills of Yorkshire may represent estate boundaries of the late Bronze Age. Around two millennia later, the Normans may have been responsible for constructing some of the linear earthworks in Ireland.

The great dykes like Offa's Dyke and Wansdyke embody an enormous amount of organised effort, and the author has estimated that the much shorter Devil's Dyke, already mentioned, would have taken a workforce of 500 labourers more than a year to build. In addition to these massive and rather mysterious frontierworks there are also territorial boundaryworks of a lesser status. In the later part of the Bronze Age, most of southern

Wiltshire and western Hampshire was partitioned by 'ranch boundaries', which sliced across the existing 'CELTIC' FIELD patterns and created a new land allotment that must almost certainly have been imposed by a powerful centralised authority. The ranch boundaries are still visible features in places like Bulford Down and the Bourne valley to the north-east of Salisbury. More than 500 miles (800 kilometres) of such ranch boundaries have been detected by archaeologists, and originally they were very prominent ditches and embankments, the ditches being about 6 feet (1.8 metres) deep and 10 feet (3 metres) wide.

A close examination of Ordnance Survey maps will show that linear earthworks are numerous, though only a small fraction of them can yet be linked to a particular historical period and political situation. All, apart from the ranch boundaries, seem to be territorial boundaryworks and all would have been difficult to defend when one considers the enormous numbers of troops that would have been needed to man such features along their entire length. They are probably best regarded as imposing and unequivocal frontierworks that symbolised the intention of communities which built them to resist incursions into their homelands. Intruders would be obliged firstly, to traverse the deep fronting ditch, and then to scale the steep bank formed of up-cast from the ditch – so they would be well aware that they had trespassed beyond a significant frontier. If the function of the frontierwork was symbolic rather than military, there remains the fact that in small-scale skirmishes the defenders manning the crest of the ditch-fronted bank would enjoy a distinct advantage – particularly in resisting cavalry attacks. The deep ditches would also impede raiders departing with booty.

*Further reading:* Malim, T. *et al.*, 'New Evidence on the Cambridgeshire Dykes and Worsted Street Roman Road', *Proceedings of the Cambridge Antiquarian Society* **85**, 27–122.
Muir, R., 'Cambridgeshire Dykes Retain Their

Secrets', *Geographical Magazine* **55**, 1980, pp. 198–204.
Spratt, D. A., *Linear Earthworks in the Tabular Hills*, Sheffield University Press, 1989.
Stoertz, C., *Ancient Landscapes of the Yorkshire Wolds*, RCHME, Swindon, 1997.

**Linhay**. A West Country hay-barn-cum-animal-shelter, with an upper level or 'tallet' serving as the open-fronted hay-barn with the livestock area beneath. Sometimes nesting niches for doves are provided in the sides of the linhay.

**Link**. In Scotland this can refer to the meanders of a river on its flood plain or to the seashore sand dunes that have been colonised with grass and which produce the open, breezy, undulating landscape greatly loved by golfers. A 'links' is also a golf-course, but 'link' may be used to describe a section of a stack of peats.

**Lint, lin**. Where these words are encountered in place-names they normally refer to the old cottage linen industries. A lint hole, lint pot or lint coble was a pond in which the flax that provided the raw material for the industry was steeped. Many 'lin' names relate to the old hemp industry, but a few refer to a lime or 'linden' tree. See also HEMP.

**Lisheen**, see KILLEEN.

**Litt**. In Northern Britain the appearance of 'litt-' in a place-name can signify the former presence of a dye-house (litt house), dye vatt (litt fat) or litt kettle.

**Litterstane**. A large walling stone carried to a builder in a litter.

**Loanin(g)**. In Lowland Scots, a field, paddock or lane. It may be a track between corn fields used by cattle brought home for milking or it might describe half of a highway, from the centre of the road to houses on one roadside. There is a distinct association with milking and a loaning-green was a milking green, while a loaning dyke separated ploughland and pasture.

*Lock-up*
A lock-up at Castle Cary in Somerset.

**Loch, lough**. Substantial natural lakes in Scotland and Ireland respectively.

**Lochan, lochen and loddan**. A small lake or loch. When the water body is just a small pool it is a loddan or lodden in Scotland.

**Lock-ups**. Before the organisation of the police forces, each village had an elected constable. If the constable was fortunate, a lock-up would be available, normally a poky little place where felons could be detained before their removal to court or where drunks might sleep off their intoxication. A few lock-ups survive, sometimes as grim little brick buildings with barred windows and bolted doors, but there are a few more dandified examples. One of the best is at Castle Cary in Somerset, a cylindrical stone structure built in 1779 housing a cell which is a cramping 7 feet (*c.* 2 metres) in diameter. Sometimes, older chambers were commandeered as lock-ups, and this was the fate of the oratory or bridge chapel at Bradford-on-Avon. At Stratton in Cornwall the south porch of the church served as a gaol, and so that no confusion might occur, the heavy timbers were studded with 240 large nails, spelling out 'CLINK', a colloquial word which still substitutes for prison. Since most fun, drunkenness and trouble would occur on market day, lock-ups (or STOCKS) were normally situated in a handy position on the market green or square.

**Lodes**. These are artificial fenland navigation channels which connected the communities of the southern Fen edge and interior of England (via the main Fenland waterways) with the North Sea trading arena. Between three and six of the lodes are thought to have been dug in Roman times, the remainder being cut in medieval or later periods. Some lodes experienced well over a thousand years of navigation, for the system remained in use until the railway era. One of the most interesting of the lodes is Reach Lode in Cambridgeshire, which is thought to be of Roman origin. At the terminus of the lode is Reach village, originally two separate settlements linked by a green, the one village serving as an outport of Swaffham Prior and the other as an outport of Burwell. Although scarcely recognisable as a riverport today, Reach was importing coal in the nineteenth century and maintained its

Reach Lode in Cambridgeshire, a Roman canal which
remained in use into the nineteenth century.

commercial life until the opening of the
Cambridge-Mildenhall railway in 1884. During
the Middle Ages, Burwell became independent
of its outpost when a direct connection to Reach
Lode was cut, and beside Burwell Lode one can
still recognise the relics of the canal basins and
the wharfs or 'HYTHES' which served the
merchants of Burwell.

**Lodge**. For monastic lodges, see GRANGE and
MOOR. On Shetland, lodges were small buildings
providing sleeping accommodation for fishermen
and stores for salt and cured fish during the
eighteenth to nineteenth centuries. They were
the descendants of the medieval BODS or
BOOTHS and were often located far from
permanent habitations on the remoter bays of
the archipelago. FAR HAAF stations were larger
fishing bases, about 20 in number and they had
seasonal populations. In addition to the far haafs
and lodges, around 80 shingle beaches were used
as places, often close to the dwelling of a

fisherman, where a boat could be beached and
where fish could be spread out to cure.

**Lodger, inmate, byhold, undersettle**. An
undertenant who would often be an outsider to
the manor concerned, and resented or treated
with suspicion because of this. Where lodgers
were tolerated their activities were likely to be
carefully regulated and they would be obliged to
get their livestock on and off the common at
specified dates.

**Loft-house**. A cottage or FARMSTEAD provided
with a loft above the living space. This might be
used for the storage of fodder or produce or be
furnished with shelves for sleeping. Spinning
lofts were a special development of the
pre-factory economy.

**Long barrow**. Long barrows are Neolithic burial
monuments and date from the period *c.* 4200–
3000 BC. They exist as elongated earthen
mounds with an appearance that has been compared to that of a basking whale. In the
stone-strewn uplands of northern Scotland the
earthen long barrows of England find their equivalents in the 'long cairns', whose mounds are
composed of scree and stone rubble.

Following prolonged erosion, long barrows are seldom visibly striking features, although they must have seemed impressive when newly built. Outwardly, they appear to be simple earthen mounds, but this apparent simplicity is misleading, for numerous excavations have shown that these monuments had complicated and variable internal structures. Long barrows were collective tombs which generally contained the remains of many corpses. After death, a body was not entombed directly in a long barrow, but apparently allowed to decompose in a 'mortuary enclosure' of rectangular or trapezoidal shape which was defined and protected by a ditch and palisade. Sometimes, these were erected before agricultural activity had removed the woodland from their surroundings. Within the mortuary enclosure, a timber 'mortuary house' sometimes seems to have existed. The disarticulated remains of corpses might be stored in the mortuary house until a sufficient amount of skeletal material was deemed to have accumulated and then the mortuary house would be entombed as work commenced on raising the earthen mound of the new long barrow. In the case of the Fussell's Lodge long barrow in Wiltshire, excavation revealed the bones from more than fifty skeletons. The mound of the long barrow often had the profile of an elongated wedge, was around 100–200 feet (30–60 metres) in length and had a shape that was trapezoidal in plan, although oval forms were also constructed. The earth used to build the mound was excavated from the flanking ditches (which are sometimes still visible as shallow trenches). 'Bank barrows' were extremely elongated forms of the long barrow and were much less common. The largest example lies within the Iron Age (later) ramparts of Maiden Castle HILLFORT in Dorset overlying the Neolithic CAUSEWAYED ENCLOSURE contained there and is about a third of a mile (1 kilometre) in length. Occasionally, the more elevated ends of long barrows seem to be directed towards features of the physical landscape, like a few granite tors on Dartmoor. The monuments were frequently placed so as to be seen silhouetted against the sky by travellers on trackways in their locality.

Long barrows differed from their equivalents in many stone-rich districts, the CHAMBERED TOMBS, in that the earthen tombs could not readily be reopened to accept new burials, though both types of monument were associated with the rite of collective burial. In a few cases, as at Winterbourne Stoke crossroads in Wiltshire, an old long barrow appears to have served as a nucleus around which ROUND BARROWS were later clustered.

There can be little doubt that the role of the long barrow was much more than that of a simple tomb. They may have been reserved to receive the corpses of members of a particular local dynasty or caste, for there were far more people living in Neolithic England than were ever buried in long barrows. There is also evidence that each long barrow was associated with a particular local community and cell of land. So, as well as serving as tombs, long barrows are now widely regarded as territorial symbols which signify the ownership of the adjacent lands by the group whose noble ancestors were entombed in the barrow concerned. Most aspects of Neolithic religion and ritual remain elusive. It is impossible for us to know whether, when the disarticulated bones were finally laid to rest under the massive mound of a long barrow, the tomb-makers regarded their task as burying people or as placing a hallowed deposit into the ground in order to appease Mother Earth for the goodness which farming had removed. Long barrows vary enormously in terms of their preservation. Some, like the White Barrow near Tilshead in Wiltshire, are sufficiently intact to display characteristic features, while others are ploughed out and can only be recorded when traces of their flanking ditches emerge in aerial photographs. Of forty-two long barrows recognised in Hampshire and the Isle of Wight in 1979, fourteen retained their prominent mounds and four of these also had visible ditches. The remainder had been damaged by a variety of later activities, mainly ploughing. See also CHAMBERED TOMB, ROUND BARROW.

*Further reading:* Royal Commission on Historical Monuments, *Long Barrows in Hampshire and the Isle of Wight*, Her Majesty's Stationery Office, 1979.

**Longhouse**. The longhouse was a frugal dwelling which, in various local forms, was common throughout medieval Britain. It provided accommodation for both a peasant family and a few of their livestock. The sharing of a home in this way is evident in the case of some excavated round houses of the Bronze Age, though the longhouse, as a low rectangular single-storey building, probably originated in the post-Roman era. However, buildings of a quite unsophisticated longhouse type were commonly inhabited in Northumberland and Westmorland until the middle of the seventeenth century. For centuries, longhouses served as homes to the more impoverished members of the farming community and also as abodes to the few beasts that they possessed. Stone-built longhouses can still be found standing today. Some of the superior 'classic' type are still occupied in Devon, while in the northern uplands of England an old longhouse can sometimes be seen serving as an outbuilding to its successor, often a farmstead of the LAITHE-HOUSE type.

Some of the earliest longhouses excavated date from the ninth century, and the footings of these boat-shaped dwellings of Scandinavian settlers can be seen at Brough of Birsay, a tidal island off the main Orkney island. The boat-shaped plan was not adopted by later longhouses, and a tenth-century longhouse of a more conventional kind has been excavated at Mawgan Porth near Newquay. It revealed the typical partitioning of the interior to provide separate accommodation both for the family and their livestock. Numerous medieval longhouses have been excavated, some with walls of turf or WATTLE AND DAUB and some with rubble walls. Typical examples had low walls supporting roofs of thatch, no windows and an entrance set

in the middle of one of the long walls. A light timber screen could provide a partition between the human and animal quarters; the domestic part of the building was warmed by an open hearth, while the warmth from the animals will have added to the fug. Such dwellings were built quickly and frugally with whatever materials were available. After a generation of occupation they would be in need of much repair and within fifty years of building they were often beyond repair and a new longhouse would tend to be built more or less on the site of its predecessor. While excavations can reveal the layout of such dwellings, old documents may tell us about the sort of animals which were housed. Thus at Wakefield court in 1316 it was alleged that William de Thurgerland 'opened the door of Peter del Grene and stole a horse and cow', and in 1323 at the same court three people were accused of breaking into a house and shearing five sheep.

The longhouse evolved in different ways and at different rates in various parts of the country. The human and animal quarters often came to be separated by a cross passage that ran from the front door, still in its traditional position in the track-side long wall, to a back door opening on to a toft or backyard. In the South-West the early type of longhouse buildings seems to have lasted no longer than the Middle Ages, and their occupants were then choosing to commandeer the space occupied by the byre and convert it into a second domestic room, while relegating the beasts to a separate, purpose-built byre. In the North-East of England, however, longhouses of the early type persisted for another century or so.

In some counties, like Herefordshire, North Yorkshire and Cumbria, a new generation of 'improved' longhouses appeared in the sixteenth and seventeenth centuries. They were more substantial dwellings, mainly built in the CRUCK-FRAMING method, and in the north the cruck frames were often encased in stone. Improved longhouses with sophistications like chimneys and attics were being built in the eighteenth century, though further improvements had already produced the 'classic' longhouse of which some examples recognised in Devon date back to the sixteenth century. The traditional open hearth was replaced by a fireplace and chimney, and the chimney-stack with its wall now separated the domestic quarters from the byre. Behind the chimney wall was a through-passage with doors leading off it to the living room and byres, while attics or upper storeys were provided. On the ground floor, in addition to the hall or living room with its hearth, there was a second room, used as a parlour or dairy. Such houses were typically built of stone, without timber-framing, and were roofed in thatch. The classic longhouses of Devon were built in the period about 1550–1700. Similar longhouses appeared in the North-West of England and were still being built in the eighteenth century, though in many cases the room which had served in the Devon examples as a byre was now used as an additional service room. See also BLACK HOUSE, LAITHE-HOUSE.

*Further reading.* Mercer, Eric, *English Vernacular Houses*, Royal Commission on Historical Monuments, 1975.

**Long strip**, see STRIP, FURLONG.

**Looker's hut**. A simple shelter erected for a 'looker' who watched over sheep. In the Romney Marsh several hundred of these huts existed in solitary locations on the marshes, providing cover for shepherding tasks as well as look-out posts. A few brick-built examples with chimneys and paling enclosures remain, but most have been dismantled.

**Lost gardens**. When confronted by a puzzling assemblage of man-made earthworks the rambler's thoughts are likely to turn to deserted villages or abandoned castles, and one may be slow to appreciate that gardens could just as easily be abandoned to dereliction as the houses that went with them. In fact, the remains of former gardens are among the most numerous of EARTHWORK monuments. If, after abandonment, the garden became incorporated into neighbouring pastures and never suffered ploughing, then elaborate complexes of terraces, moats, canals, lakes, beds, prospect mounds, lawns or pathways could be preserved beneath the turf. Such relics are fairly numerous – for example, the terraces of a sixteenth-century garden, abandoned along with its mansion in the seventeenth century, can be seen on the outskirts

*Lost garden*
At the shrunken village of Strixton in Northamptonshire sheep graze on the terraces of a lost garden of the sixteenth century. The manor house to which the garden belonged has disappeared.

*Lost village*
The excavated footings of dwellings at the deserted village of Hound Tor on Dartmoor.

of the shrunken village of Strixton in Northamptonshire. Just as surviving gardens can be interpreted according to our understandings about the evolution of garden fashions, so the character of earthworks and layout – whether formal and geometrical or picturesque and 'organic' – will inform our understanding of lost gardens. They can be of particular interests when abandoned suddenly and after only a short existence, for such gardens are likely to have escaped later modifications and to remain 'true to type'. Numerous examples have been discovered unexpectedly, while they and other examples can be studied in relation to archival materials – like estate maps, records of accounts, and artistic representations.

*Further reading*: Pattison, T. (ed.), *There by Design: Field Archaeology in Parks and Gardens*, Brit Archaeol Rep Brit Ser **267**, Oxford, 1998.

Taylor, C. C., *The Archaeology of Gardens*, Shire Archaeology Series, 1983.

Williamson, T., *Suffolk's Gardens and Parks*, Windgather, Macclesfield, 2000.

**Lost village**. Lost village sites are remarkably numerous and are amongst the most fascinating and informative of our landscape relics. Only when the abandonment of the settlement occurred in relatively recent times can one expect to see the ruins of dwellings though traces of their footings often appear in air photographs, most clearly when the buildings were of stone. Most common are the sites deserted in late medieval times, where the evidence of village life is apparent in the form of EARTHWORKS left by features such as streets, property boundaries, houses, MOATS and PONDS. If the site has been ploughed, then CROP MARKS or artefacts found in FIELD-WALKING may provide the only visible clues.

As explained in the entry on VILLAGES, there

*Lost village*
The ruined church of the deserted medieval village of Egmere, Norfolk.

is a distinction between the older and the younger villages. Prehistoric villages existed, but they, like many Roman and sub-Roman settlements, tended to be deserted as a matter of course. It was only around the eighth or ninth centuries AD that villages were established which were permanent in the sense that, barring accidents of fate, they have tended to endure. However, these accidents of fate have been many and have come in various guises. Between the late Saxon times and around 1300, thousands of new villages were founded to accommodate the rapidly swelling rural population. Even so, a number of casualties appeared in their ranks, but because the survival of documentation is slight and incomplete for the period before the compilation of Domesday Book in 1086 our knowledge of earlier desertions is meagre. Much, for example, remains to be learned about the villages (as opposed to estates) which were extinguished by the Harrying of the North by the Norman armies in 1069–71. It is clear, however, that after Domesday, a wave of early

medieval village desertions was accomplished by monks of the Cistercian order as they built their abbeys and organised their expanding estates. By 1152, Britain had gained fifty-one Cistercian foundations, and the order's desire for solitude had grim repercussions for villages whose presence was judged an intrusion on the rigorous and exclusive life of an ABBEY or GRANGE. A few dozen villages and hamlets were torn down and depopulated by the monks, the bulk of the destruction taking place in the Yorkshire heartland of the Cistercian empires, though even in Leicestershire it seems that ten or more peasant communities were evicted by the monks. One of the most picturesque of the sites is that of the lost village of Herleshow, which lay at the foot of prominent How Hill on the doorstep of Fountains Abbey. It was converted into a monastic grange after 1149. Almost all the monastic clearances took place in the twelfth and thirteenth-century period of rapid Cistercian expansion, but as late as 1489 the monks of Bicester Priory in Oxfordshire depopulated the nearby village of Wretchwich.

In contrast to the Cistercian clearances it is much more difficult to discover examples of villages which were extinguished by war. There is no doubt that many villages were plundered and burned in the course of medieval civil strife and Scottish raiding, while BATTLEFIELD ARCHAEOLOGY is demonstrating how ghastly battles, such as Towton, could be. However, it seems to have been the common and prudent practice for villagers to quit their homes and drive their cattle into the woods as the armies approached, returning later to rebuild new dwellings upon the ashes of the old. So long as good land was in short supply, then recolonisation would always take place.

Lost village sites are plentiful, and those that are known to the local populations have frequently acquired a mythical obituary that relates their disappearance to the horrors of the pestilence or 'Black Death'. This terrifying disease arrived in England in 1348 and by the end of the century it had probably reduced the population by between a third and a half. There were frequent recurrences of the pestilence until the seventeenth century and, not surprisingly, it is popularly regarded as the culprit of most village desertions. There is no doubt that it could virtually annihilate a village population, leaving the survivors too few and too demoralised to work the village lands. Even so, plainly documented cases of villages which were

*permanently* extinguished by the pestilence are remarkably few. Tusmore in Oxfordshire was one example, and in 1357 it was recorded as being 'void of inhabitants since their death in the pestilence'. Tilgardesle in the same county was another victim, and in 1359 it was reported that the village could render no taxes as nobody had lived there for the last ten years. But more typical plague histories belonged to villages like Cublington in Buckinghamshire, where a new settlement was established on a nearby site overlooking the ruins of the original settlement, or Coombe in Oxfordshire. This village was abandoned in 1350 but replaced by a planned settlement on a nearby site a few years later. As with the village victims of warfare, recolonisation and recovery were normal when the village lands were sufficiently attractive to entice new settlers. To put the plague contribution to the deserted village in perspective, one can quote the results of detailed survey work in Northamptonshire which identified more than eighty deserted village sites, but could demonstrate that, of

*Lost village*
The ruined church tower at the deserted medieval village of Godwick in Norfolk.

these, only Hale and Elkington were victims of the pestilence.

Often less dramatic but more permanent in their effects were the consequences of climatic deterioration that was intensifying during the fourteenth century. Rapid population growth in the centuries preceding 1300 had led to the establishment of small villages and hamlets in unpromising situations with thin or poorly-drained soils which could not sustain intense cultivation. As the soils wore out and the pastures were over-grazed, the worsening of climate increased the poverty of the farming, while attempts to sustain yields led to more severe levels of soil exhaustion and over-grazing. In this remorseless way, which was most severely encountered on the moorland margins, sandy heaths and heavy clay lands, hundreds of 'weaklings' were culled from the village flock, including many hamlets and destitute little villages which scarcely merited mentions in the medieval records. Death of a much more sudden kind came to many villages, mainly those sited on vulnerable terrain on the east coast of England. It came as a result of the violent storms and sea-surges which undermined cliffs and overran coastal marshes during the fourteenth and later centuries.

The cruellest round of village desertions was yet to come. The repeated onslaughts of the pestilence had transformed a situation of peasant surplus into one of labour shortage – and, not surprisingly, surviving villagers sought to exploit the new conditions by demanding more favourable terms of service. The landlord and poet Gower complained that 'The shepherd and cowherd demand more wages now than the master bailiff was wont to take; and, whithersoever we look, whatsoever by the work, labourers are now of such price that, when we must needs use them, where we were wont to spend two shillings we must now spend five or six'. A jury in Lancaster in 1350, for example, found that 'William de Caburn of Lymbergh ploughman, will not serve except by the day or the month, and will not eat salt meat but fresh;

and on this account he hath departed from the township, because no man dared to hire him on those conditions in contravention of the statute of our lord King'.

In fact, the statutes failed to temper wage rises, and landlords cast around for alternative methods of exploiting their lands. The answer was easily found, for the raising of sheep required only the employment of a few shepherds while the market for wool was as buoyant as ever. The Tudor decades witnessed a wholesale assault on 'village England', one which filled the highways of the kingdom with resentful, starving and homeless peasants. Many landlords had only one estate to clear, but there also arose dynasties of depopulators, like the Knightleys and the Spencers, who amassed great fortunes by securing agricultural estates, evicting the villagers and converting the ploughlands to sheep ranges. The scale of the Tudor sheep clearances was staggering, and in the 1480s the chantry priest, John Rous, was able to list some fifty-eight depopulated villages, all lying within a dozen miles of Warwick. The worst-affected area spanned the entire Midlands and ran northwards into the Vale of York and Yorkshire Wolds. In his *Utopia* Sir Thomas More described the contemporary situation in Tudor England: 'Noblemen and gentlemen, yes, and certain abbots, holymen God wot ... enclose all pastures. They throw down houses, they pluck down towns, and leave nothing standing but only the church, to make of it a sheephouse.'

As the economic balance between peasant arable farming and wool production changed in Elizabethan times, so the sheep evictions declined, but a new form of depopulation arose which owed more to fashion and vanity than to economics. The decline of the dynastic castle was paralleled by the rise of the stately home and the desire to surround the mansion with a large expanse of empty PARKLAND. Villages were removed from the designated parks, sometimes with a new village being provided outside the park to house the tenants, and sometimes with the unfortunate villagers being simply cast out

on the road. New Wimpole in Cambridgeshire, New Houghton in Norfolk and Milton Abbas in Dorset are some of the better-known examples of replacements for emparked villages. In this way one of the most characteristic of English country scenes was created, with the village church surviving in isolation within the park, surrounded by the earthworks of the dwellings of its congregation and overlooked by the splendid mansion. Only in Victorian times did the rise of humanitarian values bring a close to the emparking of villages in England. Subsequently a few villages have been depopulated – unfortunate victims of

*Lost village*
Earthworks of the deserted medieval village at Ogle in Northumberland. The traces of the green, individual houses and house-plots are very plainly displayed. The ridge and furrow ploughland terminates at the back of the house-plots. (CUCAP)

circumstances which happened to be in the wrong place at the wrong time. Some were industrial villages which owed their livelihood to a declining colliery or quarry, or intruded on plans for reservoir construction, although a clutch of villages in the East Anglian Brecklands and a few on Salisbury Plain were destroyed to create military training areas. In Scotland, with the worst of the CLEARANCES over, the depopulations on Skye and the removal of people from designated deer forests continued far into the nineteenth century. In Ireland, the famine of the late 1840s produced depopulations on a scale not seen in England since Tudor times, as the rural poor starved or bought passages out of the devastated land.

Thousands of deserted medieval village sites have been recorded, but a considerable number of similar sites must still await discovery. Those that have escaped later episodes of ploughing or building will display quite prominent earthworks, and with a little care one may easily discriminate between the EARTHWORKS of quarrying or LOST GARDENS and those of deserted villages. The most obvious feature is likely to be the HOLLOWAY of the former High Street, and narrower holloways will trace the courses of side-streets and back lanes. By plotting the courses of these holloways one can reconstruct the street-plan of the lost settlement. When the site is well preserved small platforms will be seen at intervals beside the holloway, and these HOUSE PLATFORMS mark the positions of former dwellings. Where stone was used for walling the overgrown walls may still form low ridges around the platform, and a gap in such a ridge may denote the doorway. Churches at deserted village sites were normally pillaged for their valuable stone, but some survive as gaunt ruins, particularly in Norfolk where most were built of worthless flint. Low banks and ditches trace property boundaries, corresponding to the limits of the CLOSES or TOFTS which contained the dwellings, while level areas beside or embraced by holloways could be GREENS. Other earthwork features that may be found in close proximity to the village relics include MOATS, FISHPONDS and MOTTES. The limits of the village and its tofts or closes may be marked by the corduroy pattern of RIDGE AND FURROW,

denoting the old open-field ploughland of the medieval community.

The sites of deserted medieval villages vary enormously, the differences reflecting the size of the settlement, its duration, the use of stone or other materials in housebuilding and the subsequent agricultural uses of the site. Most lie on private land but some are still accessible by footpaths. Probably the most visit-worthy site is that of Wharram Percy in the Yorkshire Wolds, where more than three decades of patient excavation have contributed much of what is known about the day-to-day life of the medieval village. See also EARLY ENCLOSURE, HOUSE PLATFORM, ISOLATED CHURCHES.

*Further reading*: Beresford, M. W. and Hurst, J. G.,
   *Deserted Medieval Villages*, Lutterworth Press, 1971.
Muir, R., *The Lost Villages of Britain*, Michael Joseph,
   1984.
Beresford, M. and Hurst, J., *Wharram Percy*, Yale
   University Press, New Haven, 1991.

**Lot meadow, rotation meadow, shifting-severalties**. A meadow held in common by the local community in which shares were redistributed annually by a lottery in which holders of open field ploughland all participated. See also DOLE, KEAVLE, MEADOWS.

**Lousy land**. Most field-names of this kind derive from an Old English word for a pig-sty and denote land where pigs were kept.

**Luggie**. A Small lodge, hut or cottage in a park in Scotland. See also PARKLAND, LANDSCAPE PARK.

**Lunkie**. A hole in the wall for sheep. The Scottish equivalent of a SMOOT or sheep creep.

**Lychway**, see CORPSE ROAD.

**Lye**. Pasture.

**Lyse-hay**. In Northern Britain, hay cut from land that was normally used as pasture rather than from permanent meadow land.

# M

**Macadam**. John Loudon Macadam (1756–1836) became known as 'The Colossus of Roads' because of his work in raising the standard of road-building. He came from the minor gentry of Ayrshire and worked as a youth with his uncle, a merchant in New York. His involvement with roads followed his return to Ayrshire, where he purchased an ESTATE at Sauchie. In 1798, he began work as a naval agent concerned with victualling in the port of Bristol. In 1816 he became General Surveyor of the Bristol roads and wrote *Remarks on the Present System of Road Making*, advocating, as other good road-makers, including the Romans, had, the need for good drainage and surfacing in suitably graded materials. Along with his fellow Scot, Thomas TELFORD and Blind Jack METCALFE of Knaresborough, he promoted sound techniques at a time when the British road network was emerging from a millennium-and-a-half of neglect. 'Macadamising' involved spreading a layer of small stones on a well-drained foundation and then applying pressure, so that the stones were compacted into a homogenous surface.

*Further reading*: Reader, W. J., *Macadam: the McAdam Family and the Turnpike Roads*, Heinemann, London, 1980.

**Machair**. Unusually fertile ground on the raised beaches of the Scottish Highlands and Islands. The best land of many CROFTING communities is found here, where shelly sand from the seashore has blown over the acidic peat and settled to form a sweetening layer.

**Mad, mead**. These words when occurring in place-names relate to MEADOWS.

**Mailin**. In Scotland, a farm holding held by a tenant or 'mailinder'.

**Mains**. In Lowland Scots, the HOME FARM of an ESTATE. Following the IMPROVEMENTS it became a very common place-name.

**Malm**. A word occurring in field-names that denotes light, loam soils.

**Manor**. The definition of a manor is a subject of controversy between historians. It was a feudal estate, the word deriving from the Latin *mansus*. The manor could encompass a TOWNSHIP or vill or several vills, it could embrace a village and its lands, or the village might be split between two or more manors (see OPEN VILLAGES and CLOSED VILLAGES). The manorial system was prevalent in England after the Norman Conquest, but various important elements of the system must have been established before the Conquest, perhaps long before it. Normally, the manor would comprise the lands of the lord's DEMESNE, the common ploughland and meadowland, and the common grazings and the woodlands of the waste. The lord's demesne strips were originally scattered throughout the open fields. The manor was governed by the manor court where various taxes and fines were imposed, but the authority of the manor court was compromised in certain areas, such as those concerning the rights of free tenants, by the powers of the royal court, so that the manor was not as autonomous as comparable institutions on the Continent.

The wealth of the manor derived from the produce of the demesne lands, which were worked through labour services demanded of the peasantry, and from a variety of feudal dues, rents and fines exacted by the manor court. Many lords held several widely separated manors, and a steward might preside over the manor court when the lord was absent, while the day-to-day organisation of work was accomplished by an official known as the reeve and by discussions between the peasants themselves. Each manor might develop its own particular customs, and while the manorial peasants would accept a remarkable burden of feudal exploitation they were usually steadfast in upholding the customs of the manor. These customs were well entrenched before the Norman Conquest, and the early eleventh-century author of a tract on *The Rules of Individual People* took pains to indicate that 'The customs of estates are various. Nor do we apply these regulations, which we have described, to all districts.'

Because of the difficulties inherent in trying to generalise about manors, Prof. Homans preferred to study one manor – not a typical manor, because there was no such thing. He chose Spelsbury manor in Oxfordshire as it existed in 1279. It was held by Angareta de Beauchamp who held of the Bishop of Worcester, who held of the King (similar chains of 'subinfeudation' linked all land in England ultimately to the King). The manor had three plough-lands (about 160 acres: 64.8 hectares) in demesne and worked by the lady's tenants and servants. The rest of the land was held by tenants who were socially divided into the classes of freeholders, villeins and COTTARS. The most substantial of the six freeholders held a mill and 6 acres (2.2 hectares) and paid an annual rent of 20s. 4d. (£1.02), and his only obligation was to attend the manor court on the two days of the year when it was held. Moving down the hierarchy of the manorial community the wealth and holdings of the members tended to decrease, while the duties became more onerous. Thirty-three villeins with substantial holdings were obliged to do sixty 'works' between 29 September and 1 August – tilling the demesne and other labours – plus four special days of ploughing work and one day of mowing. During harvest, between 1 August and 29 September, the burden of work increased – thirty-six works and three days of special reaping were required. These villeins were also obliged to devote three days to collecting nuts and to provide the lady with a bushel of wheat at Martinmas, and at Christmas each must give

her a hen in return for having the right to collect dead wood and also give her a present worth a penny. These villeins had holdings of about 30 acres (12 hectares), though any part of their money and goods could be taken by the lady every year as 'tallage', according to her will.

There were ten villeins who had holdings of about fifteen acres and they performed about half the labours of the thirty-three 'yardlings' who had the 'yardlands' or 30-acre (12-hectare) holdings; they provided three hens for the lady at Christmas and were also tallaged. The six cottars constituted the lowest class and were obliged to perform forty works per year plus five works of haymaking and three 'boonworks' – notionally performed out of love of the (lord or) lady. The cottars were to give four hens each at Christmas. The reeve was chosen from the ranks of the yardlings and the bedell, a subordinate official, from those of the holders of half-yardlands.

The manorial system was adept at squeezing work, rents and fines from the peasant community, but the peasants meanwhile were ingenious in discovering ways to lighten their burdens. Since only one member of a villein family was obliged to perform a work the wise family would despatch their most inept performer. Work on the demesne was likely to be accomplished without great enthusiasm, though peasants who over-exploited the system ran the risk of being fined. The author Rowland Parker discovered a number of examples when he explored the manor-court rolls of Foxton in Cambridge:

> 1326: Ten of the tenants of full holdings were each fined 2*d.* [1p] because they made their sheaves much smaller with twisted bands when they ought to have made sheaves of the same size as they did when working for the Lady. (Here they were not trying to cheat the lady, but to deprive the rector of some of his tithes.)

Other cases heard around this time included:

All customary tenants fined because they refused to carry the Lady's hay out of the water on the day when they were mowing.

William Cock in contempt in saying that the tenants did not know that they were supposed to mow in a swamp.

Nicholas Werry fined 6*d.* (2½p) because he reaped badly the Lady's corn.

Thomas Leger fined 12*d.* (5p) because he reaped the Lady's corn when the weather was considered too cold. Likewise six others.

The manorial system can only be evaluated in terms of its period and setting, so rather than stress its injustices from a modern perspective one may note the fourteenth-century commentary by William Langland in his *Piers the Plowman*:

O, my lord, I labour hard; I go out at daybreak in order to drive the oxen to the field, and I yoke them to the plough. There is not so stark a winter that I dare stay at home, for fear of my lord, but having yoked the oxen and fastened the share and coulter to the plough every day I have to plough a full acre or more ...

The manor court comprised the COURT BARON, attended by free tenants and the COURT CUSTOMARY, for the unfree and they were concerned with regulating the COMMONS and waste. Sometimes control was gained of the COURT LEET, which regulated the common arable land. The role of the manor court was far from being solely concerned with the oppression and exploitation of the feudal tenants. It played a vital role in the detailed operation of the agricultural countryside, producing bylaws to prevent the unjust expropriation of resources and worked to make the environment safer and more efficient by controlling livestock, preventing accidents, improving drainage and attempting to improve roads. See also DEMESNE, ESTATE.

*Further reading:* Homans, G. C., *English Villagers of the Thirteenth Century*, Norton, 1975.
Parker, R., *The Common Stream*, Paladin, 1976.
Williamson, T. and Bellamy, L., *Property and Landscape*, George Philip, London, 1987.

**Mar-, mare-**. Words deriving from MERE that occur in place-names and signify a boundary.

**March-dyke**. A BOUNDARY wall.

**Mark, march**, see MERE, BOUNDARY, DOLE.

**Mark Stone**, see BOUNDARY STONE, MERE STONE.

**Market cross**, see CROSSES.

**Market house (green house, fair house)**. These buildings, usually survivals of the later medieval centuries, were erected on GREENS that were the venues of MARKETS AND FAIRS. They were used for storing the components of market booths and the hurdles used for making pens on their ground floors, while there may have been an upper storey which accommodated the court of 'pie-powder'. This improbable word comes from the French *pieds poudres* or 'dusty feet', referring to the state of those who had plied the dusty lanes to reach the scene of trading. These courts levied fines against those who had broken the trading regulations and collected market rents and tolls – all valued sources of revenue to the feudal sponsors of markets and fairs. When the village market declined – as most did – the market house could experience a succession of different uses, as a store-room, guildhall, school or chapel. One of the most attractive examples, dating from about 1500, stands on the green at Elstow in Bedfordshire. See also GUILDHALLS.

**Markets and fairs**. Markets must have a remarkable antiquity, and it has often been suggested that STONE CIRCLES and HENGES could have served as ancient marketplaces, while CAUSEWAYED ENCLOSURES may have been the venues of Neolithic 'fairs'. In Saxon England the King, and subsequently nobles, bishops and abbots, controlled and organised the movement

*Market house*
The market house on the green at Elstrow in Bedfordshire.

of goods between their estates and developed markets and fairs, with royal mints being established in various places to strike coins for use in trading. Numerous markets must have existed in Saxon England and some were recorded in DOMESDAY BOOK. After the Norman Conquest some of those customary markets were regularised by the issue of a formal market charter.

Whether or not a medieval village was able to aspire to rural stardom by obtaining a market could depend largely on the entrepreneurship of its local lord and patron. Were he ambitious, he would probably seek to purchase a market charter from the King – and if the local estate-owner was also the King, then he would similarly seek to promote the commercial interests of potentially promising villages. Some market charters were granted in Norman times, but the heyday of the market was the thirteenth century when around 3000 markets were authorised, while the economic decline experienced in the next century stemmed the flood of newly created markets. There was income to be made from markets, and not only by the traders: the local lord could expect to profit from taxes levied on his markets and from the various fines erected against breaches of trading regulations – hence the proliferation of market charters. Thus, in 1282, a charter from York records that 'Robert de Plumpton gave the King ten pounds for the institution of a market on his Manor of Grassington [in Wharfedale] and a fair in the same'. Forestalling, the offence of trading before reaching an authorised market, attracted heavy fines.

The competition between local village markets was intense and often fatal, while the smaller players in the world of commerce also faced severe challenges from large and well-established urban markets and also those established in the numerous planned new towns of the Middle Ages. To alleviate competition, limits could be placed on the proximity of markets, while within a locality market days were usually staggered throughout the week. Even so, the great majority of village markets were poorly provided and faced gradual extinction. Wensley in North Yorkshire, chartered in 1202, was sufficiently important as a market centre to give its name to a dale (previously known as Yoredale or Uredale), and in the sixteenth century John Leland wrote: 'Wensedale, as some say, taketh name of Wensela Market'. In 1563, however, Wensley was hit by the pestilence or Black Death and shortly afterwards, in 1587, Askrigg, a few miles further up the dale, received a market charter and Wensley could not survive the competition. Not far away was Richmond with a market formalised in Norman times, but by 1440 there were complaints that Richmond's trade was shrinking in competition with toll-free markets established at Masham, Bedale, Middleton and Barnard Castle.

To modern eyes medieval village markets might seem rather tedious events with nothing very exciting being offered for sale. For the peasants of the day, however, they were important events which offered relief from tedious routine. The reeve might make special efforts to ensure that shepherds and cowherds did not abandon their charges to wander in the corn when lured away by the anticipated thrills of a market or fair. Occasionally the local courts would punish a miscreant by forbidding him or her to attend the market. A few villages grew on the success of their markets, gained borough status and so cast off the shackles of feudalism and prospering as market towns. More often, village markets struggled along for a century, or two or three, before fading away, so that today there are very few village weekly markets of any note and a good number of villages have followed their failing markets into oblivion (see LOST VILLAGES). Most chartered markets are recorded, and a search in the local history section of a library should reveal information about particular markets. In the countryside, the evidence of a former market can be found in village GREENS or market squares and the market CROSSES which may still stand upon them, intact or in fragments. Other relics include old market roads, like the track between Settle and Kirkby Malzeard in the Yorkshire Dales, which took travellers over high moors at heights up to 1750 feet (530 metres).

Fairs were much more important functions and were normally annual rather than weekly occasions. They were frequently held on the day of the saint to which the principal church in a town or village was dedicated. They attracted a more far-ranging class of merchants. Some fairs may have developed from village WAKES, though most were sanctioned by a special charter which specified their date and duration. While village markets could handle basic commerce in essential goods, to obtain luxuries and exotic goods one normally had to visit a fair – and village fairs could not hope to emulate the celebrated fairs of the great provincial cities or open venues, like the ancient Stourbridge fair held near Cambridge. Some fairs specialised in certain commodities and a few of these fairs proved durable – like the Tan Hill sheep fair, held high on the Marlborough Downs on St Anne's Day until the early years of the twentieth century. For lack of space in the market square, a number of town fairs were held in rural settings; Cambridge's Stourbridge fair was at Barnwell and the Easter fair of St Ives (Huntingdonshire, now Cambridgeshire) spilled beyond the town and into the open fields. Statute fairs derived from legislation in the reign of Elizabeth I that required meetings to be held in every district or HUNDRED to settle wages and appoint employees. Those in search of employment would attend with the symbol of their service – shepherds with their crooks, maids with their mops, and so on – and these

fairs (as so evocatively portrayed by Thomas Hardy in his Wessex novels) became commonly known as 'mop fairs'. A few 'Shambles' field-names may indicate the locations of medieval markets. Like the famous Shambles in York, the name refers to butchers' stalls. See also CROSSES, GREEN, VILLAGE.

*Further reading:* Taylor, C., 'Medieval Market Grants and Village Morphology', *Landscape History* 4, 1982, pp. 21–8.

**Market stance**. The field that contained the market site or 'marketstead'.

**Marlpit (dene hole)**. Since at least Roman times, and probably well before, British farmers were aware of three ways of restoring fertility to

*Marlpit*
Flooded marlpits dug into the earthworks of Godwick deserted village in Norfolk.

their fields: fallowing; manuring, that was achieved either by folding animals on deteriorated ground or by carting and spreading farmyard manure; and marling. Marling involved spreading chalky clay subsoil on to the field concerned, and if its soils were acid, the marl would help to sweeten them. LIME-KILNS were also developed to produce powdered lime for agriculture, though modern fertilisers arrive in plastic bags that tend only to have chemical contents.

Marlpits appear to have been dug in Roman Britain, while the Saxon charters make various references to the existence of marl or loam pits (*lampytt*), sometimes preserved in field-names like Lamb Pit Field. Where the chalky clay occurred close to the surface, the marlpits could exist as shallow hollows like pock marks on the face of a chalk hill, but in many places the marl could only be obtained by sinking a shaft – a chalk well or draw pit. Where such pits have collapsed a hollow or a pond will occur. In the chalk of the Yorkshire Wolds the marlpits generally have a crater-like appearance and in west Norfolk the depressions marking the old workings have often been colonised by clumps of trees. The digging of marlpits was common in medieval and later times and continued until around the end of the nineteenth century. Some old workings, like the Abbot of Fountains Abbey's workings in the Magnesian Limestone at Ripley, North Yorkshire, are extensive earthworks of considerable amplitude. On the whole, however, the marling of soil was to a considerable extent a consequence of the LIGHT LAND REVOLUTION and associated with the enclosure and the sweetening of heathland soils, which could then be brought under arable cultivation. The practice has left a legacy of field- and place-names, like Marlpit Hill in Kent and scores of Marl-, Marlpit-, Chalk- and Chalkpit field-names. The latter derive from the Old English *calc*, and some 'chalk' names must be older than the alternative Old French word *marie*, which was introduced at some stage in the Middle Ages. In 1339, a surviving record

shows that marl was selling in West Yorkshire at 2*d.* (about 1p) per cartload, though the price must have varied according to the distance from the source. Lanes known as 'chalkways' originally led to the places where marl was dug.

**Masterwork**. Before rents in service disappeared in Scotland this was work on the MAINS or HOME FARM that could be demanded of tenants from surrounding small holdings.

**Maypoles**. Where these survive, they generally represent fairly recent whimsy shared by a portion of the community. Dancing around a pole did take place on May Day in some villages as part of fertility rituals to celebrate the start of summer and the poles concerned may have been set in slots in a flat, heavy stone. A large maypole is said to have stood in the (subsequently lost) village of Clint in the Yorkshire Dales, being pulled down early in the eighteenth century after the heir to the manor had an accident of some kind when playing there. Very few maypoles appear to have survived through the period between the abandonment of ancient rites and the emergence of a fascination with folk song and dance in the late nineteenth century. Where 'may' appears in a place-name it most often relates to the hawthorn or may. Some of the names do relate to lands associated with either festivities or opening to grazing in May, but there are a few that were associated with maypoles. Field quotes a Maypole Hill at Bilsborrow in Lancashire and a Maypole Meadow at Newnham, Gloucestershire.

**Maze**. Mazes have become the subject of much colourful speculation. Perhaps this is fitting since their name derives from the now little-used word 'mazed', meaning baffled or amazed. The traditional maze was cut in turf, and although such mazes seem to have existed on various medieval village GREENS and PLAISTOWS, and could have had a much longer history, it is difficult to imagine a more perishable kind of monument, so that the antiquity and understanding of old mazes is likely to remain a matter of speculation. Pliny mentions children playing in mazes, though it is probably merely coincidental that some of the more elaborate of the prehistoric CUP AND RING MARKS somewhat resemble maze plans. The impermanence of the maze once neglected by its users is neatly summarised in Shakespeare's *A Midsummer Night's Dream* of about 1595:

> ... the quaint mazes in the wanton green
> For lack of tread are indistinguishable.

There appears to have been a fashion for mazes and maze games in later medieval times, and mazes were incorporated into church decorations, like a boss at St Mary Redcliffe church at Bristol and a detail in the world map at Hereford Cathedral. Subsequently, the ascendancy of more puritanical values, which frowned on symbolism and frolics, must have led to the abandonment of numerous turf mazes. Turf mazes exist at places such as Saffron Walden in Essex and Camerton in Avon, but most surviving mazes are likely to have been cut in post-medieval times. Hedge mazes derive from Italian fashions in gardening and were introduced to Britain in Elizabethan times, although the famous Hampton Court maze dates from the reign of William III. Former mazes may only very occasionally be denoted by 'maze' and 'Troy' place-names (a popular maze game being known as the Game of Troy), and Troy Farm at Somerton in Oxfordshire has a maze.

**Meadows.** The need for hay-meadows derives from the simple fact that under the British climate the growth of grass virtually ceases during the winter months, so hay must be grown and dried to provide fodder to keep livestock alive during the winter. Hay can be grown either in dry upland meadows, on the BANKS of fells or in damp meadows in the valley bottoms. Under the manorial system there were common meadows as well as the common ploughlands and 'wastes'. These meadows, usually on low-lying ground beside a stream or river, were divided between the tenants into strips known as 'DOLES' or 'dales' which were frequently marked by 'MERE STONES' or boundary stones, while removable fences or hurdles might be used to clarify the limits of the doles. In some places the division of the meadow was permanent, but sometimes lots were cast each year to reallocate the doles in what were known as 'LOT MEADOWS' or 'dole meadows'. The manorial DEMESNE meadow often seems to have been kept separate from the common meadow. Sometimes certain privileges were granted to peasants for mowing the lord's meadow. At Barton-in-the-Clay in Bedfordshire an official of the abbot of Ramsey's manor released a sheep amongst the mowers – if they could catch it, then they could keep it. A gift of mutton and cheese and of as much hay as each mower could lift on his scythe without breaking its shaft seems to have been the custom on various MANORS.

The typical medieval meadow was kept free of livestock until the hay crop was mown, dried and gathered and was then grazed in common by the village livestock for the remainder of the season. The hay harvest traditionally began on St John's Day (24 June), and in the words of Thomas Tusser in the sixteenth century:

> At midsummer downe with the brembles and
>   brakes
> and after, abroade with thy forks and thy rakes
> Set mowers a mowing, where meadow is
>   growne
> the longer now standing the worse to be
>   mowne.

Some meadows were known as 'Lammas meadows'. Lammas, from the Old English *hlaf-mass*, or loaf mass, was 1 August, the date on which the newly mown and cleared meadows were thrown open to grazing and work began on harvesting grain. Lammas meadows were grazed until the beginning of the re-growth of the grass at Candlemas (2 February). Lammas was also the beginning of a season of relative plenty, with new grain becoming available to replenish the empty stores.

Medieval meadows may have been ploughed periodically to revitalise the grass, though many modern hay-meadows are regularly reseeded with a grass monoculture, and it has been estimated that since 1947 we have lost no less than 95 per cent of our traditional wildflower-rich meadows. Another threat to wildlife derives from the popular practice of cutting hay early and moist for silage rather than mowing and drying it in the traditional manner. As a result, meadow-nesting birds find their habitat being cut long before the completion of nesting. The corncrake, formerly the most characteristic meadowland bird, is now largely confined to a few refuges in Cumbria and north and west Scotland. See also WATER MEADOW, LOT MEADOW.

*Further reading*: Williamson, T., *Shaping Medieval Landscapes: Settlement, Society, Environment,* Windgather Press, 2003.

**Mealin.** In Scotland, a FARMSTEAD, farm holding or farm rent. A 'mealler' is a COTTAR who works the farm free of rent for several years in return for improving the land.

**Medieval and later bridges.** In medieval times bridges were more often wanted than won. Part of the problem derived from the fact that, while travellers (notably traders, itinerant artisans, pilgrims and the noble owners of several widely separated manors) urgently desired the means to cross rivers in safety and with dry feet, the local notables who were nominally responsible for providing bridges were reluctant to bear the considerable costs of bridge-building. Meanwhile parochial attitudes might argue that the building of a bridge would only increase local pressure on

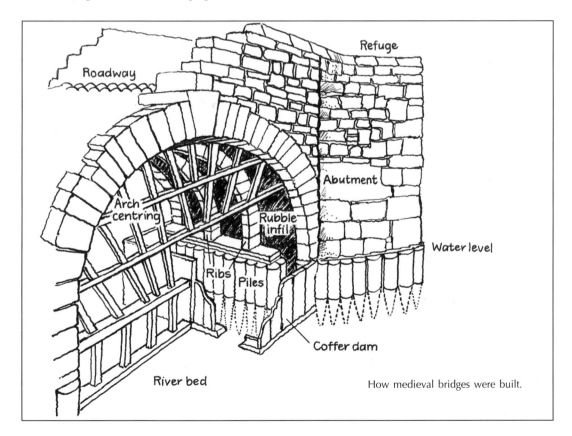

How medieval bridges were built.

the road concerned – leading to greater demands for maintenance work. The medieval authorities concerned, normally the MANORS, generally preferred short-term expedients in the form of timber bridges which would endure no longer than the next great flood. This said, where bridge-building was undertaken on a more purposeful basis (often as an attempt to stimulate a market and boost its revenue of trading tolls), the result could be a beautiful and impressive structure. Such a bridge could survive to the present day, it could be demolished to yield place to a larger, if less elegant, structure, or it could survive with substantial modifications. Preservation is often associated with a modest traffic-flow or the later development of alternative communications, such as has permitted the survival of the lovely fifteenth-century bridge at Moulton in Suffolk.

Medieval bridges vary considerably in size. Some, like the (widened) fifteenth-century bridge across the Tees at Croft, are large and imposing; others, like the one at Fountains Abbey, are bijou constructions. In some cases, bridges appear to have developed in an accidental fashion, with travellers first being attracted to a mill dam, which offered a dry crossing of a river or stream. In turn, a trackway would develop as people were drawn to this crossing point, and eventually, a purpose-built bridge could be provided. At Ripley, in North Yorkshire, the dam of a medieval fulling mill seems to have been the ancestor of the ornamental bridge spanning Ripley Beck which is the outlet of the nineteenth-century ornamental lakes in the adjacent LANDSCAPE PARK. The Medway is noted for its medieval bridges, such as the one at Teston, though the magnificent eleven-arch bridge near Rochester was replaced in 1856. Bridges of this period can generally be recognised irrespective of their size (though this does not apply to CLAPPER BRIDGES). Their

*Medieval bridge*
The medieval bridge across the Tees at Crfot, near Darlington.

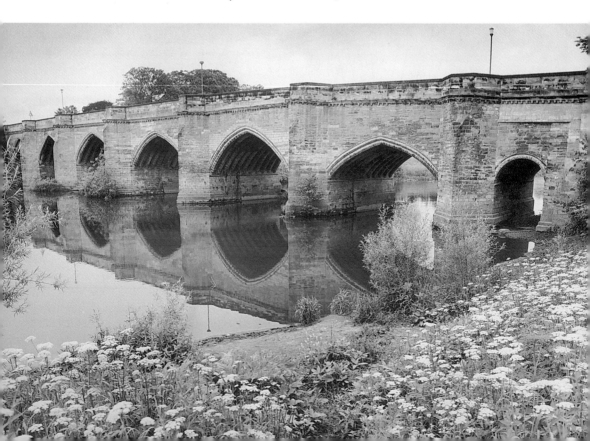

arches are often to some degree pointed rather than rounded, reflecting the Gothic fashion in church arches. Cutwaters – the projecting stone-works which split the current and divert it around the piers – are pointed, and – perhaps to economise in stone – the undersides of the arches are sometimes, though not always, 'ribbed' with projecting parallel bands of stone which follow the curves of the arches. The sequence of bridging a river could be quite complicated. Many medieval bridges succeeded old fords and a few may mark the sites of Roman timber or stone bridges (none of which survives in Britain). In turn medieval bridges could often be widened in order to accommodate the broader vehicles of later ages. In examining a bridge it is therefore necessary to look at both sides – there are several examples like the one at Croft where one side of the bridge is medieval and the other side (that is, the upstream or downstream side) is the result of later widening. Equally, a place might have experienced a succession of bridges in the course of the Middle Ages, with a stone bridge only being acquired when a shortage of heavy timber or disasters associated with wooden bridges argued for a more durable replacement. In a few cases urban medieval bridges were fortified (for example, Monmouth) or had integral bridge chapels (Bradford-on-Avon and St Ives, Cambridgeshire).

Appearances can be deceptive, but a number of post-medieval bridges carry datestones or other inscriptions (like the one on the bridge at Cowgill, Dentdale: 'This bridg repered at the charg of the West Riding A.D. 1702'), and display un-medieval features like rounded, rib-less arches. There is seldom reason to suppose that a country bridge seen is the original one to have stood at a crossing. Some simple bridges of the eighteenth and nineteenth centuries stand on routes used to connect medieval granges or link them with their abbeys. Various timber bridges may have been washed away before the surviving structure was built. Post-medieval bridges could also be successive –

one of the most successive examples crossing the Ure between Middleham and Leyburn in Wensleydale. The first bridge was paid for by public subscription and opened with a Bridge Inn and a TOLL HOUSE beside it in 1830. It soon collapsed when a herd of cattle was crossing (two cows drowned) and was reopened in 1831. During the years that followed, it provided locals with opportunities to demonstrate their ingenuity in devising ways of dodging tolls, until the bridge timbers decayed and another public subscription was required to finance the girder bridge of 1850. In 1880, the tolls of the less ingenious travellers had recouped costs and the bridge became the property of the county council – which had to foot a £500 bill for strengthening it nineteen years later. Subsequently it only proved moderately expensive.

**Medieval roads.** In the words of the historian, C. T. Flower, medieval roads 'made and maintained themselves'. During the Middle Ages, new roads were not generally the products of careful planning and earnest engineering. Instead, they appeared spontaneously when sufficient travellers had formed a consensus about the best way of getting from A to B. Not surprisingly, the old ROMAN ROADS, which had been both planned and engineered, remained as the main alignments of the national road system. At the start of the Middle Ages the importance of the Roman system was reinforced when the Norman kings restored the capital to London, which had been the hub of the Roman road system.

Where the movement of bulky goods was concerned, the RIVER TRANSPORT and coastal trading systems were more important than the inadequate and neglected network of medieval roads, so that the roads often existed as feeders to the waterways used in river trading. Even so, there was always much more land traffic than the road could cope with without causing frustration, delay and inconvenience. Country people needed to reach their local market; the market and fair traders had to arrange their affairs so that they arrived at their next destination in time for the weekly market or annual fair and not on the day after; pilgrims needed to get from one hostel to the next and not be benighted on the road; nobles with large and hungry retinues wanted to get from one manor to the next in time for supper; and so on. Meanwhile, the greatest traveller in the entire realm was the King himself, forever circulating between his many royal estates, hunting in his FORESTS and DEER PARKS, presiding over courts or enjoying the hospitality of his greater subjects – but even he was virtually powerless to effect a worthwhile road-building programme. It used to be held that four great highways were under his special protection: Watling Street, Fosse Way, Ermine Street and the Icknield Way. Recent scholarship has exposed this story as a twelfth-century myth. The extent of the dependence on pre-medieval road-making is apparent when one considers that first three were Roman constructions and the fourth was largely prehistoric in origin! Purposeful efforts in road-building during the Middle Ages seem to have been largely confined to the creation of three causeways across the Fens to Ely and the development, under Edward I, of some routes for conquest in Wales. In some parts of the country travel was hazardous in a variety of ways. In 1285, King Edward I heard of the murder by robbers of a party of Stamford merchants and he issued an edict commanding that where roads passed through woodland a zone of 60 feet (18 metres) on either side of the highway should be cleared of trees to deprive outlaws of hiding places. This seems to have caused a brief flurry of clearance, though the commandment was soon forgotten.

For evidence of the main routes used in medieval England one must rely partly upon contemporary accounts of journeys made – with there being considerable information available on the movements of the monarchs – and partly on the skimpy and unaccomplished map evidence. The crude 'Gough Map' of around 1360 attempted to depict roads, and the historian,

B. P. Hindle, has described how it reveals the importance of the four old highways, while some 40 per cent of all the routes shown were Roman in origin. The shortcomings of the land transport network must have acted as a brake on commerce, but it is notable that the most numerous and exasperated complaints about roads came from the two post-medieval centuries – the period when the system was really beginning to break down.

In medieval times, the road was not perceived as a 'made' routeway but as the King's Highway: a right of way. This right of way was a variable alignment: if the track became so muddy and rutted as to be impassable, then the traveller had the freedom to skirt the hazard via the adjacent fields. Meanwhile, the manor courts would work at the margins of the problem and attempt to remove the worst individual abuses without ever achieving general improvements. Thus at Hatfield Broadoak, Essex, in 1443, it was found that 'William Barbor junior built a latrine on his holding which runs into the King's Way to the nuisance of passers-by'. Trouble greater than mere nuisances occurred when benighted travellers fell into cess pits that had been unlawfully dug in the highway. In addition to the more important roads which were integrated into the network or terminated at a port there was a mass of other unintegrated tracks, leading from village or farmstead to fields and fisheries or from cottages to church.

Because of their undisciplined nature, medieval roads are not instantly recognisable – even though they form perhaps the bulk of our minor roads and lanes and underlie many of the more important modern routes. Many medieval roads will have been inherited from earlier periods, while today they can exist as living roads, dusty lanes, overgrown HOLLOWAYS or MULTIPLE TRACKS. Unless the highway divided or broadened to provide alternative routes across open or difficult ground it was likely to be narrow and hollowed. Where an old road has escaped 'modernisation' it may be a through-way so narrow that one can simultaneously touch the hedgerows on either side, like the nettle-infested path near Ripley, North Yorkshire, that was once the main road between York and Lancaster. Place-name evidence can be invoked, though often chicken-or-egg situations arise. There are scores of old roads and lanes with names like Arkendale Road, Aldborough Gate or Skelton Lane (to take some examples from the Boroughbridge area) which are taken from old settlements or market centres – but did the towns and villages attract the roads or were they built beside highways which could already have been ancient? In Wales place-names associated with roads include *cryw*, 'a ford'; *fford* and *heol*, 'a road'; and SARN, 'a causeway' and also a name which often attaches to Roman and other ancient roads. If there is one story that encapsulates the medieval road, it concerns the events in 1386, when the abbot of Chertsey allowed two enormous wells to exist in the high road between Egham and Staines in Surrey. After a traveller fell down and drowned in one of them the abbot added insult to injury by laying claim to his goods.

The traveller on medieval roads was likely to encounter some grim scenes. They were sometimes GIBBET SITES as well as earlier places of execution. Until the practice was outlawed by an Act of Parliament in 1823, suicides and criminals were often buried at roadsides, crossroads being favoured because it was thought that the crossing would confuse their ghosts and prevent them returning. As such a crossing, called Gallows Gate, near Fowlmere in Cambridgeshire, some 60 skeletons were excavated in the 1920s and inspection of the remains showed that some Saxons had been beheaded and later victims had been hung. In the same county, victims of a gallows maintained by Crowland Abbey were found at a crossroads near Oakington village. See also CAUSEWAY, DROVE ROAD, GREEN LANE, HOLLOWAY, PACK-HORSE ROAD, ROMAN ROADS, SALTWAY.

*Further reading*: Cooper, A. R., *Obligation and Jurisdiction: Roads and Bridges in Medieval Britain, 700–1300*, unpublished PhD thesis, Harvard University, 1998.

Halliday, R., 'Criminal Graves at Rural Crossroads', *British Archaeology*, 1997 (June), p. 6.

Hindle, B. P., *Medieval Roads*, Shire Archaeological Publications, 1982.

Hindle, B. P., *Roads, Tracks and Their Interpretation*, Batsford, London, 1993.

Taylor, C. C., *Roads and Tracks of Britain*, Dent, 1979.

**Meer.** Before the modern era, lead was mined in the Yorkshire Dales according to customary mining law whereby the ground along each vein was divided into rectangular blocks or meers. At Grassington the meer was 30 yards long with a quarter cord or 7.5 yards of land on either side of the vein as breadth. Mining grants were made in the form of blocks of meers and miners were obliged to undertake their operations, including dressing the ore, erecting buildings and stacking waste within the areas of the quarter cords. Meerstones marked the confines of the grants. In 1774, this system of linking a grant to a vein was replaced by the leasing of larger blocks of ground that might include several veins. See also BELL PIT, MERE STONE.

*Further reading*: Roe, M., 'The Changing Face of Lead Mining Archaeology in the Yorkshire Dales', LANDSCAPES 4.1, 2003.

**Megalithic tomb**, see CHAMBERED TOMB.

**Memorial stone**, see CROSSES.

**Menhir**, see MONOLITH.

**Mere, mear.** A boundary, sometimes a boundary between OPEN-FIELDS or FURLONGS and sometimes a grassy balk between lesser divisions. See also DOLE, BOUNDARY.

**Mere stone, mere stane.** A boundary stone.

*Further reading*: Brewer, D., *Boundary Markers On and Around Dartmoor*, Devon Books, Exeter, 1986.

Griffiths, D., Reynolds, A. and Semple, S., *Boundaries in Early Medieval Britain*, Oxbow, Oxford, 2003.

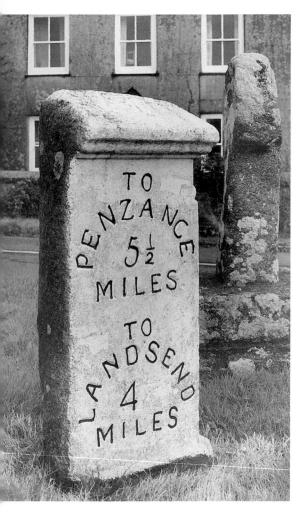

*Milestone*
An old milestone at Crows-an-wra in Cornwall.

**Messuage**. A medieval term used to denote a house, FARMSTEAD or farm. An 'ancient messuage' could relate either to a house built before the reign of Richard I or else one that was built longer ago than anyone living in the locality could remember. While often denoting a farm, the term 'messuage' when used in a narrower sense included a house, its subsidiary buildings, its yard and, if it had one, its garden.

A 'capital messuage' was a large house. See also GARTHSTEAD, MAILIN.

**Metal**. To repair a road with broken stones.

**Metcalfe**. Blind Jack Metcalfe of Knaresborough was a most remarkable man who, like MACADAM and TELFORD, prospered in the turnpike era. He was blinded by smallpox in 1723 at the age of six yet pursued a life of adventure and excitement. His interest in road building began in 1751, following involvement in the pacification of the Scottish Highlands. He inaugurated a coach service between Knaresborough and York and undertook the improvement of three miles of TURNPIKE between Harrogate and Boroughbridge. Though blind, he served as his own surveyor, employing his staff as sounding rods and relying on his sense of touch to evaluate materials. He had particular successes in driving roads across expanses of marshy ground in the Knaresborough locality. By 1792 he could claim to have been instrumental in the construction of 180 miles of turnpike and several solid bridges.

**Midden, medding**. Dung heap.

**Milestones**. The first milestones were erected beside Roman roads, some of them providing distances to nearby towns, but some only giving the name of the then current emperor. Such stones have sometimes been moved into museums, as at Caernarfon, but a few survive *in situ*, as at Chesterholm on the Corbridge–Carlisle road, or have been just slightly moved, like the one at Middleton near Kirby Lonsdale which has a brief Roman inscription, 'MP LIII', denoting fifty-three miles to Carlisle. Thereafter, very few milestones seem to have been erected before the era of the TURNPIKES. Acts of 1744 and 1766 extended the compulsion to erect milestones to all roads, and a multitude of attractive white-painted stone and cast-iron examples appeared – some made by local craftsmen who did not assist the long-distance traveller by adopting the vernacular name for places (Salisbury appearing in the ancient guise of Sarum). Connoisseurs of the genre will appreciate the stones seen beside the A10 near Cambridge, set up by the Master of Trinity College in 1728 and bearing the college crest. One now puzzling instruction is the 'Take-off' beside a minor road near Callington, Cornwall. The stone marks the spot where an additional horse, hired and harnessed to a coach for the steep climb beyond the TOLL HOUSE a mile below, was taken off or unhitched and returned to the toll house. The pillar known as 'coachman's cautionery' on the A40 between Trecastle and Llandovery was erected in 1835, the inscription provides 'a caution to mail coach drivers to keep from intoxication'. This followed an incident when the drunken mailcoach-driver, Edward Jenkins, met a cart while driving at full speed on the wrong side of the road, so that the coach was smashed to pieces at the bottom of the 121-foot (37-metre) precipice. Occasionally, milestones will remain in place after the road that they grace has become redundant. One such stone can be seen at the northern end of Ripley, North Yorkshire, signalling a former branch of the village street towards Pateley Bridge and giving evidence of a re-routing of roads. A good selection of stone milestones of the eighteenth century, like the 'Porridge Stoop', giving miles and directions for destinations in the Keighley/ Skipton locality, were put up in the Pennines on the eve of the industrial era. See also SIGNPOST, STOOP.

**Military roads**. Most if not all ROMAN ROADS were initially built as roads of conquest or occupation, though they assisted the development of the commercial functions that became more important on the lowland roads, at least. In Saxon charters certain roads are described as '*Here-paeth*' and they seem to have been associated with the movement of armies or official retinues. In fact, the designation is not really clear and many if not all of these roads will have had an earlier existence as trackways and will have been used by ordinary travellers as well as by troops. Many roads and tracks are still known as 'herepaths' or 'harepaths', such as

the Wiltshire Herepath, traversing Fyfield and Overton Down near Marlborough.

A completely different generation of military roads provides the basic road network in the Scottish Highlands. These were built by the British authorities in an attempt to police and pacify the clan territories following uprisings in 1715 and 1719. The works began in 1725, with additional routes being added in the 1740s, and road-building continued intermittently into the 1760s. An Irish general, George Wade, was appointed commander-in-chief of the British forces in the Highlands in 1724 and he ordered a survey of the country and then advocated the building of Fort Augustus and Fort George. In combination with the existing stronghold at Fort William, this chain of forts would divide the Highlands, while the new military roads that he recommended would allow the rapid deployment of forces. Several of Wade's roads have been transformed by later improvements, as exemplified by the A83 and A93, but other stretches have been abandoned or by-passed during road-straightening. One of the finest original stretches links Laggan Bridge and Fort Augustus via the 2500-foot Corrieyairack Pass.

*Further reading*: Miller, Ronald, 'The Road North', *Scottish Geographical Magazine*, 1967.

**Mince-, Minchins**. When occurring in field names these denote land once attached to a nunnery.

**Minnis**. An upland COMMON in the south.

**Minster**. Most people know that this word has some connection with the Church and, because of the fame of the cathedrals known as York Minster and Ripon Minster, many will imagine it to be simply synonym for cathedral. The answer is more interesting than this, for an understanding of the role of minsters is crucial to an appreciation of the early centuries of Christianity in Britain. The word derives from the Latin *monasterium*, though the minsters of the Dark Ages were not exactly the early equivalents of the medieval monasteries. They are best regarded as mother churches that served as centres for conversion and the organisation of worship in the centuries preceding the establishment of a system of ecclesiastical parishes with 'field', 'proprietorial' or parish churches. Christianity was brought to Britain in Roman times, and Christian worship was not entirely extinguished in the years of turmoil and decay that followed the withdrawal from the collapsing Empire about AD 410. Surviving 'Eccles' place-names, from a debased form of the Latin *ecclesia*, or 'church', like Eccles, Eaglesfield or Exley, seem to denote a few of these old centres of worship. During the seventh century Christianity was adopted in the different English kingdoms, and thereafter minsters, staffed by a priest and his small body of monastic or secular assistants, were created, while in tenth-century Wales, a number of minster-like *clasau* appeared. These were large, often cruciform churches staffed by an abbot assisted by hereditary canons.

Evidence is emerging that shows that the minsters tended to be established on royal estates. This does not simply reflect the piety and evangelical inclinations of the Saxon kings, for with their educated and literate communities, the minsters were able to offer clerical services which would be valuable to the administration of an estate and a kingdom. During the later Saxon centuries, landowners provided churches to serve their own estates, and in this way the parish church system superseded the one based on a much smaller number of minsters that had despatched clergy to preach in the broad surrounding territory.

Minsters either decayed for lack of congregations or else merged into the parochial system. One of the most fascinating minsters is at Kirkdale, an isolated site on the southern edge of the North York Moors. Here, a wonderful inscribed Saxon sundial tells how the church was bought by Orm, Gamal's son, 'when it was all broken down' and rebuilt, in 1055–65. Many of the details of the old minster network are still to be discovered. As a result of successive

rebuildings, some old minster churches, like Horningsea in Cambridgeshire, are indistinguishable. Some, like Wing in Buckinghamshire, have not had their undoubted original minster functions actually confirmed by documentary sources. The sites of a few minsters, like *Laestingaeu* – probably Lastingham near Whitby – are still disputed, while many minsters are still to be identified. Any Saxon church with a generous complement of early crosses or cross fragments, traces of an archaic layout or of architectural fragments of seventh-, eighth- or ninth-century date is very likely to have been a minster. It is also occasionally possible to identify minsters by discovering which parish churches were originally subordinate or daughter churches of another. Any church which appears to have had a leading or 'motherly' position over neighbouring parish churches probably began as a minster, though rebuildings may have removed all traces of the original masonry.

*Further reading*: Bettey, J. H., *Church and Parish*, Batsford, London, 1987.
Blair, J. (ed.), 'Minsters and Parish Churches: The Local Church in Transition, 950–1200', *Oxford University Committee for Archaeology* Monograph 17, Oxbow, Oxford, 1998.

**Moat**. Medieval people were just as status-conscious as any others, not least because social class determined one's rights and one's obligations. The greatest nobles lived in splendid if rather uncomfortable castles, with heraldic banners, battlements and moats all symbolically underlining the privilege and nobility of the occupants. The lesser lords or ambitious franklins also sensed needs proclaim and, if possible, exaggerate their importance within their localities, though lacking both the means and the rights to indulge in castle-building. They attempted, therefore, to echo the grandeur of the powerful aristocrats by living within moated enclosures. This fashion, which flourished between about 1150 and the start of the fourteenth century, must have been extremely influential, for at least 5,000

*Moat*
The moat and gatehouse at Markenfield Hall, near Ripon.

homestead moats were constructed in England and Wales, and moats were quite common in Ireland and continental Europe. They were dug throughout most parts of the English and Welsh lowlands, with particularly heavy concentrations in East Anglia, Essex, the south-east Midlands, Warwickshire and Worcestershire. Although the fashion declined in the closing centuries of the Middle Ages, some of the greater Elizabethan mansions were symbolically moated. In Ireland, the homestead moats were dug after the Normans had consolidated their hold on the land, divided it into fiefdoms and established the parochial divisions. Those excavated tend to reveal a briefer span of occupation than in England, which often began in the late thirteenth century and ended within a century or so.

If the moat was primarily a status symbol, it also had other uses. If it stayed wet throughout the year, it could be stocked with fish and also, less idyllically, be the destination of domestic sewage, while sometimes improving the drainage of the house site. It used to be thought that homestead moats were defensive constructions, protecting the household against wolves and vagabonds. However, most moats were spanned by an immobile wooden bridge and many only ran along three sides of the homestead concerned. Surviving moats come in all manner of forms. Some may be in pristine condition, like the moat around the fourteenth-century fortified manor house, Markenfield Hall, near Ripon, around sixteenth-century Kentwell Hall in Suffolk, or fifteenth-century Oxburgh Hall in Norfolk. Many of the less pretentious and more typical medieval moats are still wet and still contain homesteads. In other cases moats can be deserted, and either wet or dry; they may have been reduced to just one or two arms by infilling. Most were four-sided with access via a bridge or causeway, but as well as the three-sided forms there were also double moats and round, oval and concentric forms. In the final stages of silting and neglect, the moated site may be revealed only by a counter-scarp bank of up-cast material on the outer rim of the moat. Moats also became popular in association with elaborate water gardens, as represented by the earthworks around the fanciful stone summer house of the 1590s, Lvyeden New Bield in Northamptonshire. Where double moats are found, one might have contained the medieval homestead, and the other have protected a garden. Defensive and ornamental moats will not normally be confused, but difficulties could arise at sites such as Middleham Castle in Wensleydale, where a trough at the foot of south-facing walls seems to have been an ornamental water feature rather than a defensive moat. In Scotland, 'moat' can signify a motte.

*Further reading*: Aberg, F. A. and Brown, A. E.,
    *Medieval Moated Sites in North-West Europe*, BAR
    International Series 121, 1981.

**Model Farm**. Model farms provided the owners of the great ESTATES with the opportunities to improve the commercial efficiency of their estates and to acquire fashionably progressive images. Hitherto, the holders of feudal estates had been entirely content to let their social inferiors concern themselves with the affairs of the estate and were only concerned that each tenant should meet his or her obligations in full. A rising fashion for efficiency and wholesomeness in agriculture blossomed under the influential patronage of George III (1760–1820), who

became widely known as 'Farmer George'. Despite the madness that affected the king in his later years, his advocacy of progressive farming methods, which sat easily with his opposition to political corruption and unrestrained patriotism, remained influential. While traditional farms had evolved organically, new buildings often being added according to the confines of the village plot or placed to sit within an existing lay-out, model farms, often HOME FARMS, were set out according to a grand plan which sought to have each building in its proper place. As defined by Wade Martins the model farm was '... a steading built for a landowner who wanted to set an example to the tenantry on his estate and society at large, invariably in addition to satisfying his own taste for classical or picturesque buildings'. The landlord provided the fixed infrastructure for the farm, while the tenant worked it and provided the machinery, livestock and seed. On the great estates the model farms sometimes, and ironically, resembled the state farms of the old Soviet Union, being set amongst other farms where they were expected to serve as pacemakers where the highest standards of efficiency would be achieved and as nuclei for the diffusion of innovations. They were the places where the latest inventions were introduced and tested, with steam engines and their associated gadgets often making their debuts in the model farms of a region. Buildings were normally built of durable materials like stone or brick, soundly-roofed and well-maintained, partly according to the premise that if animals and produce were provided with better shelter then they would respond accordingly.

Amongst the model farms, the inspiration in Georgian times was the Park Farm operated by Coke of Holkham in Norfolk, where the sheep shearings served as a gathering place for the dissemination of innovations. King George's Norfolk Farm at Windsor, Lord Anson's farm at Shugborough and the Duke of Bedford's farm at Woburn were other nuclei for the broadcasting both of changes and gadgets, but also the spiritual messages of HIGH FARMING. The agricultural social climate in the years around 1800 was influenced by changes that were useful and practical and also by the positive image that was associated with an involvement in progressive and responsible farming. Formed in 1838, the Royal Agricultural Society produced publications that broadcast the messages of the 'high farming' that the new, machine-based agriculture had created. Some of the changes to the farm were necessitated by the inventions, with engines and threshing machines requiring engine houses and threshing areas. Labour was reduced while arrangements had to be made to accommodate the moving belts radiating from engines to power different machines and achieve different tasks. The speed of operation of the threshing machines when compared to the flails of the old labour-intensive threshing meant that less corn was kept in store awaiting threshing, so there was no longer a need for the enormous threshing barns inherited from medieval times. The plans proposed for model farms attempted to produce the most efficient dispositions of buildings. One, proposed by Arthur Young in 1770, had the stacks neatly arranged in open yards in an outer square. Within, two flanks were occupied by an ox house and a calf house, each with its respective food storage shed, while one end of the farm yard thus enclosed existed as a sheep yard, surrounded by its feeding ricks and facing the barn across the open farm yard. In the 'sheep corn' areas of light, sandy or calcareous soils, bullocks could be incorporated into the arrangements. Turnips were gathered and taken to the farmstead where they were fed to bullocks living in yards surrounded by shelter sheds. These yards were placed beside the threshing barn so that straw from the threshed crop could be spread as bedding in the yard, trampled in dung and later spread on the land. By the time that the Home Farm at Longleat was built in 1863, the day of the Model Farm was coming to an end. In the next decade, a series of cool, wet years combined with severe competition from agricultural producers in the new world destroyed the confidence in sound farming techniques that had buoyed up high farming and estate owners looked to other areas for investment. See also FERME ORNÉE.

*Further reading:* Wade-Martins, S., *The English Model Farm, Building the Agricultural Ideal, 1700–1914,* Windgather Press, 2002.

Mingay, G. E. (ed.), *The Victorian Countryside,* 1981, II, pp. 214–26.

**Model Village,** see VILLAGE.

**Moiety.** A share of a feudal estate, generally half the estate, but sometimes less than this.

**Monolith (menhir, standing stone).** Monoliths

*Monolith*
A Bronze Age monolith at Merrivale on Dartmoor.
A small stone circle and double stone row are nearby.

present many problems to the prehistorian; their functions are mysterious and they are normally difficult or impossible to date. A standing stone of modest proportions might have been erected by Neolithic or Bronze Age people for some now unfathomable ritual purpose or it might merely be a boundary stone or cattle rubbing-post or some other form of STOOP erected just a century or so ago. There is little reason to doubt the prehistoric provenance of the larger monoliths. The tallest example in Britain stands beside the church at Rudston near Bridlington in a locality traversed by CURSUS monuments. It stands 26 feet (8 metres) tall and is a 26-tonne slab of gritstone which was probably hauled to its chosen site from the nearest source of such stone at Cayton Bay, some 10 miles (16 kilometres) away. The Devil's Arrows, near Boroughbridge, North Yorkshire, are a trio of standing stones, the tallest towering to a height of about 23 feet (7 metres), composed of Millstone Grit slabs hauled over a distance of at least 6 miles (9.5 kilometres) before their erection. Other celebrated monoliths include the 20-foot (6-metre) Clach an Trushal stone on Lewis and the Blind Fiddler monolith and the pair of standing stones known as The Pipers, all in Cornwall. In addition to these famous examples there are scores of less imposing monoliths, a high proportion of them erected in prehistoric times, whose function is still mysterious. They might be grave-, boundary- or route-markers or objects of great ritual significance. Despite the problems of dating and attributing functions, at least monoliths would appear to be relatively unsophisticated monuments – or so it seemed until recent excavations at the site of a seemingly unremarkable monolith at Stackpole Warren near Pembroke. Here it was found that the stone, known as the Devil's Quoit, had been erected amongst an arrangement of more than 3000 small stones and placed at the rounded end of the boat- or shield-shaped assemblage. Originally, a timber post stood mast-like near the centre of the arrangement. The peculiar

monument could only be roughly dated, to the period 1700–1050 BC, and most other monoliths are assumed also to belong to the Bronze Age. It remains to be seen whether subsequent excavations may reveal similar complexities.

*Further reading*: Burgess, C., *The Age of Stonehenge*, Dent, Lodon, 1980.

Parker Pearson, M., *Bronze Age Britain*, Batsford/ English Heritage, London, 1993.

**Mool**. In Scotland, a headland.

**Moor hags**. Holes made in the MOOR by peat cutting. See also TURBARY.

**Moors**. In the common parlance of former times, 'moor' ('muir' in Scotland) was a term used more widely than today, describing not only the upland heather moors, but also lowland heaths and low, marshy or 'moorish' COMMONS. There has been considerable debate concerning whether the moors of the British uplands are natural creations or the products of human intervention. It seems to be the case that in the mountains of Scotland and in Scandinavia the ling-covered moors are the climax vegetation. However, in the uplands of England they are thought to result from the destruction of indigenous woodland by humans, a process which began with the clearing of open hunting ranges in the Mesolithic era. Deforestation, the saturation of ground following the removal of trees, grazing by sheep and cattle, and the more cyclonic conditions established in the latter part of the Bronze Age all contributed to the creation of distinctive landscapes of peat bog, cotton grass and purple moors.

The dappled appearance of most moors, resembling the patches on a camouflaged jacket, are produced by SWALING or the systematic burning of sections of heather moor. Today, this is associated with the management of grouse moors though it greatly pre-dates the fashion for grouse shooting and was originally undertaken by medieval shepherds to provide a 'soft bite' of heather by burning-off woody growth and encouraging the eruption of juicy new shoots

*Moors*

A typical upland scene near Skyreholm in the Yorkshire Dales, with the old common (now used for grouse shooting) rising above the lower walled fields and intakes.

beloved both by sheep and by grouse. Grouse shooting has led to the perpetuation and expansion of the kind of upland landscape associated with the rearing of sheep, though numerous moors are now in decline. The British red grouse is now regarded as an insular race of the Scandinavian willow grouse, and while chicks take insects, the adult birds are totally dependent on heather shoots and associated bilberries for their food. The manipulation of the upland environment to maximise the numbers of grouse supported has protected and sustained the area of heather moor, though the activity of keepers in persecuting vulnerable predators like the hen harrier, buzzard and short-eared owl has had a devastating effect. The illegal poisoning, trapping and shooting of such birds continues.

A number of factors were essential to the emergence of grouse shooting as a highly lucrative form of ESTATE management. Firstly, technology had to create guns that opened the activity to the myopic mill-owner as well as the crack-shot. Secondly, the activity ('sport' seems an inappropriate synonym for ritualised killing) had to be perceived as the sort of thing that would bolster one's manly and gentlemanly status. Thirdly, there had to be developments in the national transport system that would enable participants from all parts of the country to reach the moors in moderate comfort, and also facilitate the rapid consignment of 'the bag' to fashionable eating places. The pioneering enthusiasts shot over pointer dogs with flintlocks and it was the diffusion of new breech-loading guns of a French design in the middle of the nineteenth century that gave the mediocre shot the possibility of hitting a succession of flying birds and enabled the dedicated 'guns' to wreak mayhem amongst the bird population. (On 30 August 1888 Lord Walsingham employed four breech-loading guns and two loaders and killed 1070 birds in 20 drives on Blubberhouses Moor near Harrogate: an 'attainment' as curious as it is questionable).

The shooting of grouse began as an activity

for hardy locals who walked up to the moors with dogs and flintlocks. At the start of the nineteenth century, shooting rents were low, moors had, at least until recently, been regarded as wild and horrid places and shooting on them was confined to a muscular few. However, the challenging physical nature of the activity and the levels of marksmanship required helped the notion of it as a fitting diversion for a gentleman to take root. By the middle of the century, the pursuit was being formalised, with 'bags' being systematically recorded and compared – and this at a time when PARLIAMENTARY ENCLOSURE was privatising countless acres of upland commons. The formalisation of shooting, with its associated gamekeeping, swaling, the transportation of shooters, beating duties, loading and catering all helped to stimulate local economies in times of high rural unemployment. Meanwhile, the organised shoots associated with the great houses became meetings for the aristocratic, political and economic establishments. Grouse shooting became a ritual that cemented and regulated the affairs of the ruling class, while the owners of estates vied to provide the size of bags that would encourage titled guests, even royalty, to visit their moors.

Grouse moors had no significance if potential users were unable to reach them. In the eighteenth century, the construction of MILITARY ROADS in the uplands and Highlands of Scotland and the building of TURNPIKES in England brought the estates concerned within reach of the potential clienteles. Railways later provided fast and comfortable access to the moorland fringe. In the Yorkshire Dales, for example, seven relevant destinations acquired rail connections between 1846 and 1907. In addition, the relative swiftness of the trains allowed birds to be exported to butchers, poulterers and fashionable restaurants. In a single week in the August of 1901, a game dealer of Richmond despatched 17,352 birds to customers.

In order to serve a clientele characterised by affluence, breeding, or both, the activity had to evolve from the one that had lured the flintlock shooters and their pointers to the moors. The hardy marksmen who shot over their dogs, sometimes hitting a bird on the wing with a musket ball, were superseded by those who were conveyed to the moors in coaches and took part in 'battue' shooting. Even though the birds sped away at up to 90 k.p.h. they had become too easy to hit with the new shotguns when flying away. Now, the shooters waited in butts or behind walls for birds to be driven towards them by lines of beaters. The targets were more difficult, the guns far better and the tramping across the moor had been done away with. A few diehard estate owners persisted with shooting over dogs, but battue shooting marked the pursuit in its mature form, with jinking targets, massive bags, the management of moors as grouse factories and the organisation of shooting as a socio-political ritual of the ruling classes. Battue shooting had its own distinctive landscape of *shooting lodges, shooting houses/lunch huts* and *shooting butts.* The *lodges* began to appear as the activity gained in popularity and they provided alternative accommodation for members of shooting parties to that provided by the great house or the inns of the locality concerned. A lodge would often comprise an elegant house with numerous bedrooms, quarters for servants, stables, a coach house and a garden. Lodges became centres for commercial and political dealing, amorous assignations and status-seeking. *Shooting houses* and *lunch huts* were more functional in appearance, providing accommodation where refreshments could be consumed in the course of the day's shooting between drives. Some were purpose-built, while others were adapted from farmsteads or farm buildings. *Butts* were essential to battue shooting, providing places where the shooters could be concealed from their prey. Their positioning was not random, and took account of the flight-paths of the birds, the prevailing winds and the concern not to have birds driven away into a neighbouring estate. A variety of forms were employed: round; half-round; square;

sunken; H-shaped; or butts built from old railway sleepers. Sometimes DRYSTONE WALLS were commandeered to serve as butts, with painted numbers on the stones indicating the positions of the 'guns'. *Watching houses* were sometimes constructed in prominent places, allowing keepers to look-out for poachers.

The organisation of grouse shooting as an important and lucrative form of estate land-use helped to conserve heather moors, while drastically reducing birds that preyed on grouse. It took place against a background of PARLIAMENTARY ENCLOSURE and, by depriving ordinary people or access to the moors, it underlined the decay of public rights to enjoy the land that men and youths were expected to fight and die for. The exclusion of the public from grouse moors resulted in large-scale demonstrations concerning rights of access in the inter-war years and the problems of access are still to be completely resolved. In the twenty-first century the industry has become too small to conserve the former extent of grouse moors, while disease is reducing the numbers of grouse. A relict landscape of grouse shooting is emerging, with crumbling butts, abandoned buildings and heather moors that are going over to rough pasture. See also MOOR HAGS, MOSS.

*Further reading:* Done, A. and Muir, R., The Landscape History of Grouse Shooting in the Yorkshire Dales', *Rural History* 12, 2001, pp. 195–210.
Hudson, P. (ed.), *Grouse in Space and Time – The Population Biology of a Managed Gamebird,* The Game Conservancy Ltd, Fordingbridge, 1992.
Dunn, C. and Fletcher, M., 'The Evolution and Changing Perceptions of a Moorland Landscape', in Pattison, P., Field, D. and Ainsworth, S. (eds), *Patterns of the Past,* Oxbow, Oxford, 1999.

**Morning surprise**, see SQUATTER.

**Moss.** A moor where peat-cutting takes place. In the lowlands it may survive as a field- or other place-name after the moor has been drained and enclosed. See also MOOR, TURBARY.

**Moss thief, moss trooper**. Border riever or raider.

**Motte (motte and bailey)**. It would be wasteful of space to include a lengthy description of medieval castle types in a book on the rural landscape, but mottes and motte and bailey castles (as well as RINGWORKS) are included because they can often be encountered in countrysides as potentially puzzling earthwork features. Castles consisting of a flat-topped conical earthen mound or 'motte' (which was later often sited within or beside an embanked enclosure or 'bailey') were developed in France and the Rhineland a few decades before they were introduced to England and Wales (and later Scotland and Ireland) by the Normans. A few were built before the Norman Conquest by Norman favourites of Edward the Confessor (1042–66), the one at Richard's Castle near Ludlow being an example. Most mottes belong to the Norman period, and many of the smaller ones were built by the new Norman lords just after they had taken possession of their lands. Such mottes may have served no grander purpose than to provide the lord and a handful of followers with a defensive strongpoint from which their authority could be asserted – and readers may be surprised at how diminutive such earthworks can be, perhaps mistaking them for ROUND BARROWS or WINDMILL mounds.

About a thousand mottes were built in Britain in the early medieval centuries, many in the direct aftermath of the Conquest and others, many of them illegal or 'adulterine' castles, being erected during the anarchy of King Stephen's reign (1135–54). Not surprisingly, the entry in the Anglo Saxon Chronicle for 1137 complains that 'they filled the land full of castles. They cruelly oppressed the wretched men of the land with castle works and when the castles were made they filled them with devils and evil men and they said openly, that Christ slept, and His saints.'

Mottes were built of the earth-and-rubble upcast excavated from the surrounding MOAT, and some appear originally to have been coated in slippery clay to make it difficult for attackers to gain a foothold. The crown of the motte was ringed with a palisade of timber posts, and often a rectangular timber tower or 'keep' was erected within the palisade. Such wooden keeps would not normally be occupied, but where the motte was furnished with a bailey, then the domestic and ancillary manorial buildings would be erected within the shelter of its ramparts and palisade while the motte and its keep would serve as last-ditch defences. The conversion of timber keeps on mottes into towers of stone or donjons could present severe problems owing to the unconsolidated nature of the earthen mounds and the vulnerability of the corners of donjons. The tops of large mottes were sometimes ringed with stone walls to form circular shell keeps. At the main towns, dynastic centres and key defensive locations the earthen-and-timber fortresses would normally be superseded by stone keeps or curtain walls. Alternatively or additionally, a bailey could be ringed by a stone curtain – though the further evolution of stone castles lies beyond the scope of this book.

The mottes varied enormously in their size and importance, ranging from the modest strongholds of many rural knights to the gigantic castles at places like Ongar, Clifford's Hill in Northamptonshire, or Thetford in Norfolk, the last-named being the largest British example of a motte with a height of 80 feet (24 metres) and a base diameter of 360 feet (110 metres). Many of the small mounds were associated with the initial period of uncertainty as a Norman knight took over an English ESTATE, with such sites being abandoned for an unfortified HALL as soon as the members of the new local dynasty felt secure. In the Welsh border region mottes are known as 'tumps', and in Wales the word '*tomen*' is used. These words are not always reliable descriptions, and Hetty Pegler's Tump in Gloucestershire is a CHAMBERED TOMB. In England the word 'burgh', signifying a fortified place, is often associated with mottes. In Ireland, a flurry of motte-building followed the establishment of Norman control around 1170 and it lasted to around 1230. Thereafter, mottes lost the defensive lead to keep towers and then to curtain walls at the more significant centres. As in England, most were erected hastily to consolidate the positions of the new Norman occupiers and the concentration of mottes lies in the east of the country and outside Ulster. Attached baileys are rarer than in England, though occasionally an existing RATH was converted into a motte, as at Lismahon in Co. Down. Some mottes were built as elements in a Norman defensive design, and in Co. Wexford they formed a double line marking the frontier between the Norman-dominated areas and the north. See also BURH, RINGWORK.

*Further reading*: Brown, R. Allen, *English Castles*, Chancellor Press, 1970.

**Mount**, see PROSPECT MOUND.

**Mud and stud (clam, staff and daub)**. A cheap and poor-quality form of TIMBER-FRAMING used in low-status rural housing until the late eighteenth century. Upright posts were set directly in the earth rather than being jointed into a sill beam and were linked at their tops to a horizontal beam. The panels between the posts were filled with vertical staves and coated with a daub of clay to produce a wall.

**Muir**, see MOOR.

**Mull**. In Scotland, a promontory.

**Multiple estate**. Some of the most important influences on the history of the countryside are far less obvious than many other relatively inconsequential features. The multiple ESTATE could have existed as a crucial stage in the organisation of the landscape in England and Wales, but at present it exists more as a stimulating concept than as something that can be plainly seen in the rural setting. The term was coined by the historical geographer, Glanville Jones, whose research was partly based on medieval Welsh sources. In simplified terms,

the idea of the multiple estate sees much of Dark Age England and Wales as being divided between such estates, which were vast territories each centred on a head MANOR or caput to which all other territories on the estate were subordinate, while the estate itself was an amalgamation of many smaller land units. The lower units and settlements were responsible for providing specialised goods and services – such as horses, honey, building work and so on – to the head manor. The head manor could have taken the form of a palace or have been no more than a glorified farmstead. It was the place where the lord had his HALL and court, and its name and that of its estate would generally be the same.

The head manor would tend to occupy the best lands in its estate and from it an INFIELD-OUTFIELD system of farming would be operated by tenants living in the village that accompanied the *caput*. Meanwhile the subordinate territories with their hamlets of bondsmen would each also operate an infield-outfield system. MINSTER churches would normally be established at the head manor, and in due course daughter churches of the minster could be established at the bond hamlets. The bond hamlets would render goods and services to the head manor, some of them specialising in particular areas of work or production, while some might share certain resources of the estate, like an expanse of marshland pasture or upland grazing, these traditions of INTERCOMMONING sometimes persisting long after the fragmentation of the multiple estate.

The antiquity of the multiple estates is uncertain; some may have been formed in Roman times, while others could have originated as territories dominated by Iron Age HILLFORTS. In later Saxon times the multiple estates became fragmented as a result of inheritance, the granting of lands to monasteries and the granting away of portions of royal estates, while the old patterns were further changed by the redistribution of landholdings following the Norman Conquest. The reconstruction of the

territories of ancient estates is difficult and
demands considerable expertise, but such work is
essential if we are to be able to probe the deeper
and darker recesses of local history and develop
an understanding of the organisation of the
countryside during the Dark Ages. See also
PARISH, TOWNSHIP.

*Further reading.* Aston, M., *Interpreting the Landscape*,
    Batsford, London, 1985.
Jones, Glanville, 'Multiple Estates and Early
    Settlement', in Sawyer, P. H. (ed.), *English Medieval
    Settlement*, Edward Arnold, 1979.
Fleming, A., 'Swadal, Swar (and Erechwydd?): Early
    Medieval Polities in Upper Swaledale', *Landscape
    History* 16, 1994, pp. 17–30.

**Multiple tracks.** These are tracks that run
roughly parallel to each other or else fan out
rather like the chaotic streams in a river delta.
Though the people using the tracks would be
pursuing similar destinations, different travellers
would have different ideas about which routelet
provided the best 'going'. In summer, the Dark
Age or medieval traveller might forsake the hard
broken surface of a badly-maintained ROMAN
ROAD for the softer turf of the verge, while at
other times exploiting a succession of courses in
winter as the current track became muddy and
rutted. Within the 'zone of movement', various
versions of a road would develop, with different
ones being employed at different times.

Multiple tracks were commonly formed when
a route left the confines of a ploughed or
enclosed lowland fieldscape for the open sloping
ground of an upland COMMON. Road beds
become deeply incised into the countryside when
the route ascends the brow of a convex slope.
There, as one track became worn and difficult, a
new version of the route would be pioneered,
leading to the formation of a fan-like network of
ascending HOLLOWAYS. Multiple tracks can date
from any period from the prehistoric to the
modern and can still be impressive features on
scarp slopes in the southern chalk downlands
where short turf has so far escaped modern
ploughing. Short sections of multiple tracks may
be found where tracks from a common converge
on the slopes running down to a bridge or
fording place. Ploughing will quickly obliterate
traces of multiple tracks, but where they survive
they can be recognised as a broad zone of
ground which is striped by a series of trench-like
holloways.

# N

**Nazard or nassell horse**. A bad-natured stallion that was denied access to the COMMON.

**Neat land**. Ground where neat cattle grazed in Scotland and northern England, not to be confused with Scottish 'neaplands', where turnips grew.

**Nettle**. Now known largely for its unpleasant sting, the nettle was a useful plant that provided both dyestuff and pharmaceutical materials to the old rural communities and which could also be cooked. Nettles are potentially useful to landscape historians as clumps often flourish on the sites of former habitations and stock pens, where a high potash level in the soils meets their preference for fertile ground.

At some deserted settlement sites, roughly rectangular clumps of nettles seem to indicate the end of a house that accommodated livestock.

**Neuch, nook**. A hollow or recess, a secluded corner.

**Nock**. In Scotland, a hill.

**No Man's Land, -Patch, -Heath, etc., Norman's Field etc**. Names of this kind signify lands that had no particular claimant at the time when parish boundaries or other partitions were being set out.

**Norfolk system**, see FOUR-COURSE ROTATION.

**Norse tenure**. On Shetland, many customs inherited from the Viking settlement were preserved, including a system of tenure whereby land was held 'from the highest stone on the hill to the lowest stone on the beach'. As a consequence of this, holdings spanned a cross-section of resources, from upland pasture and peat MOOR, through enclosed areas, down to the beach, with its reserves of seaweed which could be spread on the land as a fertiliser.

**Nousts**. Boat-shaped depressions behind beaches on the Shetland Isles into which boats could be dragged, to be tied or weighted down as protection against gales. Some may date back to the Viking era.

# O

**Oast**. On Scottish shores an oast resembles a Shetlandic NOUST.

**Oast-house (hop-kiln)**. Oast is an old word for a kiln, and the oast-houses of Kent, Sussex and the West Midlands housed the kilns which were used for drying hops before they were sent to market. The hop plant is native in England but may only have been cultivated for use in brewing in the fifteenth century. In the sixteenth century the oast-house designs of Flanders were imitated as the cultivation of hops became a significant activity on various farms, though most surviving oast-houses date from the nineteenth century. In the most typical design, a

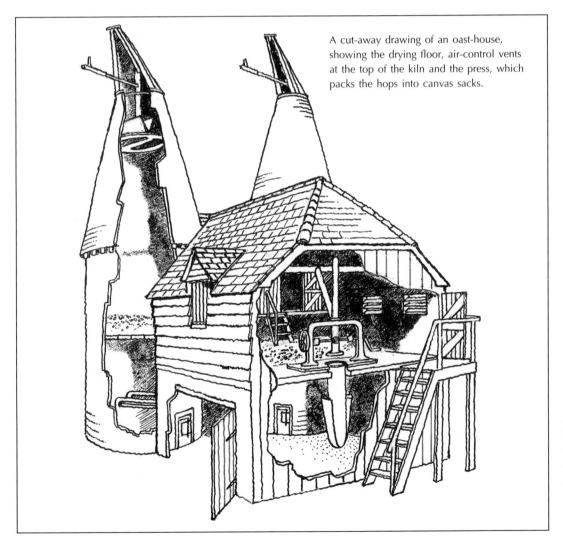

A cut-away drawing of an oast-house, showing the drying floor, air-control vents at the top of the kiln and the press, which packs the hops into canvas sacks.

drying floor was built about 10 feet (3 metres) above the firebox of the kiln. This drying floor was composed of battens separated by spaces through which the hot air could rise, and hops were spread out over a horsehair cloth covering the battens. The smoke then rose through the cone-shaped roof, the roof culminating in a revolving cowl which could be adjusted to control the draught. The kiln structure was frequently attached to a two-storey building. The lower floor was used for stoking the kiln but might also serve as a cartshed or POUND-HOUSE. The room above received the hops from the drying floor, which were cooled and then packed in long sacks or 'pockets' that hung down into the space below through a treading hole in the floor. As a pocket filled, the hops were stamped more tightly into the sack by a farmworker.

Oast-house chimneys may be square or circular. Eighteenth-century kilns had square (pyramidical) chimneys, while circular (conical) designs appeared in Kent in the first few years of the nineteenth century but were not adopted in Surrey and the West Midlands until the 1830s. Square designs again found favour in the West Midlands in the 1870s but were not readopted in the south-east until about 1910.

**Ogham**. A form of script that was developed in Ireland, perhaps as a result of contact with Latin script on the British mainland. Letters are formed by lines that intersect a 'baseline' in different numbers and at different angles. The original for ogham may have been a notched tally stick used in counting cattle. Ogham inscriptions are found on CROSSES and memorial stones in Ireland. In parts of Wales and Cornwall that may have been settled by Irish people, bi-lingual inscriptions in ogham and Latin may be found. About the eighth century, the Picts developed a Pictish version of the Irish ogham.

**Onstead**. A term for a cluster of farm buildings used in parts of the north of England and Scotland.

**Open-field farming**. In some parts of England open-field farming existed for about a thousand years, surviving in a number of parishes until the middle of the nineteenth century and lingering still in a very much modified form at a few localities, notably Laxton in Nottinghamshire and Braunton in Devon. Although outdated books repeat the claim that this form of communal farming was introduced to England by Saxon settlers in the fifth and sixth centuries AD, there is no actual support for this contention or indication that it was practised in the Anglo-Saxon homelands. Open-field farming seems to have been an indigenous product of the eighth or ninth centuries. There is as yet no real understanding of how it was created and imposed upon a large portion of the estates of lowland England. Nor does one know the motives underlying the introduction, though it may be that the concentration of arable land in two, three or more vast fields released much of the remaining area as valuable pasture. Also, the concentration of the subservient population in large, nucleated villages will have facilitated social control.

Open-field farming is so-named because the great fields were *open* – there were no internal hedges, walls or permanent fences though hedges ran around the great fields and some FURLONGS may have been enclosed. Each open field was subdivided into furlongs, which sometimes were pre-existing fields, and the furlongs were divided into the STRIPS, or 'lands', which were tenanted by the different members of the farming community. The introduction of each local system of open fields must have led to an enormous reorganisation of the countryside and community concerned, and we do not know whether the new fields were superimposed on landscapes where INFIELD-OUTFIELD farming was practised or whether the land was in enclosures resembling the so-called 'CELTIC' FIELDS. Whatever the circumstances, it is hard to imagine that the owners of the various estates did not play leading roles in effecting and imposing the transformation. Of necessity, the changes involved the desertion of many dispersed farmsteads and hamlets and the establishment of new villages at the heart of each open-field cluster. Archaeology confirms that such changes were taking place in the eighth and ninth centuries – while open-field terminology appears in charters of the tenth century, showing the system to be established on some estates. (The most succinct review of the many conflicting theories about the origins of open-field farming is provided by David Hall, in the reference below.)

Open-field farming systems varied considerably from one part of the country to another, but they shared certain features: the subdivision of very large fields into strips; peasant rights of common grazing on the stubble after harvest as well as on whichever of the great fields was lying fallow; the existence, usually nearby, of a COMMON or 'waste'; and the existence of a village assembly to organise the whole affair.

Given the complexities of open-field farming this organisation had to be comprehensive and detailed. The MANOR court was the paramount institution involved, though day-to-day operations were influenced by the reeve, an elected official, and by discussion and co-operation between the village peasants. As well as the need for each member of the farming community to observe all the intricate rules of the system, synchronise his activities with those of his neighbours and perform a range of services for the lord there was also a need to arrange ploughing covenants, for very few peasants indeed owned sufficient oxen or horses to form a complete plough team. Breaches of faith could have dire consequences, as the court at Bridge of Rastric in West Yorkshire heard in 1286: 'Richard of Tothill was the companion of Roger of the Wood to plow jointly with his plow, and at the time of plowing cast him off, so that his land lies untilled.' As a result Roger was awarded damages of 10s. (50p). The typical peasant holding in the open fields amounted to a 'VIRGATE' or 'YARDLAND', known in the

north of England as an 'OXGANG' or 'BOVATE'. Although the virgate is conventionally regarded as comprising scattered strips amounting to 30 acres (12 hectares), in practice a virgate might be little more than 15 acres (6 hectares) or as much as 40 acres (16 hectares). Some peasants had only half-virgate holdings. The virgate would consist of strips scattered through all the open fields, and in a village of average size there would be around thirty or forty peasant families holding virgates.

Because the fields were open, the growing of crops and the grazing of livestock could not take place in the same field at the same time, and for this reason a common crop rotation was applied to each field (or, in some cases, each furlong). If a village only had two open fields, then half the ploughland would lie fallow each year – and this was not very economical. Three-field systems were much more common. The crop rotation most frequently applied successively on each field in a three-field system was: wheat–legumes (pease and beans)–fallow, with oats, barley and rye sometimes substituting for wheat. Some villages had more than three open fields, though whether this was always so or resulted from the creation of new fields by ASSARTING or by the subdivision of larger fields is not normally known. Open-field farming was gradually dismantled in the course of the post-medieval centuries by enclosure of the common lands, but it survived long enough for numerous maps of village open-field systems to be compiled and so we have good visual impressions of the arrangements as they existed in the seventeenth, eighteenth and nineteenth centuries.

See also ANCIENT AND PLANNED COUNTRYSIDE, DEMESNE, EARLY ENCLOSURE, FURLONG, MANOR, PARLIAMENTARY ENCLOSURE, RIDGE AND FURROW, STRIP, SUN DIVISION.

*Further reading*: Baker, A. R. H. and Butlin, R. A. (eds), *Field Systems of the British Isles*, Cambridge University Press, 1973.

Dodgshon, R.A., *The Origins of British Field Systems:*

*an interpretation*, London Academic Press, London, 1980.

Hall, David, *Medieval Fields*, Shire Archaeology Series, 1982.

Homans, George C., *English Villagers of the Thirteenth Century*, Norton, 1975.

Rowley, T. (ed.), *The Origins of Open-Field Agriculture*, London, 1981.

Russell, R. C., *The Logic of Open Field Systems*, Standing Conference for Local History, 1974.

Brown, T. and Foard, G., 'The Saxon Landscape: a Regional Perspective' in Everson, P. and Williamson, T. (eds), *The Archaeology of Landscape*, Manchester University Press, 1998.

**Open villages and closed villages**. The concept of 'open' and 'closed' villages concerns the degree to which a single lord or squire could control and regulate the affairs of the community. Though the phenomenon was far older, the concept seems to have become current at the time of the nineteenth-century Poor Law administration, when it was apparent that in 'closed' villages, where a single squire reigned supreme, he was able to control the size, obedience and morals of the village population. On occasions where he owned all the dwellings in a village he might seek virtually to depopulate the parish, causing families which might become a burden on the rates to move into neighbouring parishes from whence their members would 'commute', to work on his lands while sparing him of any contribution to the upkeep of the weak and decrepit members of the community. However, the distinction between open and closed villages also existed in medieval times. The lord who controlled a closed village was much better able to replan the village, organise cultivation, introduce a market and manipulate the population. In more open villlages, meanwhile, the division of power between different influential landlords and the presence of independently minded free peasants or yeomen made the manipulation of village affairs much more difficult. Equally, during the post-medieval era of 'emparking' (see entry on

LOST VILLAGES) it could be quite easy to uproot the population of a closed estate village, but very difficult to dispose of that of an open one.

In a recent study of the geography of religion in England, J. D. Gray found that:

> Where the village was of the closed integrated type, the squire and parson would wield a patriarchal influence ensuring the stranglehold of the Church of England. [But] if the village was one of the open type with no dominant landlord, independent thought and action was more possible and chapels could be easily established ... In general an arable economy with its nucleated settlement favoured the Church of England, while a pastoral economy with its scattered settlement favoured the Nonconformists.

Opinions about the values of open and closed villages will vary. The writer W. H. Hudson, however, had no doubts, and in his *A Shepherd's Life* in 1910 he recalled that:

> In my roamings about the downs it is always a relief – a positive pleasure in fact – to find myself in a village which has no squire or other magnificent and munificent person who dominates everyone and everything, and, if he chooses to do so, plays providence in the community.

The distinctions between open and closed villages is less important today, though there are still some closed estate villages of tied cottages where contemporary squires are able to extend influences or impose sanctions on their tenants which many would consider incompatible with life in a democratic society. The term 'open parish' was used for a parish in which it was easier for a stranger to obtain a certificate of settlement than was possible in a 'close parish'. Once gaining a certificate, the settler could apply for parochial support.

*Further reading*: Banks, S., 'Nineteenth-century Scandal or Twentieth-century Model? A new look at 'open' and 'close' parishes', *Economic History Review*, second series 41, 51–73.

Hammond, J. L., and Hammond, Barbara, *The Village Labourer*, Longman, 1978.

Mills, Dennis R., *Lord and Peasant in Nineteenth-century Britain*, Croom Helm, Rowman & Littlefield, 1980.

**Orchard**. The living orchard is too familiar to merit a description here, but orchards are interesting in historical terms, even though their removal may leave no visible trace. While prehistoric communities will have gathered wild fruits (Mesolithic people gathered enormous quantities of hazel nuts as winter rations), it is not known if organised, working orchards existed before the Roman invasion. The Romans, who could consult a large specialist literature on fruit-growing, doubtless established numerous orchards beside their villas in Britain. Orchards were a common feature of the medieval landscape, and were not monopolised by the upper classes as there is evidence of orchards belonging to free peasants. The old documents often distinguish between the garden (*gardinum*) and orchard (*ortus*). The apple was the main cultivated fruit, grown primarily for cider-making, while wild crab apples, or 'wood apples', were also gathered. Orchards and fruit trees are often commemorated in field- and place-names. Applecross in Scotland is not such a name, the 'apple' element deriving from *aber*, the river mouth or estuary, but Appletreewick hamlet in Wharfedale is probably authentic. There are scores of Orchard field-names, plenty of Applegarth or similar field-names, and a number of Plum and Plumb ones, too. Medieval orchards and wood apple trees also gave us two common surnames: Appleyard and Crabtree.

Vineyards also existed in medieval times, even in some northern counties, where the blustery late-medieval climate must have been discouraging. Old vineyards may occasionally be signified from 'winter' place-names, deriving from the Old English name for a vineyard, though the same word also related to the season,

and field-names like Winter Close or Winter Green are ambiguous, while a name like 'Winter Beer' indicates a winter-sown crop of barley. Later field-names include Vinery and Vineyard forms and are less confusing, though it has been suggested that in Dorset the home close was sometimes called 'Vineyard'. It is commonly but quite erroneously stated that STRIP LYNCHETS are old vineyard terraces.

**Ord**. In Scotland, a steep-sided hill or mountain.

**Ordinary Landscapes**. This is a refreshing and valuable perspective on landscapes that was apparent in the writing of John Brinckerhoff Jackson in the second half of the twentieth century and which is now particularly associated with John R. Stilgoe. The emphasis of study is shifted from sites of antiquity, celebrated places and those places that are unusually beautiful or 'historic'. Instead, practitioners study and interpret the settings of ordinary, day-to-day life: streets and street furniture, used car lots, jetties, and so on. Landscape interpretation and the use of established types of evidence, like place-names, can still play parts in studies which explore the settings of ordinary people. It is an approach associated with the USA, perhaps evolving there rather than in Europe because of the shallower, less faceted nature of the American heritage. However, the potential for studying ordinary landscapes in Europe is immense.

*Further reading:* Groth, P. and Todd, W. B., *Understanding Ordinary Landscapes*, Yale University Press, New Haven, 1997.

Stilgoe, J. R., *Outside Lies Magic*, Walker, New York, 1998.

**Ornamental lakes and ponds**. These were created as elements in a LANDSCAPE PARK. They were most frequently formed by damming an existing stream, though some exploited natural springs. When encountered in the context of a LOST GARDEN, an ornamental pond lying in a valley or produced by impounding water on a valley slope can be distinguished from a FISHPOND by the level surface on the top of the retaining dam, which was employed as a walkway. Earth that was excavated in the digging of a pond was often employed in the creation of other garden features, like PROSPECT MOUNTS, in the vicinity. During the medieval period, sheets of water in the vicinity of castles and high status buildings featured in various ORNAMENTAL LANDSCAPES. One of the most bizarre water features to be constructed in the post-medieval era was a crescentic lake created in the gardens of the Earl of Hertford at Elveham in Hampshire. Made to entertain Elizabeth I in 1591, the lake had three islands, one a spiral mount, one decked out as a ship and one arranged as a fort. After the day of the Queen's visit, the whole contrivance was abandoned. In the earlier part of the seventeenth century, PARKLAND water features like geometrical canals were popular, and a straight canal formed from the canalisation of the R. Skell featured in John Aislabie's landscaping of Fountains Abbey, North Yorkshire, in the last third of the century. From around 1755, however, fashion had moved in favour of more naturalistic, curving designs and during the remainder of the century irregular expanses of water featured prominently in the creation and re-modelling of landscape parks. The naturalistic designs reflected the current enthusiasm for the landscapes associated with the Swiss and Italian lakes and the English Lake District. Tastefully disposed buildings and bridges were incorporated into the lacustrine scenes, with Chinese pavilions (Shugborough, Staffordshire), a Chinese dairy (Woburn, Bedfordshire), pagodas (Biddulph Grange, Staffordshire), authentic ruins (Fountains), synthetic ruins (Shugborough), rotundas or BELVEDERES (West Wycombe), cascades (Studley, North Yorkshire), stepping stones and rustic bridges (Studley) and imposing bridges (as built by Vanburgh at Blenheim, Oxfordshire) all gracing the lakesides. Generally, the aim in the second half of the eighteenth century was to create artificial water bodies in serpentine forms

that appeared to be features of the natural countryside. This could involve the introduction of lakes to agricultural countrysides or in the existing lawns in PARKLAND, or it might involve the reorganisation of existing lakes of an unfashionable form, as exemplified in Humphry Repton's 'before and after' plans for Garnons, Herefordshire. Of the existing rectangular pond, in 1791 he wrote in his Red Book: '... there can be no room to hesitate about destroying the pond in front of the present house ...' Instead, he preferred to create a new water feature: '... it will be necessary to raise the road to some height as a causeway over the wet part of the meadow, and very little additional expense will form a dam to support a small pool ... so small a piece of water in itself would be very inconsiderable in the extensive Park of Garnons, but its effect may be very important especially as I am of the opinion that some reach of the river Wye may be rendered visible from the house with proper management, or at least a part of the wet moor may be made to shew an apparent continuation of River'. Naturalistic forms would result automatically when a shallow valley was dammed and the water level rose to follow an existing contour, and in such cases the downstream end of the lake was formed by the straight or curving masonry of the dam.

Boat houses for craft that entered the lake from tunnels in the lakeshore could add to the interest, as at Studley Royal. Often the fall of water leaving the dam and returning to the natural water level would be exploited to produce an ornamental cascade (Ripley, North Yorks). The actual shape of an artificial lake depended partly on the natural topography and partly on the degree to which this has been altered by, for example, the scalloping of the lakeshore or construction of promontories, jetties, boat houses and so on. Lancelot 'Capability' Brown was particularly fond of elongated lakes of serpentine form. At Blenheim, in 1763, he replaced Vanbrugh's formal canal and part of his bridge with a sweeping stretch of water and at Sandbeck, Yorkshire, he swept away the old ponds and canals set in lawns and levelled the site, while creating a lake in the valley of Roach Abbey: '... beginning at the head of the Hammer pond, & continuing up the valley towards Loton in the moor, as far as Lord Scarborough's ground goes & to continue the water & dress the valley up by the present farm house until it comes to the separation fixed for the boundary of the new farm'.

*Further reading*: Williamson, T., *Polite Landscapes*, Alan Sutton, Stroud, 1995.

**Ornamental landscape**. This term has recently begun to be applied to medieval landscapes that have been manicured and embellished for recreational and aesthetic purposes. Water, in the form of ORNAMENTAL LAKES, PONDS and MOATS which are associated with carefully contrived approaches, bridges and causeways feature prominently in the arrangements. There was a tendency to regard castles and other high status buildings of the medieval period in a functional way and the considerable evidence for the beautification and dramatisation of their settings was neglected or overlooked. In fact, complex systems of ornamental and recreational features were created, including intimate walled gardens, DEER PARKS and ornamental landscapes in which water generally played a prominent part. These features were associated with castles and other prominent buildings, and these high status buildings tended to have careful arrangements for the viewing of the landscapes. At Middleham Castle in Wensleydale, for example, one could look southwards across gardens and a lake towards one of the castle's deer parks. Similarly, at Framlingham, in Suffolk, the prospect embraced a flooded area, a formal garden and a deer park. At Ripley, in North Yorkshire, a pond originating in a fulling mill dam formed the foreground to the view into the late-medieval deer park to the south of the castle. The hunting associated with the deer parks served both to symbolise the aristocratic status of those participating and to give training in martial skills, while the ornamental landscapes

were permeated with many forms of symbolism. They provided romantic settings for indulgence in courtly love and a paradise-like contrast with the harshness of any untamed wildernesses beyond – as well as being venues for boating and other pursuits. The era of the ornamental landscape spanned most of the Middle Ages and persisted until the seventeenth century, thus providing ancestry for the post-medieval LANDSCAPE PARK.

*Further reading*: Everson, P., '"Delightfully surrounded with woods and ponds", field evidence for medieval gardens in England', in Pattison, P. (ed.), *There by Design*, RCHME, London, 1998.
Everson, P. and Williamson, T., 'Gardens and Designed Landscapes', in Williamson, T. and Everson, P., *The Archaeology of Landscape*, Manchester University Press, 1998, pp. 139–65.

**Orthostat walls**. These field-walls, seen in the western uplands of Britain and parts of Ireland, are composed of large irregular boulders, often interspersed with DRYSTONE WALLING using smaller stones. Such walls are generally assumed to be very old, and one can suspect that they may incorporate the boulder litter which was cleared during an early clearance of land for agriculture. Few actual dates for orthostat walls have been obtained, but excavations at Shaugh Moor on Dartmoor suggest that a wall there was built before about 1500 BC. Some are seen as relics, others are part of the living landscape, while many examples are likely to belong to relatively recent centuries. See also DRYSTONE WALLS. In most parts of Britain where drystone walls are found, some with orthostats in their bases will be seen and these may represent an early phase of land clearance, though such walls continued to be built during the medieval centuries.

**Osier Ground, -Beds, Carr etc**. Osier field-names will normally relate to the cultivation of osier willows as a coppice crop on moist, low-lying ground, with the pliable stems being used in basket-making.

**Out-dyke**. Unenclosed grazing land.

**Outfield**, see INFIELD-OUTFIELD CULTIVATION.

**Outgang**. A track leading out from a farmstead, often continuing through the enclosed land to the COMMON. See also OUT RAKE.

**Outlet**. Pasture beside cattle sheds into which wintering cattle could be released.

**Out rake, outgang, day drift, rake**. In the northern uplands of England these were trackways used for the movement of flocks and linking the FARMSTEAD with the HEAF on the fells above that was home to its flock. Although the fells might exist as COMMONS, the manor courts of the hill farming country protected the heafs and out rakes as though they were almost part of the single farm holding and the courses of the tracks were carefully recorded. A 'day drift' was a track that was used daily in the movement of stock to and from the MOORS.

**Outrun**. In Northern Britain, pasture attached to a farm.

**Outset**. On Shetland, small enclosure on the margins of the cultivated area. In Scotland generally, land newly broken in from the waste, an outhouse or extension to a building.

**Outwinterers**. Cattle that stayed out throughout the winter.

**Overleap**. A sum of money paid by tenants from one manor to the lord of another in anticipation that their stock would stray onto his grazing. The payment of overleap avoided the more troublesome business of having stock impounded and having to pay a fine. It was encountered in uplands where two communities using a grazing resource had not developed full INTERCOMMONING rights. See also COMMONS, POUND.

**Overpress**. The misdemeanour of putting too many animals on a COMMON, for which the party concerned might be fined by the MANOR court. See also COMMONS, STINTED COMMONS.

**Oxgang, oxgate, oxengate**, see BOVATE. A broad oxgang was twice the size of a normal one and equivalent to a yardland or VIRGATE though a narrow oxgang was normally a conventional oxgang.

# P

**Pace-market**. An Easter market.

**Pack-horse bridges**. Pack-horse traders would be happy to exploit any convenient bridge, be it of the CLAPPER type or of iron, but a certain type of bridge is known as a pack-horse bridge. Though most of these bridges were probably built in association with PACK-HORSE ROADS, they will also have been used by other travellers. Pack horse trading in various forms pre-dated the commercial organisation of transport, and trade within monastic ESTATES or linking the great medieval fair centres will have involved strings of pack ponies. Today, with pack horse trading dead for more than a century, the bridges can still be invaluable to local farmers and ramblers. A few carry motor-vehicles, but often they are too narrow or too steeply humped, so that where the old pack-horse route endures as a motor-road a pack-horse bridge will frequently be seen stranded beside its younger replacement.

Pack-horse bridges are numerous – and would be much more so had it not been so difficult in the past to raise the wherewithal for bridge-building. There are a few surviving medieval bridges, like the fine three-arched fifteenth-century example at Moulton in Suffolk, which appears to have been closely associated with pack-horse trading, and in the Middle Ages the lay or ecclesiastical landlords were usually responsible for the provision and repair of bridges. At the close of the period, responsibility in England passed to local Justices of the Peace, but progress in bridge-building remained fitful. Most pack-horse bridges date from the period 1650–1800, some being paid for by a local or countywide levy, others being furnished by a local benefactor.

They tended not to be provided if a convenient fording-place was available, and the typical pack-horse bridge crosses the stream in a single span, with a steeply humped arch designed to keep the structure safely above pounding floodwaters. The use of strong abutments and the absence of piers reduced the threat from flood-borne tree trunks. The road surface of the bridge and its approaches were normally paved with stone flags or cobbled, and the parapets were originally absent or very low, so as not to rub on the panniers of the pack-horses. By keeping the parapets low the width of the bridge could be kept to a minimum, and waist-high parapets are often a later, safety-minded addition. Many rivers were too broad to be spanned by such a bridge, and in such cases the traffic would either have had to be sufficiently heavy to merit the building of a more substantial multi-span bridge (often only after great pressure from road-users), or else a fording place would be exploited. Pack-horse bridges are most numerous in the Lake District and Pennine Dales – areas with difficult terrain but a strong association with packhorse trading – although old bridges in all parts of the country are likely to have experienced regular use by the trade. See also CLAPPER BRIDGE, MEDIEVAL AND LATER BRIDGES, PACK-HORSE ROAD.

**Pack-horse road**. Pack-horse trading came to an end in the latter part of the nineteenth century, terminating a form of transport which must have existed since Bronze Age or even Neolithic times. Like the DROVE ROADS, whose tracks they sometimes shared, pack-horse roads could be conventional roads shared by many users or they could be more specialised routes used mainly by pack-horse traders. As with the drove roads, the pack-horse routes are sometimes improved and integrated into our living route network, but often they have been abandoned,

*Pack-horse bridge*
A pack-horse bridge on the track which crosses the Sty Head Pass in Cumbria.

gradually to melt into field or moor. From ancient until relatively modern times, the transport of goods was achieved by cart or waggon or by pack-horse. The advantage of the pack-horse convoys was their ability to traverse expanses of hilly, broken and muddy ground and to negotiate rocky fords or slender arching bridges that were impassable by wheeled traffic: they reached the parts that other carriers could not reach. Consequently, pack-horse roads are more a feature of the northern uplands than of the gentle English lowlands with better roads and opportunities for RIVER TRANSPORT.

While much is still to be learned about the early centuries of pack-horse trading, plenty of information exists for the eighteenth and nineteenth centuries. In the north, the man leading a chain of pack-horses was known as a 'Jagger', the word coming from the sturdy German 'Jaeger' ponies which, along with Scottish Galloways, were the favoured breed. Pack-horse teams walked in line behind a lead-horse which was decked out with bells; the size of the team would vary according to the cargo and the resources of the carrier, but teams of two dozen horses were not uncommon. The goods were carried in panniers slung on either side of each pony – small ones for heavy commodities or large ones for lighter materials – and a pony would manage a load of 100 kilograms: a weight which only a strong man could lift. The goods that were transported varied enormously, depending on the commerce of the region concerned, but in the north they included coal, metal ores and products, building materials, knitwear or household goods. The rate for transport at the start of the nineteenth century was around 1 shilling (5p) per ton per mile.

In the course of its long history, pack-horse trading had evolved but, even so, the changes were relatively modest. The Neolithic trader in stone axes or the itinerant smith of the Bronze Age needed a beast of burden to transport his wares, and we know that in medieval times the pack-horse merchants plied the lanes and open fells as traders circulating around the MARKET AND FAIR network. In the course of the Industrial Revolution the rapidly growing volume of trade and the demands for a more effective transport system encouraged TURNPIKING and gave rise to the canal and the railway. Before these changes had eroded the pack-horse system, Kendal, a hub of the carrier trade, supported some 354 pack-horses distributed amongst its different gangs. However, even when this form of trading was in its prime, in the late eighteenth century, the carriers were often part-timers, dividing their efforts between transport and small-scale farming or other pursuits. Writing in 1904, Edmund Bogg described how 'Eighty years ago, James Ibbotson, besom maker, of Ling Hall, Threshfield, having a keen eye to business, and knowledge extending beyond ling and withies, kept some thirty Jagger ponies'. The demise of the trade must have brought an unaccustomed tranquillity to remote tracks which had echoed to the bell and hoof for many generations. Geoffrey N. Wright quotes from H. Speight, who recalled the end of the era in 1897: 'When the packhorse traffic ceased hundreds of these sonorous bells [the ones worn by the lead-horses] were sold for old metal, and the brokers' shops were for a time full of them.'

Some old pack-horse roads survived the changes and exist as metalled minor roads, like the old market track from Ramsgill in Upper Nidderdale to Masham in Wensleydale. Some remain as walled GREEN LANES, others as HOLLOWAYS. Quite frequently, different sections of a pack-horse road will endure in different guises – like the ancient Craven Old Way from Dent to Ingleton in the Pennines, which leaves Dent as a metalled motor-road, becomes a walled green lane, then a holloway deeply incised into an expanse of limestone pavement, before merging with a ROMAN ROAD above Ingleton. Abandoned pack-horse roads are not always instantly recognisable without a measure of documentary research, not least since most were also used by pedestrians, mounted horsemen or, in their less rugged sections, by farm vehicles.

Usually they are narrow, no wider than was necessary to accommodate a pony and its panniers, and in places they may be punctuated by graceful little PACK-HORSE BRIDGES or crudely improved or 'causewayed' stretches paved with heavy stone flags or cobbles. As with the drove roads, wayside inns may survive to provide clues, the equivalent of 'The Drovers' being 'The Pack-horse' or 'The Packman'. Place-names like 'Jagger Lane' can be preserved, and one may also look out for ones like 'Badger Lane', 'Badger Gate' or 'Brogger Lane'. The 'badger' was a small trader who had a licence to take corn from market to customers or other markets, while 'broggers' operated perhaps a couple of pack-horses and went from farm to farm buying wool for sale to the clothiers of Halifax and Kendal. See also HOLLOWAY, PACK-HORSE BRIDGE.

*Further reading*: Raistrick, A., *Green Roads in the Mid Pennines*, 1978.

Wright, Geoffrey N., *Roads and Trackways in the Yorkshire Dales*, Moorland Publishing, 1985.

**Pad**. A footpath or the act of trampling-out a new footpath. Also a word used for an old horse or nag.

**Paddock**. Generally a small enclosed pasture for livestock close to a FARMSTEAD. In Scotland the word can denote a small farm.

**Paffle**. Small portion of land or small farm.

**Palatinate**. Territory governed by a bishop or earl.

**Palimpsest analogy**. It is often said that historic cultural landscapes resemble palimpsests, pieces of parchment that were written on over and over again with the earlier entries being obscured but never completely obliterated by the later jottings. This conveys the nature of countrysides and townscapes in which evidence of former activities 'shows through' the imprint of subsequent uses.

**Paling**. A fence made of stakes. Fields with names like 'Paled Piece' or 'Palin' were enclosed in this way.

**Pan**. A depression of a shallow, bowl-like form. When found in woodland it could mark an old charcoal-burning site.

**Pannage**. The woodland floor was a valuable source of food for SWINE, which would grub for roots and shoots and consume large quantities of acorns and beech mast. Acorns, however, were deemed to be the property of the lord and pannage was a payment paid by tenants for the right to pasture their swine in their lord's wood. The practice had to be regulated carefully as the pigs could pose a threat to game and could kill and eat newly-born deer or injure fawning does. Generally, pigs were driven into woods and WOOD PASTURES between Michaelmas and Martinmas (7 October to 19 November by the modern calendar) to feast on the acorn crop, though pannage could also involve the fallen fruits of orchards and hedgerows, as well as stubble. They were banned from the woods during the 'forbidden month', 22 June to 16 July on today's calendar. In some places a tax on pigs known as 'avesage' was imposed in the acorn season. It involved a payment amounting to very roughly 5 per cent of the value of each pig owned. See also AGIST, WOODLAND, SWANIMOTE.

*Further reading*: Rackham, Oliver, *The Last Forest*, Dent, London, 1989.

**Pant well**. A covered WELL.

**Papa, papil**. Place-name elements that are indicative of ancient Celtic churches on Shetland.

**Pargetting**. This is decorative plasterwork applied to the exterior of houses in East Anglia and the south-eastern counties during the sixteenth and seventeenth centuries. Repetitive geometrical designs may still be combed into plaster by modern craftsmen, but the old-style pargetting is in high relief and displays flowing floral or bird and animal motifs. One of the finest examples can be seen on the PRIEST'S HOUSE beside the churchyard at Clare in Suffolk. The word may derive from the French

*pour jeter* relating to the throwing of plaster on to a wall.

**Parish.** These minor administrative divisions often still support active parish councils. From about the ninth and tenth centuries onwards, the parishes existed as the tributary areas of the parish churches which were superseding the older system of MINSTERS. Since most parish churches were originally provided by the lords of the late Saxon countryside, it seems quite reasonable to presume that their parishes corresponded to the estates of the various churchbuilders. In their earlier guise as estates the parishes could be very old indeed,

*Pargetting*
Pargetting on late-medieval houses in Saffron Walden.

and Iron Age or even Bronze Age origins have been suggested. However, recent researchers have pointed out the lack of correspondence between some parish boundaries and the boundaries of Iron Age field systems discernible in aerial photographs. Even so, as discrete units of land, many parishes are likely to be very old, even if their boundaries have fluctuated. In some areas these boundaries are the same as those described in Saxon land charters that provide a written perambulation of the bounds conserved. *Parish boundaries* should be explored with care; civil and ecclesiastical parishes do not always exactly coincide, and plenty of parishes have had their bounds adjusted and tidied up on different occasions, a process that still continues. Parishes with double-barrelled names, like Knayton-with-Brawith parish, often reveal a merging of parishes following the extinction of a former parish focus – in this case Brawith is the deserted village. Parishes with peculiar shapes, particularly those of a dumb-bell outline, are likely to result from the 'capture' of the lands of a deserted settlement, and in these ways a survey of parishes can reveal deserted village and hamlet sites. In thinly-populated upland areas, a vast original parish may only gradually have been partitioned as churches were provided to serve its localities in late- or post-medieval times. It is also interesting to see how parishes – that is, ancient estates – were often set out so as to tap a range of environmental resources. Famous examples are those of the Lincolnshire scarplands where attenuated parishes run from narrow river frontages up to high grazings on the escarpments and the nine parishes which converged on the small former Breckland mere of Rymer. Sometimes parish boundaries loop out, originally in order, for example, to combine an ancient watermill with its parochial and manorial hinterland.

**Park**. An area enclosed for recreation. See DEER PARK, LANDSCAPE PARK, ORNAMENTAL LANDSCAPE, PARKLAND. The word was also used quite frequently to denote an ordinary PADDOCK or pasture, while in the north of England it could describe a playing field.

**Parkland**. Though parkland is regarded as an artificial form of countryside, evidence is emerging that the ancient 'wildwood' may have had a park-like character, with many large clearings grazed by deer, swine and aurochs. The distinction between the medieval DEER PARK and the landscaped parks of the eighteenth and

nineteenth centuries is not as clear-cut as one might imagine. Indeed, in some respects the efforts of the great landscape manipulations of Georgian times represented a re-creation of some of the scenic features associated with the old deer parks. Several medieval deer parks existed for scarcely a century, scores had vanished by the close of the Middle Ages, and by the end of the seventeenth century only a relatively small minority survived. Some new 'deer' parks had been created at the end of the Middle Ages, but these seem really to have been created for the breeding of horses, although deer could also be included. Post-medieval landscaped parks reflected the substitution of the great family mansion for the outmoded dynastic castle and the fashion for surrounding the opulent new mansion with a broad expanse of carefully contrived countryside. As the importance of deer-hunting declined, so the more civilised pursuit of enjoying the scenery of the park came to the fore. Even so, this was not a revolutionary change of emphasis, for some of the old deer parks must have been enjoyed almost as much for their beauty, as for their hunting. The lawns, groves and dappled shade of the tree clumps must have had symbolic significance that is not understood today. Some deer parks, like Studley Royal, near Ripon, were reborn as landscaped parks, and some eighteenth-century parks imitated the traditional characteristics of the deer park, though now the deer were included for their decorative attributes. One of the earliest deer-park parodies was accomplished at Holdenby in Northamptonshire, where in the 1580s Sir Christopher Hatton surrounded his new house and gardens with an ornamental deer park or land which was commandeered from the open fields of Holdenby village, converted to grass and planted with trees and spinneys.

In the late seventeenth century fashionable influences from France led to the creation of formal parks, with the extension of formal designs outwards from the garden over the HA-HA and into the surrounding park. Straight avenues, distant eyecatchers and geometrical plantations became the mode, but by the middle of the eighteenth century the more relaxed and naturalistic landscaping influences of Romanticism were in vogue and very little indeed survives intact from the formalised parks of the preceding era.

In the nineteenth century Romanticism still influenced the landscaping of parks, though the greater availability of exotic plants brought by the intrepid collectors of the age resulted in parks modified to accommodate great assemblages of alien trees and shrubs. As recently as 1871, the arbiter of taste, Robert Kerr, could write: 'The two rival styles of landscape gardening are by name the *Italian*, which is Classical or Architecturesque, and the *English* or *Natural* which is Picturesque'. Of the work of the landscape gardener Kerr wrote:

> If the estate be extensive he will look for woods through which to open up vistas and glades and peeps, as he calls them of far-off places; and the rolling pastures he will hope to be convertible into a quiet deer park, and long graceful woody drives. He will not object to broken ground, rocks, wild knolls, a gravel pit even; quite the contrary – he will convert everything of the sort into dashing bits of art. But what he will not like is such a thing as half a dozen square flat ploughed fields, bounded by trim hedge-rows, – every stick of timber cut away for the ventilation of heavy crops, – every little excrescence pared off and every rough place made smooth, – not a weed to be seen upon the land it may be, and not an inch of opportunity lost for making two blades of grass to grow where but one grew before – but nevertheless, with all its complacent material plenty, to the artist's eye a barren desolation – a vacant clock-face without a single feature upon which the ingenuity of art can hang a smile.

The history of the English landscaping tradition and of the many parks created under its influences are well recorded, but readers with an interest in the history of the countryside should always be on the look-out for the many examples of former parks which have been surrendered to more commercial uses. While the lawns may now be grazed by dairy cattle or produce crops of grain, the enclosing high park-walls with imposing gateways may survive. Clumps of native or introduced trees – elms, oaks, sycamore, evergreen oaks, limes or horse chestnuts – growing as field-trees are very often the products of a landscaping design, while really old oaks may have witnessed the coming and going of the park, being incorporated, as many already existing trees were, into the parkland scheme. For example, the seventeenth-century park of Earlham Hall in Norfolk assimilated the oak pollards formerly associated with the deserted village of Earlham and rows of former hedgerow trees graced the lawns in parks like Nidd, near Harrogate, and many others. Other indications of a former park may be provided by an isolated church, left stranded by the emparking of its associated village and, of course, the mansion which the park was created to serve. See also DEER PARK, ORNAMENTAL LAKE, ORNAMENTAL LANDSCAPE, AVENUE.

*Further reading*: Fleming, L. and Gore, A., *The English Garden*, Michael Joseph, 1979.

Taigel, A. and Williamson, T., *Parks and Gardens*, Batsford, London, 1993.

**Parliamentary Enclosure (general enclosure)**. In numerous PARISHES and regions of England Parliamentary Enclosure was the most important single factor in the shaping of the face of the modern countryside. In some others, 'barley barons' have erased the neatly hedged landscapes of enclosure and wiped away all details of rural character. But there are also many regions and localities which were completely untouched by Parliamentary Enclosure, and it has been estimated that the transformations actually only affected about 22½ per cent of the area of England. The area affected coincided with the planned or champion lands (see ANCIENT AND PLANNED COUNTRYSIDE) where most of the ploughland was still in OPEN-FIELD cultivation, although areas with extensive COMMONS, like the Yorkshire Dales, were also caught in the enclosure net. The main impact of Parliamentary Enclosure was experienced in an area lying roughly between a line drawn from the Solent to the north-eastern limit of Suffolk and another line drawn from the western limits of Dorset to the estuary of the Tees.

Parliamentary Enclosure was a means of accelerating and formalising the practice of enclosure by agreement, which had already made considerable inroads into the open-field landscape. It substituted formal parliamentary proceedings and the deliberation of independent commissioners for the informal local processes of agreement or coercion that had previously been applied to achieve the 'privatisation' of land. The first Act occurred in 1604 and affected Radipole in Dorset. A few more Acts followed, but the movement did not gain momentum until the reign of George II (1727–60), when 200 parishes experienced Parliamentary Enclosure. The period greatest of vitality for the movement was the century 1750–1850, after which the pace of enclosure decelerated, with the last Act being passed in 1914. The statistics relating to Parliamentary Enclosure are debated by historians, but one of the more thorough calculations, by W. E. Tate, estimates that there were some 5400 Acts, which affected about 7 million acres (2,832,861 hectares) of common field and common land in England after 1700. Thus the area affected was equivalent to the combined areas of the four largest and the four smallest of the old English counties.

In each parish where the leading landowners desired the enclosure of commons and common fields, they would petition Parliament to produce the necessary Act. Then commissioners, normally selected from the ranks of the nobility, the clergy and the professional farming community and often three in number, were officially ratified to produce a new allocation of land. A meeting would be held in the parish concerned, and a surveyor and a valuer would be appointed. The objective of the enclosure award which resulted from the debate, survey and valuation was to provide each lawful claimant to a share in the award with a compact holding of land which was notionally equivalent to the claimant's share in the fragmented common lands. (The organisation of Parliamentary Enclosure was affected by the General Act of 1801 which simplified the parliamentary procedures, and the General Act of 1836, which permitted enclosure by the consent of two-thirds of the interests affected without special application to Parliament.)

In effect Parliamentary Enclosure greatly favoured the larger landholders. Following the enclosure award, the recipients immediately faced bills for the cost of making the award and further bills for hedging or walling the allocated holdings. Small landholders who could not face such bills or who found that their new holdings could in no measure compensate for loss of access to the resources of the commons were often obliged to relinquish their holdings. Landless, they would seek work as farm labourers or factory workers, some heading for the rapidly expanding industrial centres, others for a berth on a ship to the New World. Cottagers who had relied exclusively on the commons could be left destitute. At the start of the nineteenth century, Arthur Young, a leading advocate of enclosure, became aware of its effects on the poor:

> Mr Foster of Norwich, after giving me an account of twenty inclosures in which he acted as Commissioner, stated his opinion on their general effect on the poor, and lamented that he had been accessory to the injury of 2,000 poor people, at the rate of twenty families per parish ... The poor in these parishes may say, and with truth, 'Parliament may be tender of property: all I know is that I had a cow and an Act of Parliament has taken it from me.

There was considerable public opposition to Parliamentary Enclosure, and the most frequent charge was that it caused a depopulation of the

*Parliamentary Enclosure*

Yelvertoft, Northamptonshire: geometrical outlines of a Parliamentary Enclosure fieldscape superimposed upon the curving corrugations of ridge and furrow, in an area of medieval arable farming that was converted to pasture. (CUCAP)

countryside. Although greed and violence have played important roles in shaping the English landscape, it is reassuring to discover that compassion has always had a part in English life. Thus, in 1772 a number of freeholders at Ackworth in West Yorkshire refused to sign a petition to enclose their commons:

> Mr Joseph White said it will injure the Poor.
>   Peter Wilson believes it for his Interest but that it will hurt the Poor.
>   Mrs Turton said she would never consent to have the Common enclosed for it would hurt the Poor.
>   Mary Rishworth's reasons were that it will injure the Poor be expense to her and that she would have things go on as they had done.

The common people tended to fear enclosure, often with good cause, and a number of stormy anti-enclosure meetings were held. At Quainton in Buckinghamshire opponents managed to delay the passing of the Act for almost forty years, while at Thornborough in the same county, enclosed in 1798, a special lamentation was composed:

> The time alas will soon approach
> When we must all our pasture yield
> The Wealthy on our rights encroach
> And will enclose our common field.

The formalities and lamentations over, Parliamentary Enclosure proceeded to dismantle the surviving medieval framework of the parish and superimpose the new award on the face of the countryside.

It is estimated that the movement resulted in the planting of over a billion shrubs in the creation of 200,000 miles (321,870 kilometres) of new HEDGEROWS. On one farm at Oakhill in Somerset about 1½ million hawthorn seedlings were said to have been planted. The countrysides created were geometrical planners' landscapes, with straight walls or hedgerows, rectangular fields and undeviating roads. At Stewkley in Buckinghamshire, for example, the Act (of 1811) required the boundaries of the holdings to be

marked with new hawthorn hedges, ditched on one side and protected on each side from browsing by post and rail fences. Such requirements were quite typical, though once his boundaries were fenced the new proprietor could establish his internal field divisions in his own time, and often large allocated fields of around 50 acres (20 hectares) were subdivided into more manageable 5- or 10-acre (2- or 4-hectare) units.

With the new field-patterns established, changes in land-use could follow, often with the old open-field ploughlands going to pasture and then being subjected to a regime of UP-AND-DOWN or convertible husbandry. The commons and wastes were now partitioned by hedges or DRYSTONE WALLS. Often the rough pasture was limed or marled, and the improvements also allowed the establishment of up-and-down husbandry on what had been barren over-grazed land. The enclosure and improvement of moorland was more difficult to achieve, and drainage, the burning off of heather and bracken, stone clearance and several bouts of ploughing and liming were required before crops could be harvested. But the high crop prices that prevailed during the Napoleonic wars often provided the incentive for moorland reclamation.

Though many contemporary critics despised the visual qualities of the newly enclosed countrysides, later generations have learned to cherish the maturing hedgerows, appreciate the way that the ascending lines of DRYSTONE WALLS detail the bare upland landscapes and admire the rectilinear patchwork patterns of the surveyors' fieldscape. Planned countryside may never be able to match the subtle curves, sunken lanes and wooded nooks of ancient countryside, but it has its own admirable qualities and plenty of niches for hedgerow wildlife. Parliamentary Enclosure was a great victory for the landlords and their vision of control and order over the collective, quasi-democratic interests symbolised by the common and its impoverished commoners. It is there that its greatest significance may lie. See also LIME KILN, MARL-PIT, HIGH FARMING.

*Further reading:* Chapman, J., 'The Extent and Nature of Parliamentary Enclosure', *Agricultural History Review* 35, 25–35.

Hammond, J. L., and Barbara, *The Village Labourer*, Longman, 1978.

Tate, W. E., *The English Village Community and the Enclosure Movements*, Gollancz, 1967.

Turner, M. E., *English Parliamentary Enclosure*, Folkestone, 1980.

Williamson, T., 'Understanding Enclosure', LANDSCAPES, I.I, 2000, pp. 56–79.

**Parrach, parrick**. A small PADDOCK, sometimes one used when a ewe is adopting a strange lamb.

**Peat**, see TURBARY.

**Peat bank**. The place where peat was cut. See TURBARY.

**Peat road, peat gate**. A track in the northern uplands used partly or mainly for conveying loads of peat from the high moors to the settlements that enjoyed rights of TURBARY there. In relatively recent times, tall conical stacks of drying turves shaped rather like Christmas trees could be seen beside the tracks that ran down from the moors.

**Pecht-stane**. In Scotland, a prehistoric stone such as a MONOLITH. The word derives from the dialect term for a Pict.

**Pele tower**. Pele towers occupy a place in the hierarchy of strongholds between the BASTLE and the castle proper. They are concentrated in northern England in the zone that was vulnerable to Scottish raiding in the centuries before the Union of 1707 and were the houses of members of the nobility (or, occasionally, of the Church) who were of less than castle-owning rank. Pele towers came in a range of forms and sizes and appeared in the mid-fourteenth century and continued to be built until the seventeenth century. Although designs varied, the typical example would exist as a thick-walled rectangular tower with small window-openings which was entered at first-floor level via an external stone staircase. The ground floor was normally used for storage, the hall was placed at first-floor level and the level above contained a tower. A walled courtyard or 'BARMKIN' with a high wall and, sometimes, a gatehouse provided protection outside the tower for livestock.

Pele towers are most numerous in Cumbria, which has about ninety examples, of which Sizergh Castle is one of the best preserved, and there is a thinner sprinkling of examples in northern Lancashire, Northumberland and North Yorkshire. One of the most southerly examples is Nappa Hall in Wensleydale, which has two towers, the west tower and attached hall being built in the mid-fifteenth century by the experienced Agincourt veteran, Thomas Metcalfe. It is associated with interesting LOST GARDEN earthworks.

**Pen**. In the Celtic languages, a head, signifying a hill, often a pointed one.

**Pen fauld**. In Scotland, a close or pen for cattle on a farmstead, but see also POUND.

**Pen head**. The part of a mill stream leading from the millpond towards the mill. See also DAMS AND WIERS, WATERMILL, FALL TROUGH.

**Penitential cross**, see CROSSES.

**Perception of landscape**. see ENVISIONING LANDSCAPE, ICONIC LANDSCAPE, THERAPEUTIC LANDSCAPE, SITES OF MEMORY, CONTESTED LANDSCAPE.

**Perch, rod, pole, perk**. A variable measure that became standardised at 16½ feet. Also a measure of area of 30½ square yards.

**Pest-house**. When occurring as a field-name this signifies the site of a hospital for victims of contagious diseases.

**Pictish symbol stone**, see SYMBOL STONE.

**Pilgrim roads**. Pilgrimage was extremely popular in medieval Britain. The spiritual aspects apart, it provided many common people with opportunities for travel which they would not otherwise have enjoyed and provided the centres of pilgrimage with substantial revenues. The favoured centres of pilgrimage had shrines with potent religious associations or relics, real or spurious, of popular saints or 'fragments of the cross'. Canterbury, with its shrine of St Thomas Becket, was the most heavily patronised of the destinations. There were many other popular centres, including the shrine of Our Lady of Walsingham at Little Walsingham in Norfolk; Glastonbury with its mythical associations with Joseph of Arimathea, Camelot and the improbable 'grave of King Arthur'; and other less accessible places, like the shrine of St Magnus in Kirkwall Cathedral, Orkney, or the saint-infested island of Bardsey off the tip of the Lleyn peninsula of North Wales.

The roads used by pilgrims most usually have been pre-existing routes, and all were shared with other travellers. A number of inns and other facilities were provided to assist the pilgrims, including wayside chapels served sometimes by hermits, hostels, a few of which survive, like the George at Glastonbury, hospices as represented by Y Gegin Fawr farm on the track to Bardsey, and infirmaries like the one at Castle Acre in Norfolk, which received ailing pilgrims destined for Walsingham. At Houghton St Giles a 'slipper chapel' remains, where the more devout of the pilgrims would leave their shoes to plod the final mile to Walsingham barefoot. A few roads used by pilgrims are still called 'Pilgrim Way', like several of the tracks near Canterbury.

**Pillow Mound**, see WARREN.

**Pinding**. The right to impound trespassing livestock and to exact a charge for their grazing. See also AGISTMENT, POUND.

**Pinfold**, see POUND.

**Pit alignments**. These are not visible from the ground, except as CROP MARKS, but are quite often apparent in aerial photographs. When newly made, in Neolithic and Bronze Age times, pit alignments consisted of long chains of pits. Their function is still largely mysterious. The most widely supported explanation argues that pit alignments were dug to mark out boundaries, though it has also been argued that they were tree-planting holes (the interpretations are not mutually exclusive). They may represent an early phase in the partitioning of territory.

*Further reading:* Pollard, S. J., 'Iron Age Riverside Pit Alignments at St Ives, Cambridgeshire', *Proceedings of the Prehistoric Society* **62**, 1996, pp. 93–116.

**Pit stones**. Stones that mark out the boundaries within a peat moss. See also TURBARY, MOORS.

**Place-names**. Numerous references to place-names appear in different sections of this book, and place-name evidence can be very helpful. It can provide important clues to features of the landscape which are no longer obvious or which existed long ago. At the time when it was given, every name had a meaning in the language of the person who provided the name. However, many place-names today are distorted or seem to be gobbledegook because the spoken language has changed completely or evolved considerably. A place named for a Saxon sheepfold (*eowestre*) could, as language evolved, become Oyster Field or Close. Relatively few place-names that are really old are readily intelligible today and even some post-medieval examples are perplexing. Experts attempt to find the best-fit translations. Thus, Handing-Post Piece is likely to be land near to a spot where a signpost with pointing hands had stood. Very often, though this seldom emerges in the literature, the proper interpretation of a place-name is largely a matter of opinion, even where expert knowledge of old languages and the evolution of pronunciation is applied. Frequently, a number of possible translations are available and there is no certain clue as to the one which is correct. The most respected experts will prefer to study the present appearance and topography of a locality before opting for a particular choice. For example, words which include the element 'Ram-', like Ramsdale or Ramsey, could, as seems most obvious, relate to the male sheep, but they could equally derive from the Old English *hramsa*, referring to ransoms or wild garlic, or they might include a contraction of the Gaelic *ràth*, a circular fort, as with Ramornie in Fife, which may mean 'the fort of a member of Clan Morgan', while Ramsgate in Kent is thought by some to include a personal name – Hraefn's gap or *geat* – and to relate to the gap in the cliffs.

As well as evaluating the locations concerned, place-name experts search the old documents for the earliest recorded form of a name, so reducing the guesswork concerning the development of language and pronunciation. Thus, for example, Milton in Cambridgeshire, which one would normally regard as an easy translation – the settlement (*ton*) or vill with a mill – is recorded in DOMESDAY BOOK as *Middeltone*, meaning 'the middle settlement', while Duxford in the same county appears as *Dochesuitorde*, the name-ending, normally written as 'worth', denoting an enclosure rather than a ford – even though the village is at a fording site on the River Cam. To add to the confusions, attempts to establish a chronology of Saxon place-names have been completely revamped as experts have reinterpreted the evidence. In their turns, names including the elements *ing* or *ham* and those which describe topographical features have each been held to denote names established during the primary Saxon settlement. In seeking a translation of a particular place-name the best that the interested novice can do is to consult a number of place-name dictionaries and, where they offer alternative translations, pick the most likely candidate. The forms of names as recorded in Domesday Book can be found in H. C. Darby's and G. R. Versey's *Domesday Gazetteer*, Cambridge University Press, 1975. Despite all the problems posed by place-names, their usefulness is described in many of the entries in this book.

*Further reading:* Gelling, Margaret, *Place-names in the Landscape*, Dent, 1984.
Gelling, Margaret, *Signposts to the Past*, Dent, 1978.

**Plain-stanes, plane-stanes**. In Scotland, a pavement or flagged roadway.

**Plaistow (plastow or plaster)**. These are places (now mostly only remembered in place-names like Plastow Green, Kingsclere, in Hampshire) which were used for games and, sometimes, for the meetings of medieval courts. The names derive from the Old English *Pleg-stow* – 'a place for sport'. At Selborne in Hampshire the words evolved into Plestor and here the open area, once shaded by a massive oak which Gilbert White described, was used for the village markets as well as for recreation. In Cornwall circular plaistows exist at Perranzabuloe, St Just-in-Penwith and inside the ROUND known as Perran Round. Tradition associates these sites with the performance of miracle plays, but they probably had broader uses. Other place-names which can denote old sporting venues include not only the obvious ones, like 'Football Close', 'Playing Close' or 'Bowling Close', but also some 'Camp-' place-names, deriving from the camp or field where camp-ball, a primitive kind of football, was played. A cluster of Camping Close field names is found in Cambridgeshire, as at Histon. The West Yorkshire place-names Follifoot and Follithwaite seem to indicate the sites of early medieval horse-fights between pairs of stallions (sometimes their owners, too), while the Hesket and Hesketh placenames of northern England may denote horse-racing courses of the same period. Lancashire has Hesketh Bank and Hesketh Lane and Heskin Green, while Cumbria has Hesketh High and (perhaps aptly) Hesketh Newmarket.

**Plank**. In Northern Britain, an oblong field or a BALK. To plank is to consolidate inter-mixed holdings in a communal field so that each tenant has a compact tenancy.

**Planned countryside**, see ANCIENT AND PLANNED COUNTRYSIDE.

**Plantation**. The essential difference between a plantation and a wood is that while woods were harvested they were not – so far as we know – deliberately planted, but with proper management they provided an infinitely renewable source of timber. Plantations, on the other hand, have been planted and they may not renew themselves once felled without deliberate replanting. A number of plantations were previously woods, which were felled and cleared to remove the native hardwoods and subsequently replanted with alien softwoods, of which larch is the least offensive (see CONIFERISATION). Parts of the New Forest and other historic woods have suffered coniferisation in this way. Plantations come in many different forms, ranging from the unsightly modern conifer plantations (whose practical function often has more to do with the harvesting of elaborate tax concessions than with the growing of useful timber) to SHELTER BELTS, woods planted to enhance PARKLAND or other ornamental tree-clumps, and skyline plantings of the eighteenth and nineteenth centuries. A special form of plantation is the type planted with a commemorative or a humorous intent. At Blenheim in Oxfordshire the victor had trees planted to represent the disposition of forces at the start of the Battle of Blenheim and at Douthwaite Hall, Kirkby Moorside, North Yorkshire the plantings were supposed to represent a fleet of ships. Naming plantations gives some scope for a sense of fun, for example the plantation at Ripley, North Yorkshire, called 'Sir Henry Wood'.

*Further reading*: Skipper, K. and Williamson, T.,
  *Thetford Forest, Making a Landscape, 1922–1997*,
  Centre for East Anglian Studies, Norwich, 1997.

**Plantation of Ireland**. During the seventeenth century, land ownership in Ireland was transferred to English and Scottish Protestants who controlled communities of Irish tenants. The indigenous communities lived in settlements dominated by nearby castles or by the settlers' manor houses and their courts. In Munster, leading English colonists or 'undertakers' arrived as landlords responsible for settling 90 families on their 'seignories' of around 12,000 acres. The conquest of Ulster was followed by more extensive plantations, with settlers, particularly from western Scotland, arriving to displace indigenous communities, reclaim land and replace the pastoral bias in farming with an arable one. Nucleated settler villages and small towns of up to 40 households were established, guarded by castles and bawns and provided with churches, court houses, prisons and mills. These changes provided the structures under which the agricultural improvements of the eighteenth century could be imposed, with the enclosure of land, the consolidation of tenancies and the growth of nucleated settlements.

**Planting**, see PLANTATION.

**Plashie**. Marshy.

**Plash-mill**. Scottish term for a FULLING MILL or WALK MILL. See also WATERMILL.

**Plastow, plaster**, see PLAISTOW.

**Pleuat, plood**. Scottish term for a piece of living turf used for rural roofing.

**Pleuch-gang, pleugh-gate**. In Scotland, the amount of 'pleuchland' that a single plough can till – around 40 Scottish acres. See also HIDE, VIRGATE.

**Ploughland, ploughgate**, see HIDE.

**Plough ridge**, see RIDGE AND FURROW.

**Plump**. A clump of trees.

**Policies**. The pleasure grounds of a rural mansion in Scotland. See also IMPROVEMENTS, PARKLAND. In England a similar word may evolve from medieval words for a hedge or small wood with pollards.

**Polissoir**. These are stones which were used for sharpening weapons and tools and which display smoothly polished grooves which result from long use in the sharpening process. The oldest examples result from the sharpening of flint and stone axes; a few of the stones in the Avenue at Avebury are grooved in this way, and there is a very good example of a polissoir boulder inside the great chambered tomb known as the West Kennet long barrow, overlooking the Avebury area. Later polissoirs were used for sharpening swords and arrows, and some churches and church porches have had their fabrics scarred in this way. Hard, fine-grained stones imported for doorposts or lintels might be particularly favoured.

**Pollard**. One method of obtaining a regular crop of timber poles was by maintaining a COPPICE. The disadvantage of the coppice was its susceptibility to severe damage to soft low growth by browsing animals during the decade which followed felling, so that animals had to be excluded from the coppice. Pollarding was an alternative method of producing light timber in a way that was compatible with grazing. A suitable tree – often an oak, elm, hornbeam or beech – was cut at a height out of reach of browsing, normally at about 8–12 feet (2.4–3.7 metres) above the ground. The pillar-like trunk that remains after pollarding is known as a 'bolling'. New growth would not tend to develop from the sides of the bolling, but from its crown. After perhaps ten or twenty years the poles or loppings would be cut, and the cycle of pollarding would begin again. Pollards were also exploited, particularly in DEER PARKS, as sources of 'greenhews' or leafy fodder. Medieval illustrations suggest that pollards were extremely frequent, while leases of the period sometimes allow tenants to cut fronds or greenhews, but forbid cutting in ways that would damage the trees.

When grazing pressures removed the WOOD PASTURE trees from the wooded COMMONS, HEDGEROWS surrounding the growing numbers of enclosures and ASSARTS provided alternative sources of light timber, as did the increasing COPPICES. Pollards growing in hedgerows in the eighteenth and nineteenth centuries tended to suffer severely in areas where agriculture on heavy soils gravitated towards arable uses. The trees were considered to damage the crops by shading them and by taking nutrients from the soil.

Today the practice of pollarding has been virtually abandoned in woods, parks and hedgerows, though willows growing beside the more carefully managed angling rivers are still pollarded, as are lime pollards lining many suburban streets. In Epping Forest a number of old hornbeams have been experimentally pollarded after many years of neglect, and the old bollings could soon be seen crowned in a fuzz of new growth. Formerly, pollarded trees were very numerous, and although many will not have experienced lopping for over a century they can still be recognised by the branches, now often only 3, 4 or 5 in number, all arising from one level which corresponds to the height at which pollarding used to take place. See also WOOD PASTURE.

*Further reading*: Read, H., *Veteran Trees a Guide to Good Management*, English Nature, London, 1999.
Muir, R., 'Pollards in Nidderdale, a Landscape History', *Rural History* 11.1, 2000, pp. 95–111.

**Pond**. Ponds exist in a wide range of shapes and sizes; and, although some kinds of pond can be identified with ease, others are hard to distinguish. Sometimes it is even difficult to differentiate between man-made and natural ponds.

*Natural ponds* will form in any depression which lies below the level of the watertable, while a variety of natural ponds owe their origins to glacial events.

*Meres*, which can be pond-sized or lake-sized, can form in several ways, though many, like those of northern Shropshire, formed in the immediate aftermath of glaciation as waters from the melting ice-sheets accumulated in hollows in the hummocky terrain of the 'drift' or boulder clay that the ice had dumped. Where such drift covered frozen ice-bound ground, the thawing of the permafrost could cause subsidence and the formation of *kettleholes*. In the Brecklands of East Anglia the meres are thought to have originated as 'pingos', lens-shaped blisters of subterranean ice which grew and bulged upwards before eventually melting. The melting produced a circular, water-filled hollow with a seemingly artificial but deceptive raised girdle of earth that had slumped around the margins of the pingo. Because the movement of water in the underlying chalk is complex, the level of water in the Breckland meres is difficult to predict, and high levels may sometimes coincide with periods of low rainfall.

While the meres of the Breckland are natural but look man-made, many meres or *flashes* in South Lancashire and Cheshire seem to resemble the glacial meres of Shropshire, but are in fact human-made, resulting from the sagging and flooding of the land-surface following a method of salt extraction whereby the rock-salt was flushed out in the form of brine.

Silting and the colonisation of their margins by vegetation eventually lead to the shallowing, contraction and eventual disappearance of meres, and sometimes 'mere' place-names, like Hanmere in Shropshire, may mark the sites of lost meres, while some 'moss' place-names signify a late stage in the life of a mere, that of a damp peaty hollow. (However, 'mere' names must be handled with care as a high proportion derive from an Old English word for boundary: *meare*.)

*Swallowholes* are features of chalk and limestone country, these rocks being soluble in rainwater, particularly if the solution has become acidic through trickling through humus or acid rocks or sands. Swallowholes are solution hollows that may appear as dramatically gaping shafts, like the Buttertubs in North Yorkshire, or as fairly circular water-filled hollows or sinkholes. Water flowing in then usually percolates underground through the subterranean network of fissures and caverns.

*Artificial ponds* have been constructed at all periods since the Iron Age and for a wide variety of purposes. Sometimes it is possible to link a pond to a particular origin and role – as with millponds and fishponds – but frequently the age, origin and function of a pond will remain a total mystery. This is the case with many field-ponds, which could, on the visible evidence available, be sinkholes, artificial cattle-watering ponds or industrial ponds.

The most obvious function for any *prehistoric pond* would be that of providing a reliable source of drinking water for people, cattle or both. While it is hard to imagine that the simple necessities of life would not have led to the building of such ponds in large numbers, it is almost equally difficult to prove the ancient origins of many ponds: archaeologists usually have more urgent commitments, though only excavation can provide the answers. Oliver Rackham has quoted the case of an apparently artificial watering hole in a wood near Salisbury which pre-dates the Bronze Age LINEAR EARTHWORK of Grim's Ditch, the earthwork making a detour in order to bisect it. The first industrial ponds to be built in Britain were probably the work of the Romans. At Dolaucothi goldmines in Dyfed, waterwheels were used for draining the Roman mine workings and a system of aqueducts and reservoir ponds was built to assist the mining processes.

In Wessex several ponds, isolated and incongruously placed on barren chalk hilltops or plateaux, have supported villages since Saxon and, perhaps, Roman times. Ashmore (that is, 'Ash mere') is the most picturesque example. Such ponds appear to be natural or largely natural features associated with pockets of water-retentive clay. *Dew ponds* have acquired a similar mystique and result from a human application of the same natural principle. Particularly where the underlying rock is calcareous and the countryside therefore deprived of natural water supplies, circular hollows were dug, often in the bottom of a natural dell, and the bed of the intended pond was lined with puddled clay or with puddled clay and straw coated with loose flints. Dew had little role to play in the filling of such a pond, this relying mainly on the capture of run-off from rainfall. Despite the air of mystery popularly associated with dew ponds, the makers of such ponds

could be employed until as recently as the Second World War – though this is not to deny the probability that the craft originated in prehistoric times. The circular village pond at picturesque Newton-on-Rawcliffe, on the scarp of the North York Moors above Pickering, would seem to be of this type and might possibly be as old as the Norman or Late Saxon settlement.

*Millponds* were constructed from Roman times right through until the water-powered phase of the Industrial Revolution, when thousands of new examples appeared, many served by an elaborate system of leats. At the deserted medieval village of Wharram Percy on the Yorkshire Wolds, the pond of the Saxon and medieval village mill has been excavated and restored. In its most simple form the pond which provided the mill with its regulated head of water was formed by damming the chosen stream to create a triangular pond, though more circular forms could result from a natural or

*Pond*
The earthworks of a medieval fishpond at Landbeach in Cambridgeshire.

artificial broadening of the valley just upstream from the dam. Where the earthworks are quite well preserved it may be possible to recognise the nicks or clefts representing the old sluices, or the silted channels of any leats which were used to supplement the supply of water. (See DAMS AND WIERS)

*Hammer ponds* were a form of millpond associated with the old iron industry and are most numerous in the narrow valleys of the Weald. Dams or 'bays' were built of clay (or sometimes of brick or stone), and the supply of water could be increased by lining a string of ponds along a valley. In close proximity to the Wealden hammer ponds are *furnace ponds*, built to provide a reliable head of water to drive blast-furnace bellows rather than the

trip-hammers of a forge. All such ponds can be difficult to date but mainly belong to the sixteenth, seventeenth and eighteenth centuries: the blast furnace was introduced at the end of the fifteenth century, and the last forge in the Weald closed in 1820. During the early, water-powered phase of the Industrial Revolution, industrial ponds proliferated while some existing ponds were developed for new uses; dams in Sutton Coldfield Park, Birmingham, were probably built in the early fifteenth century to serve fulling mills but then served sword- and button-making mills.

*Armed ponds* have irregular shapes rather like amoebas, with projecting lobes. They were probably provided or modified for the watering of livestock. Where old field-boundaries survive armed ponds will commonly be seen straddling a boundary so that the animals in adjacent fields can drink from different arms or lobes.

*Fishponds* are mainly of a medieval date, though in recent years the vogue for fish-farming and day-ticket angling has resulted in the creation of a new generation of fishponds. Medieval fishponds, providing the lord of the manor with an assured supply of carp for feasts and for Fridays, when meat could not be consumed, were normally shallow embanked structures. Today, following the decay of their sluices and the silting of any leats which fed them, these ponds are usually dry, though a few wet or seasonally wet examples can be seen, as at the

211

deserted village site beside Cublington, Buckinghamshire. The forms of such ponds varied, but the most typical layout involved a rectangular or trapezium-shaped main pond, flat-bottomed and with water retained by earthbanks around 3–4 feet (1 metre) high, with an adjacent chain of two or three small stew ponds, where young fish were raised. Often the main pond contained an artificial mound that served as a secure island roost for wildfowl. Other fishpond forms can be encountered, like the hillside scoops at Bolton Priory in Wharfedale. Carp were probably the most favoured fish, though different medieval documents mention the taking of young pike, eels, perch, bream and trout. Often, fish were caught by nets or by angling in nearby rivers, with the fishpond being used as a form of store. The 'fish on Friday' convention buttressed the importance of the fishpond, though some remained in use after the Reformation and a new fishpond was built amid the ruins of Wormleighton village in Warwickshire after its depopulation by the Spencers in the 1490s. With the hunting out of so much wild game in the earlier medieval centuries and the uncertainties attached to the contemporary methods of preserving meat in brine, any source of fresh protein was highly valued. The pond and its produce were the property of the manorial lord or monastic landowner. Poaching was a problem and ponds were usually situated within sight of the MANOR house so that the earthworks of fishponds and homestead MOATS are often seen together. Sometimes a protective hedge surrounded a pond. A few ponds were found close to towns and, in 1316, John de Amyas was fined at Wakefield manor court after he had meddled with the water-course of his fishpond and inadvertently flooded one of the town's main streets. See also DAMS AND WEIRS, WATERMILL.

**Poor Man's Land, Poors Piece, etc.** Names of this kind will usually refer to charity lands whose profits were left to support the poor.

Occasionally, the words will relate to the poor quality of ground.

**Portal dolmen, quoit.** A form of megalithic tomb with an entrance formed by two large portal stones which help to support a huge, sloping capstone. Numerous in Ireland and the west of Britain, these tombs may have been associated with a ritual in which the corpse was exposed for defleshing by scavengers before the bones were interred in the burial chamber. A few are associated with CUP MARKS. See also CHAMBERED TOMBS.

**Post mill**, see WINDMILL AND WIND PUMP.

**Post and pan.** Scottish term for a method of building using upright posts linked together with wooden crosspieces or 'pans' to create a framework which could be filled with rubble, mud and clay. See WATTLE AND DAUB, CLAM AND STAFF.

**Pot.** A small still.

**Pottery**, see FIELD-WALKING.

**Pou, pow.** In Northern Britain, a slow-moving stream or a place with pools of stagnant water.

**Pound.** The pound or pinfold was an essential adjunct to OPEN-FIELD FARMING. A pound would normally exist on any medieval manor, while long after the decay of the manorial system pounds were still needed so long as unenclosed strip-fields survived. They were needed because open fields were *open* – there were no hedges between the field strips, so that stray cattle or sheep could cause a great deal of damage to the growing crops. Similarly, in upland areas, animals straying back over the HEAD DYKE in summer were very destructive. Livestock were all privately owned, and their owners were responsible for ensuring that they were to be found in their proper places: grazing on whichever open field was being fallowed; feeding amongst the stubble of an open field after harvest; away on the COMMON, or confined in one of the hedged CLOSES beside the village.

The lord of the manor kept the pound, and straying beasts were captured and confined by an official called a 'pinder', who was appointed each year by the manor court. Studies of the records of the old manorial courts show that the peasant owners of livestock were frequently fined for the depredations of their animals. Given that a pound was an indispensable feature of open-field farming and that everyone in a village could identify the owner of a cow or goat, it is remarkable how often villagers were fined for pound-breaking. In 1327 Alice, wife of John de Heton, was fined 12*d.* (5p) in the Ossett district near Leeds because she was forever letting her cattle trespass on her neighbour's property, 'and when her cattle were impounded for damages, she broke the pound and drove them off without making any compensation to those who had impounded the beasts'. In 1189 the abbot of Croyland impounded peasant cattle caught on a disputed fenland grazing – and was then confronted by an armed peasant mob, claimed to be 3000-strong; eventually the royal court found in the abbot's favour. In 1280 the tenantry of Mickleover lost a lawsuit against Burton Abbey in Staffordshire and the abbot defrayed his costs by impounding all the village's 800 livestock. The peasants adopted a more imaginative approach than that of the Croyland mob, taking to the road, women, children and all, to follow and pester the King, who eventually issued a writ for the return of the cattle. Yet the Mickleover people, who were the serfs of the abbot, in feudal terms owned only their own stomachs, so after winning the final legal round on this basis, the abbot relented, exacting nominal fines but seizing half the growing corn from the two ringleaders.

The medieval pinder was a much-abused but essential member of the community. Sometimes he needed special protection, as at Mid-Merrington township in Durham, where it was ordered that 'none should assault the pinder at his duty nor curse him'. Medieval pounds will normally have existed as small, fenced or hedged enclosures. A number of villages still preserve later pounds of stone or brick, as at Laxton in Nottinghamshire, and it is likely that the seventeenth- or eighteenth-century survivals often mark the site of their medieval predecessors. At Raskelf, near Boroughbridge, there is a very well preserved pound, a small open polygonal brick structure with arched and barred door and window openings. There was no set design; the pound at Newnham-on-Severn near Cinderford is square and of brick, the one at Hutton-le-Hole near Pickering is circular and of stone. Field- or street-names like Pinderfield, Pound Piece or Pinfold Close indicate the locations of former pounds.

**Poundhouse (cider-house).** A small rectangular farm building associated with cider-making which housed a donkey-powered apple-crushing mill and a fermenting room. The cider-mill consisted of a vertical stone wheel that revolved around a circular trough. A horse or donkey was harnessed to a beam that projected from a central spindle; as the beast walked round and round, so the crushing stone rolled around the trough. The crushed apples were then transferred to a cider-press and juice from the pressing was poured into barrels to ferment.

**Prairie fields.** These visually sterile and featureless expanses of 'countryside' are created by the destruction of hedgerows, woods and ponds in order to produce the vast tracts of land associated with late twentieth-century mechanised, subsidised farming. Although farmers have been heavily criticised for the vandalisation of scenery and obliteration of wildlife, many were simply following official Ministry advice – and some deeply regret the consequences of hedgerow removal.

In 1984 the Nature Conservancy Council estimated from a study of aerial photographs that, of around 500,000 miles (804,675 kilometres) of hedgerow existing in England and Wales in 1946–47, 150,000 miles (241,400 kilometres) had been removed by 1974, all but 20,000 miles (32,190 kilometres) of the destruction being wrought by farming. In 1986, research on

'Monitoring Landscape Change' produced by the Countryside Commission and Hunting Technical Services estimated that between 1947 and 1985 the absolute length of hedgerows in England and Wales was reduced by 22 per cent or 190,000 miles (305,775 kilometres). The rate of destruction accelerated to 4000 miles (6440 kilometres) per year in the early 1980s.

Estimates of the absolute lengths of hedgerows existing at different post-war periods are:

| 1947 | 1980 | 1985 |
|---|---|---|
| 495,000 miles | 406,000 miles | 386,000 miles |
| (796,630 km) | (653,395 km) | (621,210 km) |

The most barren and uncompromising prairie-field landscapes are found in the East Midlands and East Anglia; Cambridgeshire and Bedfordshire have been rendered almost as monotonous as Oklahoma; while Suffolk, formerly one of the loveliest English counties, has had the greater part of its rural beauty extinguished. Meanwhile in Wessex the prairie has engulfed expanses of DOWNLAND pasture and destroyed many fascinating CELTIC FIELD networks. Doubtless the historical and aesthetic sterilisation of the English countryside seems set to continue although the economic crisis in the Common Agricultural Policy and the resort to set-aside schemes to reduce the burden of subsidy have changed the direction of changes. The modern experience has shown that western governments readily subordinate issues of ecology, aesthetics and culture to the profit motive and the powerful pressure group.

*Further reading:* Blunden, J., and Turner, G., *Critical Countryside,* British Broadcasting Corporation, London, 1985.

Countryside Commission, *The Changing Countryside,* Open University/Croom Helm, Beckenham, 1985.

Countryside Commission, *Agricultural Landscapes: A Second Look,* Countryside Commission, 1984.

Shoard, M., *Theft of the Countryside,* Maurice Temple Smith, London, 1982.

Shoard, M., *This Land is Our Land,* Gaia Books, London, 1997.

**Preaching cross**, see CROSSES.

**Prebendary manor**. A prebend or MANOR that supports canons or members of the chapter of a cathedral or collegiate church.

**Preceptory**. A house of the Knights Templar which was staffed by a small complement of Knights, their chaplain and servants, and which usually served like a MANOR as the centre for managing an estate, and sometimes operated as a recruiting centre of the order. After 1312, the order was suppressed amid bizarre accusations and the preceptories were transferred to the Knights Hospitaller, though continuing to be known as preceptories rather than as COMMANDERIES. Some were granted actually to friends of the King, and for several decades the Hospitallers attempted to recover them. Many 'Temple' place-names are associated with bases of the Knights Templar, such as Temple in Cornwall, Templeton in Devon or Temple Guiting in Gloucestershire. The word 'Temple' also survives in field names.

**Prehistoric track**, see ANCIENT TRACKWAYS.

**Pressland, Press Field, etc**. Land that was associated with the GLEBE of the priest.

**Priest's house**. The medieval equivalent of a vicarage or parsonage. Priest's houses generally stood close to churches, sometimes in the CHURCHYARD. It was the home of a clerk who would normally have worked his GLEBE much as the villagers in his congregation worked their holdings.

**Priory**. A priory was a monastery that was governed by a prior or a prioress and which, generally speaking, ranked below an ABBEY, whose abbot or abbess enjoyed higher status and which had greater independence. Some priories were dependencies of prestigious abbeys, and the offshoots or daughter houses of abbeys usually began as priories but could aspire to abbey rank. However, all Carthusian houses and most of those of the Canons Regular (Augustinian, Gilbertine and Premonstratensian Canons) were priories. A priory could also be a small cell of a mother house, which managed remote lands or served as a penitentiary, retreat or convalescent home for members of the parent foundation. Alien priories were direct dependencies of Continental houses, mostly established by Normans who donated parts of their newly won ESTATES in England to monasteries in their home-lands. Some were little more than MANORS, others supported a prior and a substantial monastic community. More than a hundred alien priories existed in the early medieval period, but they fell from favour during the wars with France because of their strong continental links and uncertain loyalties, and various restrictions were imposed in 1295. Some became independent priories, others dependencies of English houses, and by 1414 alien priories were extinct in Britain. Priories can survive as impressive ruins, like Bolton Priory in Wharfedale or Castle Acre Priory in Norfolk, or be completely destroyed, like many priory cells.

**Promontory fort (cliff castle)**. This is a form of HILLFORT that is fortified by constructing a set or several sets of ramparts across the neck of a cliff-girt promontory. Promontory forts are very numerous along the western and south-western shores of Britain, where the coastal terrain greatly favoured this form of defence. Amongst the best-known examples are the fort on Gurnard's Head near Zennor and The Rumps near Polzeath, both in Cornwall. Some of the Cornish promontory forts may have been constructed by settlers from Brittany during the Iron Age, while evidence of occupation during the Dark Ages has been found at various of these strongholds. In Ireland, promontory forts are numerous on the southern and western coasts and also in the vicinity of Dublin. Several of these sites were in direct contact with the Roman world during the Roman occupation of England and Roman artefacts were discovered in promontory forts like Loughshinny, near Dublin.

**Prospect Mound or Mount**. An earthwork taking the form of a domed or flat-topped conical mound that was used in the formal gardens of the sixteenth, seventeenth and eighteenth centuries as an elevated vantage place from which to enjoy views of the surrounding lawns, hedges, beds and canals. Some of the larger examples were 'spiral mounts', ascended via spiral paths, while some acted as platforms for BELVEDERES. If the associated gardens fall out of use and revert to countryside, the mounds might be mistaken for MOTTES or ROUND BARROWS. Low, slightly domed mounds were sometimes planted with a circular clump of trees to add interest to the interior or approaches to a LANDSCAPE PARK.

**Prospect tower**, see FOLLIES

**Purlieu**. An area originating as an unlawful addition to a FOREST or else land bordering a medieval forest.

**Pyle**, see PELE TOWER.

# Q

**Quarries**. This section does not concern working or recently disused quarries, for their nature and function are obvious. The landscape of Britain is littered with long-abandoned quarry workings, for in medieval times any small community which had access to a resource of passable building stone would have its local quarry. The stone quarried could be of indifferent quality but it would be exploited, particularly for parish church-building works, since the costs of transporting stone, other than for special components, like lintels, were prohibitive. Other, grander quarries, like those at Barnack and Ketton near Peterborough, Portland, or Corfe in Dorset were of a different magnitude of importance, exporting stone for use in the great and prestigious medieval building works. Where a region was deprived of suitable building stone, then high-quality stone might be moved over great distances, using RIVER TRANSPORT wherever possible. Thus East Anglia, with little

*Quarry*
The old village chalk (clunch) quarry at Orwell in Cambridgeshire.

available but chalk and flints, imported building stone from quarries like Barnack along the river and LODE system. Villages in Cambridgeshire like Reach and Cherry Hinton used the same system of waterways to export chalk 'clunch', which was soft yet amenable to carving and valued for protected interior church masonry.

Medieval village quarries can be found in many guises and present puzzling appearances once the shallow pits, working faces and spoil-heaps have been overgrown. At first glance the relics may be confused with other earthworks, like those of deserted farmsteads or villages, though on closer inspection they will be seen to lack any regularity of form. In the cases of a few of the grander quarries the relics can be quite spectacular, as can be seen in the great expanse of bumps and hollows on the outskirts of Barnack village. In general, those who worked local sources of stone in the medieval period sought outcrops of near-horizontal strata. These were exploited with rows of wedges, blocks of rock being split-off from a scarp-like face and then sledged away. This technique avoided the digging of pits, with the associate problems of hauling quarried stone out from the hole. At old quarry sites a search should be made for an administrative area, where the stone was stacked awaiting removal. Shallow, overgrown heaps of chippings from the work on squaring blocks of stone may also be seen. Because of the severe shortcomings in the transport system, medieval builders would seek to employ the nearest suitable outcrop of stone that could be found. Stone from a quarry can normally matched to any medieval buildings surviving in its vicinity. Many communities enjoyed the right to quarry building stone, and old records relating to Yetminster village in Dorset tell that 'there are customary quarrs lying in the east downs which is in the lords [demesne] and is known by the name of Quarr Close in the which it is lawfull for the tennants to dig and to carry away at all times such stone as they shall need to build or repair there houses'. Field-names like 'Quarr Close' are good indicators of former quarrying sites, and other examples include Quarhill Field, Quarr Leaze and various 'Standells' or 'Standles' names, which also relate to quarrying.

# R

**Rabbit**, see WARREN.

**Rag-fallow, rag-fauch.** A hay field which has been ploughed after mowing and is then ploughed for two more seasons before being manured and returned to grass.

**Raine**, see STRIP LYNCHET.

**Raith**. A Scottish term for RATH.

**Rake.** A path or animal trackway, also an expanse of hill grazing for cattle or sheep.

**Rammel, ramle.** Stone rubble from ruined buildings or a loosely-built rubble wall.

**Ranch boundary**, see LINEAR EARTHWORK

**Rannoch.** In Scotland, BRACKEN.

**Rape-thackit.** In Scotland, house thatch that is held-down by weighted ropes. See also BLACK HOUSE.

**Rath.** A rath was a lightly defended Irish farmstead, now usually recognisable from the circular bank-and-ditch earthworks that enclosed the perishable house and buildings within. Raths coincide with the areas that were most heavily settled in prehistoric times, but date from the fifth to the tenth centuries AD. The great bulk of them seem to be associated with a rapid expansion of farming in Ireland in the fifth century AD, which may have been linked to the arrival of Christianity and closer contacts with the Roman world. More than 18,000 rath sites have been identified on the ground and a further 28,000 are known from maps and air photographs, many of them distinctive earthworks, though others now much degraded. The circular enclosures are around 100 feet (*c.*30m.) in diameter and will have served as a farmyard. The raths avoided uplands but seem to have favoured swells in the topography that allowed better visibility. A few larger and bivallate raths generally occur within the pattern of 'standard' examples, and these may have been the high-status settlements with better defensive properties. 'Rath' place-names are extremely common in Ireland, deriving from the Gaelic *rath*, 'a circular fort', and the word also occurs occasionally in Britain, in examples like Rathillet, 'the fort of the Ulsterman', near Cupar in Fife. In the Irish literature, raths are commonly described as 'ringforts'. See also CASHEL.

*Further reading*: Stout, M., *The Irish Ringfort*, Dublin, 1997.

**Rean.** A ribbon of unploughed land in the OPEN FIELDS. See also BALK, MERE.

**Reaves.** These are low tumbled banks of boulders, rubble and earth which were constructed in the Bronze Age, around 1600 BC, as part of a systematic demarcation of communal territories and fields in Dartmoor. The major reaves can follow ridges for several miles to mark out the main ancient territories, while the subdivisions are marked by systems of parallel reaves which leave the major reaves at right angles. Other quite prominent reaves can be seen on either side of the River Dart below Dartmeet. Today, most reaves are rather difficult

*Reaves*

A system of reaves on Mountsland Common, Ilsington, Devon. Note the regular, planned character of the Bronze Age field-system. Low walls of rubble define the fields and originally they may have been capped with earth and have existed as hedgebanks. (CUCAP)

to discern at a distance except in favourable winter conditions, but originally the banks are likely to have carried hedges and would have resembled the fine living hedgebanks of the countrysides which border on the moor. See also CO-AXIAL FIELDS.

*Further reading*: Fleming, A., *The Dartmoor Reaves*, Batsford, London, 1998.

**Reeve, reive**. In Northern Britain, a cattle pen or sheep FOLD, also a circular ditched prehistoric enclosure, see RATH.

**Relief**, see ENTRY FINE.

**Rendal, rennal, rundale**. In Scotland, land in a field fragmented between different tenancies. See also RUNRIG.

**Represented landscapes**. Landscapes as depicted in paintings, photographs, maps and literature. They contrast with real or 'material' landscapes.

**Rib**. To half-plough land by leaving alternate furrows untilled.

**Rickle-dyke**. In Scotland, a field wall with a firmly-built base but an upper section consisting of just a single thickness of loosely-stacked stones. See DRYSTONE WALL.

**Rick place**, see STACK STAND

**Ridding**, see ASSART.

**Ridge and furrow**. When travelling through countrysides of old pasture, particularly when a low sun is casting long shadows, the rambler is almost sure to notice that the surfaces of some fields seem to have a corduroy-like texture. Similarly, in winter curving stripes of melting snow will pattern a field, the snow remaining in the sheltered dips of the furrows after it has melted from the slight ridges on either side. These are the legacies of a very common form of medieval arable cultivation but only survive as plainly visible features in places where the old patterns have been preserved from later ploughing and protected by the sward of pasture or parkland. Plough ridges and their adjacent furrows were deliberately produced by a particular method of ploughing, and their main advantage appears to have been the improvement of drainage which resulted from creating a corrugated land-surface, the ridges generally being aligned down slopes. Also, in years of drought a portion of the crop might survive in the damper ground of the furrows, while ridging would also have helped to define the limits of the STRIPS, lands or selions. Plough ridges were as long as strips of which they were parts – a strip could encompass one, two, three or more adjacent parallel ridges.

The ridging of land was most pronounced in the poorly drained clay lands, while in some parts of the well-drained lowlands of the East Midlands and East Anglia there seem to have been strips without lasting ridges. During the ploughing of fallowed fields in May there was the 'casting of the tilth' down from the ridge into the furrow by ploughing around the ridge in an anticlockwise manner and redistributing the topsoil. Later in the season, two clockwise ploughings, with the mouldboard of the plough turning the soil towards the centre of the ridge, would establish the domed cross-section. The crest of a plough ridge could stand 3 feet (1 metre) or more above the furrow. Since long teams of six or eight oxen were used to haul the plough it was necessary to begin the turn at the end of a ridge well before the HEADLAND was reached. The turn to the left is represented in the 'reversed-S' shape of the typical ridge.

Ridge-and-furrow cultivation probably became widespread in the late Saxon period although the practice of ridging land could be much older than this and examples have been discovered beneath Hadrian's Wall and now the CORD RIG that has been found on some upland slopes is considered to be prehistoric. The ridging of land was extensive in medieval times, and some plough ridges were still being perpetuated in the traditional manner in the early years of the nineteenth century. Victorian STEAM PLOUGHING could produce a form of ridge and furrow in which the ridges and furrows were

exactly straight, while the corrugations of LAZY BEDS for the cultivation of potatoes were produced by a spade rather than a mouldboard. Some plough ridges had working lives that spanned a thousand years, and in the course of such a long period, a variety of modifications could appear. For example, after a long period of cultivation, a few metres at the end of a set of strips could be left as grass, and this would result in the development of 'small heads' at the ends of the original ridges and the development of a new HEADLAND further down. In places on the upland margins, like the Yorkshire Dales the medieval arable interlude may have been short and have been terminated by the Black Death before ridges with proportions anything like those of the Midlands had been able to develop. In the Dales, the ridges tend to be shallow, with distances of about 4.5m from furrow to furrow. It is not possible to date particular examples from their visible appearance, though generally speaking medieval plough-ridges tend to be broader than the later 'narrow rigg' of the eighteenth and nineteenth centuries. In Scotland the terms 'rig and fur', RIG AND RENNET and RIG AND RENDAL are used. See also OPEN-FIELD FARMING, RUNRIG, STRIP.

*Further reading*: Hall, D., *Medieval Fields*, Shire, Aylesbury, 1982.

Rowley, T. (ed.), *The Origins of Open Field Agriculture*, Croom Helm, London, 1981.

**Rig and rennet, rig-and-rendal**, see RENDAL.

**Rigg, Rig, Ridge**. Rig is a Scottish and northern term for a ploughridge. See also RIDGE AND FURROW, PLOUGH RIDGE, RUNRIG, CORD RIG, LAZY BED, STEAM PLOUGHING.

**Rights of servitude**. These constituted the Scottish equivalent of COMMON rights, including

*Ridge and furrow*
The corrugations of ridge and furrow at Frisby in Leicestershire with possible windmill mounds, lower right. (CUCAP)

rights to graze animals and to dig peat. As in England, the rights were restricted to those who held land in the estate concerned and were regulated by the manor courts.

**Ring**, see RATH.

**Ring dyke, ring garth**, see HEAD DYKE.

**Ring fort**, see RATH.

**Ringwork**. Ringworks are somewhat puzzling defenceworks which consist of a circular embankment, normally originally palisaded, which was composed of upcast materials from the surrounding moat or ditch. There is some controversy concerning whether such defensive earthworks preceded the Norman Conquest, but there is certainly archaeological evidence to show that existing ringworks were sometimes redeveloped as the sites for MOTTES. At Aldingham, on the shores of Morecambe Bay, a ringwork was probably built around 1100, and in the middle of the twelfth century the interior of the ringwork was filled with earth to form a low motte. The earthwork known as The Crump, near Berden in Essex, is a fairly typical example, while the most impressive ringworks are the Peel Ring of Lumphanan in Grampian, which was developed as the stronghold of the famous Durward dynasty, and the massive and unusual earthworks surrounding the stone keep at Castle Rising in Norfolk. At Middleham in Wensleydale a large ringwork is seen to cut pre-existing ridge and furrow and it was superseded by a hall keep on lower ground, the sequence of events helping to date the feature by relative means. Though enjoying an elevated plateau-edge situation it was served by its own spring, which may have powered a horizontal mill wheel in the moat. See also RAM, ROUND.

*Further reading*: Welfare, H., Bowden, M. and Blood, K., 'Fieldwork and the Castles of the Anglo-Scottish Borders', in Pattison, P., Field, D. and Ainsworth, S. (eds), *Patterns of the Past*, Oxbow, Oxford, 1999.

**Ritual landscape**. There has been a tendency for sacred monuments to be considered individually and in isolation, but during the 1980s a strong interest in ritual landscapes developed. Assemblages of monuments were regarded as having collective significance and as reflecting distinctive ways of organising the natural and cultural contents of landscapes for ritual purposes. However, it would be unwise to imagine that ancient, pre-industrial communities perceived sharp distinctions between the arenas of belief and the locations of day-to-day existence. Instead, facets of the scene like trees, pools, springs, caverns and so on were often regarded as being the abodes of spirits or as having consciousness of their own. Whatever the sacred elements present in a landscape might be, in many places throughout the world efforts were made to heighten any existing sanctity through the creation of carefully-contrived systems of monuments. In the vicinity of the R. Ure in North Yorkshire there is a collection of once-impressive henges and (originally) a quartet of large monoliths, all, presumably, enhancing the sanctity of the river. Various interpretations have been given for the association of a CAUSEWAYED ENCLOSURE, artificial hill, CHAMBERED TOMB, avenue, HENGE and STONE CIRCLE at Avebury in Wiltshire, while the studious and incredibly costly positioning and re-arrangement of stones at Stonehenge implies a carefully organised ritual landscape. In contrast to the situation at the more prosaic sites, ritual landscapes, by their very nature are very difficult to decipher. They must all have had a certain, calculated significance, but this significance existed in the minds of the believers and perished when they did. Perhaps the locations chosen for the development of ritual landscapes were those where the existing features imparted a certain drama or mystery. In some cases, perhaps the selected places were thought to be those where some form of 'otherness' was thought to burst through conventional space?

Landscape could also be invoked to further less mystical interests. Various hermits and mendicants exaggerated the hardship of their lives and settings, while the Cistercian communities established in northern England developed a variety of fanciful foundation myths. These dramatised or falsified the hardships and dangers that the founders had experienced whilst establishing houses in supposedly wild and threatening situations. In such ways the resourcefulness and fortitude of the monks was highlighted in a way that would have attracted potential benefactors.

*Further reading:* Bradley, R., 'Monuments and Places' in Garwood P., Jennings, D., Skeates, R. and Toms, J. (eds), *Sacred and Profane*, Oxford University Committee for Archaeology Monograph 32, 1991, 135–40.
Barrett, J., Bradley, R. and Green, M., *Landscape, Monuments and Society: the Prehistory of Cranborne Chase*, Cambridge University Press, 1991.

**River transport.** The former significance of inland waterways, including rivers, artificial waterways and some navigated stretches of water that were scarcely more than ditches was, in large measure, an expression of the inadequacies of the land transport network. Roads had an advantage over rivers in that they were not so susceptible to gradients, did not have problems associated with rapids and portages and went fairly directly in the direction desired. However, they had to be made and once made, they had to be maintained. Both these requisites were severely neglected in the centuries between the waning of Roman power and the growth of turnpikes, almost 1½ millennia later. Roads, however deficient, were preferred by human travellers, like kings or nobles circulating between manors or for tasks of light transport, such as PACK-HORSE teams might accomplish. It was in the movement of heavy, bulky loads, like building stone, clay, coal or timber that the waterways had an advantage. Also, medieval sea-going vessels could navigate in just a few feet of water, placing towns and cities like York in direct contact with the international commercial highways. Where cities lacked direct access to the sea, they might be served by outports on navigable rivers or cuts. Thus, Lincoln was linked by the Foss Dyke to its doomed outport of Torksey on The Trent, the canal becoming silted after Boston captured Lincoln's wool trade. The Foss Dyke was part of the Roman Car Dyke system of artificial waterways and was built soon after the conquest. Waterways could also extend the hinterland of an international port, in the way that transhipment to smaller vessels allowed goods to be taken up the river Ouse to the river port of Nun Monkton at its confluence with the river Nidd. When the river network failed to meet the needs of human commerce, difficult portages between systems were needed. Some problems with gradients were solved by simple '*flash locks*', involving movable barriers to pond-back the flow, gaps through which boats would shoot downstream on a flood and gruelling man-hauls up the shallows. Most primitive of all was the 'cow flash' whereby the water in a difficult shallow stretch was deepened by wading a herd of cattle into the stream.

The most successful of the river ports had great international fairs, like the Stourbridge fair on the banks of the Cam. Such fairs received international commodities carried by sea to the estuaries on the navigible rivers. Lesser river ports, some ABBEYS, like the one at Reading, the dwellings-cum-warehouses of merchants and even some MANOR houses had their HYTHES and sometimes a basin where goods could be unloaded. Sometimes the goods would be transferred to panniers and the network of PACK HORSE ROADS. The river transport system survived until the era of the canal in the eighteenth century, and most of the early canals that were built served as feeders to the existing river system.

**Rockman.** One who catches seafowl on the cliffs of Northern Britain.

**Rod,** see PERCH.

**Roddons.** These are natural landforms of the East Anglian Fens. They are composed of tiny silt particles swept upstream on the ancient fenland rivers by the tides and deposited on the riverbeds. Following drainage and the shrinkage of the fenland peat, the silt-plastered riverbeds now stand above the surrounding black lands like whitish, sinuous ridges. They date, very roughly, from the Iron Age.

**Roe.** This occurs in field-names and derives from an Old Norse word signifying a nook of land.

**Roman roads.** Although Roman roads have become the subjects of various myths, it would be difficult to exaggerate the importance of the network that the Romans provided in England, Wales and southern Scotland. The Romans were not the first road-builders in these islands – far older were the timber trackways which have recently been excavated in the peat of the Somerset Levels and which date to various prehistoric periods from the Neolithic onwards. Not all the roads and trackways used by the Romans in Britain were built by them, for they would have exploited the multitudes of lanes and field-tracks which, though seldom if ever engineered or improved to any impressive degree, had formed the means for communication in the Iron Age chiefdoms. Such ancient routeways continued to provide the local links in the Roman system, and a proportion of them must still exist, unrecognised, in the living network of minor roads and byways. Roman roads are vital because they provided the first coherent 'national' transport system and because they were so well engineered and orientated that, despite centuries of minimal maintenance, they continued to serve as the basic communications system until the turnpike era, while many of the Roman alignments are still reflected in modern trunk roads.

Most of the main Roman roads were acquired at a fairly early stage in the occupation of Britain, for they were initially intended as military highways which could support and sustain regional conquests by assuring the rapid movement and deployment of troops – and each soldier was equipped and trained for

*Roman road*
A Roman road which ran towards a fort at Bainbridge in Wensleydale appearing in the guise of a fieldtrack.

road-building works. The roads are aligned upon their targets with an uncanny certainty; and, although the effective surveying techniques employed are not entirely understood, they must have involved the use of a chain of sighting points – slight kinks in the alignments sometimes occur where 'dead ground' was encountered. Typically, a road was built with a raised bed or 'agger' formed from materials excavated from the flanking drainage ditches, and this would be covered with free-draining sand or gravel and rubble and the surface could be cobbled or paved. One of the most celebrated stretches of Roman road can be seen in the North York Moors on Wheeldale Moor, where the rubble foundations of the road are exposed. The best-known stretch of paving is on Blackstone Edge near the Yorkshire–Lancashire border, close to Littleborough, and although the Roman credentials of this road have been questioned it probably is authentic.

It is a remarkable fact that virtually no new roads were *built* in Britain between the Roman and TURNPIKE eras. This is not to say that the situation remained stagnant: new routes could be forged spontaneously to serve new villages and market towns, and diversions could loop off from the Roman routes to link with a growing settlement or avoid a badly degraded stretch of track. But, while the main roads of Roman times were coherently planned, carefully built and (usually) effectively maintained, those of the succeeding centuries were pragmatic, often unmade and generally badly cared for. Roman roads remained the essential framework of the land transport system, but they did not retain their original Latin names. Stangate combined the Viking word for a road (*gata*) with 'stane', so it was 'stone street'; the ancient trackway which the Romans improved in East Anglia became 'Peddars Way', the road of the pedlars; Fosse Way was named after its flanking fosses, or ditches; and Ermine Street and Watling Street bear names derived from Saxon communities. Many Roman roads became known as 'streets', a word that comes from the Latin *via strata* via the Old English *straet*.

Any Roman roads which are encountered in the course of a ramble can usually be recognised, and both 'living' and relict examples are often identified on Ordnance Survey maps. ENCLOSURE ROADS might be mistaken for Roman ones, but reference to books like the Margary volumes (see below) will resolve such doubts. Some Roman roads may not be recognised by those who believe that such roads were always dead straight. Even the Roman route-ways would curve or weave to exploit a valley or pass or traverse difficult ground. When surviving within the modern road system, Roman roads tend to have a 'hyphenated' appearance. Straight sections where the alignment survives are often interrupted by curving sections representing the places where the crumbling track was abandoned in favour of a diversion. There are many places where a stretch of Roman road has vanished completely into the fieldscape and some lesser Roman roads will probably have escaped discovery or recognition. 'Lost' (or imagined) Roman roads have attracted much attention, but to be credible any candidate must link destinations that one would expect to be linked. In some cases, old hedged headlands, which had become the repository for stones tossed away by ploughmen, have been mistaken for Roman roads. Seeing a straightish ridge resembling an AGGER, the investigator imagines his/her suspicions to be vindicated when a dig reveals a mass of cobbles. Perhaps the greatest difficulty of interpretation occurs where paved tracks or CAUSEWAYS exist which might be Roman or else the result of

paved causeway construction in the medieval period or right through to the eighteenth century.

*Further reading:* Margary, I. D., *Roman Roads in Britain*, 3rd edn, J. Baker, London, 1973.
Davies, Hugh, *Roads in Roman Britain*, Tempus, Stroud, 2002.

**Roo**. In Scotland this denotes either a heap of drying peats – see TURBARY – or a pen ('wroo') in a pasture where cattle are kept at night. Further south, 'Rue' field-names usually reveal places where rue was grown, sometimes as a pharmaceutical and sometimes for strewing on floors, where it was thought to act as a disinfectant.

**Rood**. Quarter-ACRE.

**Round**. Small native settlements of the Roman period, quite common in Cornwall. A simple roughly circular bank and ditch provided modest shelter for a small cluster of oval stone dwellings within. See also RATH.

**Round barrows**. Round Barrows are mainly associated with the Beaker period, around 2700–2000 BC, although the building of round barrows continued for a few centuries after this date. Whether the introduction of the new 'Beaker' ideas and culture was effected by a major invasion and settlement of so-called 'Beaker people', or whether the indigenous people of Britain simply adopted a fashionable package of beliefs which was circulating on the Continent has been debated but is likely to be the kind of problem that genetic fingerprinting may soon resolve. In either event, the old CHAMBERED TOMBS and LONG BARROWS became redundant and the change in belief found expression in the countryside with the appearance of the round barrow.

These were not the first dome-shaped burial mounds to be built in Britain, for much more massive circular mounds had covered some of the great passage graves, like Maes Howe on Orkney (see CHAMBERED TOMBS). The round barrow was associated with a more solitary form of burial, many of the mounds covered individual graves, though frequently later burials or cremated materials were inserted into the sides of an older barrow. In a typical burial associated with the Beaker tradition, the corpse was placed in a crouched position, sometimes in a stone-slab box, or 'cist', and was accompanied by a few possessions, perhaps including a copper dagger or flint knife, as well as a finely decorated beaker, a drinking vessel which probably contained a ritual libation. The cist might be sealed with a slab, but normally the burial would be covered with a domed earthen mound. In fact the burial rite associated with round barrows was quite varied. In some cases a vessel which may have contained food was provided instead of the beaker, and the associated body was sometimes cremated. Occasionally, corpses were buried in tree-trunk coffins, or cremated remains contained in a leather pouch might substitute for the corpse. Not all the original burials were of solitary individuals, while pits were sometimes sunk into existing round barrows to incorporate new inhumations.

In Wessex, a range of 'fancy' barrow types was adopted, and groups of barrows of different shapes can be found together in some favoured burial grounds. The 'standard' bowl-shaped barrow could be ditched or lack a ditch; the 'bell' barrow had a narrow 'berm' of level ground between the mound and its encircling ditch; 'saucer' barrows had low broad mounds surrounded by a ditch with a raised outer rim; 'disc' barrows had small mounds ringed by wide berms that were bounded by ditches with raised rims; while 'pond' barrows had sunken centres surrounded by raised rims. The significance of the different Wessex barrow forms is still a mystery. In Wales, Scotland and the north of England the barrows were built to the bowl standard, but groups of round barrows were sometimes associated with doughnut-shaped 'ring cairns', circles of turf and rubble faced on their inner and outer faces with revetments of boulders. The ring cairns seem to have acted as

religious focuses within the barrow cemeteries. Ring ditches are also found in association with barrow cemeteries and most are probably the remains of flattened barrows. Although the essentials of belief may have changed, the metal-working communities still respected and revered the sacred sites of the Neolithic period. Their barrows often clustered round ritual monuments that were already ancient, like the Dorset CURSUS, to produce multi-period RITUAL LANDSCAPES.

Excavations have revealed that even the typical bowl-shaped barrows could be quite complicated constructions. Sometimes, a barrow began as a small turf mound covering the original burial; concentric rings of stakes might be placed around this mound before the final covering mound was built. There were also cases where corpses were cremated by firing timber mortuary houses, the relics of the conflagration being entombed when the covering mound was raised. In the course of the Bronze Age, the ritual of barrow burial gradually died out. In some places, cremated remains were buried in large urns in 'urnfield' cemeteries. The demise of the round barrow probably indicates a major shift in religious belief, and theology may have evolved to favour water gods. Imposing funerary monuments ceased to be built, and it is possible that corpses were cast into rivers, lakes and marshes, as were valuable items of metalwork, some ritually-broken.

During the Roman period a few gigantic round barrows were built, the four finest examples of which can be seen at Bartlow Hills in Cambridgeshire, where the tallest of the mounds towers to a height of about 45 feet (14 metres). Three other barrows in the group were destroyed by railway-building operations. Barrow burials were occasionally built in Dark Age times, the most notable examples being at the famous Sutton Hoo royal ship-burial site in Suffolk, which is currently undergoing a new excavation. As with the earlier long barrows and chambered tombs, the round barrows of the later Neolithic and early Bronze Age period were the burial places of a favoured elite in society. It has been guessed that less than the top 10 per cent in Bronze Age society qualified for barrow burial, and archaeologists have wondered about how the remaining corpses were disposed of. However, excavations of field-ditches dating from around 2000 to 1000 BC at Fengate, near Peterborough, found a number of human burials in what had been open ditches. The corpses were placed there in crouched positions, but there was no evidence of any funeral ritual or grave-marking. Sometimes the barrows are grouped together in barrow cemeteries, like the ones grouped around Stonehenge or visible at the Lambourn cemetery in Berkshire, but more frequently they were solitary monuments, frequently placed in eye-catching positions. On the high watershed of the North York Moors chains of round barrows marked the boundaries between adjacent communal territories. They superseded earlier, less prominent forms of boundary-marking and might represent an intensification of competition for territory. Most domed mounds encountered in a country ramble are likely to be round barrows, but not all will display the characteristic rounded form. Up to 20,000 round barrows are known in Britain, many of them destroyed and only evident in aerial photographs. Although the barrows are generally protected monuments, farmers often clip the margins of a barrow, reducing it in the course of successive ploughings, while barrows in moorland settings, which lack a stabilising covering turf, may erode into low, rather formless mounds of rubble. Both MOTTES and WINDMILL mounds could be mistaken for round barrows. See also CHAMBERED TOMB, LONG BARROW, SQUARE BARROW.

*Further reading*: Burgess, Colin, *The Age of Stonehenge*, Dent, London, 1980.

Bradley, R., 'Mental and Material Landscapes in Prehistoric Britain' in Hooke, D. (ed.), *Landscape, the Richest Historical Record*, Society for Landscape Studies, 2000.

**Rubbing stone**. These are stone pillars that are worn smooth by cattle that have used them to ease the irritation of parasites. Whether such a post was provided for that purpose, or whether it originated as a gate post, or STOOP, a MILESTONE or a MONOLITH could be impossible to tell.

**Ruech**. In Scotland, a hill grazing for cattle or SHIELING.

**Rundale**. Old system of farming in Ireland and Scotland associated with the periodical redistribution of STRIPS in the INFIELD in areas of marginal land. See also RENDAL, RUNRIG.

**Runrig, run-rigg run-ridge**. This was a form of INFIELD-OUTFIELD farming operated in Scotland in the centuries preceding the CLEARANCES and IMPROVEMENTS. The system was operated by the tenants of a 'group farm', which was a multiple tenancy often equating with a CLACHAN or fermtoun accommodating up to a dozen households. The infield or 'mucked land' was kept in continuous production by manuring and was divided into between two and five 'breaks', where oats, barley, pease and rye were the main crops cultivated. Frequently, a simple rotation of two crops of barley followed by one of oats was practised. Within the infield, the land of individual tenants was distributed 'runrig', meaning dispersed through the field in strips. The strips existed as massive ridges of ploughsoil, up to 6 feet (1.8 metres) in height, 30 feet (9 metres) broad and perhaps half a mile (0.8 kilometre) in length. The land ridging was accomplished by an unusually heavy plough hauled by a team of ten or more oxen, though on the most intractable terrain the farmers were obliged to resort to spade cultivation. The massive dimensions of the ridges ensured that a crop could be harvested on the crests of the ridges even in the wettest summers when the remainder of the field was waterlogged. Runrig extended into the Scottish Borders, where strips were reallocated on an annual or a biennial basis. Beyond the INFIELD or 'in-by' was the

OUTFIELD or 'out-by' and beyond this the common grazing of the MOOR or 'muir'.

Within this group farm the pattern of tenancy could be complex, so that while one household might lease a third of the infield strips and be able to employ a landless cottar to help with the farm work, another might only lease a twenty-fourth share. Meanwhile the year-long leases provided may have served to discipline the tenancy through threats of their imminent non-renewal, but they removed all incentive for tenants to attempt long-term improvements. Being poorly adjusted to the fragile agricultural environments of Scotland, as well as to the social and economic aspects, runrig farming was associated with exploitation, poverty, famine and disease. While the runrig system was either eradicated cruelly, by clearances, or in a more enlightened fashion, by improving landlords, overgrown relics of the great plough ridges can be seen in areas which have escaped more modern systems of ploughing. A law introduced in Scotland in 1695 allowed existing runrig land to be divided, and the process of ENCLOSURE in the early decades of the eighteenth century saw much runrig land being repartitioned between more commercial farm units as part of the process of IMPROVEMENT, with dispersed farms and estate villages replacing the old CLACHANS and FERMTOUNS. See also CLACHAN, CLEARANCES, IMPROVEMENTS, INFIELD-OUTFIELD CULTIVATION.

*Further reading:* Dodgshon, R. A., *Land and Society in Early Scotland,* Clarendon Press, Oxford, 1981.

**Rush.** Rushes were found on land that was too poorly drained to be of great value to farmers. However, the rushes could be harvested and spread on floors or fashioned into candles. They could also be used as a rather poor thatching material, the reeds of the fenlands being much better in this role. Rushes appear very commonly in field-names, like Rush Leasow, Rashes, and so on. Where land has subsequently been drained, the rush names reveal its former nature.

**Ryfe out.** In Northern Britain, to break up land and reclaim land from the waste.

# S

**Sair-six**. A crop rotation used in Scotland involving two grass crops, two cereal crops, turnips and another cereal crop. See also IMPROVEMENTS.

**Saltern, salting, salt pan**. A site at or close to the coast owned by a 'salt master' where salt was produced by evaporating brine (though a coast may have moved as much as 15 miles since the early days of salt-making). In times before refrigeration, salting, drying and pickling were the only means of preserving perishable food stuffs, so that the saltings and the SALTWAYS radiating out from them were indispensible to day-to-day life. Salt-making was a common activity amongst the winding creeks of salt marshes. Encroaching sea water was directed by channels and retained in embanked enclosures, with banks that rose to about waist-high and thus exposed the trapped waters to evaporation. In the British climate, evaporation alone was often considered insufficient to allow efficient salt production and the Romans introduced the practices of evaporating brine in iron pans, using coal as the fuel. The final stages of drying were accomplished by putting the wet salt in wooden moulds which were dried in a hot room until the salt set in hard blocks. During the medieval period turf and charcoal were employed as fuels. Salt water was evaporated and filtered to produce a stronger concentration of brine, which was then heated in a peat-fired boiling house. A technique of salt-making employed in East Anglia required just three pits and the warmth of the sun. Seawater was run into the first, where it remained until the silt had settled. Then it flowed into the second and gradually became more saline. Then it was run into the third and was exposed to the sun until the remaining water had evaporated and salt crystals were formed. As well as a legacy of 'Salt' place-names, salt-making has left a number of landscape features. De-salted silt forms low ridges along the coast in regions like East Anglia becoming covered in grass and serving as sheep pasture and coastal defences following its use in salt-making. The Red Hills on the coast of Essex contain silt and residues from Roman evaporating hearths. Old salt-making sites abound in the former marshes of the Stour valley in Kent. The fragments of old retaining banks seen in association with low mounds or black patches of burnt materials are also indications of former salterns.

**Saltway**. Saltways are roads which had a sufficiently strong association with the salt trade for the old trade to be fossilised in their names, and examples such as Saltergate or, as a result of later misunderstandings, Psaltergate are remarkably common. Such names may be medieval or earlier, for even in the disruptions of the Dark Ages the salt trade remained active. The salt concerned came from inland saltfields associated with places like Middlewich, Droitwich, Nantwich and Northwich in Cheshire and from coastal SALTERNS, where brine was evaporated. To understand the importance of the salt trade we must remember that it thrived in days long before the invention of refrigeration and before the importation of oriental spices, when salting was essential for the preservation of meat. Of course, saltways were used by all kinds of other travellers besides the traders in salt.

**Sanctuary cross**, see CROSSES.

**Sarn**. In Wales, an old CAUSEWAY, sometimes a ROMAN ROAD.

**Sauch, sauchen tree**. A willow tree.

**Saw pit**. These pits were generally found in

association with the workshops of joiners, cartwrights and estate carpenters. Planks were sawn from heavy logs and trunks by two sawyers, one perched relatively comfortably on a platform at the top of the pit, but the other being showered with sawdust and sawing in the heat and gloom of the pit. Towards the end of the nineteenth century most pits were superseded by mechanical saws. 'Saw pit' field names are quite common.

**Scaling**. A medieval term used to describe a tract of summer pasture. Many 'scale' names derive from an Old Norse term for a summer hut. See also SHIELING, AGISTMENT.

**Scaps**. A landscape, in Lowland Scots.

**Scar**. In Northern England, a steep exposure of strata on the flanks of a fell or valley side caused by differential erosion or glaciation, from a word signifying 'bare' or 'precipitous'. It emerges as 'scarrie' and 'scaured' in Scots, adjectives meaning rocky or cliff-like.

**Scattalds**. Rough hill grazing on Shetland. Scattalds land was separated from inbye enclosures by a HEAD DYKE. This could be a turf wall or 'fealy dyke'.

**Schugh**. In Scotland, a furrow or ditch.

**Sclender**. In Northern Britain, a scree.

**Scotch mile**. A distance of 1984 yards, 1814m.

**'Scot'- names**. These field-names usually refer to medieval taxation rather than to Scottish nationals. Scutage or 'shield-money' substituted for a tenant-in-chief's military obligations and was recovered by him from his tenants.

**Scowb and scraw**. A traditional method of thatching in Scotland involving wattle and straw or strips of turf. The scowb or scob is a wand of willow or hazel used as a spar to pin down the thatch and the scraw is a thin strip of turf. See also THATCHING.

**Scrogg**. In Northern Britain, stunted shrubs or land covered with such trees and thorn scrub.

**Scug**. A hollow in a hillside.

**Seat house**. MANOR house on a Scottish ESTATE. See also HOME FARM, MAINS.

**Seaweed**, see KELP.

**Sea wynd**. An alley leading down to the sea.

**Selion**, see STRIP.

**Set aside**. A movement existing in numerous countries which reflects the public's inability to consume, and the inability of governments to continue to subsidise, the production of western agri-business industries at existing levels. Set-aside land that has temporarily been taken out of intensive production may offer some advantages to wildlife over a limited period. The historical and aesthetic cases may be less clearcut. Agri-business may already have destroyed the interest that existed, while even where it has not, there are no guarantees that it will not do so in the future.

**Setr**. Shetlandic place-name element indicative of pasture, or of pasture that subsequently attracted a settlement.

**Shade**. A cultivated field.

**Shaw**. A wood or GROVE, also sometimes a flat piece of ground at the foot of a slope. See also WOODLAND.

**Sheep-corn lands**. The light lands of lowland England were the downland chalk soils and heathland sands that were easy to work, but hungry. They were often fertilised by folding flocks of sheep on the ploughlands destined to raise the next cereal crop. Their character was transformed by the MARLING and other improvements associated with the LIGHT LANDS REVOLUTION, FOUR COURSE ROTATION and HIGH FARMING.

*Further reading*: Allison, K.J., 'The Sheep-corn Husbandry of Norfolk in the Sixteenth and Seventeenth Centuries', *Agricultural History Review* 5, 12–30.

**Sheep creep**, see SMOOT.

**Sheep faws**. Lowland places where the hill sheep from the MOORS can shelter in winter.

**Sheep ree, sheep stell**. In Scotland, a pen for sheep built from turf or stone.

**Sheep-rodding, sheepwalk**. Sheep track.

**Sheep tathing**. Land on which sheep are folded in order to manure it.

**Shelter belts**. These are alignments of trees which have been planted primarily to protect exposed fields against wind erosion and crops and livestock against wind damage and wind chill – though many shelter belts have an important secondary role as game cover. The most impressive sequences of shelter belts are the eighteenth- and nineteenth-century alignments of Scots pines which protect the loose, sandy soils of the Brecklands of Norfolk. Some of these belts were originally managed as hedgerows. Around the little daffodil fields of the Scilly Isles the tall hedges of *Escallonia* and *Pittsporium crassifoliam* reach heights of 20 feet (6 metres) and have the dimensions of shelter belts. High hedges of hawthorn and other native species shelter the hop fields of the Weald and West Midlands. In lowland areas varieties of poplar have been planted as shelter belts, some of the densest plantings forming protective curtains around Kentish orchards. Most shelter belts date from the eighteenth and nineteenth centuries, though occasional examples are still planted, particularly in association with new fruit farms.

**Shieling**. The movement of members of a stock herding community and their animals to temporary settlements among upland grazings certainly existed in the early medieval centuries, though by then the custom was probably already ancient. Growing population pressure in the two-and-half centuries following the Norman Conquest of England may have led to an increase in temporary migrations to the high pastures. However, the disease and climatic changes of the fourteenth century will have opened many holdings to new tenants in the lowlands and have discouraged upland lifestyles. In northern England and southern Scotland, the custom of transhumance continued through the Middle Ages but gradually declined during the closing medieval centuries and disappeared in the seventeenth century. In the last year of the sixteenth century, Camden described seeing 'a martiall kinde of men in the Scottish Borders, who, from April to August went 'summering' with their cattle in little cottages that they called 'Sheales' and 'Shealings'. A shieling was a summer settlement usually located on high grazings. On some manors in northern England, members of the farming community would be fined by their manor courts for remaining in their lowland farmsteads and hamlets in the summer when other members of the communities were in the hills. Growing crops needed little attention until the harvest and the livestock were conveniently past the HEAD DYKE and far away in the hills when these were vulnerable to grazing. In some places, each man had his own 'shealrowme' on which to settle, as well as his own ground where his beasts could feed.

Shieling grounds survived as a feature of the living, working landscape in the Scottish Highlands and Ireland until the nineteenth century. In the Highlands, the migration of a large proportion of the CLACHAN community and their livestock to their shielings would normally occur on May Day, a date coinciding with the pagan festival of Beltane. The shieling consisted of simple stone or turf-walled huts known as 'bothies' and served as a centre for controlling animals on the summer grazings and for the making of cheese and butter. In addition to this dairy activity, sometimes a small crop of oats or rye would be sown and harvested in little fields beside the shieling.

In the Scottish Highlands and Islands, the seasonal occupation of shielings persisted until the sad times of the Highland CLEARANCES on the mainland, and until the mid nineteenth century in the Outer Hebrides, but in the hill country of southern and Midlands England the 'transhumance' system of seasonal migration perished before the close of the Middle Ages. Throughout Britain and Ireland, the old traditions are evidenced by a number of Dark Age or early medieval place-names. Old summer pastures may be recognised from '-erg', '-airey' and '-arrow' names, deriving from the Celtic *airidh*, 'a shieling or summer hut', like Sizergh in Cumbria. The Scandinavian word for a spring shieling, *saetr*, appears in '-satter', '-seat' and '-sett' place-names, like Appersett Pasture, near Hawes in Wensleydale, and the outliers of principal farms or shepherds' huts were known as *skali*, producing '-scale' names, like Seascale in Cumbria.

In Wales the transhumance lasted longer, persisting into the nineteenth century in Snowdonia. Here *meifod* names denote 'middle' or 'May' dwellings which were staging posts *en route* to the high pastures and the summer settlement or *hafod*. In Celtic parts of Ireland a similar arrangement endured into the seventeenth and eighteenth centuries, and the equivalent of the shieling or *hafod* was the *buaile*, or in English, 'BOOLEY houses'. Beehive-shaped huts of prehistoric appearance served as bothies on shielings in Lewis and are thought to have been used as recently as 1859. Today, those who ramble across the uplands of the Celtic counties can expect to see numerous ruined shielings, hafods or booley houses. What cannot be recovered is the senses of joy and rapture which, according to various different accounts and recollections, were associated with the summers of rustic simplicity spent in the thyme-scented air of the high pastures. See also CLACHAN, INTER-COMMONING, LODGER, SHIRE MOOR, SUMMER FARM, SUMMERING.

*Further reading.* Miller, R., 'Land Use by Summer Shielings', *Scottish Studies* 2, 1967, pp. 193–221.

**Shire**. An Old English word for a boundary. See also MERE-STONE.

**Shire moors**. In the Lake District and other northern uplands, shire moors were blocks of MOOR associated with INTERCOMMONING by all the communities on an ancient estate. By the close of the Middle Ages, the old shire moors had been divided between the different settlements.

**Shooting butts**, see MOORS.

**Shooting house**, see MOORS.

**Shooting hut**, see MOORS.

**Shot**, see FURLONG.

**Signpost**. Signposts were the only indications of direction to be found in the medieval period, with MILESTONES, which had punctuated ROMAN ROADS, not appearing again until the seventeenth century or becoming numerous until the eighteenth century. However the provision of these posts was sporadic and erratic in the Middle Ages and examples have not survived; the oldest of those that do survive date almost entirely from the eighteenth century, when distances were often given in furlongs. The 'Porridge Stoop', a squared stone pillar at the junction of two ancient roads above Lothersdale, a market for oatmeal and salt carried there by teams of packhorses, gives directions from Skipton to Colne and from Keighley to Clitheroe in the form: '8 miles to Keighley' followed by an open hand indicating the direction to travel. See also STOOP.

**Signal station**. During the latter part of the Roman occupation of Britain the Romanised lands faced mounting threats from barbarian sea-raiders. Advance warning was provided by scouting ships and by signal stations erected after AD 369 on some of the most vulnerable stretches of the coast. The most impressive system of signalling stations was erected on the north-eastern coast of England, which was exposed to Pictish raiding, and stations occupied prominent headlands between Goldsborough and Filey. All are now in ruins, but it has been possible to reconstruct the appearance of Scarborough station, which consisted of a tall stone watchtower standing in a courtyard which was defended by walls with corner towers. Although the stations were fortified against attack, it appears that the defenders at both Goldsborough and Scarborough were overwhelmed and slaughtered by raiders. The exact technique for relaying messages is not known, and the stations were only intervisible under clear conditions, but they seem to have been erected to provide warnings of attack to the garrisons at Malton and York. Other signalling stations stood at intervals along Hadrian's Wall, in Cumberland and at points on the south-western cliffs.

A much later series of signal stations was built in the 1790s for communication between the Admiralty and the naval ports, involving wooden buildings which carried frames of shutters, and those were replaced by flat-roofed buildings which supported semaphore equipment.

**Sike, syke**. A small stream or beck. Some with names associated with colours, e.g. 'Black Sike', seem to be associated with ancient boundaries.

**Sites of memory**. These are places with strong historical associations, these often being associations closely linked to the sense of national identity. They include places that might otherwise seem unremarkable were it not for the presence of a prominent monument – as at battlefield sites, and other places, like historic ruins, cathedrals and so on which obviously connect with the past. See also BATTLEFIELD LANDSCAPES, ICONIC LANDSCAPES, CONTESTED LANDSCAPES.

**Skaithie**. A fence made of stakes and bundles of straw or turf and placed outside the house door in windy northern regions as protection against the wind.

**Skeoch**. In Scotland, a very small cave.

**Skir**. A rock or islet in the sea.

**Slack, sloak, slough**. A deep glen, pass or hollow between hills in Scotland. In England, 'Slough' often denotes a mire, while 'Sleight'

derives from a different Old English word and denotes a sheep pasture.

**Slake**. Both a rugged hill and the inter-tidal section of a beach.

**Slap**. As slack, but also a gap or break in a HEDGEROW.

**Sluice**. Gated gap for regulating the movement of water in and out of ponds, leets and canals. Long after the waters have drained away and the timber of the sluice gates has decayed, the location of sluices may be recognised as notches in the earthworks built to contain water bodies.

**Smearing house**. A hut that was used for smearing sheep with an ointment made from tar and either train oil or butter in the days before chemical sheep dips were employed.

**Smockmill**, see WINDMILL AND WIND PUMP.

**Smoot, sheep creep, hogg hole**. A small gap in the foot of a wall sufficient to allow the passage of a sheep. The wall above is supported by a stone slab which serves as a lintel and the smoot is easily blocked to confine sheep, as necessary. The Yorkshire Dales name 'hogg hole' refers to hoggets or yearling sheep.

**Smuggling.** Long stretches of coastal landscape in Britain derive much of their content and identity from the practice of smuggling. It underpinned numerous businesses and establishments and produced great quantities of disposable wealth that could be invested in agriculture or buildings. The activity was particularly rife on the Channel coast of England. Here, the trade was not confined to the illicit importation of commodities that carried high levels of duty, like tea or spirits, for there was a long tradition of illegal exporting. The 'owlers', who were said to communicate by imitating owl calls, sought to evade bans on the export of raw wool and were active in the later Middle Ages. Their activities peaked in the early decades of the eighteenth century, when they connived with the sheep farmers of the Downs and Romney Marsh. As their operations subsided, the work of smugglers importing brandy from French distilleries deliberately sited on the coast for the export trade, tobacco, tera, wine and lace increased. By the middle of the century, as many as 20,000 men in Kent and Sussex may have found employment as smugglers, their imports dominated consumption of luxury goods in southern England, while the numbers of revenue officers confronting them were minute. The smugglers employed fast boats with bowsprits that were lengthened to carry larger headsails. Landing in sheltered coves, or more blatantly, in established ports, the boats would be met by teams of pack-horses, and their contents stored in inns, warehouses or even churches and distributed to the public at large. In his *Smugglers' Song* Rudyard Kipling described the five and twenty ponies trotting through the dark and the child told to 'Watch the wall, my darling, while the Gentlemen go by'. The trade had and retains a frisson of glamour, but like most illegal enterprises it was rooted in fear and intimidation. Geography ensured that the most intense activity would be found in the narrowing of the Channel fringed by Romney Marsh and the old Cinque Ports, but other localities also had high levels of illicit trading, which extended up the North Sea coast and westwards to Land's End. In Scotland it was sometimes regarded as the national vice. Dutch and English textiles, Irish cattle and corn as well as the highly-taxed alcohol and tobacco all entered the country illegally. Spirits, which were subject to a Malt Tax, were particularly remunerative to the smugglers. There was also an internal revenue problem posed by the multitude of illicit stills in the Scottish Highlands that the Small Stills Act of 1816 attempted to tackle.

*Further reading*: Bretnall, M., *The Cinque Ports and Romney Marsh*, John Gifford, 1980.

**Socage**. Free tenure without an obligation to render military service. It was abolished in 1660. See also FREEHOLD, SCOT NAMES.

**Sokeman**. A free tenant in the feudal world who owed only light obligations to his lord.

**Solskift**, see SUN DIVISION.

**Sonk dyke**. A wall with stone or turf to one side and an earth bank to the other.

**Soot house**. These are only known to survive on Achill Island, Co. Mayo. They are low, rather house-like structures supporting a roof of timber and sods which were allowed to smoulder through the winter, the soot and ash being gathered from the floor and used as a fertiliser

**Soum**. In Scotland, 'soum' relates to the number of sheep that can be kept on a pasture.

**Souterrain (fogou, weem)**. Souterrains remain a source of puzzlement to archaeologists. They are well-constructed underground passageways, which may be of a zigzag, curving or bottle-like form, and which led from native Iron Age dwellings and went to nowhere in particular. Their length varies, but they can be up to 196 feet (60 metres) long. In Scotland and Ireland these underground passages are normally referred to as souterrains, but in Cornwall they are known by the local name of 'fogou'. In Scotland, where souterrains may also be known locally as 'weems' or 'earth houses', around 200 examples are known. Those on Orkney and Shetland tended to be fully subterranean chambers and were roofed with horizontal flags, while those in eastern Scotland were sometimes only partly subterranean and must have had visible timber roofs. The Scottish examples date roughly to the period of the Roman occupation, and small items of Roman manufacture have been found in some of them. They were originally regarded as 'earth houses' or as hiding places but are now generally interpreted as storage areas which were associated with small settlements.

In Ireland, where there was no Roman occupation so that the Iron Age life persisted, the souterrains, which now number more than 3,500, have yielded significantly later dates, from the sixth to the twelfth centuries. They are found in four great clusters, roughly corresponding to the cardinal points and this, plus the lack of a clear association with contemporary RATHS, remains puzzling. However, the souterrain associated with the royal ringfort of Rathmore in Co. Antrim was built on a fitting scale, being a tunnel 130m in length. Here they may have been used to shelter cattle, but were mainly regarded as cool storage areas for dairy products, though Irish opinion on souterrains appears to be swinging back towards a defensive interpretation. They can be interpreted as comprising refuge chambers that could only be reached via a narrow passage that rendered invaders, advancing in single file, vulnerable to attack. Defence against Viking raiders is put forward as an explanation. In Cornwall, the fogous are associated with small settlements of Romano-British date and, again, the storage explanation is the most popular, though it has been argued that fogous, like the one that can be visited at the Carn Euny native settlement site, may have been associated with rituals of some kind. Souterrains seem to have been associated with a great many late Iron Age and Romano-British settlements but most are still hidden or have been filled in for reasons of safety to livestock. Interesting examples can be explored at places like Carn Euny, Rennibister on Orkney, or Ardestie and Carlungie in Tayside.

**Sow-kill**. A simple LIME KILN dug into the ground in Scotland.

**Spinning gallery**. An open-sided gallery attached to a farmstead or wool-barn in northern sheep-farming areas, notably the Lake District. The gallery could have provided a well-lit working area for spinning, but its main use appears to have been the drying of fleeces in sheltered but airy conditions.

**Square barrows**. The nature of burial in Iron Age Britain is largely mysterious, perhaps reflecting a situation where bodies were left exposed to scavengers or cast into rivers, lakes or marshes. A localised exception to the mystery is represented by the square barrows of the Yorkshire Wolds and the immediately surrounding areas, which were probably built by an intrusive population of Celtic settlers. These small barrows are usually only visible as damaged features identifiable in aerial photographs. However, excavations have revealed a great deal of interest and a few square barrows have been found to cover 'chariot burials', where the corpse was accompanied by a dismantled light cart or chariot. See also ROUND BARROW.

**Squatter**. In post-medieval England, squatters occupied the lowest rung in the rural social hierarchy, but today it is not unusual to see a squatter cottage, built illegally but now gentrified to become a bijou period residence, sell for a very good price. Known at the close of the Middle Ages as 'selfehulles', squatters were landless peasants who tended to gravitate to the margins of COMMONS, where they hoped to secure access to the common grazings or acquire land in the form of INTAKES. Although such activities were generally illegal and unwelcome

*Squatter*
This deserted dwelling, near Llanddewi Brefi in Dyfed, succeeded a much smaller squatter cottage which now lies in ruins beside it.

since they reduced the amenities enjoyed by those who had authentic rights on the common, the practice was difficult to control in over-populated countrysides. Cottage hovels could be erected very quickly, and if their occupants were local people, then demolition and eviction would only increase the burden of the poor rate, which was borne by the less impoverished members of the parish. One callous approach by the local rural establishment was to offer employment to the squatters in a neighbouring parish, while demolishing their dwellings before they could return. Some landlords accepted the presence of squatters or COTTAGERS, choosing to allow them to put a few beasts on the common or to take a small rent from their intakes rather than face higher poor rates. Fairly typical were the problems faced by the Honour Court of the Forest of Knaresborough, which periodically attempted to crack down on illegal cottages and intakes. In 1560, for example, William Deane and Thomas Joye, who had made an intake in Clint township, were each ordered to return the land to the common by Michaelmas of the following year or face a fine of 6*s.* 8*d.* (34p). In 1592, the same court toyed with the idea of taking all squatter cottages into the possession of the Queen, allowing their poor occupants to live out their lives in them, and then demolishing the dwellings when the squatters died. The idea was less ingenious and humanitarian than it seemed, for its enactment would have created a burden of homeless descendants of the 'nationalised' cottagers.

Tens of thousands of squatter cottages were erected in the seventeenth and eighteenth centuries, either beside common-edge intakes or broad roadside verges. Some developed into hamlets with, as the geographer Brian K. Roberts has described, 'their names – Fen End or Stockley Bottoms – often being slightly derogatory, fit residences for "a poore beggerley sort of people apt to run in Arrears"'. Frequently such settlements developed in association with woodland craft industries like

clog- or hurdle-making and turnery or pottery, mining and quarrying based on the non-agricultural resources of the common.

In the eighteenth century, respectable society tended to see the commons as breeding grounds of indolence and lawlessness, their attitudes being reinforced by the Board of Agriculture reporters, like the author of the report on Shropshire which appeared in 1794:

> Let those who doubt go round the commons now open, and view the miserable huts and poor, ill-cultivated, impoverished spots erected, or rather thrown together … which … affords them a very trifle towards their maintenance, yet operates upon their minds as a sort of independence; this idea leads the man to lose many days' work, by which he gets a habit of indolence; a daughter kept at home to milk a poor half starv'd cow, who being open to temptations soon turns harlot, and becomes a distrest mother instead of making a good useful servant.

Such attitudes had been current for a long time, for the preamble to the Poor Law of 1662 complained that:

> … poor people are not restrained from going from one parish to another, and therefore to endeavour to settle themselves in those parishes where there is the best stock, the largest common or wastes to build cottages, and the most woods for them to burn and destroy; and when they have consumed it, then on another parish, and at last become rogues and vagabonds.

PARLIAMENTARY ENCLOSURE spelled disaster for those cottagers who relied solely on common rights, legal or otherwise, but dealt less unkindly with those who had secured their rights to an intake. Today squatter cottages may be seen as overgrown ruins or may appear, after various extensions and rebuildings, as extremely desirable residences. Any cottage or string of cottages occupying a site which corresponds to the margins of an old common may quite easily have been founded by squatters, while squatter encroachment can sometimes be seen or detected on some of the larger village GREENS.

In Wales there is the tradition of the *ty unnos*, 'the house of one night' or 'morning surprise', a squatter cottage built in the belief that if the house could be built overnight and smoke be seen issuing from its chimney in the morning, then squatter rights had been established. Whatever the basis of this belief, examples can be found in many parts of Wales, often with the original *ty unnos* existing as a ruin or an outhouse beside its more commodious successor. Closely linked to the *ty unnos* tradition was the myth that the successful squatter could claim ownership to all the land around his cottage as far as an axe could be thrown. See also COMMONS, INTAKE, PARLIAMENTARY ENCLOSURE.

*Further reading*: Hammond, J. L. and Hammond, B., *The Village Labourer*, Longman, London, 1978.

**Stack stand.** Place where stacks were stood at medieval farmsteads, sometimes recognisable as earthworks in the form of small, slight mounds. Known in Scotland as 'stewles' and as 'stagerths' in northern England.

**Staddle-stones.** These mushroom-shaped stones, reminiscent of the mushrooms sheltering elves in fairy stories, are often seen as garden and forecourt ornaments. Their original purpose was to raise granaries and ricks above the reach of rats and mice, which, it was hoped, could not negotiate the overhang between the stem and rounded cap of the stones. See also GRANARY.

**Stadir, bolstadir.** Place-name elements indicative of homesteads associated with farmland in the Shetlands.

**Staithe.** A landing place, sometime with a jetty or small dock and associated warehouses. Often associated with inland transport using natural waterways. See also RIVER TRANSPORT.

**Stake and rice hedge/fence**, see GARTHING.

**Stance.** The word has various meanings, including the field where a fair or cattle market is held.

**Standard.** Standards are timber trees that are allowed to grow freely. In former times, when deciduous woods were carefully managed to meet the insatiable need for timber of all kinds, standards were frequently cultivated in association with a COPPICED understorey. The understorey timber would be harvested according to a 10–20-year coppicing cycle, while the standards – most frequently oak – were felled every 80–100 years to provide heavy structural timber. After felling, a new crop of standards would be planted or allowed to grow from saplings, even though those who planted them would never expect to live to see them felled. For example, in 1629 the Earl of Huntingdon leased Buddon Wood near Loughborough to two developers on condition that they left twelve 'samplers or standalls' (saplings) growing in each acre for the duration of the lease and protected the woodland from browsing by keeping its walls and fences in good repair. Old woodland standards can frequently be seen growing today above the tangle of neglected coppices, while both STANDARDS and POLLARDS are seen as field and hedgerow trees.

**Standing stone**, see MONOLITH.

**Stane.** A stone, the word sometimes being associated, like STREET, with ROMAN ROADS that had metalled surfaces.

**Stank.** A redundant name for a pond in Northern England and still current in Scotland, where it also denotes a marsh. It often survives in field-names in places where industrial ponds or FISHPONDS formerly lay.

**Starr.** The word denotes sedges and appears in place-names.

**Statesman**, see INLAND.

**Stead, steading.** A word which denotes a place, usually one associated with settlement. The

*Stinted commons*
Sheep on the high pastures above Grassington, where a new system of stinting the common or moor was adopted in 1860 following severe overgrazing.

settlements concerned were often solitary farmsteads and manors and the common place-name 'Halstead' can be a useful indicator of a medieval manor site.

**Steam ploughing**. A mechanised form of ploughing employed in the nineteenth century involving the hauling of a plough between steam engines. Land ploughed in this way could be ridged-up, superficially to resemble RIDGE AND FURROW, though the ridges were quite narrow and completely straight. They did not have the reversed-'S' plan associated with medieval ploughing by oxen. Ploughing of this kind can sometimes be seen fitting exactly into new fields produced by PARLIAMENTARY ENCLOSURE, while the planned field boundaries cut-across medieval ridge and furrow.

**Stig, sty**. A lane or track that ascends a hillside. 'Anstig' or 'Anstey' may relate to narrow paths where people went in single file.

**Stint**, see STINTED COMMONS, GATE, SURCHARGE.

**Stinted commons**. It seems likely that the regulation of grazing on COMMONS by stinting began to spread in the thirteenth century. During the Middle Ages and the centuries which followed, both stinted and unstinted common pastures existed. Where there was no stinting arrangement to regulate the grazing and management of the common the deterioration of the pasture, to the detriment of all users, through over-stocking and over-grazing was always a threat. The ancient common known as Port Meadow near Oxford is unstinted and has been used by freemen of the area since time immemorial, and unrestricted grazing has greatly impoverished the pasture. On the stinted common the grazing was reserved for farmers ('gate holders') who had specific rights to pasture a given number of animals. On unstinted commons a form of regulation was sometimes applied according to the principle that the number of animals put on the commons in summer could not exceed the number that a farmer or peasant kept on his holdings in the same lordship during winter (see LEVANCY AND COUCHANCY).

Stinted commons had a more rigorous organisation – for example, in Upper Nidderdale the stinted pastures were 'firthed' or cleared of stock to allow a strong regrowth of grass on 25 March and about a month later the cattle were introduced in the numbers determined by the stint. At Michaelmas or Martinmas, according to prevailing conditions, the commons were thrown open to sheep from the hills, which could graze there in unrestricted numbers until the spring, and the cattle meanwhile were fed on hay and oat straw in the lower, enclosed fields. Severe over-stocking afflicted Grassington moor in Wharfedale in the 1860s and a meeting was held to work out stinting arrangements, which were calculated as being proportional to the amount of Land Tax each farmer paid, one 'sheep gate' being permitted for every £1 9s. 0d. (£1.45) of tax. Sheep were the main consideration, but arrangements for other animals were calculated in sheep equivalents: 1 beast (a cow or bullock) = 5 sheep; 5 sheep with lambs = 5 sheep; 1 horse = 10 sheep; 10 geese = 1 sheep. A shepherd was appointed to supervise the arrangements, which then remained intact for about a century. The 'gate' referred to was the right to graze one adult beast (beast gate) or sheep (sheep gate). Sometimes a gate would cover a sheep plus her lamb until a date in July, when the growing lambs were calculated at the rate of two to a gate.

Different attempts at stinting developed in different places at different times. For example, on Landbeach manor on the edge of the Cambridgeshire fenland grazings it was demanded in 1548 that 'no tenant or inhabitant of the aforesaid town shall keep upon the commons there above the number of three sheep for an acre under pain of forfeit unto the lord 20*d.* [9p] ... it is [also] ordained that no tenant shall take into feed upon the commons of this town the sheep of any stranger above two sheep for an acre and to take of the lord's farm three for every acre upon pain to forfeit 11*d.* [5p]'. Where elaborate and comprehensive stinting arrangements were in force, it is debatable whether a common really was a common. See also COMMONS, INTERCOMMONING, SHIRE MOOR, TURBARY.

**Stitching, stetching**. A method of assisting surface DRAINAGE employed in East Anglia and the East Midlands and recorded in the early seventeenth century. The surface was ridged up into temporary corrugations that might only last for a year or a few years. See also RIDGE AND FURROW.

**Stocks**. Medieval punishment was harsh (though not necessarily harsher than that of the eighteenth century), and the severity of the punishments must partly be explained by the very low rates of capture. Stocks provided both confinement and the opportunity for public humiliation throughout most, if not all, the

medieval period and onwards until the start of the nineteenth century. One of the earliest mention of stocks comes from 1201 where, in Middleton near Pontefract, Adam de Beeston accused William le Gramaire of having taken his forester – and William was put in the stocks. The word comes from 'stocks', or tree-stumps, which equate to the upright posts supporting the leg-clamping boards. Peasants were forever being put 'in mercy' of their manor courts for petty offences, but this meant they were fined or obliged to perform certain works; it was relatively unusual for the crime to merit them being put in *compedibus*, in the stocks.

However, when the establishment turned its thoughts towards punishment it had some rather fearsome gadgets at its disposal. Wakefield

*Stocks*
The old whipping post at Stow in Lincolnshire.

*Stone axe factory*
The Neolithic axe factory on Pike o'Stickle in Cumbria. The snow-covered scree trail to the right of the summit is largely composed of debris from axe making. This unstable area is unsafe for visitors.

gained a pillory (*collistrigium*) at a cost of 20*s*. 2½*d*. (£1.1 [?£1.06?]) in 1270, and it was repaired in 1454. In the year that the pillory was made stocks were also built at Wakefield, costing 20*d*. (9p). A cucking stool existed nearby at Thorner in 1556, for the punishment of local gossips. The cucking stool resembled a pillory in function, and the victim was secured in it either at his or her own front door or in some public place. In contrast, the ducking stool was a chair held over a pond on a pivoted post, allowing the victim to be ducked in and out of the water. These devices certainly existed beyond Hollywood reconstructions of medieval life, and in 1593 Margaret and Elizabeth Longfellowe were sentenced by Wakefield court to be ducked three times before Christmas 'because they are scouldes'.

A remarkable number of village stocks survive, and this must reflect the fact that this rough-and-ready form of punishment by public humiliation endured until the start of Victorian times. It is unlikely that the wooden components of stocks still displayed at some places date right back to the Middle Ages. Some of the best examples are those seen in the marketplace at Ripley in North Yorkshire, St Feock in Cornwall, Little Budworth in Cheshire and, under a canopy, at Offery St Mary churchyard in Devon. A more brutal aspect of medieval and later punishment is represented by the whipping posts associated with stocks at Aldbury in Hertfordshire and Meldreth in Cambridgeshire.

**Stone axe factory.** This name is given to sites where the raw materials for stone axe making were quarried or obtained. The users and makers of stone axes developed a detailed knowledge of the qualities and locations of different raw materials and would go to considerable lengths to obtain the best. Those chosen were selected for their workability, largely determined by the manner in which the stone fractured when struck in the proper manner, enabling axes to be shaped; their durability under use; and, in some cases, their aesthetic qualities – since a minority of the axes made were beautiful ceremonial and status objects rather than working tools.

Two basic types of material were used: firstly, flint, obtained in 'commercial' quantities from FLINT MINES, and, second, hard igneous or metamorphic rocks, obtained from a variety of axe factories. A number of axe-factory sites have been identified in the Langdale Pikes area of the Lake District, yielding a volcanic tuff which was probably roughed into shape at the factory site and then taken to the Cumbrian coast for grinding and polishing on the red sandstone outcrops before export. Other axe-factory sites among the thirty or so discovered included Tievebulliagh Mountain in County Antrim, Mynydd Rhiw on the Lleyn peninsula of Wales, and the greenstone outcrops of Cornwall. Stone axes from these and other axe-factory sites have been found widely dispersed from their places of origin, demonstrating an active trade in this essential commodity of Neolithic (and Bronze Age) life. The means and nature of this trade have been much debated; some archaeologists believe that axes circulated as tribute goods passed from one chieftain to the next, but the majority today favour the idea of a systematic trading system which would have involved boats and itinerant traders. Axe factories are, along with flint mines, our oldest industrial centres, and reminders of the sophistication and ingenuity of our Neolithic forebears. When visited, the factory sites seldom display more than a litter of discarded stone flakes; some are in quite elevated and dangerous situations, and visitors are now discouraged from exploring the best-known site on Pike o' Stickle in the Langdales, for reasons both of conservation and of safety. When viewed from a sensible distance

– the ridge known as 'The Band', offering splendid vantage-points of the high flanks of Pike o' Stickle – one can see a long tail of whitish scree which is being extended gradually down the mountain by participants in the dangerous pastime of scree running. This scree consists of flakes of debris from axe-making, and an expert from Reading University has estimated that Pike o' Stickle scree represents the waste products of 45,000–75,000 completed stone axes. These figures become even more impressive when additional waste material at the head of the gully is taken into account. About 200 axe-flaking sites have now been identified in the Langdale Pikes area, and a further 350 lie between Bow Fell, Scafell Pike and Glaramara – so it seems fair to regard the Lake District as one of the earliest industrial regions. See also FLINT MINES.

*Further reading:* Bradley, M. and Edmonds, M., *Interpreting the Axe Trade*, Cambridge University Press, 1998.
Edmonds, M., *Stone Tools and Society*, Batsford, London, 1995.
Fell, C., 'The Great Langdale Stone-Axe Factory', *Transactions of the Cumberland and Westmorland Antiquary and Archaeological Society*, new series 50, 1964.

**Stone circle.** Stone circles date from about the period 3200 BC to 1800 BC and seem to have evolved from the embellishment of HENGE monuments with standing stones. Although they have inspired an enormous literature (much of it ridiculous), we are still uncertain as to the exact purposes of stone circles. They were certainly associated with religion and ritual, though they could also have had subsidiary roles as meeting and trading places. These monuments experienced their greatest and most grandiose development during the Beaker period, around 2700–2000 BC, when Britain, along with other parts of western Europe, was exposed to the Beaker 'cultural package' of beliefs and rituals. (Whether there was a large-scale invasion and settlement of actual 'Beaker people' is now disputed). During the currency of the Beaker culture the older collective tombs, the CHAMBERED TOMBS and LONG BARROWS, were abandoned in favour of more solitary burials covered by ROUND BARROWS, with the corpse usually being provided with a finely made clay beaker, which may have contained a ritual beverage. The archaeological evidence seems to suggest a fairly drastic change in religious belief after the dawning of the Beaker period, although the continuing interest in henges, cursüs and collective tombs and circles implies a perpetuation of many indigenous ideas about ritual centres.

The dividing line between the stone circle and the henge embellished by standing stones is a difficult one, particularly since some henges, like Mayburgh in Cumbria, are known formerly to have displayed more stones than are present today. Stonehenge began its ritual life as a henge

monument, while at Avebury the henge earthworks, though eroded, are still at least as impressive as the stone circles contained within. In the cases of some smaller circles the stones are the prominent features and there are no associated henge earthworks. Several of the more diminutive of the monuments once classed as 'stone circles', like the ring at Yockenthwaite in the Yorkshire Dales, may not be stone circles at all, but the relics of a kerb of stones originally erected around a (now eroded) round barrow.

Stone circles vary so greatly in size and form that one may wonder whether the differences seen are those of kind rather than of degree. Circles like the famous Ring of Brodgar on Orkney with its great rock-cut ditch and

*Stone circle*
Castlerigg stone circle in Cumbria could have been a venue for axe trading.

twenty-six of its original sixty flagstone blades still standing, Castlerigg perched on a plateau amidst an amphitheatre of Lakeland mountains, and the smaller Swinside circle near Broughton-in-Furness, all epitomise the popular perception of a stone circle. But there are also several much less conventional 'circles': they include the spectacular Callanish monument on Lewis, with its central CHAMBERED TOMB, giant central MONOLITH, and the three short stone rows and the stone-studded avenue which radiate outwards from the thirteen gnarled pillars of the circle; Stonehenge, with its lintels and complicated evolution; and Arbor Low in Derbyshire with nearly fifty stones and stone fragments lying horizontally on a central platform within a gigantic henge. Some circles, like the Ring of Brodgar or the Rollright Stones in Oxfordshire, have associated outlying stones, while at the Cumbrian circle known as 'Long Meg and Her Daughters' Long Meg is a tall sandstone slab that stands apart from the circle of dumpy granite daughters. Then there is the special group of 'recumbent stone circles' associated with North East Scotland, with an altar-like recumbent stone set between upright flankers within the circumference of stones. The stones themselves diminish in height away from the recumbent stone, while excavations revealing cremation debris link these monuments as closely to tombs as to circles.

More than 900 stone circles are known in Britain, though some of those listed are surely the kerbs of cairns or barrows rather than genuine stone circles. Yet if these kerbs are disregarded the remaining circles appear as an extremely heterogeneous collection. Even so, it has been argued that most were built to a precise range of circular, egg-shaped or 'flattened circle' plans, and detailed surveys of some circles do offer support to the contention. Rather weaker is the evidence for the incorporation of astronomical alignments in stone circles, not least because the massive unshaped boulder scarcely lends itself to the sighting of precise celestial alignments. Stonehenge does incorporate

*Stone circle*
The tilted central stone at Boscawen-un stone circle in Cornwall.

a well-surveyed rectangle in its design, and at the summer solstice there the sun would have been seen by an observer in the centre of the circle to rise *almost* above the outlying Heel Stone. The remaining astronomical arguments attract less credibility and can be contradictory or else contradicted by new understandings of the age of the monuments. Stone circles can most simply be regarded as the places used by late Neolithic and early Bronze Age communities and their religious leaders for the observance of certain rituals. These rituals may have been performed on certain occasions during the year – like the winter solstice, marking the death of the old year and the birth of the new. But the nature of these rituals and the most basic questions about belief – like whether people worshipped the sun, moon, earth or water – remain unanswered. Perhaps the antiquarian John Aubrey (1626–97) was being a little ambitious 300 years ago, when he wrote on stone circles: 'This Inquiry, I must confess, is a gropeing in the Dark: but although I have not brought it into a clear light; yet I can affirm that I have brought it from an utter darkness to a thin mist.' See also HENGES.

*Further reading:* Burgess, Colin, *The Age of Stonehenge*, Dent, 1980.

Burl, Aubrey, *The Stone Circles of the British Isles*, Yale University Press, 1976.

**Stone rows**. These alignments of quite small boulders are a feature of Dartmoor, where

*Stone rows*
One of the two double stone rows at Merrivale, showing the triangular terminal blocking stone.

around seventy examples are known. They appear to belong to the so-called Beaker period, around 2700–2000 BC, and pre-date the adjacent Bronze Age field-networks of the moor which are defined by low walls or 'REAVES'. Sometimes the rows are single, though there are double and a few triple examples. Two double-stone rows can be seen at Merrivale, there is a good double row on Huston Ridge, a fine single row near Down Top and a complicated system of rows on Shovel Down. The rows are not always arrow-straight, undermining astronomical explanations, and the double rows are too narrow to have served as processional ways – often also having their ends blocked by larger terminal stones. The rows therefore remain tantalisingly mysterious.

**'Stoned horse' field-names**. These indicate former horse studs and are often associated with former deer parks.

**Stool**. The stump of a tree cut close to ground level in a coppicing cycle. A new crop of poles will spring forth from the stool after coppicing.

**Stoop, stoup**. Dialect term in Northern England and Scotland signifying a stone post, often a gatepost or stone milepost or boundary stone. See also MILESTONE, MONOLITH, SIGNPOST.

**Store farm**. An upland farm consisting of an extensive sheep walk.

**Storth**. A name of Old Norse origins associated with brushwood and young woodland.

**Stoup**, see STOOP.

**Strae kiln**. A corn drying kiln dug into the face of a slope and covered in branches. The grain was put on a bed of straw resting on the branches and heat from a fire at the front of the kiln was drawn towards an opening at the back.

**Straker way**. A track across open country, the word denoting an excursion across a tract of land. See COMMONS.

**Straith, strath**. A broad valley or plain traversed by a river.

**Street**. An Old English word associated with paved roads and usually linked to ROMAN ROADS. See also STANE.

**Striferiggs**. Areas of common or disputed lands.

**Strip (land, selion)**. The basic unit of farming and tenancy in the days of OPEN-FIELD FARMING was the strip. The strip was a long, narrow ribbon of land which did not have a standardised size. In the Midlands it was usually about 220 yards (200 metres) in length (a furlong or 'furrow long'), or slightly shorter, and about 8 yards (7 metres) in width, with an area of one-third of an acre (0.13 hectares). Thus a tenant who held a fairly typical 'virgate' holding amounting to about 30 acres (12 hectares) might work as many as ninety different strips. These were scattered throughout the open fields (possibly being dispersed in this way to ensure that each member of the community shared both the good and poorer plough soils), though holdings of 40–80 strips were more normal.

The origins of open-field strip farming remain mysterious but are probably to be found in late Saxon times. Evidence is emerging from East Yorkshire and one or two other locations that the 'conventional' strips of medieval farming were preceded by 'long strips' which could be over 1000 yards (915 metres) in length and grouped together in long FURLONGS. Thus, many later strips resulted from a subdivision of the older long strips. Long strips recognised in the Yorkshire Wolds measured 1100 yards by 10 yards (1006 metres by 9 metres). There is also evidence that strips were apportioned in an organised and regular manner, as described under SUN DIVISION. Currently, interest is reviving in the question of how older elements of the farmed countryside were incorporated in the open field systems of the mid- and late Saxon eras.

Each strip consisted of one, two or more 'plough ridges', and further details of these are provided under RIDGE AND FURROW. There were generally no divisions between strips other than the furrow of the ridge-and-furrow undulations. Consequently – there was a temptation – usually resisted – to behave like the dishonest fourteenth-century peasant described in *Piers Ploughman*: '... if I went to the plough I pinched so narrowly that I would steal a foot of land or a furrow'. Many field strips survived until the PARLIAMENTARY ENCLOSURE movement of the eighteenth and nineteenth centuries, and there are numerous surviving post-medieval maps of strip patterns. Often they show strips of varying width within the furlongs of the open field, showing that there had been amalgamations of adjacent strips at one time or another. See also RUNRIG, BALK

*Further reading*: Hall, David, *Medieval Fields*, Shire Archaeology Series, 1982.

Rowley, T. (ed.), *The Origins of Open Field Agriculture*, Croom Helm, London, 1981.

Harrison, S., 'Open Fields and Earlier Landscapes', LANDSCAPES 3.1, 2002, pp. 35–54.

**Stripe**. A small stream or sometimes a STRIP.

**'Striped' farms**. A form of settlement pattern and land-holding found in Ireland, particularly in the western coastal zones as the result of the reorganisation of RUNDALE holdings. Farmsteads have roadside frontages, with long, straight ribbons of land that are subdivided into fields running back at right angles to the routeway. See also LADDER FARM.

**Strip lynchet, raine**. Of all the fossilised field systems, those composed of flights of strip lynchets are visually the most impressive. Hillsides displaying a staircase of long terraces are redolent of landscape history and many must have wondered how such bizarre landforms were created. The popular explanation, that strip lynchets represent the terraces of Roman or medieval vineyards, is quite untenable – one would be hard pressed to raise a decent cabbage let alone a vine on flights of northern strip lynchets, like those of Wharfedale and Wensleydale.

Each strip lynchet, or 'raine' as it is known in northern England, is composed of an artificially created level cultivation-surface, or 'tread', and a steep slope just below it, a 'riser'. They seldom occur singly but are usually seen in stepped flights with each strip lynchet in the flight running very roughly parallel to the contour lines of the hillslope and having a length of between about 60 yards (55 metres) and 250 yards (229 metres). There is little doubt that strip lynchets were created by ploughing, smooth hillsides being given their staircase profile by repeated episodes of ploughing in a consistent direction, which notched the hillside and turned soil outwards to expand the level surface of the tread. Plainly such arduous efforts to form plough terraces would not be countenanced by communities which enjoyed adequate resources of OPEN-FIELD ploughland, so strip lynchets are associated with marginal hilly or steeply undulating country where suitable level and low-lying ground was in short supply. Also, given the immense efforts needed to carve out the terraces and the meagre returns that could be expected from cultivating many of the northern and south-western flights, it seems likely that many systems of strip lynchets exist as memorials to communities afflicted by overpopulation and landhunger. Since the strip lynchets are seen to cut older CELTIC FIELD systems in several different locations they can safely be regarded as the creations of medieval peasant farming. This is supported by the fact that the earthworks of strip lynchets can be found 'fossilised' in DEER PARKS, like Studley

*Strip lynchet*
Strip lynchets and later field-walls near Linton in Wharfedale.

Royal. They most probably date from the period before the arrival of the Black Death in 1348, when the rural population had begun to outstrip the agricultural resources of the countryside and new sources of both ploughland and pasture were desperately needed.

One of the finest systems of strip lynchets can be seen above Linton in Wharfedale and another excellent example is carved into the coastal slopes at Worth Matravers in Dorset. In a few places, like Coombe Bisset in Wiltshire, modern

*Strip lynchets*
Medieval strip lynchets which were worked from a former hamlet pleat on the hillsides at Challacombe, Devon. (CUCAP)

farmers have continued to cultivate the treads of a strip lynchet system, but usually where the terrain is reasonably gentle the effect of modern ploughing has been gradually to obliterate the staircase patterns. In the undulating Gog Magog

Hills area of Cambridgeshire the old strip lynchets may now only be visible as faint ridges, though in a few post-medieval woods here the stepped profiles of medieval strip lynchets are very clearly preserved. A good description of the then much more obvious strip lynchets was provided early in the nineteenth century by William Marshall:

> The artificial surface which meets the eye in different parts of these hills, forcibly arrests the attention. It occurs on the steeper slopes, which are formed into stages or platforms, with grassy steeps, provincially 'linchets', between them. The stages or platforms are equally commodious for implements of tillage, as for carriages; besides retaining moisture better than sloping surfaces; while the grassy steeps, between the arable stages, afford no inconsiderable supply of herbage; on which horses are tethered or tended, while corn is in the ground; and which gives pasturage to sheep at other seasons. This sort of artificial surface is common in different parts of the island.

**Stroud, strode**. The southern English equivalent of northern CARR: brushwood and alder marsh.

**Summer farm**. A separate sum or rent paid to the lord of a MANOR by tenants using the SUMMERING. In the north of England these practices varied and in some localities no summer farm was paid, it being assumed that rights to the summer grazings were covered as appurtenances to holdings within the MANOR. See also AGISTMENT, SHIELING.

**Summering or shieling grounds**. The high grazings on a manor in the northern uplands of England where livestock were pastured in the summer months. See also SHIELING, WINTERSTEEDS.

**Sun division (solskift)**. This was a precise arrangement of the holdings of villagers within the surrounding OPEN FIELDS according to a regular order of rotation. It is known to have

existed in Scandinavia during the Dark Ages, but now most experts also accept its existence in late Saxon and medieval northern England. The order of plough STRIPS in a FURLONG corresponded to that of the TOFTS in the adjacent village, so that a peasant working one of his strips in the open fields had the same neighbours on either side as he did when resting at home in the village. The direction in which the ordering applied corresponded to the course of the sun.

The English origins of sun division have not yet been identified, but the system does indicate an orderly planning of the fields and villages of some feudal ESTATES. The evidence for such organisation is very strong in Holderness, but it can be recognised in documents relating to other parts of England. For example, in the fourteenth century the lands of John Moldeson of Winslow in Buckinghamshire comprised seventy-two half-acre strips scattered around the village fields, and sixty-six of these strips were next to the strips of a villager called John Watekyns. Clearly, however precisely a sun-division system was designed at the time of its introduction, within a few generations the accidents of inheritance would cause it to blur, but the numerous similar examples discovered in medieval documents argue strongly for the existence of sun-division planning. The old documents also frequently describe the position of lands in relation to the sun, in phrases like 'towards the sun', probably meaning to the south-east, or 'towards the shade', probably meaning towards the north-west. It is likely that the scattering of strips and the perpetual grouping together of neighbours would help to ensure that each villager had a fair share of better and poorer lands. It was thought that the precise allocation of land would probably date from the late Saxon era, but now later dates are favoured. Few events are so well-attested as the Harrying of the North, but its severity currently being out of favour with historians, the twelfth rather than the eleventh century is advanced as the time when *solskifte* was introduced.

**Surcharge**. Overstocking of the common grazings.

**Swail**. An undulation.

**Swaling**. This is a traditional method of maintaining moorland grazings through controlled burning. It is declining in many areas but can still be employed in areas like Exmoor and the Millstone Grit areas of the Pennines. If left to grow unchecked, heather becomes woody and stalky, but controlled burning, which preserves a living root, will promote lush new growth and revitalise the plant. Swaling was widely practised in the medieval period and documents going back to the sixteenth century record how the burning of ling is followed by a season in which a good grass crop springs from the ground that had been overgrown by heather. Molinia grass pasture, which dies off in winter with the dead growth forming a soggy mat which suppresses the emergence of better grasses, also benefits from swaling. Evidence of swaling can be seen in MOORS that have a dappled appearance. Black patches represent recent burning, lighter green patches denote fresh new growth and darker patches, areas which have not been burned for some time. Swaling takes place in an environment of delicate ecological balances, and if mismanaged an excessive burning of the heather exposes the ground to erosion and can lead to gullying of the land surface. Also, the heather grows in a carpet of peat that may be several feet thick. The peat is highly combustible, and once established, underground fires in the peat beds can smoulder for weeks. At the end of the nineteenth century, a moorland fire on the Dallowgill estates of the Earl de Grey and Ripon produced such a conflagration that the smoke gave rise to complaints in Ripon, some ten miles away. In both England and Scotland, statutes controlled the burning of heather. In Scotland, from 1424 onwards, various laws prohibited moor burning from the end of March until the harvest and in England an Act of 1609–10 outlawed it between the start of April and end of September. See also TURBARY.

**Swanimote**. Meeting three times a year, the Swanimote regulated the use of royal Forests. In the autumn, the court organised pannage and later met to collect the dues, which in early summer it arranged for the woods to be closed to prevent swine killing fawns and pregnant hinds.

**Sweat house**. The BURNT MOUNDS of northern England and the Irish supposed cooking sites are likely to be the remains of prehistoric saunas. In Ireland sweat houses were also numerous in the historical era, especially in the northern half of the island. They are small structures of dry-stone walling with low, lintelled doorways and roofs that were sometimes corbelled and covered in sod, as with the typical CLOCHÁN. Inside was a stone-flagged floor on which fires were lit. The heat from the floor stones caused naked participants to sweat, and after enduring the heat for a while they would cool in a nearby water body. Numerous examples survive, sometimes now serving as animal shelters.

**Swile**. A boggy patch in a meadow.

**Swine**. Pigs were important components of the old peasant economy, but they were also, along with GOATS, the most destructive of the farmyard livestock and had to be closely controlled. They fed on acorns, beech mast and other woodland resources, but normally regulations governing PANNAGE were in force to ensure their removal in summer around the time of fawning. They were also a threat to crops and to HEDGEROWS and in some communities swine could only be kept if the neighbours gave their consent. Rings inserted in the snouts of the animals prevented them from destroying the sward by rooting, while pigs were frequently fitted with triangular wooden collars, the projecting ends of which prevented them from barging through hedges. Many communities would employ a swineherd to drive the pigs away from the ploughlands and enclosed fields and guard them on the WASTE or MOOR from springtime until the harvest was safely in. Places associated with pannage and the keeping of swine are recalled in numerous place-names, like Swincliffe, Swinehead, Swinfen, Swinden (valley of the pigs) and Swinburn, while field names like Boar Butts, Boar Garth, Pigs Park and Sow Croft also recall domestic pigs. In Scotland, a 'swine ree' is the enclosure within which the swine sty stands. See also SWANIMOTE.

**Swire**. A mountain pass or col; the downslope used in a descent or a bowl-like depression near the hill top.

**Symbol stone**. The symbol stones which were erected in the Dark Ages on the lands of the Pictish peoples of Scotland constitute one of the most fascinating and tantalising mysteries of the British countryside. The Pictish nation appears to have gelled from a fusion of Iron Age tribes in the part of Scotland lying to the north of the Forth–Clyde isthmus during the Roman occupation of England and (periodically) of southern Scotland, with the Pictish heartland spanning north-east Scotland. The Picts were regarded as being rather bizarre by their literate contemporaries living in other parts of Britain; their territory was apparently divided into northern and southern 'kingdoms', and these were subdivided into provinces, all except Caithness apparently having a major and minor component, such as Buchan and Mar, Angus and Mearns, Atholl and Gowrie. The Pictish culture seems to have had archaic features, such as the tracing of descent through the female line, and also seems to have been rooted in Bronze Age rather than Celtic origins. The language of the Picts may not have been Celtic, but is only known through a few place-names, most notably those with the 'Pit' element, like Pitlochry, which seems to denote a place or land-holding. Around AD 843, the Scots,

advancing from south-west Scotland, occupied and assimilated Pictland and the Pictish culture vanished, leaving behind a residue of mysteries.

Perhaps the greatest of these mysteries concerns the remarkable symbol stones which were erected in the years after AD 600 or AD 650. These are divided into three, presumably successive, classes. Class I stones are unshaped slabs which display only pagan symbols; Class II stones have a juxtaposition of the cross and the pagan symbols while what were described as Class III stones are early Christian crosses which are closely linked to the broader British tradition. Naturally it has been assumed that the evolution of the stones reflects the Christian conversion of Pictland.

The symbols carved on the stones comprise *real animals*, such as the sea-eagle, now re-established in the north-west, and the reindeer, extinct in Scotland by or during the Middle Ages; *mythical animals*, the 'S-dragon' and the 'swimming elephant'; *real objects*, notably mirrors, combs and cauldrons; and, most mysteriously, complicated *abstract symbols*, such as the 'crescent and V-rod', the 'serpent and Z-rod' or the 'spectacles and Z-rod'. The carved

*Symbol stone*
The 'notched rectangle and Z-rod' and the 'mirror case' symbols on a Pictish symbol stone at Aberlemno near Forfar.

crosses, in contrast, appear to be influenced by the Christian decorative style of Northumbria.

The actual purpose of the symbol stones is still debated. The most popular interpretation at present regards the Class I stones at least as memorial stones to the dead, though not necessarily graveside stones though they could have had tribal and territorial rather than personal associations. The meaning of the symbols themselves remains completely mysterious, and they have also been found on Pictish metalwork and cave carvings. They are fluent and consistent and probably had an intelligible meaning to the Picts. They might be an early form of heraldry or could derive from body tattoos – the Picts were known to the Romans as 'Picti', or 'painted ones'. (Although

there can be no direct connection with the Picts, a frozen corpse of the fifth century discovered in a barrow in the Altai Mountains was tattooed with highly stylised animal symbols.) There are about fifty symbols in the Pictish repertoire and several hundred symbol stones. Some of the finest stones are displayed in Scottish museums or churches, but most stand, mainly solitary, in the countryside, though whether any individual stone has been moved from its original site is virtually impossible to know.

*Further reading*: Henderson, I. M., *The Picts*, Thames & Hudson 1967.

Thomas, Charles, *Celtic Britain*, Thames & Hudson, 1986.

# T

**Tacksman**. Member of the lesser gentry in the clan society of the Scottish Highlands. The tacksmen provided the bridge between the chieftains and the clansfolk, served as an officer caste in times of war and held their ESTATES from the chief, dividing them into numerous sub-tenancies which were let-out to lesser members of the clan.

**Tan-**. When appearing in a field or local name, this may refer to a tanyard associated with leather working, though some names could come from the wildflower, tansy.

**Tathe faud, taithe faud**. In Scotland, a field in which livestock are folded in order to enrich the ground with their droppings.

**Tatie-grun**. Potato ground, land where potatoes are grown.

**Teasel**. This plant was grown commercially, with its prickly seed heads being used to comb woollen cloth to raise its nap. In the latter part

of the eighteenth century it played a large part in the economies of a few villages, like Biggin, near Selby, where there were heavy clays that were more favoured by the plant than were the soils in the West Riding textiles belt itself. Rare field-names that incorporate 'Tessil' denote land where the teasel was grown.

*Further reading*: McMillan, R. A., 'The Yorkshire teazle-growing trade', *Yorkshire Archaeological Journal* 56, 1984.

**Telford**. Thomas Telford (1757–1834) was, like MACADAM and METCALFE, instrumental in promoting superior techniques of road construction at a time when the land transport network was expanding after many centuries of neglect. A Scot from Eskdale, Telford was apprenticed to a stone mason and then set to work building a model VILLAGE at New Langholm on the estates of the Duke of Buccleuch. He worked as a mason at the building of the new town in Edinburgh, then at

Portsmouth dockyard and in Shropshire but he did not gain prominence as a road-builder until the start of the nineteenth century, when he was employed by the Commissions for Highland Roads and Bridges and the Caledonian Canal. He supervised the construction of numerous roads, harbours and bridges in the Highlands and worked on canal projects in England and Sweden as well as initiating work on the Caledonian Canal and he built the Holyhead road in Wales. See also TURNPIKE.

*Further reading:* Rolt, L. T. C., *Thomas Telford,*
  Penguin, Harmondsworth, 1985.

**Tent, Tenter-field**. Field-names like 'Tenter Green', 'Tentry Croft' and others of this type are quite common and are associated with places where, in medieval or later times, there were cloth-stretching frames furnished with tenterhooks which were used to stretch pieces of drying cloth.

**Terraces**. Landforms of a stepped nature can result both from natural and from cultural processes. River terraces are step-like shelves on the flanks of valleys and they represent *cycles of erosion* in relation to different *base levels*, with the changes in base level normally being caused by rises or falls in the land relative to the sea. If there is a rise in the land or fall in the sea then the erosive power of the river is *rejuvenated* and erosion in relation to the new sea level will gradually spread upstream. The level sections on old river terraces represent the river flood plains as they existed before the rejuvenation of the river concerned. Occasionally, river terraces may form a staircase on the face of a river bluff, otherwise terraces may be absent in a valley or lateral movement of the river may have eroded away one or both of matching sets of terraces. *Terracettes* are little steps just a few inches in width seen ascending steep slopes, particularly in downland. They result from a downward, rotational creeping of the soil, but their form can be intensified when sheep use the 'tread' components as paths. STRIP LYNCHETS may superficially resemble river terraces, although the

tread sections rise and fall markedly from the horizontal, systems on opposite sides of a valley cannot be matched and the lynchets occur in other locations as well as the flanks of valleys. *Garden terraces* form much more localised and much more rigidly geometrical sets of terraces and they represent relics from abandoned formal gardens of the seventeenth and early eighteenth centuries. Such relics are not uncommon though the extent to which their forms are blurred by erosion varies considerably. When they are well-preserved, the earthworks may preserve the traces of shallow ponds and knot gardens. Examples include the traces of Sir Christopher Hatton's garden terraces of the 1580s at Holdenby in Northamptonshire or the relics of sixteenth-century garden terraces of the manor house in the LOST VILLAGE at Strixton in the same county. See also LOST GARDENS.

**Thack, theak**, see THATCHING.

**Thackstone**. In northern England and Scotland, a slab of fissile stone, usually sandstone but not true slate, that was used for roofing. The use of such materials in vernacular architecture depended on the availability of stones of the right type, but such roofs were common in the Yorkshire Dales and were built until the extension of the railway network allowed the importation of slate from Cumbria and North Wales.

**Thatching**. In prehistoric times the roofs of dwellings could have been covered in a variety of material – thatch from the straw of cultivated grains, reed, sedge, turf, rushes, fern or heather. Straw or reed thatch was the popular roofing material in Dark Age and medieval Britain, though turf and ling were still used and slates and stone tiles were popular where available; wooden shingles were also employed, and fern seems to have been used widely to cover the humbler dwellings. The word 'thatch' or 'thack' derives from the Old English *þæc*, which referred to roof coverings in general, not just to straw or reed.

A disadvantage of the thatched roof has

*Thatching*
Thatching in progress at Barrington in Cambridgeshire.

always been its vulnerability to fire, which could rapidly traverse the roofs of closely clustered dwellings. Records of the London Assize of 1212 recognised the risk and provide us with a description of the varied roofing materials then in vogue:

> whosoever wishes to build, let him take care, as he loveth himself and his goods, that he roof not with reed, nor rush, straw nor stubble, but with tile only, or shingle or boards, or if it may be, with lead or plastered straw ... Also that all houses which till now are covered with reed or rush, which can be plastered, let them be plastered within eight days, and let those which shall not be so plastered within the term be demolished by the alderman and lawful men of the venue.

Thatching has experienced rises and falls in popularity. Currently it is favoured by the more affluent and worldly members of the rural community, not only for its handsome and

'authentic' appearance, but also because thatched 'period' cottages command high prices. Meanwhile, the less prosperous villagers dread the high cost of rethatching that will be incurred every fifteen to thirty years. Consequently, many thatched roofs have been stripped, slated and tiled. Roofs which were formerly thatched can usually be recognised from their steep pitches of about 50°, needed to shed water from the thatch, while tiled roofs have angles of about 45° and slated roofs may have a pitch of only 30°.

Regional preferences in thatching have developed. In East Anglia the roofs have high pitches and sharp-edged gables, the thatching of the roof ridge sweeping upwards near the gable ends to throw back water that might otherwise run down the tall gable-end wall and damage the plaster or daub. In nearby Sussex, however, the thatch of the ridge is often carried around the gable. In other parts of England, as in Kent and Wessex, hipped roofs were favoured so that the thatch has a pie-crust effect or seems to warm the whole house like a tea-cosy.

In England, thatchers now use wheat straw or reed. Good thatching straw is not easy to obtain, and thatchers seek out crops of 'long straw' types of wheat with flexible stems which are cut with an old-fashioned rather than a modern combine harvester. Reed for thatching is still cultivated at Wicken Fen nature reserve in Cambridgeshire. In parts of Ireland, oat straw is still sometimes used, and the thatched roofs have a paler, rather shaggy appearance. Reed produces roofs of a darker hue and is generally regarded as providing a more durable form of roof. To thatch a roof in the English manner the thatcher carefully sorts his straw or reed into small bundles of parallel stems known as 'yelms'. The first yelms are tied to the purlins and laths of the bare roof, and then, as the thickness of yelms attached builds up, additional yelms are firmly tamped home and pegged down with 'spars'. These are 'staples' made by splitting wands of hazel or willow, sharpening each end of the spar and twisting and bending it in the middle. Spars are also used to peg down 'liggers', lengths of hazel laid over the ridge area of the roof to protect this, the most vulnerable part of the thatch. Underlying layers of thatch may be secured by long hazel 'sways', which are hidden and held by hooks to the roofing timbers. On roofs thatched in reed, tough sedge may be used to thatch the ridge, while some ridges are raised 3–4 inches (about 10 centimetres) above the main roof-level and their edges cut to form decorative points or scallops. The thatched roof is finally shaved to a trim finish and may then be covered with wire netting as protection against sparrow damage. In the Celtic lands spars are generally known as 'scollops' and in areas exposed to Atlantic gales the thatch may be held in place by ropes tied to stone pegs in the walls and gables or else tied at

each end to heavy stones. There are numerous regional variations and in parts of Scotland 'stob-thacking' was employed, with stobs or posts being used to hold down the straw. See also SCOWB AND SCRAW.

*Further reading*: Billett, Michael, *Thatching and Thatched Buildings*, Hale, 1979.

**Therapeutic landscapes**. These concern the notion that certain landscapes exert a positive psychological effect on some sufferers from physical and, particularly, mental illnesses. The idea has been explored by researchers in medical geography and the geography of health care who are interested in benefits that may be derived from landscape associations. It has also been realised that therapeutic landscapes may be incorporated into literature. In times of stress and illness our minds may wander back to happy childhood locations and it has been suggested, for example, by Daniell and by the geographer, Philo, that when John Buchan needlessly set so much of *The Thirty-nine Steps* in Galloway he was 'escaping' from his sick bed in Kent and the threat of impending war and retreating into his Scottish identity.

*Further reading*: Daniell, D., 'The Scottishness of The Thirty-nine Steps' in Herbert, W. N. and Price, R. (eds), *Gairfish: Discovery*, Gairfish, Bridge of Weir, 1985.

**Thieves' Lane**. Names such as this may denote routeways that were particularly prone to the activities of thieves and vagabonds, though the Thieves Road near Attleborough on the Thetford-Norwich road was associated with the transportation of prisoners to the Lent Assizes at Thetford. On a former waste near Harrogate is 'Turpin's Lair' reflecting a (perhaps apocryphal) link with the York-born highwayman. References to Robin Hood are much less convincing. Where 'Thieves' occurs in field-names it may be derogatory and the land steals labour or fertiliser.

**Thirlage**. In Scotland, an obligation to grind one's corn at a particular mill. 'Outsucken' was

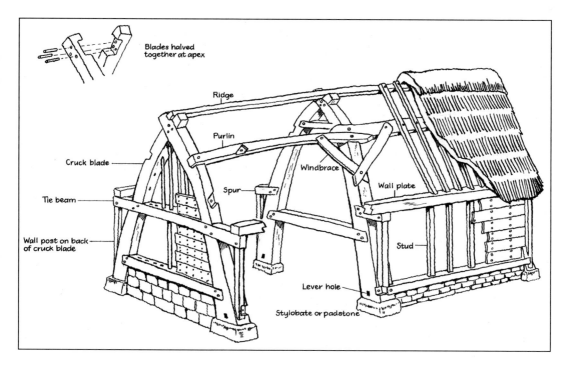

**Blades halved together at apex**

**Ridge**

**Purlin**

**Cruck blade**

**Windbrace**

**Wall plate**

**Spur**

**Tie beam**

**Wall post on back of cruck blade**

**Stud**

**Lever hole**

**Stylobate or padstone**

the freedom from such duties and an 'outsucken', was someone not thirled to a thirling mill. In England the tenant's obligation to grind corn at the lord's mill was known as 'millsoke' or 'suit of mill'.

**Threshing barn**, see BARN.

**Through-gang**. A way through, a passageway.

**Tide mill**. These mills derived power from the natural energy of the rising and falling of tides. Water from the incoming tide would be trapped by sluices and used to revolve one or more water wheels as the tide fell and the water was allowed to drain back to the sea. Devon and Cornwall had three tidal mills in the thirteenth century and nine by the close of the Middle Ages. It is a form of renewable energy that is ripe for re-development.

**Timber-framing (half-timbered, or black and white houses)**. Britain still contains a wealth of timber-framed buildings and, although the dates concerned range from the twelfth or thirteenth to the nineteenth centuries, most examples

encountered range in age from the fourteenth to the seventeenth centuries. Most surviving medieval timber-framed houses were the homes of the moderately affluent or prosperous members of the community. Until the fifteenth century people of low social status inhabited rather fragile hovels, and so it is unusual to find surviving examples of modest timber-framed cottages of pre-fifteenth-century date.

Timber-framed buildings differ from those built of materials like stone, brick or COB in that they consist of a structural load-bearing framework of timber, with the spaces between the timbers having an infill of WATTLE AND DAUB, subsidiary timbers, brick or lath and plaster. There are numerous different techniques of timber framing which reflect the differences in period, place and prestige, but the most fundamental distinction is between buildings

*Timber-framing*
Close-studding in the late-medieval houses at Lavenham in Suffolk.

which employ the cruck-framing method and those built in box-framing. Cruck-framing is not commonly seen today. This is largely because the style became mainly confined to small and humble houses, many of which have been demolished, while in the north of England most cruck-framed houses are encased in stone, so that the timber-framing is invisible from outside. This form of framing involves the use of pairs of massive slightly curved 'blades' of timber which are joined at their apices to form 'A'-shaped frames. A house of one bay would derive its main structural strength from two such 'A'-shaped frames erected at either end of the house with the upper part of the 'A's forming the gables. A house of two bays would employ three 'A' frames, and so on.

Cruck-framing came to be associated with lower-class housing, but this was not originally true, for in the fourteenth century it was employed in some prestigious dwellings and fine barns, like the Glastonbury Abbey tithe barn. It was only in the sixteenth century, or later in the north, that cruck-framing became relegated to the humble homes, so that cruck houses displaying heavy well-shaped frames ceased to be

built. The basic deficiency of this form of timber-framing derived from the fact that the width of the house was governed by the length of oak blades available to form the 'A'-frames. Extra height could be obtained by raising the bases of the crucks. In a 'full cruck' design they are raised on low stone plinths, in the 'raised cruck' form the frames are carried on low walls, while in 'upper cruck' designs the cruck frame is carried on taller walls and so forms the roof of the building. Cruck-framing was once extremely common in the dwellings of the poorer rural classes. In the Yorkshire Dales in the eighteenth century hundreds of thatched cruck-framed houses were replaced by cottages and farmsteads of stone, while many of the clansfolk evicted during the CLEARANCES retreated carrying the cruck frames of their former dwellings with them, so valuable were the timbers.

While the origins of cruck framing are hotly debated, houses employing box-framing were built in Roman Britain, although no pre-medieval box-framing survives. Where this form of timber-framing is employed, the main structural components of the house – the principal upright posts, the ground-level horizontal 'sill beam' and eaves-level horizontal 'wall plate' into which the posts are jointed and the 'cross rail' which links the back and front of the house – combine to form a box-like framework. The strength of this box is increased by lesser vertical and horizontal timbers and, often, by diagonally curving braces. Box-framing can be seen in many different forms; the technique evolved considerably through time, particularly in the use of different types of joint; there were great regional variations, as well as others which depended on the status of the occupant. 'Large framing' is the commonest form of framing seen in houses dating from before about 1450, and here the frame is very open, some of the large wattle-and-daub panels between the sturdy framing timber being traversed by curving braces. Where 'small framing' is employed the timber frame is divided up into small square panels by numerous horizontal and vertical timbers. Square-panel framing in both the large and small form is most common in the Midlands, south and south-west, while in the east and south-east, particularly East Anglia, 'close studding' was frequently preferred. Here the frame is divided into long, narrow, vertical panels by numerous closely spaced uprights or 'studs'. Often the studding was closer than was necessary to satisfy structural needs and was a means of proclaiming the affluence of the occupant – for timber was never cheap. This form of timber-framing was current in East Anglia from about the thirteenth to the seventeenth centuries, though beyond the region it tended to be popular in prestigious buildings from the early fifteenth to the early seventeenth centuries. 'Paycocke's' at Coggeshall in Essex is a fine example. Decorative framing can involve 'close panelling', which exaggerates the appearance of 'small framing' and may display four panels per storey of height, or

appear as small framing with each square panel packed with decorative bracing patterns, as displayed in various ornate timber-framed buildings, like Little Moreton Hall in Cheshire. Most of the framing is purely for decorative effect, and the style enjoyed popularity in buildings of high status from the late sixteenth to late seventeenth century and was mimicked in some showy nineteenth-century urban buildings.

While East Anglia is associated with close studding, and large framing with heavy timbers is normal in the medieval farmsteads of the West Midlands, the boundaries between the different timber-framing styles are not rigid; close studding can be seen in both the West Midlands and Yorkshire. By the late seventeenth century timber-framing was distinctly unfashionable. Prosperous people chose to build in brick or stone, while superb timber-framing was often masked by a plaster façade. From the late seventeenth to the early nineteenth centuries timber-framing was still used in much low-quality housing, though these buildings normally reveal a miserly use of poor timbers. Even so, they become 'desirable period dwellings' when offered by estate agents.

Oak was almost invariably the main structural timber grown for the medieval building industry, although black poplar may occasionally have been used and elm was employed in internal work. The woodland historian, Oliver Rackham, has estimated that the construction of a typical West Suffolk farmhouse might devour around 300 oaks and 30 elms. Most timber-framed buildings were prefabricated at sites close to where the timber was felled and unseasoned timber was used, the only seasoned oak in a newly built house being reused material garnered from dismantled buildings.

The use of prefabrication and the modest dimensions of peasant dwellings allowed such houses to be relocated after they had been erected and occupied. For example, in 1297 Peter the Shepherd paid 6*d.* (2½p) to Wakefield manor court for the right to buy a house and move it to a new location some distance away,

while around 1327 Thomas Tanner bought a
house in a now deserted hamlet, uprooted it and
carried it out of Wakefield manor. He was fined
for buying it without licence from the manor
court. In the houses of the poorer medieval
people – dwellings too mean and feeble to
survive to the modern age – timber other than
oak must have been used. In 1303 at Halton in
Buckinghamshire the court rolls relating to a
widow's dower record that 'Hugh will give to
said Alice two marks and a half of silver and
three ash trees of the better sort at Merdene in
order to build a house on the messuage farm
that is called "Stotkeslond".' See also GREAT
REBUILDING, HALL, WATTLE AND DAUB,
WOODLAND.

*Further reading:* Harris, Richard, *Discovering*
  *Timber-Framed Buildings*, Shire Publications, 1978.
Mercer, Eric, *English Vernacular Houses*, Her Majesty's
  Stationery Office, 1975.

**Timty**. A method of cultivation to improve
coastal land on the Isle of Lewis, involving
digging the land and covering it with a form of
marine algae.

**Tirl mill**. Primitive form of mill on Shetland
from a word signifying rattling or revolving.
See also CLICK MILL, WATERMILL.

**Tithe barn**, see BARN.

**Toft 1**. In many medieval villages the houses
were arranged in rows along the margins of the
village through-road, which generally doubled in
this section as the village High Street, while
behind each house a narrow ribbon of land, a
toft, ran back at right angles to the road. All the
tofts, or all those on one side of the street,
would be of about the same length, and they
often terminated at a *back lane* which ran
parallel to the High Street. Thus each village
house stood within but at the end of its own
toft and each house was freestanding rather than
being part of a terrace. The farming of the toft,
which could have been used for hay, small
livestock and poultry or for vegetables and herbs,

was the concern of the individual tenant, so that
the tofts were not integrated into the OPEN
FIELDS. In relevant medieval charters the phrase
'toft and croft' was often used. Elongated tofts
were a common component of northern villages,
many of which were carefully planned in early
medieval times while rectangular CLOSES were
more characteristic of the Midlands and south.
Even so, villages with houses in tofts and with
closes lying just beyond the tofts were common
throughout most of England. In the sixteenth
and seventeenth centuries toft extensions known
as *garthends* or *garrends* could be enclosed from
the adjacent field to carry tofts beyond the old
back lane. Examples can be found at a number
of northern English villages, like Middleton near
Pickering. Old tofts survive at many villages and
can easily be recognised, though most represent
the amalgamation of two or three neighbouring
tofts and so are broader than the original ones.

*Further reading:* Roberts, B.K., *The Making of the*
  *English Village*, Longman, 1987.

**Toft 2**. A house, normally of the more modest
sort. The toft could survive the abandonment
and decay of the house, with rights to use the
common remaining attached to the house site.

**Toft 3**. In Scotland the word is sometimes
associated with abandoned ploughland or a bed
for vegetables, like cabbages.

**Tollgate**, see TOLL HOUSE.

**Toll house**. Although a few toll houses and toll
booths still operate, taking tolls from the users
of privately owned roads and bridges, the vast
majority are now redundant and adapted as
conventional homes. They originated in the
great TURNPIKE movement and served as the
home and workplace of the keeper who collected
tolls at his *tollgate* and *ticket window* from
travellers in order to recoup the costs of
road-building that had been incurred by the
turnpike trusts. The first tollgates are believed to
have been erected in 1663 at Wadesmill in
Herefordshire. Given the woeful nature of many

roads at the dawn of the turnpike era, the new system should have been welcomed by all and sundry, though, of course, people would plumb the depths of their ingenuity to evade the payment of tolls. Minor roads which could be followed to circumvent a toll house and tollgate were sometimes closed and barred with chains – look out for the various local routes now called 'Chain-Bar Lane'. On the whole, the turnpike-and-tollgate system was progressive rather than exploitative although in a few places the exactions were unjust.

The 'Rebecca Riots' of 1839 and 1844 began in the Preseli foothills of South Wales as a result of the excessive number of tollgates erected. Following bad harvests, impoverished farmers rioted and destroyed a number of them. As true Welshmen they took their inspiration from the Bible: '... they blessed Rebekah, and said to her, may your descendants possess the gates of those who hate them'. To emphasise the rather convoluted biblical connection the rebels actually wore female clothing to enact the role of Rebekah. The sabotage continued until a parliamentary commission accepted the extortionate nature of the tolls.

Toll houses were always conspicuous. Occasionally they were placed in the middle of a road or in a road junction, as near Stanton Drew in Avon. Usually they were placed beside their gates and abutting directly on to the roadside with the ticket-window facing the road. A wide range of fancy, whimsical and polygonal designs were employed, and houses with three-sided frontages were quite common. With their gates gone, ticket-windows blocked off or replaced by conventional window-frames and the boards giving the toll rates removed, the toll houses are much less obvious today, but several are likely to be passed in the course of most long rural rides. Watch out for small, sometimes rather bizarre houses standing end-on to the highway and usually close to the roadside or even projecting into it.

**Tomen**. A Welsh word applied to MOTTE mounds.

**Toonmels**. In northern Scotland this is the ancient core or arable land, which often became pasture for tethered milk cows which grazed beside farmsteads established on the former ploughsoil.

**Toot hill**, see BEACON.

**Torr**. High rock, rocky ground.

**Tower house**. A dynastic stronghold of a simple tall and rectangular form that is reminiscent of the Norman donjon or keep and which had a remarkably long currency. Tower houses accommodated minor aristocrats in late medieval England and Highland clan chieftains in the centuries before the defeat at Culloden in 1746. Thousands of examples can be found in Ireland, where they arrived as the strongholds of Norman colonists. They were adopted by the Gaelic nobility in Ireland in the late medieval period before the Tudor conquests.

**Tower mill**, see WINDMILL AND WIND PUMP.

**Town, toon, toun**. In old usage these words referred to all nucleated settlements, including quite modest villages. They give rise to a variety of place-names, like toon foot, toun land, town head, town dyke, and so on.

**Township (vill)**. Townships were the fundamental building blocks of countryside and community. Most are ancient, but quite how ancient is hard to know, though Roman and prehistoric origins must often apply. Townships were generally much smaller than parishes, and when ecclesiastical parishes developed in late Saxon and medieval times they could incorporate whole handfuls of townships – Halifax parish ran across twenty-two townships and Lythe parish on the North York Moors included nine townships and eleven villages. Township communities were often scattered between a number of neighbouring farmsteads and hamlets but could be organised together by a township assembly. In Roman times townships could have existed as components of estates, these estates subsequently fragmenting. In due course, portions of the Roman estate might exist as a MANOR consisting of one or several townships, while gradually the progressive provision of churches in the more out-of-the-way places gave the parish ascendancy over the township.

A glance at a modern map should reveal the survival of many township names, which now describe geographical localities within a parish. The word 'vill' was, in its early usage, often used in relation to a township rather than a village, while 'township' has affinities to the Old English *tun*, a farmstead settlement, which also formed the '-ton' ending of scores of village names. The township is best regarded as a little geographical cell of land which has sustained a small community for a very long time. In Scotland under the RUNRIG system, a township could be a group farm occupied by two or more families of farmers living in the same CLACHAN or FERMTOUN, while in the Highlands under the CROFTING system it was a small crofting community.

*Further reading*: Winchester, A. J. L., 'Parish, township and tithing: landscapes of local administration in England before the nineteenth century', *Local Historian* 27, 1997, pp. 3–17.

**Transhumance**, see SHIELING.

**'Tre-', 'Tref-' place-names**. In Wales and Cornwall, place-names beginning in this way usually derive from a P-Celtic word signifying 'a farm', like Trefeglwys, near Montgomery. Elsewhere, a variety of derivations are possible, including ones from the Old English word for a tree or post.

**Tree hole**. When a tree falls and its roots are torn from the ground a large quantity of earth and stones is likely to be removed. A saucer-shaped depression will mark the position of the tree long after the timber has decayed or been sawn-up and removed. Where a tree has been felled, the stump will gradually decay but

may be recognised for decades after the felling incident. In some cases, grass gradually colonises the decaying stump and a slightly domed, turf-covered feature will result. Within a single small grove of trees all these forms may be present to indicate the former extent and density of the wood.

**Tree surgery**. Surgery of the terminal variety tends to flourish in areas where the authorities are lax in matters concerning tree preservation orders, both in terms of the designation of trees and the enforcement of preservation orders when faced with spurious felling claims.

**Trust road**. A TURNPIKE.

**Tryst**. A Scottish cattle market or fair. The word signifies an appointment to meet, often in a romantic sense. See DROVE ROAD.

**Tump**. A domed mound, see MOTTE.

**Tumulus**, see LONG BARROW, ROUND BARROW, SQUARE BARROW.

**Turbary**. A turbary (from the Latin *turba*, or 'turf') was a peat-digging, and most medieval peasants enjoyed a right of turbary wherever the COMMONS yielded a supply of peat fuel. Peat was a valuable source of fuel, and the manor courts would impose quite heavy fines on those who abused the rights to take turfs. The majority of turbaries were of a small scale and may not even be discernible today, but there is one gigantic exception to this rule: the Norfolk Broads. The digging of peat there on a considerable scale was probably begun in Roman times, but the massive operations which created the Broads took place in the twelfth, thirteenth and fourteenth centuries, when peat-digging affected an area of about 2600 acres (1052 hectares). The working of peat on a grand commercial scale was developed by the local monastic communities employing peasant labour, with the priory of St Benedict (St Benet's) obtaining turbary rights spanning a dozen parishes. Norwich was the prime market for the fuel, and records show that its cathedral priory alone could consume 200,000 turfs or blocks of peat in a single year. It is estimated that at least 9 million cubic feet of peat was extracted from what then became the Norfolk Broads. Initially the peat-diggings were dry and will have resembled grander versions of the turbaries which can still be seen in operation in Ireland and the Scottish Highlands and Islands. However severe flooding was recorded in 1287, and a relative rise in sea-level was beginning to inundate the turbaries. For some decades efforts were made to scour peat from the beds of submerged workings, but by the fifteenth century the attempts were abandoned and the Norfolk Broads had come into existence. At this time the Broads were more extensive than today, with the lakes or broadenings on the rivers Bure, Yare and Waveney having neat outlines and vertical edges which clearly betrayed their origins as peat-cuttings. Gradually, however, silting and the colonisation of the margins of the Broads by reedbeds and then alders restricted the area of the Broads and produced a deceptively 'natural' appearance of irregular lakes hemmed by reed and 'alder carr' vegetation. Although suggestions that the Broads might be man-made were made in the 1830s, it was only in 1960 that the true story was actually established.

Much fainter traces of former peat-cuttings are evident in some other places. On the MOORS of the Lizard peninsula in Cornwall faint striations on the land-surface, which are only really visible from the air, reveal a paring away of the surface peat layers which may have been practised until quite recent times, and there are also room-sized rectangular depressions on these moors which seem to represent hearths or PANS used for making peat charcoal. Evidence of medieval turbaries in various parts of Britain can sometimes be found in road names like Turf Road, Turbary Road or Turfgate.

Extensive, active peat workings can be seen in west and central Ireland and in the Highlands of Scotland, in places where the peat has formed over many centuries in waterlogged lowland basins or on rain-lashed upland plateaux. Until relatively recently, upland communities in general depended quite heavily on access to peat beds for fuel. Where peat was not found, and where it had all been removed from locations close at hand then it had to be brought in from more distant beds. On Fetlar in the Shetlands, for example, it was transported for many miles by boat and pack-horse following the working-out of accessible supplies. In the cases of some smaller islands, the exhaustion of peat supplies was followed by desertion, while people on Papa Stour shipped peat in from other islands. Areas associated with the digging of peat or 'turf' were normally COMMONS where certain arrangements for sharing the resource had been established. Writing of an expanse of land between the foot of Bishop Hill and the shores of Loch Leven in Scotland, Munro explains: 'Although sheep were pastured on the common during the winter, the Portmoak Moss was primarily used as a source of peat for the fire. Cut in the spring after sowing the grain, the moss was divided into 16 slices like a huge round cake, each slice of the moss being allocated to a village or a farm. The slices of uncut peat, which reached a depth of nearly 20 feet in places, were collectively known as 'heads', while the adjacent land on which the peat was stacked to dry was divided into an equivalent number of sections called 'spreads'. A moss grieve appointed by the Kinross Estate made sure that the peat was cut properly and that everybody had their fair share in the form of headroom and spreadroom. In the Lake District manorial officials known as 'mossmen', 'moss lookers' or 'mossgraves' allocated shares or 'rooms' in the retreating peat resources to tenants in the seventeenth century.

*Further reading*: Lambert, S. M., Jennings, J. N., Smith, C. T., Green, C. and Hutchinson, S. N., *The Making of the Broads*, Royal Geographical Society, 1960.

Munro, D., *Loch Leven and the River Leven: A Landscape Transformed*, River Leven Trust, Markinch.

**Turnpike roads**. The term 'turnpike' appears to have been in use in the fifteenth century to describe the gated entrance to a walled town, but it subsequently came to be associated with the tollgate and with the roads which were financed by tolls. MEDIEVAL ROADS were generally inadequate, and in 1555 the onus for road maintenance was placed on the parishes under the terms of the new Highways Act. By and large, the resources of the parishes were unequal to the task, or else the obligations were simply ignored according to well-established parochial tradition. In 1663, an Act was passed which enabled the Justices of the Peace in three East Midlands counties to levy tolls for repairs to their sections of the Great North Road, the major but none the less decrepit routeway of England. Wadesmill in Hertfordshire obtained the first tollgate or turnpike – a bar that could be opened or closed to control traffic. The revolutionary consequences of this innovation were not realised at this time, and the tollgates installed were removed.

By the end of the century, however, new Acts had created seven turnpike trusts for road improvements, and the following century witnessed a great proliferation of such trusts, each one exacting tolls to finance road improvements. Groups of trustees, usually local business people with a stake in transport, would seek to raise capital to finance their 'diversion' or improved road by offering interest rates of 4–5 per cent, the income for repayment deriving from the tolls charged on road-users. At first they tended to employ their own turnpikemen, but later they would often auction off the right to collect tolls to speculators, who would hope to raise more from the tolls than had been bid at auction. Each toll house displayed a graded list of charges, and on the side of the former toll house at Templecombe in Somerset such a carved board survives.

The trusts still tended to rely on traditional methods of construction, ploughing out ruts and tipping baskets of stones into the holes, but considerable straightening and widening operations were accomplished, so that turnpiked roads did not exactly follow the lines of their predecessors. Although the general conditions of roads had been poor, there was often a multiplication of routes – and so toll-dodgers would resort to the poorer tracks in order to circumvent a TOLL HOUSE. As a consequence of this, the turnpiking of one road often led to the barring of alternative tracks: look out for 'Chain-Bar Lane' and 'Bar Lane' names. In open country with firm 'going' it was very easy to detour around a tollgate. At Newmarket, gaps in the great LINEAR EARTHWORK known as Devil's Dyke, which divides the race courses, were sealed to prevent their use by refugees from a nearby toll house – but then the Jockey Club complained that racegoers could not get to the courses, so the gaps were unsealed and barred with gates which were only open on race days.

In fact, the turnpike movement was a considerable success, and by about 1820 the improvements had transformed about 20,000 miles (32,000 kilometres) of road in England and Wales. The turnpikes were so successful that they generated a mass of new traffic – but by this time canals and the new railways were beginning to shoulder their share of the burden. The competition of the railway completely undermined the coaching trade, which had enjoyed a period of expansion and improvement during the turnpike era. Roads were dis-turnpiked, the toll houses were closed down, and the last turnpike ceased to exist in 1895. The tolls had proved a lucrative and effective means of raising revenue, but will not always have been missed by the travelling public at large: in 1856 a carriage and pair paid the then princely sum of 9*s*. 4*d*. (47p) in tolls for a trip from Keighley to Kendal. All this coinage had another side, and a broadsheet printed in support of this road argued: 'Good Roads would lower the Price of Coal at least one Third ... Goods may be conveyed from one place to another in Carriages with less than Half the Number of Horses now employed in carrying Packs and consequently at half the Expense.' It is interesting to note that the trustees of the Keighley-Kendal turnpike included several men with mining interests – and how else can one explain the anomalies in the tolls charged at Craven Cross Bar?

| Two horse cart | 1s. 1½d. |
| Two horse *coal* cart | 0s. 3d. |

Generally the trusts accomplished a considerable transformation of the conditions of road transport, in spite of resentments and occasional criticisms that people should get better value for their tolls. Arthur Young, the distinguished writer of agriculture commentaries, had this to say:

> The turnpikes! as they have the assurance to call them; and the hardiness to make one pay for. From *Chepstow* to the half-way house between *Newport* and *Cardiff*, they continue mere rocky lanes, full of hugeous stones as big as one's house, and abominable holes. The first six miles from *Newport*, they were so detestable, and without either direction posts, or mile-stones, that I could not persuade myself I was on the turnpike, but had mistook the road …

In their heyday the turnpikes also had repercussions for town, village and commerce. In the northern Pennines, for example, Sedbergh grew after 1761 because it lay on a turnpike, while Dent, which did not, declined. Enquiries in the local archives will soon reveal whether a particular road was or was not a turnpike; most former turnpikes look much like any other modern road. The traveller should keep an eye open for converted toll houses and for old MILESTONES which may have survived. These can be of stone or cast iron, and sometimes the name of the road is recorded around a semicircular panel atop the stone. It is interesting to look at the subsequent fates of routes abandoned by turnpikes in favour of new courses and the way the system, though quite short-lived, evolved. For example, in Nidderdale the emergence of several water-powered industrial hamlets led to an upland section of turnpike being replaced by one that followed the valley to link-up these places. In this locality it also appears that ancient roadside POLLARDS indicate sections where a turnpike adopted the course of an older road without greatly modifying it. See also TOLL HOUSE, MACADAM, METCALFE, TELFORD.

*Further reading.* Albert, W., *The Turnpike Road System of England, 1663–1840*, Cambridge University Press, 1972.

**Ty unnos**, see SQUATTER.

# U

**Ui**. In Scotland, a narrow isthmus.

**Understanding the past**. As itemised by the landscape historian, Brian Roberts, in general terms a spatial and environmental understanding of the past must be structured in terms of four conditions:

*Conditions of antecedence*, what came before: this *always* frames what comes later.

*Conditions of change*, the advent of new skills and new drives, new pressures, within the matrix of time, affecting the use of space.

*Conditions of stability*, the fundamental need for continuity in farming life and sustaining soil fertility within all regions: failure results in serious social and economic dislocation. Thus we should never forget that stability is a dynamic process.

*Conditions of contingency*, linkages, sometimes deliberate, sometimes fortuitous, between the natural environments and human activities and events.

*Further reading*: Roberts, B. K., 'Space, Place and Time: Reading the Landscape' in Reading the Landscape, *Journal of the Scottish Association of Geography Teachers* **32**, 2002.

**Up-and-down husbandry**. Under OPEN-FIELD FARMING the peasants took every opportunity to introduce livestock on to the ploughlands, and beasts would be turned on to the stubble after harvest, and would graze whichever of the open fields was undergoing its fallow phase. By the close of the Middle Ages a considerable amount of open-field land had been enclosed to form privately owned fields. The system of up-and-down husbandry seems to have been adopted in the sixteenth century and enjoyed great popularity in the seventeenth. It involved

growing a cereal crop on a field until there were signs of diminishing fertility and then allowing the field to revert to pasture, when the manure from the grazing livestock would replenish the ground. Where a farmer had a small set of fields at his disposal he could organise a simple rotation between corn and pasture. Variations of the system survive today under names like 'alternate husbandry' and 'ley farming', the main difference being that after cropping the field is sown with selected grasses rather than the farmer relying on natural regeneration of pasture or the broadcasting of hayseed.

The up-and-down system was recommended to farmers by the agricultural writer John Fitzherbert around 1539:

> if any of this three closes that [the farmer] hath for this corn be worn or worn bear [*sic*], then he may break and plough up his close that he had for his leys, or the close that he had for his common pasture, or both, and sow them with corn and let the other lie for a time, and so shall he have always rest ground, the which will bear much corn with little dung.

The leys of grass were usually left unploughed for six or seven years and then perhaps ploughed and cropped for three or four years, or up to twice as long if marl had been spread on the ground. At its best, the system could produce a twenty-fold yield over the seed sown, compared with a tenfold yield normal with the open-field ploughland. See also FOUR COURSE ROTATION, LIGHT LAND REVOLUTION, SHEEP-CORN LANDS.

*Further reading*: Broad, J., 'Alternate Husbandry and Permanent Pasture in the Midlands, 1650–1800', *Agricultural History Review* **42**, 1980, 20–37.

# V

**Vaccary.** A medieval farm or *vacaria* specialising in cattle. These were frequently established in deer parks and often took over as the main activity in a former deer park. The term is sometimes used for simple cattle enclosures. In some parts of England, like the Yorkshire Dales, and Swaledale in particular, vaccaries could be the most important component in the medieval farming landscape. Some of the COW PASTURES of the Yorkshire Dales may have originated as vaccaries.

*Further reading:* McDonnell, J., 'Upland Peasant Hamlets', *Northern History* **26**, 1990.

**Vermin traps,** see WOLF PIT.

**Vernacular buildings.** These are buildings of various dates that embody the particular building tradition of a region or locality. They incorporate traditional forms and materials, the latter almost invariably being obtained within the close vicinity of the building site. They are expressive of the regional heritage and preferences in building and may display features which are more closely related to tradition and habit than to the particular local environmental circumstances, and which are seldom if ever encountered outside their region. The third main characteristic of vernacular buildings is that they tend to be relatively modest dwellings which did not adopt the national or international fashions which often found expression in the designs of mansions and other grand buildings.

The vernacular building tradition gradually perished in the late eighteenth and nineteenth centuries as improvements to the transport system allowed the nationwide distribution of 'alien' materials like brick and Welsh slate and when local builders began to adopt standardised architectural plans rather than persisting with traditional local designs. Much vernacular building still survives, although the cottages of the lowest classes in rural society, which tended to be cheaply and poorly built, have largely disappeared. See also GREAT REBUILDING, TIMBER FRAMING, THATCH, HALL.

**Vill,** see TOWNSHIP.

**Villa.** A villa was the country house and estate centre of an immigrant of substance from the Roman empire or of a noble or prosperous Romanised Briton. Villas have conventionally been compared to the mansions inhabited by the rural aristocracy of later centuries, but recently a school of thought has emerged which sees closer similarities between villa society and the extended family relationships of the native Iron Age hamlet. In Britain, villas engaged in commercial farming operations of various kinds and were associated with the more fertile and politically stable conditions of the English lowlands. In the uplands of the north and west they are few or absent. They varied considerably in their size and importance, and in the sumptuousness of their equipment and furnishings, while some villas began as quite modest residences and expanded to become palatial abodes. For all this, the lines of demarcation between villas and other substantial contemporary farms could be quite blurred. Normally a villa would have walls of stone rendered within with painted plaster, tiled roofs and mosaic floors. Additional refinements included 'hypocausts', or heating systems. By successive improvements a more modest farm could acquire the trappings which brought it up to the villa rank. A villa might begin as an alignment of four or five rectangular rooms, then gain a veranda and corner towers to enhance the façade. Mosaics and pavements could mark improvements in the fortunes of the owner, a bath wing might be added, and the villa could culminate as alignments of rooms surrounding a rectangular central garden courtyard. Much is still to be learned about the social life of the villa. We know that both privileged foreigners and native aristocrats and entrepreneurs enjoyed the pleasures of villa life. However, it is not clear whether the occupants should be regarded as a family comparable to that of a post-medieval English squire, or whether they were members of an extended family perpetuating the kinship traditions of the earlier era.

The heyday of the Roman villa in Britain came rather later than that of the Roman town, and when towns were tending to become run-down and less well populated in the fourth century AD there was still a spirit of optimism in the countryside and fortunes were still being plunged into ambitious villa-improvement schemes. Like many much later mansions, the villa was both a prestigious country residence and the nerve centre of a commercial agricultural estate. As buildings, villas crumbled in the decades bracketing the Roman withdrawal from British affairs, but sometimes their tradition of leadership over the surrounding countryside seems to have persisted at their sites. Several excavations have shown evidence of later settlers camping or building flimsy dwellings amongst the ruins of a decaying villa, and in a few cases medieval MANORS are known to have occupied villa sites, as at Wharram Percy in the Yorkshire Wolds. While the villas undoubtedly perished, their ESTATES often seem to have survived. At Rivenhall, in Essex, excavation revealed an Iron Age farmstead, a Roman villa, and a succession of Saxon halls and medieval manors, all built in slightly different positions, but each perhaps presiding over the same ancient estate territory, while a study of Withington parish in Gloucestershire by Professor A. P. R. Finberg suggested that before becoming a parish the area had consisted of an estate that centred on a Roman villa. Although Roman villas are not a prominent part of the visible countryside, their influence as the centres of durable estates

may still be considerable. Villas may be found today as excavations which are usually covered once they have yielded archaeological information. In a few cases, like North Leigh villa in Oxfordshire or Lullingstone villa in Kent they are seen as public showpieces of the Roman period. Most usually they are found as crop-mark sites which are only identifiable when seen from the air.

*Further reading:* Rivet, A. L. F., *Town and Country in Roman Britain*, Hutchinson, 1964.
Dark, K. and Dark, P., *The Landscape of Roman Britain*, Sutton, Stroud, 1997.
Branigan, K. and Miles, D. (eds), *The Economies of Romano-British Villas*, J. R. Collis, Sheffield, 1989.

**Village**. The story of the village can explored through both time and space, for while villages have evolved through the passing centuries there are also variations from place to place, the large and strongly nucleated villages of the Midlands contrasting, for example, with the smaller, sometimes looser settlements that are characteristic of ANCIENT COUNTRYSIDE.

*Ancient villages.* Permanently rather than seasonally occupied settlements have existed in Britain since the fifth millennium BC, yet until the latter part of the Dark Ages villages always played a minor role in the pattern of settlement of societies which traditionally favoured HAMLET and FARMSTEAD life. And so, if one looks at the broad span of human occupation in Britain, one could argue that the rural ascendancy of the village is merely a development of the last thousand years or so – and one which breaks with a long-established preference for life in small dispersed settlements. Knowledge of the early days of village life is poor. Farmsteads, hamlets and villages certainly existed, but the places where they stood are likely to have been eroded down below the bases of the dwellings or buried by accumulations of eroded material, or else the evidence is likely to have been obliterated by heavy sedimentation or the effects of later phases of farming and settlement on the

*Village*
The idyllic setting of Duddington in Northamptonshire.

sites concerned. Even where evidence does survive, it sometimes exists only in the form of deep pits, which were dug for the storage of grain and subsequently abandoned and filled with household rubbish. The discovery of more than 200 such pits at a Neolithic site near Mildenhall in Suffolk implies a settlement here of village-like proportions, though like other settlements of its day, it may have known only a few years of occupation before the largely unexplained ancient habits of abandonment and resettlement were asserted.

In contrast to this meagre evidence of Neolithic domestic life in England, a few sites in Orkney, notably Rinyn and Skara Brae, have left the most remarkable relics. The village of Skara Brae was engulfed by sand and re-exposed when the dune shifted in the mid nineteenth century. This settlement of fishers and farmers had an unusually long life and was occupied from about

3100 BC to 2500 BC. It existed as a cluster of
subrectangular huts with thick DRYSTONE
WALLS built of the local flagstone, which were
linked by narrow passageways and fitted out
with cots, cupboards and other furnishings all
fabricated from 'planks' of stone. One of the
units appears to have been a workshop where
tools of chert were made rather than a dwelling.
Although it now has a coastal situation, the
village was set back from the sea during its
occupation, perhaps with a freshwater loch in
the intervening space. Unfortunately, the
remoteness and insularity of Skara Brae
combined with the unusually amenable stone
resource in a largely tree-less setting prevents this
village from serving as a model of what was
typical in the Neolithic countryside. It certainly
did not correspond to modern notions of a
village. The different dwellings were tightly
clustered together, almost like rooms in a house,
while the accumulation of a shell midden over
the settlement made it almost subterranean in
character. The community concerned must have
been a remarkably close-knit one.

Near Holyhead on Anglesey another glimpse
of ancient farming life is provided by a series of
HUT CIRCLES on Holyhead mountain, some of
them excavated, which date from the end of the
Neolithic period and which are scattered along
the hillside in the form of a straggle of
farmsteads rather than a tight little settlement of
the Skara Brae type. During the Bronze Age, the
preferences for farmstead and hamlet life
remained, though some village-like settlements
were also built. Their traces are best preserved in
upland areas like Dartmoor, which have largely
escaped the destruction of the evidence by later
phases of settlement and cultivation. Most
typical are the almost ubiquitous patterns of
REAVE-girt fields with isolated farmsteads and
tiny hamlet clusters appearing in field-corners or
within little paddocks abutting the fields. But
there are also a few more substantial settlements,
sometimes existing in enclosing stone compound
walls to produce 'pound villages' like Riders
Rings, South Brent, or the celebrated

Grimspound below Hookney Tor. The Riders
Rings settlement has about thirty-six hut circles,
some of them built against the compound wall,
which was about 6–7 feet (2 metres) thick, but
only about 3 feet (1 metre) high, and other
dwellings dotted about within the compound.
Throughout the Bronze Age the already ancient
general tradition of living in small short-lived
farmsteads and hamlets persisted, but there was
also the pioneering of life in HILLFORT villages
and, from evidence exposed at Runnymede
Bridge on the Thames, the appearance of large
bustling river trading ports. By the dawn of the
Iron Age, most countrysides in Britain were
heavily populated and heavily worked, though
villages remained the exceptions in the
settlement pattern. Many of the largest
agglomerations of dwellings were found within
the ramparts of hillforts, where they may have
flourished as local capitals and trading centres;
later, on the plains below, the farmsteads or
VILLAS of the Romanised elite added an extra
element in the favoured lowland farming
country. Some of the villages which flourished in
Roman Britain were rooted in native traditions,
like the villages of COURTYARD HOUSES still
visible at Chysauster and Carn Euny in
Cornwall or the hillfort village on Tre'r Ceiri on
the Lleyn peninsula, where around 150 stone
dwellings stood within the ramparts. But new
types of village also appeared, sprawling
industrial villages producing pottery in the East
Midlands, commercial roadside villages, or *vici*,
which could be planned or straggling, parochial
or endowed with minor administrative functions.
Where the villages of pre-Roman Britain were
not numerous, normally small and completely
unplanned, the Roman era seems to have
witnessed the imposition of systematic planning
on some villages. At Claydon Pike, in
Gloucestershire, the site of an Iron Age
settlement was redeveloped shortly after the
conquest. At least six small 'residential blocks'
were set out, beside a straight throughroad, their
sides defined by side-streets, and at the core of
the village was an open square.

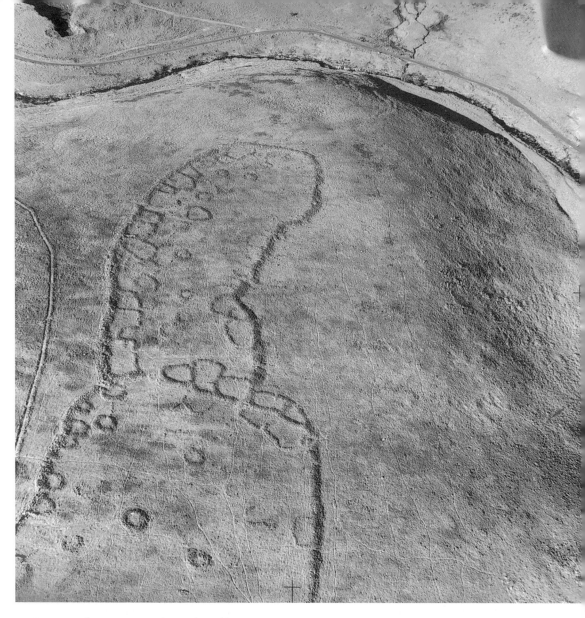

However, the Roman tendency for village growth, specialisation and planning did not survive the collapse of the Empire in Britain, around AD 410. During the occupation, the population may have risen to include perhaps 5 million souls, yet at the time of DOMESDAY BOOK of 1086 England may have contained no more than 2–3 million people. Conventionally it was said that massive Anglo-Saxon invasions during the fifth century AD resulted in the creation of 'village England' by Germanic

*Village*
The Bronze Age village at Riders Rings, Dartmoor. The settlement was surrounded by a low wall. Some circular dwellings and irregular stock pens are built against this wall, whilst others are freestanding. (CUCAP)

settlers, though this is disproved by archaeology. In fact the centuries following the Roman collapse were times of turmoil, disease, decay and economic depression, when woods and thorns recolonised the Roman fieldscape and settlements were small and loose.

*The rise of the village.* The Saxon settlement seems to have been modest, piecemeal and sporadic. Often the settler communities were relegated to the least inviting corners of run-down ESTATES; in some places they lived peacefully alongside the indigenous 'sub-Roman' or British communities, and the main element of their eventual conquest may have been the linguistic one. On the whole, they seem to have respected the ancient preference for farmstead and hamlet life, though a few early Saxon villages have been identified. At West Stow, in Suffolk, a small Saxon community – immigrants or retired mercenaries – settled in a neglected backwater of an estate and established a haphazard group of around six farmsteads with their buildings. This tiny village existed from about AD 400–650 before being abandoned, and recently it has been undergoing a fascinating reconstruction. It had no green, no orderly layout, and no evidence even of a village street has been recognised, so it bore scant resemblance to any surviving English villages. Other early Saxon villages have been recognised, and they, too, tend to be small and lacking in structure and several lie on poor rather than choice farmland. Chalton, in Hampshire, occupied a windswept chalk slope and almost fifty rectangular buildings of different sizes existed there; but, again, there were no streets, green or coherent form.

The real dawning of village England may have begun around the eighth century, have gained impetus in those which followed, and continued into the early medieval centuries. These were troubled times and, although the peasant population was slowly recovering from the terrible decline of the preceding centuries, civil wars and Viking raids and conquests still created great instability. It can hardly be accidental that the eruption of thousands of villages coincided with two other vital developments in rural life – the building of parish churches and the establishment of OPEN-FIELD FARMING. There seems to have been a far-reaching reorganisation on thousands of ESTATES that resulted in a concentration of tenants in the new agricultural villages from which the new farming systems were worked.

It is not known whether the new churches were built in already-established villages or if they already existed and acted as magnets or foci around which the village founders could arrange their estate settlements. Both processes could have occurred, but the open-field farming innovations may have been even more important. Where there were estates sufficiently large to accommodate a complete system of open fields, pastures, meadows and commons a reorganisation of the local settlement pattern appears to have been accomplished. Presumably the lord or his agents composed a strategy that concentrated settlement into a substantial 'nucleated' village located at the core of the open fields. Equally, where the patterns of land ownership and tenancy were complicated and fragmentary the open-field model could not be fully adopted and the small village, hamlet and farmstead tradition must have survived. Or so one must suppose.

*Village names.* It is sometimes implied that the village name itself provides one with comprehensive information about the origins of a village – and such simplistic notions are fraught with danger. It is certainly true that every name was meaningful at the time when it was given. Thus Norbiton, Surrey, was *nord bere-tun* in Old English, 'the northern corn farm'; while Ramsbottom, Lancashire, is the 'bottom' or dell of either the ram or the wild garlic (ramsons). It is also true that the older of the village names are mainly in the recognisable languages of settlers such as the Anglo-Saxons or English, the Norse Vikings or Danish Vikings. Walsingham, for example, is formed in Old English, from *Wael-ingas-ham* – the *ham* (a farmstead or homestead) of Wael's people; while Grimsby is an Old Danish name – the *by*, or

*Village*
Part of Weobley, Herefordshire.

settlement, of Grim. Scores of village names in England combine the name of a local patriarch with an '-ington' or '-ingham' ending, and even Birmingham began as the homestead of Beorma's kin or folowers. But even with such obvious examples one can easily make mistakes, so that Heslington, near York, is probably not the '*tun* of Hesla's folk' but more likely derives from the Old English *haeslen tun* – 'the farm where the hazels grow'. Numerous books provide translations of village names. They can be very useful, but one is well-advised to regard all translations as educated guesses. British place-names derive from a variety of languages – various 'P' and 'Q' forms of the Celtic tongue, Latin, Old English, Old Norse, Old Danish and Old French – spoken by different people at different times. Even so, it is ridiculous to employ them to represent each village as the creation of a distinct and exclusive national group. For example, in the Yorkshire Dales, villages with Old English names are interspersed with those with Scandinavian and, occasionally,

part-Celtic names. The different ethnic groups overlapped and co-existed and one cannot imagine that each group of settlers remained aloof and distinct. It is more reasonable to think that the names reflect a time when language was in the melting pot and words circulated freely between the communities. Indeed, hybrid names are quite common: Somerleyton in Suffolk is perhaps the Old English *tun* of a Viking called Sumarlidi, or 'Summer Warrior'.

Many place-names can be interpreted in a variety of different ways, and one may never be sure which way is correct. However, perhaps the greatest problem with village place-names comes from the assumption that these names were originally given to villages rather than to the TOWNSHIPS or ESTATES or localities in which villages appeared, or were adopted from earlier farmsteads. Sometimes it is plain that the name does not describe a village but, rather, a natural feature, tree, cottage, farm, homestead or district, and that the name has devolved upon the village at some later date. Researchers normally seek for the oldest recorded form of a village name, and as often as not this is the one appearing in DOMESDAY BOOK. Yet the names in Domesday refer to estates, not necessarily to villages. Generally one cannot tell whether or not an estate itemised there contained one or several villages, or no village. Village names are both meaningful and interesting, but they are also likely to confuse and mislead. Rather than attempt a rough-and-ready translation it is better to consult a number of authoritative place-name dictionaries – if only to discover the range of interpretations available.

Frequently one will find two or more villages sharing a common name component, like the Raynham and the Burnham villages in Norfolk. Usually, they have originated on an ancient estate of the same name, and simple prefixes or suffixes like Greater and Lesser, North and South, Magna and Parva serve to identify particular villages. Sometimes CHURCH DEDICATIONS are used to discriminate, as with Ilketshall St Andrew and Ilketshall St Lawrence in Suffolk. A number of village names have a 'feudal affix' which denotes the feudal dynasty which owned the village, Eastleach Turville and Acton Turville in Gloucestershire both being properties of the de Turville family. These could also sometimes serve to identify the village concerned, and in the same county Guiting Power was held by the le Poers family and Temple Guiting was owned by the Knights Templar.

*Village forms.* Villages are found in many different forms and lay-outs, and some of the more fundamental differences are explored in the entry on ANCIENT AND PLANNED COUNTRYSIDE. From the available archaeological evidence it seems that the pattern of a countryside dominated by HAMLETS and farmsteads with smaller numbers of ephemeral

villages began, in the middle Saxon times, to change to countrysides which were frequently but not invariably dominated by numerous permanent villages. In late Saxon times, thousands of new villages were established, and the process of village creation continued through the Norman period. Throughout the Middle Ages the village was volatile. It could fail completely, shift, shrink, expand or change its shape, and villages only seem to have settled down into their more durable forms towards the latter part of the Middle Ages. Much more recently, the modern development of village housing estates or piecemeal infilling have added a new dimension of change. Yet careful research and examination of the evidence can reveal much about the evolution of a particular settlement.

*Planned villages.* Village planning was probably first attempted in Roman times. The existence of Saxon village planning is disputed, though the Saxon king Alfred and his heirs certainly planned the forms of a number of fortified towns or BURGHS such as Lydford in Devon and Wareham in Dorset. Scores of villages founded or redeveloped by Norman masters were planned, as were some later medieval foundations and, of course, many post-medieval estate villages. Planning is normally evidenced by regular proportions, straight alignments, the creation of house-plots of equal size, roughly geometrical GREENS and orderly layouts. Planning presumes a masterplan, and a masterplan presumes a master – but if the master chose to build to an irregular or disorderly plan, then the evidence of planning could never be recognised! In fact it is remarkable how planned village layouts that were implemented in Norman times can be plainly evidenced today in the fabric of the surviving village. It is surprising that the notion that medieval villages in England could be planned seems to have gained widespread acceptance following June Sheppard's analysis of Wheldrake near York in 1966. Norman village planning is most obvious in Yorkshire and Durham, particularly in the Vale of York, where the majority of villages seem to display the vestiges of a Norman plan. This was the area devastated during the Harrying of the North of 1069–71, and it seems sensible if unfashionable to argue that the village planning reflects the efforts of Norman landlords to repopulate and redevelop their ravaged estates. Here, the planning was so precise that measuring rods were sometimes employed and village dimensions were related to the tax assessments recorded in Domesday Book. Various plans were employed, the most popular being the building of dwellings in lines which faced each other across a straight through-road which was sometimes flanked by ribbons of green and with long narrow TOFTS of equal size running back from the dwellings to terminate at a back lane.

Medieval village planning was by no means confined to the Norman period and the north of England, and it did not always affect the whole of a village. Folkingham in Lincolnshire seems to have been focused on a now rather peripheral church but was transformed by the addition of a large rectangular market green or square – the addition probably dating to an initiative in the twelfth century by Henry de Beaumont, the village lord and the builder of a nearby castle. Careful examination of a village map will sometimes show a juxtaposition of planned and unplanned, or 'organic', components – and one is then left to ponder whether the planned area was added to or knocked into an unplanned village, or whether a planned village has gained an irregular extension? Some of the most neatly planned villages are, in fact, the failed new towns of the Middle Ages that have never outgrown their original layouts or never quite managed to fill them. South Zeal in Devon is a stagnated medieval borough that was remodelled in 1299.

*Polyfocal villages.* A village could materialise almost overnight as the product of a comprehensive act of planning. There are also scores of villages that developed gradually from the merging of a series of distinct centres. The polyfocal village has grown from a number of such foci. Perhaps the most polyfocal of all is Shrewton in Wiltshire, which, as described by archaeologist Mike Aston, consists of an amalgamation of no fewer than eight intact or decayed hamlets. Three of these hamlets – Maddington, Shrewton and Rollestone – had churches and a fourth formerly had a chapel. In the case of the polyfocal Cambridgeshire village of Cottenham, Dr Jack Ravensdale has shown how a phase of twelfth-century village growth along a road crossing village fields united two villages which had been established in Saxon times, while contemporary growth in another direction defined a new triangular green. Polyfocal villages can often be recognised on the ground or on the map by the churches, manor houses and separate greens which formed the original components. They may also be detected by the gaps or breaks in street alignments marking the divisions between original hamlets, as at Hutton Buscel near Scarborough, where the incorporated hamlets of Hutton, Preston and Newton are still recognisable components. It is not sufficiently appreciated that numerous polyfocal centres dated from the Industrial Revolution, with different forms of industrialisation providing the energy to forge a merger of hamlets, mills and churches and produce a nucleated settlement.

*Shifted villages.* The typical medieval village normally contained only one building of great value – the church – and only one or two more buildings of real substance – its manor houses. Otherwise, the dwellings were flimsy and short-lived. Thus the village community was not anchored by valuable fixed property. Some villages would drift towards promising destinations, so that new streets would sprout at one end of the settlement and old ones would wither and decay at the other. A wholesale migration of a village could result from the desire to set up home beside a promising area of

pasture, while a reorientation of the settlement might follow a change in the importance of local routeways. An oft-quoted example concerns several villages in the Cam valley in Cambridgeshire which were aligned along tracks leading to fords in the river. Gradually, roads *following* the river became more important than tracks *crossing* it, so that the riverside villages

*Village*
Earthworks flanking the old through road mark the former extent of the village of Kilpeck, Herefordshire. The Norman motte mound can be seen near the top of the picture, and just below it is the church, which is renowned for its Norman carvings. (CUCAP)

began to expand along the valley rather than at right angles to the river. Such shifting was a gradual and piecemeal affair, but there were a few cases when a movement of the settlement was imposed from on high. This occurred at Caxton in Cambridgeshire after Baldwin de Freville gained permission to hold a market in 1247 and decided to shift the nucleus of the village a distance of a quarter of a mile in order to tap the bustling trade on the Old North Road. Most shifts occurred during the Middle Ages, but in the late eighteenth century the enclosure of its common and the development of two TURNPIKES induced the villagers of Killinghall, North Yorkshire, to gravitate from a common-edge to a roadside situation.

*Shrunken villages.* Village populations grew steadily in late Saxon times and then very rapidly during the first medieval centuries. In the thirteenth century MARKETS proliferated and ASSARTING expanded the cultivated area. The fourteenth century, however, was a time of economic decline, worsening climate, with the slow decay of many villages being accelerated by the repeated onslaughts of the pestilence or Black Death, which arrived in 1348. In previous years land-hunger had caused the establishment of new villages on unpromising lands, and these weaklings in the village flock were particularly vulnerable. But other, more venerable and substantial villages could suffer from the gradual decline of their markets or the enclosure of ploughlands, pastures and COMMONS by feudal masters who were eager to exploit the high prices offered for wool. Some villages decayed completely, and deserted villages are described under a separate entry (see LOST VILLAGE). Others, like Flecknoe in Warwickshire, collapsed to such a degree that their original layout is hard to recognise, while many more shed streets and became punctuated by empty house-plots, tofts or closes. Evidence of shrinkage can be seen in abandoned or reduced churches and in the earthworks of former streets and house-plots which may be visible nearby.

*The younger villages.* The process of village formation continued long after the passing of the Middle Ages and is even represented today with the building of a few detached residential suburbs, like Bar Hill near Cambridge. Most of the post-medieval villages were either replacements for predecessors which had been demolished in the creation of a landscaped park; completely new villages provided to accommodate communities of estate workers; or industrial villages built at the behest of a local entrepreneur. Virtually all such villages were thoroughly planned, though sometimes the planning represented a bizarre attempt to sentimentalise the ethos of village England. At Old Warden in Bedfordshire, Lord Ongley prettified his village with picturesque additions in the mid-nineteenth century. Among the most celebrated villages that are replacements for settlements removed in the creation of a splendid park are Harewood near Leeds, Milton Abbas in Dorset, New Houghton in Norfolk and Nuneham Courtenay in Oxfordshire. Estate villages are quite numerous, including Waddesdon in Buckinghamshire, built in the Arts and Crafts style of the 1880s, Blaise Hamlet in Gloucestershire, an extravagant and influential picturesque creation built in 1810–12 to house elderly retainers of the Blaise Castle estate, and Holkham which stands, deferentially, outside the gates of the great Norfolk park. Purpose-built industrial villages are also quite common, including such examples as Stewarthy in Bedfordshire, built in 1927 for employees of the London Brick Company, Bromborough Pool in Cheshire, provided for the employees of a candle factory in the 1850s, a large number of now ill-fated colliery villages and, most impressive of all, the textile village of Saltaire near Bingley.

The most significant recent work on villages in England was accomplished by Brian Roberts and Stuart Wrathmell. It concerns the way in which the distinction between woodland and open country was apparently marked before the Roman era and that there are clear links between cleared land recorded in the

Anglo-Saxon period and a belt of nucleated settlement running through England from Dorset to Northumberland.

See also DOMESDAY BOOK, GREENS, GREENS AND ENDS, LOST VILLAGE, MARKETS AND FAIRS.

*Further reading:* Aston, Michael, *Interpreting the Landscape*, Batsford, 1985.

Darley, Gillian, *Village of Vision*, Granada, 1978.

Taylor, Christopher C., *Village and Farmstead*, George Philip, 1983.

Muir, R., *Landscape Detective*, Windgather, Macclesfield, 2000.

Roberts, B. K. and Wrathmell, S., 'Peoples of Wood and Plain: an Exploration of National and Local Regional Contrasts' in Hooke, D. (ed.), *Landscape the Richest Historical Record*, Society for Landscape Studies Supplementary Series 1, 2000, pp. 85–96.

Rowley, T., *Villages in the Landscape*, Orion, 1978.

**Village green**, see GREEN.

**Vineyards**, see ORCHARDS.

**Virgate, Wista, Yardland, Yoke**. A variable area of land, normally 30–40 ACRES in extent, but the limits ranged more widely than this, with virgates tending to be smaller on the better soils and larger in the poorer settings.

**Vitrified forts**. These are largely confined to Scotland and are HILLFORTS which were built with ramparts of rubble that were stabilised by an interlacing of timbers. The deliberate ignition of the lacing timbers, with the conflagration probably enhanced by bonfires of brushwood heaped against the ramparts, generated sufficient heat to melt the rubble to form a 'vitrified' or glassy mass. Since vitrification did nothing to improve the defensive quality of the sections of rampart affected and since the defenders of a hillfort could hardly be expected to stand idly by while attackers went through the procedures of igniting their ramparts, the vitrified forts constitute a considerable archaeological mystery. A high proportion of Scottish hillforts experienced vitrification, and vitrified sections of ramparts can be recognised by the scorched and glassy nature of the building materials. See also HILLFORTS.

**Voe**. A bay, from the Norse dialect of Shetland.

# W

**Waar, ware**. In Scotland, to manure coastal land with sea wrack. A 'waar strand' is a beach on which the weed is cast up and it was heaped in 'waarcaists' for spreading on the land.

**Wait, wamflet**. The mill stream departing from a mill. See WATERMILL, FALL TROUGH.

**Wake**. This is a word that is archaic but not entirely extinct, and it derives from the treat of remaining out of bed late on the eve of village celebrations that was enjoyed by medieval peasants. Although the roots of rural wakes may burrow down into pagan gatherings, wakes were theoretically held on the feast day of the saint who was the subject of the local CHURCH DEDICATION, so that after the wakeful vigil the villagers would troop along to mass on the morning of their wake day. Then dancing, drinking and sports would follow, either in the CHURCHYARD or on the GREEN or PLAISTOW. During wake day the village might play host to visitors from neighbouring parishes, an occasion fraught with the potential for violence. Some medieval fairs could have had their origins in the fun and social contacts associated with wakes. In time, the purpose and timing of wakes became blurred, but although Henry VIII attempted to standardise wake days on Michaelmas his orders seem largely to have been ignored and the staggering of the celebrations enabled neighbouring parishes to enjoy each other's wakes.

**Walk mill, wauch mill**. Walk mills are occasionally commemorated by place-names, like Walk Mill Ing (meadow) at Ripley, North Yorkshire. They were primitive FULLING MILLS in which the pounding of the cloth underwater was accomplished not by water-driven paddles, but by the trampling action of human feet. Some of these mills seem to have survived into the later stages of the Middle Ages, though some others were superseded by mechanised mills. See also WATERMILL, DAMS AND WIERS.

**Walls**, see DRYSTONE WALLS.

**Wapentake**, see HUNDRED.

**Ward hill, wart hill**, see BEACON.

**Ware strand**. In Lowland Scots, a beach on which ware or seaweed is washed up. See also WAAR.

**Warp**. An embankment associated with land reclamation made with piles and brushwood.

**Warren**. It is rather odd how the real nature and purpose of the warren has been forgotten. When people use the word today they are usually describing the burrows of wild rabbits. However, just a few generations ago commercial rabbit warrens were prominent in the economy of areas like the East Anglian Breckland and Dartmoor and true warrens were important features of most countrysides from Norman to Victorian times. The warren was an area specially set aside for the raising of rabbits, often with protected boundaries and purpose-built accommodation both for the rabbits and for their custodians. Originally, the word referred to hunting rights to small game, and nobles paid to enjoy the right of 'free warren' on their estates, but the word was soon associated specifically with the hunting and keeping of rabbits.

The popular perception of the *rabbit* has also changed remarkably. In the decades preceding the introduction, in 1953, of the terrible myxomatosis, which killed 99 per cent of British rabbits, the animals were seen in their hundreds or thousands and were perceived as vermin and a major threat to farming. Whole fields seemed to be edged by a shifting brown carpet of rabbits, and cheap rabbit pies and stews substituted for chicken on countless cottage tables. Yet if we go back to the first two or three post-medieval centuries, the rabbit was generally thought of as a useful product of farming, while to the medieval mind it was a delicacy which required careful protection and nurture. The rabbit is not native to Britain, but was introduced, perhaps from Spain, by the Normans around 1100, and warrens became quite numerous during the thirteenth century. For a long time, the word 'rabbit' only applied to the baby animal; the adult was known as a 'coney'. One should not expect to find 'rabbit' place-names, though 'Coney' ones exist and Coneysthorpe village near York might be one. As with all place-names, they must be handled with care and can be confused with 'king' place-names, coming from the Old English *cyning* and the Old Danish *kunung* – so that Conisbrough in Yorkshire is the BURH, or stronghold, of the King and not a fortress manned by rabbits, or a 'coney burie', a man-made home for rabbits as described below. (This sort of linguistic confusion must have existed for some time, for when in Holland the author was told how when, a French king was imposed on the country by Napoleon, he announced in halting Dutch to an assembly of his subjects that he was their new rabbit.)

Today 'rabbit' is used to describe the inept novice and the wimp. In this sense coneys *were* rabbits during their early years of residence in the harsher climates of Britain. They could not burrow, were sometimes fed on hay in winter and generally needed cossetting. Two and a half centuries seem to have passed before the animals were capable of causing problems on tenant holdings, but eventually a more robust British strain evolved. In 1340 the men of West Wittering in Sussex complained that 'the wheats in the said parish have been devoured year after year by the rabbits of the Bishop of Chichester, and thereby lessened in value £7 6s. 8d. [£7.34]'. The thousands of miles of PARLIAMENTARY ENCLOSURE HEDGEROWS planted in the eighteenth and nineteenth centuries must have

encouraged the spread of rabbits, while at the same time the growing popularity of pheasant-shooting led to the ruthless extermination of predators by gamekeepers. But only in the two most recent centuries did the rabbit emerge as a very serious pest – and now myxomatosis keeps most populations in check and the animals most likely to avoid infection are those learning to live a more solitary existence in the open or to colonise DRYSTONE WALLS.

In this way the rabbit evolved from being gourmet fare to peasant fare and vermin. Because of their unusual history, the value of rabbits has tended to remain constant through centuries of inflation. A Victorian cottager could buy the main ingredient of stew for about the same price that a rabbit cost in the thirteenth century (though the difference being that medieval cash incomes were far lower). In 1300, for example, the wage of the warrener on Oakham manor was 6s. 5d. per year (about 32p), and if he wanted to buy a rabbit at market it would probably have cost him 4d. (about 2p). This was more than he could earn from the warrening work in a fortnight. It is unlikely that rabbit will regain its place on the rural menu before the passing of the generation of countryfolk who can remember the horrors of myxomatosis.

A warren could be no larger than a paddock or could cover an extensive tract of land and was often known as a 'coninger', 'clapery', 'coning-erth', 'coneygarth' or 'conerie', all of which can emerge in place-names. Lords seem to have had the right to set up their warrens on common grazings, where the rabbits will have shared the heaths with peasant livestock, while a high proportion of warrens were established in or close to DEER PARKS. Normally, however, the breeding area of the warren was ditched and banked, fenced or hedged. The accounts of Fountains Abbey for 1457–58 record the expenditure of 11½d. (about 5p) for 'making hedges around the garden of the coneys'. Such barriers were needed to keep out predators in

both the human and animal guises.
Rabbit-poaching had already become an
established part of country life – for example, in
1268 poachers invaded the warren of the Earl of
Cornwall at Isleworth in Middlesex. Poaching on
both the large and small scales persisted
throughout the Middle Ages. One interesting
case has been described by Professor J. C. Holt
in his *Robin Hood* (Thames & Hudson, 1952).
In 1417, a royal writ recorded that one 'Friar
Tuck' was leading a gang of murderers and
vagabonds in Sussex and Surrey, where they had
entered warrens and chases to hunt and had
burned the lodges of warreners and foresters.
Friar Tuck was still at large in 1429, by which
time his true identity as Robert Stafford,
chaplain of Lindfield, Sussex, had been
established. (The first appearance of the surname
Robynhood or Robinhood occurred in 1296 in
Fletching parish, which bordered on Lindfield. If
Robin Hood was a real person, he probably
lived in the Barnsdale area of South Yorkshire in
the thirteenth century, but Robert Stafford could
well have been the original Friar Tuck and his
exploits become woven into the Robin Hood
legends.)

While rabbit warrens were a very common
adjunct to manorial life almost everywhere in
Britain south of the Forth and Clyde, certain
localities were particularly favoured. They
included the Scilly Isles, where rabbits were
introduced in 1176; the Farne Islands; Skokholm
off the Pembrokeshire coast; the Breckland;
Ashdown and Hatfield Forests; Dartmoor; and
Epping Forest, where the artificial mounds
associated with warrens abound. In the
Breckland, an enormous area of more than 2200
acres (890 hectares) was enclosed as Lakenheath
Warren by over 10 miles (16 kilometres) of bank
and ditch, much of these earthworks still
surviving. Sometimes, the limits of a warren
were marked by stones, and on Dartmoor near
Postbridge an old roadside cross, Bennett's
Cross, carries the later inscription 'W.B.'
('warren boundary'). The extent to which
warrens or the breeding areas within warrens

*Warren*
Bennett's Cross on Dartmoor, dating back to medieval
times. It was adopted as a boundary marker of
Headland Warren. The initials 'W.B.' are faintly
discernible on its western face.

were enclosed by artificial banks is uncertain,
particularly for post-medieval times; on at least
three occasions the earthworks of medieval
rabbit-enclosures were excavated in mistake for
other features. In medieval times, the rabbit was
a delicacy and it also yielded a soft fur which
could be used for lining garments. In addition,
bracken gathered from the warren could be used
for bedding or compost. Later, when the rabbit
had become a source of cheap meat, its fur was
still useful; it could be trimmed and varnished
and used in the manufacture of top-hats. In the

Middle Ages, as later, coneys were caught by ferrets and nets, though those lords who enjoyed a right of free warren seem to have regarded the rabbit as poor quarry, preferring to hunt the hare.

Contemporary illustrations suggest that women rather than men were frequently involved in the ferreting and shooting. It is said that during the Peasants' Revolt rebels at St Albans marched behind a rabbit tied to a lancehead, symbolising their claim to the right to hunt over the Abbey lands.

Characteristic features of warrens are *pillow mounds*, low mounds which often have an oblong pillow-like plan or may be cigar-shaped. They are usually about 100 feet (approximately 30 metres) long and not more than 30 feet (approximately 10 metres) broad and bounded by shallow ditches. They are sometimes known locally as 'buries' or 'berries'. Until quite recently they were thought mysterious, were sometimes confused with Neolithic or Bronze Age barrows and in at least one case, are still described as such, even after excavation. Pillow mounds in Epping Forest were interpreted as the sites of Iron Age funeral pyres in the 1920s by one Hazzledine Warren – whose own mail and signature must daily have provided clues to their real function. Even more surprising is the fact that while he was excavating the pillow mound several old fellows sidled up and told him that he was wasting his time as the mounds were only old rabbit warrens and they could remember them being built. Their helpful advice was scorned. Elongated pillow mounds can be seen on the land overlooking Wensleydale, right beside the ringwork at Middleham.

The craft of burrowing was only gradually acquired by the British rabbit, and they found it easier to scrabble in the soft soil of an artificial mound. Sometimes an internal structure of tunnels was also provided. These tunnels, provided either as artificial burrows or to improve drainage, could be lined with stone or exist as boreholes. In Tudor times, the accounts of Hampton Court Palace note a payment to

blacksmith Robert Bing for 'a great long auger of iron to make and bore coney holes within the King's beries new made'. Most pillow mounds appear to belong to the post-medieval centuries, though the rectangular mounds and large square mound at Sutton, North Yorkshire, appear to be medieval and a mound furnished with stone tunnels excavated at Bryncysegrfan in Dyfed produced a fourteenth-century date. A final feature of pillow mounds is the way that they show how amazingly short and unreliable the human memory can be: 'working' pillow mounds were still numerous in the nineteenth century, but in the twentieth century the mounds had become an archaeological mystery, even though a few buries in Wales were still in use in the 1930s! To give just one example, at Ravenstonedale near Appleby in Westmorland pillow mounds were functioning as part of a working warren until at least 1797, but by 1860 the local people had lost all memory of what their 'mysterious' mounds might be.

There are many parts of the country like Dartmoor and Epping Forest where warrening has left its marks on the landscape, but there are two localities where the remains are particularly interesting: the Breckland and Dolebury Warren in Avon. In the Breckland heaths at least a dozen vast warrens appeared in the Middle Ages, the names of some of them, like Wangford, Santon, Bodney and Lakenheath warrens still surviving. The prior of Ely established his Lakenheath Warren at the end of the thirteenth century, by which time at least seven other warrens existed in the vicinity. More than 600 years later Breckland warrens were still yielding about ten rabbits to the acre, so that a large warren might produce around 25,000 rabbits each year. Warrening was big business, and the profits were always threatened by poaching. Warren lodges like miniature castles were built to accommodate the warreners and provide them with refuges against the more threatening bands of marauders. Most have disappeared or exist only as tumbled ruins, but the prior of Thetford's fifteenth-century warren lodge still stands as a square two-storey building with thick flint walls reinforced with Barnack stone. On the upper floor the lonely warrener would huddle in the gloom, well aware of the organised and brutal nature of poaching gangs.

Dolebury Warren is an Iron Age HILLFORT with the bank and ditch and counterscarp bank enclosing about 20 acres (8 hectares) of the summit. The flanks of the hill are patterned with 'CELTIC' FIELDS which could well pre-date the hillfort. Inside the ramparts, a series of elongated banks running at right angles to the long axis of the enclosure are pillow mounds. The antiquity of warrens in the Mendips is not known, for although Thomas de Berkley obtained a licence to hunt in the area in 1283, providing he kept out of the King's warrens, one cannot know whether this referred to rabbit warrens or FOREST where the King monopolised the right to free warren over all small game. These pillow mounds probably date from the seventeenth century, and it was common practice to exploit the ready-made perimeter defences for a rabbit-breeding area that were provided by the ramparts of an ancient hillfort. As recently as 1903, this warren was yielding around 200 rabbits each year. In the highest part of the hillfort one can see the stone foundations of the house of the warrener, which stands beside the remains of a circular enclosure, which may have served as his garden. To make the interpretation of all the different features more difficult, the area is striped by troughs cut into the limestone rock, and these result from the mining of lead veins, probably in the eighteenth and nineteenth centuries.

In the post-medieval period, warrens produced rabbit pelts for hat-making – a practice continued into the modern era by the Lingwood factory at Brandon in Norfolk – as well as masses of cheap meat. Interest in the potential of the long-established rabbit producing areas was revived during the AGRICULTURAL DEPRESSION at the end of the nineteenth century, when shooting and the renting of shooting rights injected much needed income

into the distressed economy. On the sandy soils of the Brecklands on the Norfolk/Suffolk border landowners experimented with asparagus and blackcurrants, but it was found that forestry and the archaic activities of rabbit farming and game shooting provided the best means of muddling through the crisis. The devastating effects that gamekeepers had had on native predators had allowed the rabbit population to soar. The Elveden Hall estate was acquired by Maharajah Duleep Singh in 1863, and in any of the years that followed up to 75,000 rabbits might be shot as well as almost 10,000 each of pheasants and partridges and 3,000 hares. The economic viability of the rabbit was demonstrated in these lean economic years and by the end of the century about half of its area was devoted to rabbits.

*Further reading*: Sheail, John, *Rabbits and Their History*, David & Charles, 1971.

**Washfold**, see WASHPOOL.

**Washpool, wash dub.** Before the introduction of toxic chemical sheep dips, it was necessary to wash greasy, tangled fleeces before shearing took place. A deep pool, usually in the bed of a river or stream was selected. Sometimes a washpool was made by artificially deepening or by damming an upland stream, often on the COMMON, just above the HEAD DYKE, but sometimes a natural lowland river or beck was used. About Midsummer or just after, sheep were driven into a pen or 'washfold' on the bank. Then they were driven individually into the chilly waters and a shepherd standing with water over his knees would duck each sheep and release it to struggle to the far bank. About a week later, the sheep were sheared. In many places the tumbling walls of washfolds can be found, some dating back to the end of the medieval period. They can be pear-shaped, with the narrow end leading down to the pool or 'dub'. In other cases they are tadpole-shaped, with the 'tail' being formed by a DRYSTONE WALL that diverts sheep towards the fold.

**Waste**, see COMMONS.

**Water corn**. A payment by farmers for the maintenance of mill dams and leets associated with the WATERMILLS to which they were bound.

**Watergate**. A track leading to a place where animals could be watered.

**Water meadow (floated meadow)**. Some low-lying riverside meadows flood naturally during the cold wet months when rivers spill over their banks. Gentle flooding of this kind could be advantageous, for the percolating mineral-rich water warms frozen roots and stimulates grass into early growth. From about the sixteenth century artificial methods of controlled flooding were developed to provide a flush of spring grazing for sheep and lambs, which were sometimes folded away from the meadows on the fallowing arable fields at night so that their dung could enrich the soil. Meadows might be flooded again in April to foster a hay crop in June.

Water meadows of this kind were most numerous in the chalk counties of Wessex but could be found in other regions, such as East Anglia, Devon and the East Midlands. Some quite elaborate systems for water control were developed in the seventeenth, eighteenth and nineteenth centuries. 'Flooding upwards' involved constructing a dam to pond back waters that would flood meadows lying upstream. 'Flooding downwards' involved damming a river and leading the impounded waters away through a canal or 'head main' which had outlets to a network of low ridges or 'carriers' with channels running along their spines. The water would thus circulate from the dam to the head main, along the carrier, across the meadow and back into the river. In the West Country, springs arising at the base of a steep hillslope would be captured by a horizontal leat, and when the leat had filled the water would overflow and run down across the meadow to the river.

Such artificial flooding techniques have fallen into disuse, but in old, unploughed water meadows the earthworks of leats, carriers and sluices may still be identified from the irregularities in the meadow.

*Further reading:* Bettey, J. H., 'The Development of Water Meadows in the Southern Counties', in Cook, H. and Williamson, T. (eds), *Water Management in the English Landscape*, Edinburgh University Press, 1999, pp. 175–95.
Cowan, M., 'Floated Meadows in the Salisbury Area', *South Wiltshire Archaeological Society Historical Monograph* 9, 1982.
Wade-Martins, S. and Williamson T., 'Floated Water-Meadows in Norfolk: a misplaced innovation', *Agricultural History Review* 42, 1994, 20–37.

**Watermill**. Watermills were almost certainly introduced to Britain by the Romans, and archaeological evidence of such mills, which were associated with serving the Hadrian's Wall garrison complex, has been found on three different streams and rivers in the area. They became quite numerous in Saxon times, the earliest recorded mention of a watermill dating from 792, when the use of a mill was granted to a district just east of Dover. Domesday Book of 1086 mentions 5,624 English watermills, though the actual total will have been higher since the recording of such assets was not systematised and comprehensive.

Under the feudal system milling was a monopoly of the manorial lord, though the mill was often leased to a miller. 'Milling soke' was not ordained by statute law, and the monopoly was not claimed on every MANOR, but on most it was a manorial custom and peasants were obliged to take their grain to the lord's mill and a grinding toll, or 'multure' conventionally one-sixteenth of the grist ground, was exacted. The lord had prior claim to the use of the mill for grinding the DEMESNE crop and was responsible for major repairs, while his tenant miller normally had to pay for lesser repairs and maintenance and sometimes had to pay for the millstones.

After the thirteenth century a money charge for milling often replaced the payment of the toll. Peasants could be fined for grinding their corn at home using archaic 'quern' stones or for patronising a rival mill. Thus, for example, on Wrington manor in Avon it was required that 'the customary tenants are bound to grind their corn at my lord's mill, or to pay a yearly tribute in money, viz. each holder of a yardland [about 30 acres – 12 hectares] 2s. 8d. [14p] ... down to the lowest cottar at 4d. [2p]'. In 1274, the abbot of St Alban's Abbey, Cirencester, demanded that all his manorial tenants should hand over their hand querns. The response was not very enthusiastic, and eventually the abbot decided to mount

*Watermill*
The weatherboarded watermill at Houghton in Cambridgeshire includes seventeenth-century elements. A watermill has existed here since Saxon times.

a search of the peasants' homes – and around eighty illicit querns were discovered! They were confiscated and used to pave the floor of the abbey.

Milling was, in fact, a controversial activity; milling soke was resented, while millers were rightly or wrongly suspected of taking an excessive multure. The contemporary stereotype of the rascally miller was immortalised by Chaucer around 1386–89 in his 'The Reeve's Tale':

> A thief he was sothe of corn and mele
> And that a sly, and usuant [accustomed] to
> stele.

In 1395 the mayor and citizens of Chester petitioned Richard II concerning the extortionate practices of the tenants of the mills on the River Dee:

> Youre pore leges and supplycants … showe that the mylners of yor milnes of dee do take from day to day divers owtragiouse partes over the right toll … graunt unto theym to have ther come and malt grounde at yr milnes for the xvj greyne [the sixteenth part conventional toll] without any other tole parte or any thyng over …

In later years popular prejudices against millers were expressed in taunts like:

> Miller-dee, miller-dee, dusty poll
> How many sacks of flour hast thou stole?
> In goes a bushel; out come a peck
> Hang old miller-dee up by the neck!

Further arguments were ever likely to erupt concerning mill weirs and their effects on navigation (see DAMS AND WEIRS).

Although the size of watermills and the sophistication of their mechanical gearing would vary enormously, the essential principle remained the same, with the power of falling or running water being captured by a waterwheel and harnessed, via various cogwheel gears, to the task of revolving the grindstones between which the grain was milled. The smallest and most primitive form of watermill was the CLICK

MILL, which had its wheel, which had angled blades like a turbo-prop, set horizontally in what could be a very humble stream and which turned the millstones via a vertical shaft. Many of the mills in Saxon England will have been of this type, while the Irish evidence spans from AD 630, the approximate date of the earliest excavated click mill, to the click mills which were still operating in the nineteenth century. Similar mills in Scotland may have had a comparably long history, and just one restored example survives, near Dounby on the main Orkney island.

More sophisticated watermills had vertical waterwheels driving horizontal shafts, and they varied according to whether the water, flowing in a trough, struck the top of the wheel (the *overshot* type), struck just above the middle of the wheel (the *breastshot* type) or struck the bottom of the wheel (the *undershot* type). All these types of watermill existed in medieval England, the most efficient undershot design being illustrated in the Luttrell Psalter of around 1338, and the three forms with vertical waterwheels were enlarged and developed in the course of the following centuries. During the Middle Ages other power was also harnessed to drive fulling mills, which were introduced in the thirteenth century and employed a moving beam fitted with hammers to beat woven cloth underwater to drive out the grease and grime. Water-powered forge-hammers were introduced around 1200 in association with the iron industry in areas like the Weald, and in the fifteenth century water power was applied to drive the bellows of the new blast furnaces. Watermills provided the main sources of industrial energy until the Industrial Revolution and the adoption of steam power, when industry began to migrate from the sources of waterpower to the coalfields. The reasons for the decline of watermills in the grinding of grain are similar to those which affected windmills (and are described in the WINDMILLS entry).

A considerable number of watermills of various post-medieval dates survive, though very

*Watermill*
The great waterwheel at Foster Beck Mill, near Pateley Bridge in North Yorkshire, served the hemp mill which was operational until the 1960s.

few indeed are still operational. There are many examples of mills which have been stripped of their wheels and milling gear and converted into domestic use; look out for tall stream- or river-side houses clad in weatherboarding. Where mill buildings have disappeared completely there may still be traces of the ponds and channels associated with the former mill. Place-name evidence can also be useful; the word 'goit', meaning 'water channel', is still in use in the north of England and derives from the Old English *gota*. Names like Steener and Steaner can derive from the Old English *Stæner*, which literally denotes a rocky place, but is frequently associated with the islands created when goits were dug to divert water from a river to a mill. The significance of 'mill' and 'wheel' place-names is more obvious, though names incorporating 'walk' can sometimes derive from *walc* and *walcere*, old names associated with the fulling industry. See also DAMS AND WIERS, WINDMILL AND WINDPUMP)

*Further reading*: Syson, Leslie, *The Watermills of Britain*, David & Charles, 1980.

Shaw, J., *Water Power in Scotland*, Edinburgh University Press, 1984.

Holt, R., *The Mills of Medieval England*, Oxford, 1988.

**Wattle and daub**. In TIMBER-FRAMED buildings the heavy oak posts, sill beams, wall plates and braces provided the structural framework of the house, and the panels between these timbers required an infilling. Wattle and daub was the most widely used infill material. The wattle component consisted of hazel or ash wands cut in a nearby coppice. The tips of the wands were set in holes drilled in the framing timbers and the wands were woven to produce a basketwork filling for each panel. Daub, usually a mixture of clay, dung and chopped straw, was then applied as a plaster to both faces of the wattle, and when dry, this plaster was sealed and protected by coats of limewash or paint. In some cases upright staves of oak substituted for wattle, while in some East Anglian houses oak staves were set horizontally across each panel and wattles of ash or hazel were tied to them. Where 'close studding' of closely spaced upright posts was adopted, short oak laths were set horizontally to receive the daub. In areas with easy access to stone, a packing of stones could substitute for wattle. In East Anglia and the south-east, brick, often laid in herringbone patterns, was adopted from the late fifteenth century onwards and panels of 'brick noggin' were sometimes introduced into older buildings when the wattle-and-daub panels needed to be renewed, even though the brick was more water-retentive than limewashed daub. Wattle and daub has a very long history, and at Fengate, near Peterborough, a dwelling dated to about 2500 BC was built of wattle and daub on a wooden frame structure. See also MUD AND STUD, CLAM AND STAFF.

**Wayside cross**, see CROSSES.

**Wealden house**, see HALL.

**Weem**, see SOUTERRAIN.

**Well**. A dependable supply of water was a prerequisite of every settlement. Roman towns had lead water-pipes – and the drinking of lead-contaminated water is one of the more esoteric explanations for the decline of Roman civilisation. Some medieval towns had water piped through bored-out logs, but villages and farmsteads relied on water from wells and springs. If there was not a convenient spring, then it was necessary to dig a well, its depth depending on that of the summer watertable. A number of medieval wells have been excavated, and several examples explored were bottle-shaped. Sometimes the shaft was faced with stone, while the mid-Saxon well at Udell in Bedfordshire consisted of a pit in which a large wicker basket was suspended to serve as a water-filter. Many villages have names ending in '-well', from the Old English *wella*, 'a well or spring', or *æwell*, 'a stream', like Prittlewell in Essex ('the prattling or babbling spring') or Temple Ewell in Surrey ('the stream owned by the Knights Templar'). See also HOLY WELLS.

**Went, tewer**. Dialect terms for narrow lanes. A 'twissell' is a Redge-girt footpath.

**Wheelhouse**. The wheelhouse is a form of dwelling that developed in Scotland around the third to fifth centuries AD. Some of the excavated examples have been found at the sites of BROCHS where they seem to represent the next stage of occupation following the abandonment of the defensive towers. At Clickhimin, on Shetland, a wheelhouse was built inside a derelict broch. Wheelhouses were circular stone-built dwellings with their interiors partitioned by radiating piers of masonry like the spokes in a wheel to create a series of cells or cubicles. An early variation of the design is the 'aisled wheelhouse' in which the piers are not linked to the wall of the house to leave a narrow circular aisle around the inner perimeter of this wall. In both cases the hearth was placed in the centre of the dwelling.

**Whipping post**, see STOCKS.

**White horses**, see HILL FIGURES.

**Wick**. A word which frequently appears in place-names, but which has a variety of meanings. These include an isolated farm specialising in dairy products, a roadside village established during the Roman occupation or a place were salt was produced. In Scotland it denotes both a creek and a farmstead and it can also derive from a Norse word signifying a bay.

**Windmill and windpump**. The history of the windmill in Britain is rather uncertain so far as the initial stages are concerned, but it is clear that windmills were very numerous in the later medieval centuries. There is a record of a windmill grant to the abbey of Croyland in 833, but this document is certainly one of the quite numerous forgeries by which monasteries attempted to claim ancient privileges. The earliest genuine reference to a windmill that seems to exist relates to the year 1191 and was chronicled by Jocelin of Brakelond. His story is worth repeating, because it suggests that windmills were already well established by this time and that 'adulterine' mills, which undermined the privileges of lawful manorial mills, were becoming a nuisance. Jocelin relates a conflict between Abbot Samson of Bury St Edmunds and the dean:

> Herbert the dean erected the windmill upon Haberdon. When the abbot heard of this, his anger was so kindled that he would scarcely eat or utter a single word. On the morrow, after hearing Mass, he commanded the sacrist that without delay he should send his carpenters thither and overturn it altogether, and carefully put by the wooden material in safe keeping. The dean hearing this came to him saying that he was able in law to do this upon his own frank fee estate, and that the benefit of the wind ought not to be denied anyone. He further said that he only wanted to grind his own corn there, and no one else's, lest it should be imagined that he did this to the damage of the neighbouring mills.

> The abbot, his anger not yet appeased, answered, 'I give you as many thanks as if you had cut off both my feet. By the mouth of God I will not eat bread until that building be plucked down ... Nor is this without prejudice to my mills, as you assert, because the burgesses [townspeople] will run to you and grind their corn at their pleasure, nor can I by law turn them away, because they are free men. Nor would I endure that the mill of our cellarer, lately set up, should stand, except that it was erected before I was abbot. Begone,' he said, 'begone: before you have come to your house, you shall hear what has befallen your mill.' But the dean being afraid before the face of the abbot, by the counsel of his son Master Stephen, forestalled the servants of the sacrist, and without delay caused that very mill which had been erected by his own servants to be overturned.

It is fairly safe to assume that a number of windmills existed in England by the late twelfth century, and the most popular explanation is that such mills imitated Continental examples which had been seen by Crusaders in the course of their travels to the Holy Land. The innovation must have been popular, and numerous windmills were recorded in the thirteenth century – like the three windmills standing in townships adjacent to Wakefield in 1270. A number of contemporary medieval illustrations of windmills exist, the earliest known being in the 'Windmill Psalter' of about 1270. The first generations of English windmills were small timber structures of the '*post mill*' type, in which the entire body of the mill carrying the sails is revolved upon a strong central post when the mill is orientated to catch the wind. Should such a mill have been wrongly orientated, a strong gust from behind could blow it right over. A later refinement involved providing the mill with a stable body, in which the grinding machinery was housed, and fixing the sails to a revolving cap. Where the rigid tower was of timber the mill was a '*smock mill*' (because the tapering or flared tower resembled a peasant smock), and when it was of brick or stone the mill was a '*tower mill*'. Mills of these types seem to have developed during the latter part of the Middle Ages, and a tower mill is represented in fragmented church glasswork of around 1475 found at Stoke by Clare, in Suffolk.

No medieval windmills survive today, though numerous later examples of all three types can be seen in ruined or restored forms. The oldest surviving structure is thought to be the post mill at Bourn in Cambridgeshire, which already existed in 1636. Any tapering cylindrical towers encountered are most likely to be the decapitated remains of old tower mills, and the oldest surviving relic consists of two floors of a stone tower mill of the fifteenth century at Burton Dasset in Warwickshire. The oldest surviving smock mill is the restored example of about 1650 at Lacey Green in Buckinghamshire.

The decline of the windmill was a gradual affair, and a considerable number of windmills still operated commercially in the early decades of the twentieth century. The invention of steam power provided an alternative source of energy in milling, and after 1784 milling engines were introduced in several towns. Portable engines, which allowed milling to be carried out at the farmstead, followed, while the development of roller milling at centralised milling locations with attendant economies of scale came about in the 1870s. Restrictions on flour production in 1916 put most of the surviving rural windmills out of operation during the First World War, and few of them returned to business after the war. About 350 windmills were operating in 1919, but only about fifty still operated in 1946, and by 1953 the number of operating windmills had dropped to twenty-one. The commercial demise of the windmill was followed by the emergence of a number of conservational groups devoted to the restoration and preservation of windmills, and it is thanks to their efforts that a large selection of windmills survive, some of them restored to full working order.

The power of the wind could be caught by

sails and harnessed to uses other than the turning of millstones. A tower mill on the shore at St Monans, Fife, was used to raise seawater to evaporating pans for the manufacture of salt. The much acclaimed drainage of the Fens under the direction of the Dutch drainage engineer Cornelius Vermuyden in the middle of the seventeenth century had, by the early years of the eighteenth century, proved to be a failure through a neglect of the environment factors. The salvation of the Fen drainage system was achieved by the use of windmills in their role as windpumps, power from the sails being used to operate scoopwheels which lifted water from one drainage level to the next. By 1748 no fewer than 250 such windmills were operating in the middle section of the Fens alone. They were not entirely a new phenomenon, for an early windpump was recorded in the Fens in 1604. The weakness of the windmill operating in this and other capacities was its impotence under windless conditions and after 1820 steam engines began to replace the Fenland windmills. The sole survivor of the system is a windpump from Adventurers' Fen which has been restored and re-erected at the Wicken Fen nature reserve in Cambridgeshire. Here it performs a reverse role, scooping water into rather than out of the Fen to preserve the environment in times of drought. A variety of windmills, mostly formerly used as windpumps, like the Berney Arms example, survive in the Norfolk Broads.

At sites where windmills have previously existed – usually hilltops or exposed areas of level ground – obvious clues may be left in the form of the common 'Windmill' and 'Windhill' place-names. Post mills were normally built on earthen mounds which often survive and can easily be mistaken for ROUND BARROWS. Where the mound concerned is a windmill mound it may still be possible to recognise a cross-shaped depression, left by the timber cross-trees which were used to anchor the post of the mill, though sometimes these features are only apparent after excavation. See also WATERMILL.

*Windmill*

An isometric drawing of High Mill, Berney Arms, Norfolk. The different parts are as follows: scoop wheel (A); stage (B); gallery (C); fantail (D); fan drive (E); curb (F); hemlath (G); whip (H); bay (J); shutter (K); wind shaft (L); poll end ( M); stock (N); clamps (O); front striking gear (P); striking chain (Q); fan stage (R); chain guide (S); cap (T); sheer (U); brake wheel (W); brake (WW); wallower (X); upright shaft (Y); scoop wheel driving shaft (Z).

*Further reading:* Wailes, Rex, *The English Windmill*, Routledge & Kegan Paul, 1954.

**Winter-haining**. Land, sometimes a COMMON, enclosed in winter with a view to taking a crop of hay from it in the coming season.

**Winterslap**. A gap in an enclosure that can be opened to allow cattle to roam freely in winter.

**Wintersteed**. The low-lying component of a manor in the northern uplands of England that contained the arable lands and the more sheltered fields where the livestock were over-wintered.

**Withershins**. Movement against the sun's course, sometimes considered chaotic or unlucky.

**Wobble road, bridle path, halter path, sheer gate, sheer way**. A track for use by pedestrians and riders but on which vehicles are banned.

**Wolf pit**. Early in the nineteenth century and for many years before, VERMIN-TRAPS were constructed at vulnerable points in WARRENS to reduce the incursion of predators, and this recalls the pits dug in earlier times, when animals more fearsome than stoats and weasels were abroad. In fact the wolf does not seem to have been generally common in medieval England and Wales and was exterminated before the period had run its course. A wolf bounty was paid in Surrey in 1212, and in 1281 Edward I employed one Peter Corbet to kill all the wolves of the Welsh Marches. In Yorkshire, wolves held out for longer, and in 1394–96 some thirteen wolves were killed in the Whitby area. *Wolf pits* or wolf falls do not appear to survive as recognisable earthworks, but there are various records of their being dug – for example, at least eight were made at Woolley Edge in west Yorkshire between the late twelfth and late fourteenth centuries (Wooley = the glade or countryside of the wolves). Wolf place-names are not uncommon, coming from the Old English *wulf.* They include Wooden, or 'Wolf Valley', in Northumberland and the self-explanatory Woolpit in Suffolk. But, caution is advised, and

Wolverhampton takes its name from an identified twelfth-century lady, Walfrun, some 'wool' names relate to a trade in fleece and '-wulf' was also a common component of personal names in Dark Age England. Approximate dates for the extinction of the wolf in Britain are 1000 in Wales, 1300 in England south of the Humber, 1400 in northern England, 1500 in the south of Scotland, and 1682 or 1743 in the Scottish Highlands. In Ireland, wolves were slain until early in the eighteenth century.

The Old English word for a snare or trap was *wöcig*, and this may give us the village of Wookey in the Mendips. Vermin traps which were recognised amongst the pillow mounds at Trowlesbury Warren on Dartmoor, built to protect rabbits against rats, weasels and stoats, consisted of a trap at the centre of a cross-like arrangement of low granite walls. These intercepted the predators and directed them towards the trap. More than eighty examples of these eighteenth-century stoat and weasel traps have been discovered on Dartmoor. On Thetford Warren, the rabbits themselves were caught in deep flint-lined pitfalls covered by trapdoors.

**Wonning**. In Scotland, a dwelling or farmstead, sometimes the HOME FARM.

**Wood acre**. A land measure used in wooded or Forest country that was almost 40 per cent larger than the normal ACRE.

**Woodbank**. Medieval woods usually had their boundaries protected and marked by massive woodbanks. This is not surprising, since a well-managed wood could often yield more profit than a similar acreage of ploughland. Many surviving woods still sit exactly or substantially within their ancient woodbanks, and the presence of a bank and its relationship to the wooded area can provide vital evidence about the antiquity of a wood and any phases of expansion or contraction that have taken place over the years. Most of the early woodbanks are very massive features consisting of a great curving earthen rampart and an external ditch. The present appearance of a woodbank will depend upon a number of factors – its original dimensions, the degree of erosion and silting of the ditch and the levels of maintenance or neglect which the bank has experienced since its construction. Woodbanks varied in appearance; some were double, some walled or faced with stone, and in a number of cases there is evidence that the crown of the bank formerly carried a stout fence or a well-maintained hedge.

Occasionally records survive to show that the making or repair of a woodbank was a considerable undertaking. In 1391 at Oatwood near Alverthorpe in West Yorkshire repairs involved digging or scouring the ditches surrounding the 18 acres (7.28 hectares) of wood and planting a hedge on the woodbank, while six cartloads of posts and boards were used in repairing the pale. It is hard to picture the wood-bank defences involved, but they must have been complex, for the document mentions ditch, bank, hedge, pale and palisade as distinct elements.

The outer woodbank was mainly needed to prevent trespass by animals from the surrounding fields, but many woods also had smaller internal banks which defined the HAGS or divisions into different COPPICES which were felled according to different rotations. To make matters more complicated, some woods have been planted on abandoned farmland or have been allowed to colonise former fields, often to produce game cover on the least productive land. In places where the old fields were bounded by hedgebanks confusion can result – but the hedgebanks incorporated in the new

*Woodbank*
A section of an internal woodbank at Burnham Beeches in Buckinghamshire.

wood will be steeper and less massive than woodbanks and may still carry trees which have grown up from their hedgerows. Woodbanks sometimes have rows of old POLLARDS growing upon them, standing like ancient sentinels ranged around the historic wood. Quite frequently the property boundaries would be disregarded and the names of those fined in MANOR COURTS for illegal felling can be revealing. The medieval records of Wakefield court show that the theft of woodland resources was very common and also indicate what the stolen timber was being used for. In 1329, William and Rose le Turnour were, as one might expect, wood-turners, and stole timber from Sowerby Wood to make dishes. In 1337, William and Roger Cooper and their servants must have been coopers, or barrel-makers, but were noted in the records as making large pails. Adam de Coventre and his sons made planks for chests from stolen oak; John Piper stole it for planking; Thomas del Bothe cut wood to make spoons; Hugh Adamson cut alder and hollowed trunks to make water-pipes (although bored-out elm was usually favoured for this role); while William Turner was caught repeating his crimes in 1337. Cases such as these show that wood was regarded as a valuable resource, and the awareness of the need to conserve woodland goes back much further than many may imagine. In the years around 1100 the Bishop of Norwich wrote as follows to one of his officials:

> To William the monk. Concerning the giving of Thorpe Wood to the sick I gave no commands, nor do I give nor shall I give; for I appointed thee guardian, not uprooter of the wood. To the sick I will give not wood, but money, when I come to Norwich, as I did last year. Give them this answer and no other. Meanwhile do thou guard the wood of the Holy Trinity even as thou wouldst wish thyself to be guarded by the Holy Trinity, and to keep my love.

**Woodland**. Woods, as opposed to PLANTATIONS, are relics of a long-established, if now largely forgotten, need for a wide range of woodland products. Many woods have occupied their existing boundaries since early medieval times or for much longer. Today the demand for the traditional products of deciduous woodland is modest, and very few landowners are prepared to tolerate the long periods of waiting for a return on capital which are demanded by the slow rates of growth associated with hardwood trees. Consequently woods tend either to be destroyed, to be tolerated but not maintained or to serve in inessential roles as game cover. It is a stark fact that since 1947 we have lost between 30 per cent and 50 per cent of our ancient woodlands. These woods stood where they did because of a longstanding consensus that the land concerned was most suitable for the harvesting of woodland products. However, the modern quest for quick returns on investment, the distortion of values by C.A.P. cereal subsidies and the exploitation of complicated tax concessions which could be gained by clearing and coniferising old woodland have all conspired against the ancient woodlands. When looking at the distribution of the surviving old woods in a locality one usually finds that they stand on the land that is least inviting to farmers – like the steeper valley sides of the Yorkshire Dales, the most sandy and barren lands of Hampshire or the heaviest of the East Anglian boulder clays. Yet, despite being relegated to the least promising farmlands, woods were the cornerstones of life before the Industrial Revolution, and when properly managed they could yield a higher income than the adjacent ploughlands and pastures.

The essential feature of a wood (in contrast to a coniferous plantation) is that it is self-perpetuating. This does not imply that the woods that we see today are living relics of the primeval *wildwood*, which colonised Britain as the climate warmed after the last Ice Age. By definition wildwood would be unaffected by the influence of humans and their domesticated animals, and it is difficult to imagine that any

Standards with coppiced underwood, producing scenes like this section of Wolves Wood in Suffolk, was the commonest form of medieval woodland management.

living wood could have enjoyed such immunity. At the same time it is unlikely that the majority of our old woods were actually planted. It is true that after felling the STANDARDS in an old wood, saplings to replace them would sometimes be planted or encouraged to develop at a density of about a dozen to the acre. However, the COPPICED underwood, which was the primary resource of many old woods, was probably developed from natural process of seeding and

colonisation. It can also be seen that when deciduous standards, like oaks, are felled, unless measures are taken to kill the stump then a vigorous regrowth of shoots from it will be seen.

In the course of time, the tree composition of

a wood may evolve, and both human and natural agencies can be responsible. The pry or small-leafed lime has never regained the ascendancy which it enjoyed in the wildwood of the Mesolithic period, and its seeds germinate less freely in the cooler climates of today. The invasion by elm of many woods in the recent era may be partly a natural process, but one that will end as a result of another environmental phenomenon: the relentless advance of Dutch elm disease. Hornbeams only seem to have become prominent in Epping Forest since medieval times, and perhaps this represents human intervention, while many ancient woods contain beech, larch and sycamore. In the north of England, beech seems to be an introduction and it has difficulty in colonising in the cooler regions. In the eighteenth and nineteenth centuries stands of both beech and larch were frequently inserted into older woods, while sycamore, traditionally considered to be an alien introduced in the late sixteenth century (but could all the medieval references to maple refer to field maple?), has successfully seeded and flourished in many old woods.

The extent of woodland has also varied. It is possible that clearances designed to create open grazings and hunting ranges in the Mesolithic period prevented the expanding wildwood from establishing itself on some upland plateaux. In the course of the Neolithic period, very extensive areas were cleared for cultivation, and this process of clearance continued until the Ages of Bronze and Iron, so that most Iron Age countrysides were only lightly wooded. By Roman times the extent of woodland could have been even less than today. In the course post-Roman centuries, woodland advanced across countless troubled and depopulated countrysides, and this woodland would often be removed by the process of ASSARTING in the course of the Middle Ages. Between the Middle Ages and the early years of the twentieth century, many medieval woods endured, even though the traditional crafts and commerce of woodmanship were gradually declining. Meanwhile, various

new commercial, ornamental and recreational plantations were established and in some marginal places woodland colonised land which had been under cultivation. During the eighteenth century some landowners sought to improve the appearance of the countryside by planting clumps or belts of trees on hilltops or the crests of ridges. These tended to be places where exposure and thin soils reduced the quality of the farmland, but where the presence of woodland would raise the skyline and magnify the apparent height of the eminences. Woodland remained a good investment and in the years around 1800, the Ingilby dynasty at Ripley, North Yorkshire, was saved from bankruptcy, the consequences of a dowry that did not result, by the sale of ESTATE timber.

When exploring a wood a variety of clues may be significant. Some woods stand on land that has never been cleared for arable farming, although it is virtually impossible to tell (without recourse to scientific analysis of preserved pollen grains) whether the land concerned was never cleared for grazing or ever existed as WOOD PASTURE. Sometimes, the woodland floor will be littered with boulders, like glacial erratics, that would have been removed prior to any cultivation that could have taken place, while bumps and hollows which are a legacy of glaciation and the freeze-and-thaw regime of its periglacial aftermath would have been smoothed out in the course of ploughing. Conversely, some woodland floors reveal the corrugations of RIDGE AND FURROW ploughland and in a number of woods one can also recognise fossilised hedgerows, hedgebanks or field-walls, all indicating an earlier agricultural existence.

Particular attention should be paid to earthworks specifically associated with woods. A massive WOODBANK could easily date from the early medieval period, though the wood could be much older than its boundary bank. Some woods still fit their ancient girdle perfectly, while where wood and woodbank do not match one may look for evidence of the grubbing up or expansion of a wood.

Caution is advised, for woodbanks may be confused with the banks of internal compart-ments and some earthworks that seem to bound woods are those of DEER PARKS or important property boundaries of a different nature. Old maps may help to chart the history of a wood, while old documents can provide detailed infor-mation of the management of a wood and the trade in its products.

Several Old English words related to woodland; 'wood' derives from the word *wudu*. *Graf* survives as 'grove', and *holt* endures in many place-names although its meaning, a thicket, has been forgotten. Other Old English wood-names have acquired more specific associations, *scaga* emerging as 'shaw', a word used to describe some northern sloping woods and the narrow woodland belts of the Weald, while *hangr* has become 'hanger', a word relating to woods, often of beech, found on steep chalk slopes in Sussex and Wessex.

Much more information about woodland features and related topics is listed under: AGIST, ASSART, COCKSHOOT, COPPICE, DEER PARK, FOREST, HUNTING LODGE, PANNAGE, POLLARD, STANDARD, WOODBANK, WOOD PASTURE.

*Further reading*: Loughborough Naturalists' Club, *Charnwood Forest: A Changing Landscape*, Sycamore Press, 1981.
Rackham, O., *Trees and Woodland in the British Landscape*, Dent, 1976.
Rackham, O., *The Last Forest*, Dent, London, 1989.
Dyer, C., *Hanbury: Settlement and Society in a Woodland Landscape*, Leicester University Press, 1991.

**Woodland countryside**, see ANCIENT AND PLANNED COUNTRYSIDE.

**Wood pasture**. This is a form of land-use that was widespread in medieval and earlier times, but is seldom seen in an authentic form today, though PARKLAND with grazed lawns punctuated by large POLLARD or STANDARD

trees offers a loose visual approximation of wood pasture. Current research shows that natural woodland may have resembled wood pasture, with grazing and other natural processes opening up clearings. Medieval wood pasture was an unnatural association between trees and livestock, and good management demanded the perpetuation of the delicate balance between the components. If grazing was too heavy, then browsing would kill all the vulnerable saplings needed to maintain the woodland, while a withdrawal of grazing from parts of the wood pasture would result in the formation of a more conventional, dense shady woodland and the shading out of nutritious grasses.
Normally it was the woodland element that suffered, with the eventual conversion to open pasture.

Wood pasture appears to have been quite common in Saxon and Norman England and is sometimes noted in DOMESDAY BOOK as *Silva pastilis*, and much of the 'woodland' of this time may actually have existed as wood pasture. However, the extent of wood pasture seems to have diminished throughout the Middle Ages, and at the close of the period the first great topographical English poet, Michael Drayton of Warwickshire, wrote of Charnwood's Hills in the following way:

> Fine sharp but easy hills, which reverently are crown'd
> With aged antique oaks, to which thy goats and sheep
> (To him that stands remote) do softly seem to weep,
> To gnaw the little shrubs on their steep sides that grow.

Much of the land used as wood pasture was COMMON land. The commoner would usually enjoy rights to the grazings, while the trees – normally pollards – and any specially protected areas of COPPICED underwood – would belong to the lord. Peasants would normally have the right to take wood for fuel ('firebote'), for houses ('hosbote'), for ploughs ('ploughbote')

Wood pasture scarcely exists today, though it will have resembled this view in the former deer park of Bolton Abbey in Wharfedale.

and for building fences ('hedgebote' or 'heybote'), and could, for a price, exploit the pannage by allowing their pigs to eat the acorns which fell – a variable feast which could be significant or meagre depending on the recent climate. The various rights may not always have been clear-cut, as a case considered by the manor court of Minchinhampton in Gloucestershire in 1273 suggests. William de la More was accused of felling a young tree: 'He admits that he did so and calls Henry of Burley, underwoodward, to warrant, and says that he was in such business because the beam of his plough broke near the wood and the tree was given him to repair this. And because he well

knew that the woodward might not warrant such a gift, he remains in mercy.' William was sentenced to perform one day's work of ploughing.

Research by the author in the Yorkshire Dales suggest that wood pasture ceased to be a commonplace sight there as a result of the sale of old trees of poor quality – the last of the wood pasture – to timber merchants in the